TEXT 2

TARGETS OF VIOLENCE
AND AGGRESSION

ADVANCES IN PSYCHOLOGY

76

Editors:

G. E. STELMACH

P. A. VROON

NORTH-HOLLAND
AMSTERDAM • NEW YORK • OXFORD • TOKYO

TARGETS OF VIOLENCE AND AGGRESSION

Edited by

Ronald BAENNINGER
*Department of Psychology
Temple University
Philadelphia, Pennsylvania
U.S.A.*

1991

NORTH-HOLLAND
AMSTERDAM • NEW YORK • OXFORD • TOKYO

NORTH-HOLLAND
ELSEVIER SCIENCE PUBLISHERS B.V.
Sara Burgerhartstraat 25
P.O. Box 211, 1000 AE Amsterdam, The Netherlands

Distributors for the United States and Canada:
ELSEVIER SCIENCE PUBLISHING COMPANY, INC.
655 Avenue of the Americas
New York, N.Y. 10010, U.S.A.

Library of Congress Cataloging-in-Publication Data

Targets of violence and aggression / edited by Ronald Baenninger.
      p.   cm. -- (Advances in psychology ; 76)
   Includes indexes.
   ISBN 0-444-88483-1
   1. Violence. 2. Aggressiveness (Psychology) 3. Victims of
 crimes.   I. Baenninger, Ronald. II. Series: Advances in psychology
 (Amsterdam, Netherlands) ; 76.
 HM291.T34 1991
 303.6--dc20   90-20291
                                                                  CIP

ISBN: 0 444 88483 1

© ELSEVIER SCIENCE PUBLISHERS B.V., 1991

All rights reserved. No part of this publication may be reproduced, stored in a retrieval system, or transmitted, in any form or by any means, electronic, mechanical, photocopying, recording or otherwise, without the prior written permission of the publisher, Elsevier Science Publishers B.V./ Physical Sciences and Engineering Division, P.O. Box 103, 1000 AC Amsterdam, The Netherlands.

Special regulations for readers in the U.S.A. - This publication has been registered with the Copyright Clearance Center Inc. (CCC), Salem, Massachusetts. Information can be obtained from the CCC about conditions under which photocopies of parts of this publication may be made in the U.S.A. All other copyright questions, including photocopying outside of the U.S.A., should be referred to the copyright owner, Elsevier Science Publishers B.V., unless otherwise specified.

No responsibility is assumed by the Publisher for any injury and/or damage to persons or property as a matter of products liability, negligence or otherwise, or from any use or operation of any methods, products, instructions or ideas contained in the material herein.

Printed in The Netherlands

Table of Contents

List of Contributors.. vii

Acknowledgements.. ix

Chapter 1	Introduction: Aggression and its targets ....Ronald Baenninger	1

Aggression Toward Defenseless Targets

Chapter 2	Violence toward other species ....Ronald Baenninger	5
Chapter 3	Victimization among school children ....Dan Olweus	45
Chapter 4	Victim risk factors in the physical abuse of children....................John F. Knutson, Helen A. Schartz, and Lisa Y. Zaidi	103

Violence and Social Institutions

Chapter 5	Institutional violence directed toward children: The case of corporal punishment in schools ,......................................Irwin A. Hyman, and Jacqueline Clarke	159
Chapter 6	Athletes as targets of aggression ....Gordon Russell	211
Chapter 7	Aggression on roadways ....Raymond W. Novaco	253
Chapter 8	Violence toward clinicians ....Burr Eichelman	327

Gender-related violence

Chapter 9	Gay-Bashing: Violence and aggression against gay men and lesbians................. *Peter M. Nardi and Ralph Bolton*	349
Chapter 10	Aggression by women: Mores, myths, and methods.. *Luci Paul and MaryAnn Baenninger*	401
Chapter 11	Violence, aggression, and targets: An overview.........*Ronald Baenninger*	443
Author Index	....	461
Subject Index	....	469

List of Contributors

MaryAnn Baenninger, Department of Psychology, Washington College, Chestertown, Maryland, USA

Ronald Baenninger, Department of Psychology, Temple University, Philadelphia, Pennsylvania, USA

Ralph Bolton, Deparment of Sociology and Anthropology, Pomona College, Claremont, California, USA

Jacqueline Clarke, Deparment of School Psychology, Temple University, Philadelphia, Pennsylvania, USA

Burr Eichelman, Deparment of Psychiatry, Dorothea Dix Hospital, Raleigh, North Carolina, USA

Irwin Hyman, Department of School Psychology, Temple University, Philadelphia, Pennsylvania, USA

John Knutson, Department of Psychology, University of Iowa, Iowa City, Iowa, USA

Peter Nardi, Department of Sociology, Pitzer College, Claremont, California, USA

Raymond Novaco, Program in Social Ecology, University of California at Irvine, Irvine, California, USA

Dan Olweus, Department of Personality Psychology, University of Bergen, Bergen, Norway

Luci Paul, Department of Psychology, Temple University, Philadelphia, Pennsylvania, USA

Gordon Russell, Department of Psychology, University of Lethbridge, Lethbridge, Alberta, Canada

Helen Schartz, Department of Psychology, University of Iowa, Iowa City, Iowa, USA

Lisa Zaidi, Department of Psychology, University of Iowa, Iowa City, Iowa, USA

Acknowledgements

I am grateful for the two very different kinds of inspiration provided by my father, Hans Baenninger, and my "father-figure", Keck Moyer. On a more practical level, the book would never have reached production without the computer and word processing skills of Monica Greco, Jane Burrell, and MaryAnn Baenninger, to all of whom I am sincerely grateful.
RB

1

Introduction:
Aggression and its Targets
Ronald Baenninger

With the publication in 1966 of Konrad Lorenz's *On Aggression* there was a renewal of popular interest in this topic that stimulated both social and biological scientists. Books, empirical and theoretical papers, and monographs on aggressive behavior in the quarter of a century since have focussed primarily on possible sources of aggression that stem from internal drives and instincts (as emphasized by certain physiologists, ethologists, and psychiatrists) or on aggression as a response to environmental events, tempered by cultural and individual learning (as emphasized by most anthropologists, sociologists, and psychologists).

One of the earliest attempts to define a taxonomy of aggression was that proposed by Moyer in 1968. Based largely on case histories of human psychosurgery and laboratory data from nonhuman species, Moyer's classification emphasized qualitative differences in kinds of aggression. He identified seven kinds of aggressive behavior, based on the stimuli that elicited them and on what was then known about their physiological mechanisms. In the years since 1968 Moyer's classification has appeared in textbooks for introductory and advanced students. His seven kinds of aggression have become part of psychology, despite the fact that Moyer initially proposed the taxonomy as a very tentative, exploratory hypothesis.

The concepts and categories we devise for research affect the way we perceive the reality of what we investigate. By proposing his taxonomy Moyer affected the way many researchers think about aggression, and the kinds of research they did. One of the purposes of the present volume is to cast doubt, by the very diversity of the targets discussed, on the validity and utility of such taxonomies.

Years ago (Baenninger, 1974) I proposed a classification based on the distinction between respondent and operant behavior (elicited versus emitted aggression), while Brain and Benton (1981) distinguished between reproductive and non-reproductive aggression. Such descriptive categories are probably harmless because they are so general. They have only minor effects on the epistemological reality that we construct, and do not limit the theoretical or empirical work of aggression researchers. Zillmann (1979) has argued that most human aggression is either inadvertent, or the result of temporary annoyance, anger, or irritation. With the possible exception of relatively rare, pathological brain disorders, human aggression appears to be the outcome or expression of underlying emotional states - such as anger or hostility - in a social and cultural context. People play different roles in complex and varying contexts with a virtually limitless array of possible targets for anger, hostility, and aggression. How, then, should aggression researchers proceed?

I have assembled a group of authors whose research work has emphasized the aggression-eliciting characteristics of people and other animals, the traits that make them targets of aggressive behavior. Despite my own own background as a comparative psychologist, the clear emphasis of the book is on aggression by humans, although some of the authors may refer to data from other species. Obviously there are additional targets of aggressive behavior that I have not included because they are not emphasized in the research literature of psychology. Since the major concern of psychological science is with the behavior of individuals rather than groups, I have specifically excluded topics such as racial violence, warfare, and political violence. Are there common elements to be found among the diverse targets of aggression to be discussed by these authors? One thing the reader will not find is any emphasis on the unproductive innate/learned controversy that plagued much of the earlier literature on aggression. In the concluding chapter I try to draw together some of the diverse strands discussed by the various authors. But I am afraid that after 25 years of research on aggression I still cannot offer The Answer. And the questions continue to fascinate all of us.

REFERENCES

Baenninger, R. (1974). Some consequences of aggressive behavior: a selective review of the literature on other animals. *Aggressive Behavior, 1*, 17-37.

Brain, P.F. and Benton, D. (Eds) (1981). *The Biology of Aggression*. Aalphen an den Rijn, Netherlands: Sijthoff & Noordhoff.

Lorenz, K. (1966). *On Aggression*. London: Methuen.

Moyer, K.E. (1968). Kinds of aggression and their physiological basis. *Communications in Behavioral Biology, 2*, 65-87.

Zillmann, D. (1979). *Hostility and Aggression*. Hillsdale, NJ: L. Erlbaum.

2

Violence Toward Other Species
Ronald Baenninger

Other species belonging to the animal kingdom are our only living companions on this planet, but ancestral hominids and *Homo sapiens* have shown much violence toward them, according to both historical and fossil records (Dart, 1953; Ruspoli, 1987). The reasons for this are many and complex, and in this chapter I plan to examine some of them. Much of the violence was not intentionally cruel; we interacted with other animal species in furthering the survival of our own, and as in many other interspecies interactions there was damage caused.

While it is true that early hominids and humans frequently had to defend themselves against attacks by their contemporary species (especially carnivores), such dangers to modern humans are largely imaginary; unprovoked attacks on the people of industrial nations by the species that we fear (e.g. sharks, crocodiles, bears, lions or wolves) are now statistically rare events (Caras, 1964). Human violence toward members of other species in the modern world is only rarely a matter of protecting ourselves. People may perceive certain animals as a threat, and behave accordingly, but healthy wild animals are rarely a legitimate danger to us.

In fact, the balance of power has swung in our favor to such an extent that the very survival of other species is a subject for debate among residents of many modern nations. Difficult choices must sometimes be made that involve striking a balance between conservation of animals and protecting human welfare. For example, in Ranthambore National Park (one of 16 national parks in India) Project Tiger has been effective in doubling the number of Bengal tigers since it began in 1973. At the same time, the number of villagers killed by tigers has increased from 18 in 1973 to 60 in 1987. Humans are not permitted to carry weapons in the Park, but many poor Indians venture inside its boundaries to grow crops that people need. Carnivores can still pose a threat to humans.

In the United States we routinely kill millions of animals intentionally, but we do not think of it as aggression. Human predation on other species is a mechanized industry, and extermination of animal competitors by farmers and ranchers is widely accepted. Unwanted pets are killed on a large scale. Wildlife that wanders too close to human dwellings, roads, railroads or airports is killed accidentally, or it is shot, poisoned, or transported elsewhere. Our right to kill members of other species, and to appropriate their habitat, is questioned only in societies that have advanced well beyond minimum subsistence, and to whom alternatives are available.

While violence toward animals has occurred since the evolutionary divergence of our species from our fellow primates there has been remarkably little scientific research explicitly dealing with the topic. Aggressive behavior among members of our own species has been extensively studied, as well as aggression among members of many other species of mammals, birds, fish, reptiles, amphibians, and invertebrates. But interspecies aggression has frequently been considered simply as predation (Lorenz, 1966) and has been ignored, or taken for granted. Of the five basic types of interspecies interactions that have ecological significance only three (competition, predation, and parasitism) are potentially harmful to the interacting species. In all three types of interactions aggression is clearly not a primary motive, the injury or harm being incidental to competing successfully for limited resources of some kind, gaining a meal, or gaining a host. Human motives for violence and aggression toward other species have been largely ignored by science, a fact that may reflect our relative independence of other animals in the late 20th century (Baenninger, 1988).

Many of our interactions with other species are much more complex than the classic ecological categories, and do not fit them neatly: e.g. our emotional attachments to animals (Levinson, 1983), our uses of them as symbols in the arts (Carr, 1965; Lonsdale, 1981) and religions (Campbell, 1983), or as models in science and medicine (Holden, 1988), the variety of ways in which they contribute to human entertainments, circuses, and sports, and our historical dependence on them for work (Hyams, 1972). Such interactions have made possible varieties of human violence and aggression toward other species that are not shown by other predators, competitors, or parasites.

In this chapter I plan to examine some historical aspects of our violence, aggression, and cruelty to other species. I will then examine the hypothesis that we generalize our treatment of animals to humans (or vice versa). Do children who abuse animals grow up to behave violently toward humans? Unlike the other targets of violence and aggression discussed in this book, we routinely kill animals and eat them. Are hunters and slaughter house employees unusually violent toward other animals and people? Finally, I will discuss anthropomorphism, cruelty, intentionality, and the potential benefits for humanity of human aggressive acts toward animals.

THE HUMANE MOVEMENT

In response to the violence and cruelty often shown by humans toward other animal species a powerful movement to protect them arose during the 19th century. In the absence of systematic data on the abuse of animals the history of this "humane" movement provides abundant case histories that are relevant to the ways that our species has treated others. The laws and strictures that developed tell us by implication of the abuses that they were drafted to correct.

The roots of kindness toward animals extend back thousands of years to the centuries when beasts were essential for all human industry, agriculture, transportation, and communications. In Exodus 20:8-10 and Deuteronomy 25:4 there were injunctions to set aside a weekly day of rest for working cattle. Oxen and asses were never to be yoked together lest the smaller animal be hurt when the plough hit buried rocks, and their feed was to be "clean provender which has been winnowed with shovel and fan". "A righteous man hath regard for the life of his beast..." (Proverbs 12:10). There were biblical criticisms of the ritual killing of animals as religious offerings - "I delight not in the blood of bullocks or of lambs or of he-goats"; "He who slaughters an ox is as if he slew a man; he who sacrifices a lamb, like him who breaks a dog's neck (Isaiah 66:3)". Such injunctions were not unique to the Judeo-Christian religions: Zoroaster also denied that evil deeds could be atoned for by animal sacrifices, and Gautama (the founder of Buddhism) viewed the killing of animals as a sin, although this was because of his belief in the transmigration of human souls after death. He did not declare the mistreatment of animals to be a sin. Mahavira, the founder of Jainism, considered animals to an unusual degree; Jain priests wore mouth covers to minimize the death of insects by swallowing them, and built hospitals for sick and injured animals.

In the Western world cruelty to animals was routine, but there were also exceptions. Among the ancient Greeks, Pythagoras and his followers were vegetarians, who bought live animals in the marketplaces in order to set them free. Areopagus, a member of the Athenian supreme court, executed a farmer who had skinned a ram alive, and a boy who had blinded a bird. By contrast, ancient Rome is now justifiably famous for the brutality shown toward animals (and toward humans) in its circuses. During the reign of Caesar Augustus (from 29 B.C. to 14 A.D.) he held 26 *venationes*, in which close to 3500 hippos, rhinos, lions and leopards were "hunted" and killed in the arena ring by army deserters, Christians, or trained gladiators (Fisher, 1967). But Cicero (as quoted by Pliny the Elder) remarked that, "...It was the last day of a venatio for baiting animals, and it brought much wonder to the common crowd, but no pleasure at all. Indeed a certain sense of pity set in, and a sort of feeling that there is a kind of fellowship between that great [baited] animal and the human race."

The record is mixed with respect to the humane sentiments of early Christians, although many saints expressed kindness to animals (Waddell, 1934). St. Paul was apparently neither tolerant nor humane, and is known for asking sarcastically "Doth God take care of oxen?" But St. John Chrysostom, a Bishop of Constantinople who lived between 300 and 400 A.D., is quoted as saying that "Surely we ought to show them great kindness and gentleness for many reasons, but above all because they are of the same origin as ourselves". The Cistercian monastic order was founded in 1098 by sheep farmers, and the Franciscans were founded about 1200 by St. Francis of Assisi, renowned as a friend of animals. St. Thomas Aquinas taught indifference to "brutes" but criticized outright cruelty to them because he believed that it would generalize to our treatment of humans. Pope Urban II, at the Council of Clermont in 1095, extended the right of sanctuary to all oxen, plough horses and harrowing horses, as well as to the men who guided them.

Among philosophers, one extreme was Descartes' view that animals were unfeeling automatons and that "any assimilation of man to animals" had to be prevented. He asserted that, "After the error of atheism there is none which leads weak minds further astray from the path of virtue than the idea that the minds of animals resemble our own, and therefore that we have no greater right to future life than have gnats and ants." Near the other extreme were philosophers like John Locke, who insisted that children should be bred to abhor the torment of *sensible* creatures. John Wesley maintained a belief in animal souls, and the possibility of their redemption.

The way in which animals were classified by early natural philosophers played a role in these debates. One of the reasons Albertus Magnus was banned at major European universities in the 13th century was his revival of the teachings of Aristotle, including his "pagan" view that humans belonged in the same taxonomic system as the beasts, a view that survives in the modern taxonomy based on Linnaeus's system. But Albertus did relegate other animals to lives based on instinct rather than reason, a view which permitted his student, St. Thomas Aquinas, to argue that indifference to "brutes" was justified since they lacked reason.

Humans put animals to work, and without their efforts humanity would have been unable to accomplish agriculture, build towns, or make war on a large scale (Campbell & Lasley, 1985). By the late 11th century over 70% of the power available in England came from the work of animals like oxen and horses. The remainder was provided by mill wheels and by men and women who could not afford the investment or upkeep of animals (Langdon, 1986). Inevitably, those who relied on the work of animals frequently demanded too much work from too few animals; suffering and cruel treatment for domestic animals were the result even in peacetime. During wars, vast numbers of horses, oxen, camels, and donkeys were used by armies for transport of supplies and shelter, armaments and ammunition (Braudel, 1981). A military manual from France's army (in the 17th century, under Louis XIII) noted that at least 25 horses were required to draw each of the largest field artillery pieces, plus at least a dozen more to carry the powder and shot for it. These beasts of burden hauled the requirements for every battle, and like the thousands of cavalry horses, were also under fire during all the battles all over Europe. "Horsepower" used to have a living definition.

Popular pastimes and amusements of ordinary people have also involved animals. Rodeos, bull-fights, cock-fights, dog and horse races, and steeplechases are still popular in many cultures. Cruelty to animals occurs in some of these activities, but is not necessarily a central aspect. But in bull-baiting, for example, a tethered bull was bitten on the nose by a bulldog, which then hung on while the bull attempted to dislodge it. This cruel practice was a widespread entertainment of medieval England, and early in the 13th century King John provided meadows for bull-baiting after finding it amusing. In Cromwell's England bull-baiting was still popular, as were bear-baiting, badger-baiting, cock-throwing, and cock-fighting. During this period (mid-17th century) butchers in England were prohibited by law from slaughtering a bull which had not been baited, since it was believed that the process improved the meat and the bull's health, as well as providing great entertainment for the masses (Niven, 1967).

American views toward animals were strongly influenced by the frontier experience, involving as it did the protection of loved ones, domestic livestock and crops from carnivorous predators, as well as the hunting and trapping of wild animals (which in most states are still classified as "game", "furbearers", or "vermin"). In agricultural, rural societies predation and competition are facts of daily life, and wild animals pose a threat to human physical or economic survival. But rural Americans also devised some cruel entertainments including "coon on a log" (in which a dog swims out to attack a raccoon trapped on a small floating log), or "snatch the rooster" (in which a galloping horseman snatches a rooster that has been buried up to its neck). People such as bounty hunters or trappers make their living by capturing or killing wild animals, and cannot afford to be squeamish about the way their victims feel. As North Americans increasingly moved to cities or towns organizations such as the Anti Steel Trap League attracted more members, and once-popular pastimes and practices were declared illegal.

The German philosopher Schopenhauer in *Geschichte der Tierschutzes (History of Animal Protection)* remarked that "He who is cruel to animals can be no good man". While individual rulers in Germany were friends to animals, and occasionally decreed that cruelty be stopped, there were no universal principles arrived at by societal consensus. Frederick the Great is quoted as saying that "Since I know men I have learned to love animals". A similar remark is attributed to Balzac, and the English writer John Galsworthy said, "If I were condemned to spend 24 hours alone with a single creature I would choose to spend them with my dog". Misanthropic sentiments thus were not unique to any nation of Western Europe, but distinctions between rejection of humans and attraction to animals are not always easy to draw.

It was in Great Britain that legalized animal protection first went furthest. Jeremy Bentham, in *Principals of a Penal Code* listed cruelty to animals as a crime "cognisable by law". In 1766 Dr. Humphrey Primatt wrote "A Dissertation on the Duty of Mercy and the Sin of Cruelty to Brute Animals". Thomas Young wrote *An Essay on Humanity to Animals* in 1798 but in 1800 Sir William Pulteney's bill to restrict bull-baiting was defeated in Parliament, largely because such entertainment for the lower classes was considered important; the advice of Roman emperors to give the populace "bread and circuses" was still heeded. By 1809 a bill to prevent "wanton and malicious cruelty to animals" passed in the House of Lords, but was defeated in Commons. This occurred again in 1810. Finally in 1821 Richard Martin managed to have a bill passed in the House of Commons that protected horses and cattle. Martin's impassioned argument provoked laughter among other Members of Parliament, and the protection of "asses" was gratuitously added to the bill, which passed in the House of Lords the following year.

After these precedents the stage was set for creation of the Royal Society for the Prevention of Cruelty to Animals in 1824. The early participants in that society were wealthy and influential - William Wilberforce, Sir James Mackintosh, T.F.Bruxton, and Lewis Gompertz (an eccentric philanthropist who refused to eat meat or ride in horsedrawn coaches). Only the advent of steam railroads made it possible for people like Gompertz to travel without relying on animal work. RSPCA discussions centered on topics like animal cruelty, the abolition of slavery, alleviating the lives of the poor, and criminal code reform. But the time was right for such concerns, and in a relatively short span of time it became unfashionable to display cruelty to animals, even among the British public. In 1854 a cat skinner was jailed under a 1835 law that forbade cat-skinning, dog-fighting, badger-baiting, cock-fighting and brutality to cart dogs; the convicted cat skinner was attacked by a street mob and vilified by the other prisoners. Not only eccentric British intellectuals were concerned with animal cruelty by the latter part of the 19th century (Niven, 1967; Lansbury, 1985; Ritvo, 1987).

As early as 1822 cruelty to animals was punishable in Nova Scotia by public whipping. In the United States the humane movement was active by the latter part of the 19th century. Henry Bergh, while Secretary of the U.S. Consulate in St. Petersburg, observed cruelty to animals that led him to promote animal welfare reform upon his return to the U.S. In 1866 New York State enacted a law declaring it a misdemeanor "to maliciously kill, maim, injure, torture, crowd, or cruelly beat any horse, mule, cow, cattle, sheep or other animal belonging to himself or another". Other states followed suit, and all states now have such laws, although their enforcement is inconsistent.

The New York Society for the Prevention of Cruelty to Children was begun only in 1876, ten years after the law governing animal cruelty. The humane movement was thus roughly contemporary with the movement to abolish slavery, and preceded the movement to protect children from abuse. In 1874 the officers of the American Society for the Prevention of Cruelty to Animals were confronted with the case of "little Mary Ellen" who was beaten daily and tormented cruelly by her stepmother. Since there was no law covering children in these circumstances the concerned people turned to Henry Bergh and the ASPCA. A separate society for preventing cruelty to children was formed as a result. In 1873 Jacob Riis' book *How the Other Half Lives* (illustrated with many of his own photographs) brought to the attention of American society just how abysmal were conditions for children of poverty. Only in 1904 was a National Child Labor Commission set up, by Felix Adler, and McCrea (1910) found that in 1908 there were 104 humane societies that dealt exclusively with animals, but only 45 that were devoted exclusively to the welfare of children. The first Federal law governing child labor conditions was the Fair Labor Standards Act of 1938.

The single greatest force for the humane treatment of animals was probably the increasing mechanization of agriculture, communications and transportation, which affected beasts of burden more than children. An overloaded truck or bus may suffer broken springs or engine problems, but when Henry Bergh blocked the path of overcrowded street railroad cars in the late 19th century he was concerned with living horses that were often grossly overburdened. There were financial incentives for overloading and overworking the helpless animals, but as industry and the colonial system generated wealth for Europe and the U.S. the protection of helpless innocents became increasingly possible. MacCrea (1910) reported the existence of a Home of Rest for Horses, The Drinking Fountain and Cattle Trough Association, and the London Cart Horse Parade Society.

ARE ANIMALS LIKE HUMANS?

Why should people concern themselves with cart horses and cattle troughs? The history of comparative psychology has reflected the size of the gap perceived between ourselves and other members of the animal kingdom (Warden, Jenkins, & Warner, 1935). At times, and by some people, they have been seen as just below us, while for others a great unbridgeable chasm has separated us from animals. They are perceived by most people now as somehow similar to us, although precisely how varies in different subcultures. This fact raises two important issues: 1) how and where do we draw the lines between us and them? 2) does their similarity to us really make any difference in how we treat them? Does our perception of them as similar or different contribute to better or worse treatment?

The treatment of human slaves and children was not always humane, and "man's inhumanity to man" has been notorious throughout our history. Many people, such as Charles Dickens (1866) have been concerned with humane treatment of both animals and people, but some are kinder to animals than they are to other people. It is not uncommon to find dislike or hatred of people among those who loudly profess their love for animals (e.g. Lillie, 1954).

When we gratuitously attribute human motives, thoughts, or emotional experiences to members of other species it is called anthropomorphism. The rules of science require that data be public and, since thoughts and feelings are not public, we can never be scientifically certain that other species really share those that we have as humans. As a result, modern science generally holds anthropomorphism in low esteem. Muckerman (1906) even argued that anthropomorphic thinking is an inevitable consequence of materialism in science. As a vitalist, who believed that a "vital essence" differentiated "Man and Brute", Muckerman reasoned that materialists (who do not accept this idea of a vital essence) have no basis for distinguishing humans and animals, and must therefore be anthropomorphists, an almost whimsically illogical conclusion.

Materialists like Descartes viewed other species as mere machines composed of hydraulic equipment and systems of levers. Such a materialistic belief was no doubt intended to reduce anthropomorphism. Like most pet owners, Descartes may have been anthropomorphic about his own dog ("Monsieur Grat"). But his intellectual compatriot Malebranche is said to have kicked his dog just to hear what he called "the creaking of the machine". Pope Pius II likened the deaths of animals in laboratories and slaughterhouses to metal being hammered in a forge, seeds rotting in storage, branches being pruned, or grain being harvested and milled. While progress in the biological sciences has been enhanced by avoiding anthropomorphism, the resulting view of animals may be scientifically incomplete (Baenninger, 1990; Griffin, 1984) and lends itself to cruelty toward them. Aggressive or violent behavior toward animals is surely easier for those who believe that other species do not experience pain or have feelings of fear, terror, misery or rage.

During the 18th century wealthy amateur "physiologists" tortured animals for the amusement of their guests; they carved up, dismembered, gutted and abused living animals in what Pepys called "pretty experiments" staged for entertainment at home (Niven, 1967). Boyle's invention of the air pump lent itself to this debasement of science, and it was used to suffocate a great many living animals for no purpose beyond demonstrations that lacked any educational or training significance. These people avoided anthropomorphism, and apparently were unmoved by Plutarch's comment that, "Boys may kill frogs for fun, but the frogs die in earnest".

Generalization is normally based on stimulus similarity; the more similar two stimuli are the more likely we are to respond similarly to them. If we perceive members of other species as similar to humans will we generalize our responses from human to non-human? If a child learns to behave violently or cruelly toward animals, will such responses generalize to humans, as Thomas Aquinas asserted? Is it possible that the violent aggressive acts of some adults are simply examples of negative transfer, whereby such people are continuing to respond aggressively to humans as they learned to behave toward animals while they were children, without learning to make the distinction made by most adults? Alternatively, it is certainly plausible that children who grow up in circumstances where violence toward other people is common will respond in the same way toward animals.

The question of stimulus similarity is thus a critical one.

Seeing animals as different from us may underlie some of the violence and aggression toward them in cultures (or subcultures) where violence toward people is minimal. In aggressive, warlike cultures aggression toward animals might occur because they are perceived as similar to the normal human targets of aggression. One way to test the hypothesis might be to examine historical variation in cruelty and variations in perceived similarity of humans and other animal species. In violent (warlike?) cultures cruelty to animals should have been most prevalent during those periods that perceived the greatest *similarity* between humans and other species. In relatively peaceable cultures animal cruelty would be more likely in eras where they were perceived as *dissimilar*. Lacking the skills, knowledge, and resources for undertaking a huge historical investigation we can still ask, "What are some of the dimensions on which humans are perceived as similar to other species?".

(1) Appearance. Except for certain non-human primates most animals do not look much like us, although pet owners are often said to resemble their pets. The facial expressions, movement, and gait of individual people may resemble certain other species (e.g. some people may be "bear-like" while others may move like gazelles or swans). Such similarities are more likely to provoke mirth or admiration rather than violence and aggression. It is doubtful that similarity of appearance promotes generalization, although it surely suggests many similes and metaphors, and helps to create symbolic roles for animals in tales for children and adults (Bettelheim, 1976).

(2) Sensory experience. Aristotle believed that animals are like children in their capacity for sensation but. However, in the absence of any objective way to verify subjective experience of another creature, this issue has been debated for centuries. Animals may behave as if they are experiencing pain, by whining, screaming, or seeking to avoid the stimulus. Most of us are convinced that animals experience pain, and most objective scientists believe that animals can feel pain. Their position is simply that it cannot be demonstrated objectively. Midgely (1983) has characterized this position as absurd.

(3) Mind, or thought processes. The study of animal mind and thought is now a flourishing area of experimental psychology. The data emerging from research on other species provide evidence of similarities and differences in cognitive processes that is more convincing than the assertions or attributions of philosophers (Shepard, 1978). Montaigne, for example, explained the ancient Thracian legend of the fox which refused to cross thin ice by attributing to it a remarkable logical sequence: The fox listens to the roaring of water and then considers the logic of the situation in the following manner - "Whatsoever maketh a noise moveth, whatsoever moveth, is not frozen, whatsoever is not frozen is liquid, whatsoever is liquid yields under any weight". Another strange attribution of intelligence has been the writing of letters to (or from) animals. The *Baltimore Sun* for Feb. 21, 1888 carried a story about a letter that was left for rats in a home infested by them. The homeowner instructed the rats to leave and make their way to the home of a Captain Low (directions to which were included).

E.L. Thorndike (1898) suggested that "Human folk are as a matter of fact eager to find intelligence in animals.... Thousands of cats on thousands of occasions, sit helplessly yowling, and no one takes thought of it; but let one cat claw at the knob of a door, supposedly as a signal to be let out, and straightway this cat becomes the representative of the cat-mind in all the books."

(4) Possession of a soul. Philosophers and theologians have differed on this issue, and science has little to offer. The denial that animals had souls was an important matter for theologians, and was one basis for the pervasive cruelty and neglect of animals in the middle ages.

The view prevalent in medieval Europe that the world was a vale of tears to be traversed as quickly and painlessly as possible naturally led to contempt for natural phenomena, including animals. If animals possessed reason it would imply that they knew right from wrong, and thus had moral responsibility, which in turn would endow them with the possibility of redemption and immortality, or of damnation for their sins on earth.

Persecution of animals by good Christians (and horribly cruel acts toward animals) were made respectable by denying the existence of animal souls. In 13th and 14th century France cats were believed to be agents of the devil, and were tortured and crucified (Barloy, 1978). Even cat owners were sometimes hanged or burned at the stake for harboring them. The city council of Cahors annually lit "The Stake of St. John" in which six cats were burned alive in a basket on top of a stake. After much singing and dancing the crowds pulled the charred remains from the embers to bring good fortune. In Metz cats were burned alive to stop an epidemic of St. Vitus' Dance, and the custom persisted until 1773, watched by kings and commoners alike. The shrivelled remains of cats have been discovered in medieval ruins; they were buried alive during construction because it was believed that they would strengthen structures. The heretical cults of Freya and Holda, two goddesses who kept cats as companions, provided justification for these cruel customs, which were not unique to medieval France (Barloy, 1978). Animals that are "sacrificed" alive, whether for Science, Religion, or some other deity, must surely suffer. Those who inflict such suffering may have a variety of motives that underlie their acts.

(5) Possession of a moral sense. Knowing right from wrong is sometimes taken as a basic criterion for normal mentality. This view is embodied in the McNaughton Rule, in which aggressive criminals are classified as insane by virtue of their inability to make this distinction. Swedenborg, the founder of a flourishing Christian sect, argued that animals are similar to humans except for their inability to distinguish right from wrong. But others did not hesitate to attribute this ability to animals. During the middle ages animals that were deemed to be wilful lawbreakers were tried in courts and tribunals complete with witnesses, judges, and all the trappings of legal prosecution (Evans, 1904; Beach, 1950). Guilty animals were sentenced to various punishments, including death, for crimes involving property or personal damage toward humans. Sometimes animals were executed as accomplices, as in the case of "...one Hachett, a servant in Salem...found in buggery with a cow upon the Lord's day". The unlucky Hachett and the cow were both executed for their immoral activity on a Sunday (Winthrop, 1853).

DOES CRUELTY TO ANIMALS GENERALIZE TO HUMANS?

If animals are perceived as similar to people (whatever the basis of such similarity may be) then the responses that are made toward animals may generalize and similar responses will be made to people. In other words, positive transfer should occur whether the childhood responses involve kindness or cruelty toward animals. Margaret Mead (1964) asserted that torture of animals by children was a precursor to adult violence in a variety of cultures. In recent years a small research literature has developed on the question of whether children who develop habits of cruelty to animals will become adults who aggress against their fellow humans. The alternative question is also of great interest, that is, whether adult violence can be ameliorated by encouraging children to show kindness and empathy toward animals. Is generalization of kindly responses easier or more likely than generalization of cruel or aggressive responses? The only study I have found that is at all relevant to such matters was reported by Lester (1988); he found that ownership of cats and dogs was positively related to the homicide (but not the suicide) rate in 15 industrialized nations.

In modern industrial societies most adults have little to do with any animals except for pets, and this lack of serious interaction may have effects on people. Therapy for pets is now a thriving enterprise, While therapy with pets apparently benefits people who are mentally ill or retarded, aged, or alone (Levinson, 1969; 1983). But many American adults seem to associate animals with childhood and childishness, and it is clear that children's toys, clothes, stories, TV shows, movies, room decorations, etc. normally have animal themes and motifs. This is probably true because adults assume that children are attracted to animals. To what extent this is true has seldom been examined scientifically.

Leaving aside the question of generalization for the moment, what kinds of responses do children make initially to animals? Are their initial responses to animals kind or cruel? Montague (1982) argued that cruelty to animals is learned, implying that kindness or neutrality toward them is the natural, unlearned response. But it may be that kindness or empathic treatment of animals is learned, while violence, cruelty or aggression are the natural, unlearned responses. Edwards (1986) found that parental sanctions, rather than internalized rules, determined the control of aggression toward animals among children of the Oyagi in Kenya. There does not appear to be a research literature on these questions. A considerable body of knowledge exists regarding the development of empathy, altruism, and prosocial responses among humans (Bryant, 1987; Edwards, 1986; Eisenberg & Mussen, 1989, Hoffman, 1977; Radke-Yarrow, 1983), but the possible role of animals in the childhood development of empathy has been virtually ignored.

Whether empathy is defined as a cognitive ability to recognize and understand the thoughts, feelings, or intentions of another individual, or as the vicarious experiencing of the emotional state of another individual, it seems to me that childhood interactions with animals would be a relevant kind of learning experience. Can children improve their empathic responses when the individuals with whom they interact belong to other species? There seems to be no answer in the psychological literature, and this gap strikes me as evidence of how unimportant animals seem to research psychologists. If it is true that little children really are attracted to animals (a sentiment that is almost universally attributed to them) then surely animals could play a role in developing empathy and altruistic responses of children toward other children. The only relevant study I have found was done over 50 years ago by Bathurst (1933); preschoolers with pets showed more "sympathetic" responses to their peers than did children who did not have pets. A totally separate literature exists on helping behavior among members of various other species, particularly non-human primates who show food-sharing, grooming, care-giving, and various nurturing activities toward the young of other individuals. But, once again, interspecific interactions have been ignored.

Ascione (1984) surveyed samples of children from kindergarten and Grade 2 and found that 75% agreed with the proposition that some animals are not nice, 88% would not be sad if a horse fell down, and 64% denied that dogs hate to sit in cars on hot days with the windows closed. Ninety percent of a sample of 4th and 6th graders disagreed with the statement that animals should not be used in entertainment for people if it was dangerous for the animals, and only 22% of these children thought that watching birds with binoculars is more fun than shooting pheasants. While even these preliminary data are interesting, it is not clear whether they indicate much about a lack of humane attitudes of children; they may simply indicate ignorance, or the inability to imagine future consequences of their actions, or an inability to take the perspective of another individual. And such attitude scales tell us nothing about how children actually behave when they see a live animal suffering. Many urban children have never seen animals other than rats, stray dogs, cockroaches, or starlings, and know of more attractive creatures only from television programs. After rock-throwing children killed a large number of flamingoes at the Philadelphia Zoo, my conversations with staff members indicated that protecting animals from children who torment or injure them is a serious problem in all American zoos.

We have very little information about normal, initial attitudes of children toward animals. This means that any generalization of aggressive acts could be from animals to people, or from people to animals. In 1806 Pinel described the case of a highly aggressive man, who eventually killed a person, and noted that "If a dog, a horse, or any other animal offended, he instantly put it to death." Some of the most notorious mass and multiple murderers reportedly had behavior patterns of excessively cruel behavior toward animals as well. According to Felthous and Kellert (1987) such observations are suspect for a number of reasons: the empirical surveys are often contradictory, and psychiatrists are unwilling to attach great importance to single symptoms. There is a danger of sampling bias in such surveys, since those who are not currently violent toward other people are seldom asked whether they were previously cruel to animals.

Felthous and Kellert (1987) surveyed the few studies on whether childhood cruelty to animals was associated with adult violence toward people. They concluded that results were generally inconclusive because of serious flaws in much of the work. Some studies reported a fairly clear relationship, while others found no relationship at all. Then Felthous and Kellert reported on a study that they carried out, using interviews rather than retrospective questionnaires, and concluded that "Prediction of a single act (e.g. homicide) on the basis of a preceding act (e.g. animal abuse) would be risky indeed. However, further acts of cruelty can be reasonably expected in a child who has already demonstrated an ongoing pattern of animal cruelty. In addition, although an isolated violent act in an overcontrolled individual would be difficult to predict, one could say that someone with a pattern of repeated assaults is more likely to commit assault again than someone who has never committed assault...The literature suggests an association between a pattern of cruelty to animals in childhood or adolescence and a pattern of dangerous and recurrent aggression against people at a later age."

Climent, Hyg, and Ervin (1972) studied 40 violent and 40 nonviolent patients by administering a questionnaire that included 14 "neurotic childhood traits". While stubbornness, temper tantrums, and emotional deprivation were associated with the violent group, animal cruelty was not. In studies where data were gleaned from charts, hospital records or questionnaires, there was often no way to know whether animal cruelty had not occurred, or whether it had never been recorded. The fact that it failed to differentiate violent from non-violent people is not surprising. The prediction of violent behavior is highly uncertain at best (Dutile and Foust, 1987).

In controlled studies in which childhood cruelty to animals was predictive of adult violence researchers collected data by using interviews, so that explicit questions could be asked about incidents of cruelty. In several studies an association emerged between adult violence and an interesting triad of childhood behaviors: fire-setting, bed-wetting, and cruelty to animals (Hellman & Blackman, 1966; Wax & Haddox, 1974). In the Hellman and Blackman study 75% of 31 aggressive male prisoners gave histories involving this triad, while only 15 % of 53 nonaggressive prisoners did so. Animal cruelty was reported by 52 % of the aggressive, but only 17% of the nonaggressive prisoners. Thus, the results of interview research contradict the findings from questionnaire studies. In their study of 152 men Felthous & Kellert (1987) asked interview questions about specific childhood involvement with animals (i.e. pet ownership, raising livestock, training animals, trapping and hunting, attending dogfights, cockfights or bullfights). They found that 25% of the aggressive criminals had abused animals 5 or more times as children, while only 5.8% of the nonaggressive criminals had done so, and none of the non-criminals. Of the 20 prisoners who reported a "pattern of deliberately, repeatedly, and unnecessarily hurting vertebrate animals in a manner likely to cause serious injury" there were 16 who belonged to the most violent group, while only 4 fell into the nonaggressive category. Kellert & Felthous (1985) defined "cruelty" as "willful infliction of harm, injury or intended pain on nonhuman animals". Thus, there does appear to be an association of childhood cruelty to animals and violent adult criminality, but it is by no means an unambiguous relationship.

SLAUGHTER AND SLAUGHTERHOUSES

None of the other targets of violence and aggression discussed in this book are routinely killed and eaten by normal humans; as facultative (rather than obligate) carnivores we eat meat if we can obtain it. This predatory aspect must have some implications for our attitudes towards animals as targets for violent, aggressive acts. Hunting wild animals for meat has been an important activity of our species for most of its history (Nitecki & Nitecki, 1987), but hunting has become less important as the raising and slaughtering of domestic animals has been relegated to specialists (Baenninger, 1987). But the industrialization of animal slaughter has made meat relatively abundant in affluent societies.

Hunting

Predation, interspecies aggression and hunting all result in the deaths of animals, but differ in a number of respects, including their motivation (Baenninger, 1987). At least for those who live in a cash economy, hunting is no longer a necessary activity. Kellert (1978) identified three modern types of hunter, based on a survey of hunters and non-hunters in the United States:
(1) Utilitarian hunters are those who supplement their diet by shooting game for the table. Their attitudes about killing animals are not those associated with aggressive acts; they view game animals as a crop to be harvested, and are likely to have low incomes, and live in rural areas. This pattern undoubtedly characterized most hunters prior to the modern era. **(2)** Naturalistic hunters, as identified by Kellert, are people with close ties to, and appreciation for, nature. They are likely to be knowledgeable about animals, and engage in other activities associated with nature and ecology (e.g. camping, bird-watching), and think of themselves as part of natural cycles of birth and death. As the writer Ortega y Gasset (1972) put it, "One does not hunt in order to kill; rather one kills in order to have hunted". Neither Utilitarian nor Naturalistic hunters can be characterized as cruel toward animals, despite the fact that they kill them. **(3)** Kellert's third type of hunter, the Dominionistic, seeks to dominate animals and nature, while being quite ignorant about them and their ways. He is more likely than the others to have served in the military, and to be more involved with firearms. Kellert's data suggested that these people are more concerned with exerting mastery and power over animals, and their motivation in hunting appears to be more aggressive than the other kinds of hunter. It would be interesting to know if they were also more likely to have

criminal records (particularly convictions for aggressive acts). To what extent were their acts of violence directed to people *or* animals, or were they violent to both? Perhaps dominionistic hunters are aggressive to people initially, and sublimate these responses by hunting animals. Relevant data are not readily available, and there does not seem to be an empirical literature on the topic.

Slaughterhouse Activities

Most of us think about slaughter houses as little as possible, preferring to find our meat wrapped in plastic and attractively displayed in a supermarket (Herzog & McGee, 1983). We generally hope that the killing is done humanely, and that the brutal, disgusting conditions described by Upton Sinclair in *The Jungle* (1906) no longer prevail.

Grandin (1988) pointed out that careful, humane treatment of animals may make economic sense. She found that slaughterhouse conditions are generally better when meat is sold on the carcass, rather than on a live-weight basis. In the carcass system ownership changes hands after slaughter so the seller must pay for bruises to the meat. Japanese customers, for example, reject bruised pork, and slaughtering plants exporting to Japan have better handling of live animals as a result. Between 1975 and 1987 Grandin (1988) visited federally inspected US and Canadian slaughtering plants for at least 2 days.

She found that 32% of the plants tolerated deliberate, repeated acts of cruelty, while 12 % permitted rough handling on a regular basis, and 56% showed good to excellent behavior of employees. Grandin reported regional differences, with better handling in midwestern and more northerly regions of the U.S. Internationally, it is her impression (as a major manufacturer of stockyard systems) that concern for livestock is higher in cooler parts of the world. In northern Australia animal handling is much rougher than in the cooler southern areas, and she reports a trend for slaughter plant managers in Scandinavia and Canada to be more concerned about humane handling than US managers. Dutch and Swedish plants were "very civilized", with employees who were concerned about animal welfare, and managers who were concerned about employee welfare. She reported that conditions at Mexican slaughterhouses were "dreadful". In general, it is Grandin's belief that societies which treat people humanely do the same to animals. It is surely also true that economic conditions play a role, and more temperate climates are associated with the greater affluence that is needed to care for animals. Societies in which subsistence of humans is problematic may believe that they cannot spare the financial resources for animal welfare.

Grandin found three general categories of treatment by slaughterhouse employees. Most common was *mechanical* handling, in which killing is done efficiently by production line workers who chat and banter among themselves, while using the painless techniques required by law to "process" hundreds of animals daily. *Sadistic* handling was consistently found in a small minority of workers (about 4%) who behaved with deliberate cruelty toward animals. Animal handling as a *sacred ritual* was the third category found by Grandin, and in some ways the most interesting psychologically. It is reminiscent of the ritual slaughter practiced by orthodox Jews and Arabs, and is accompanied by self-imposed limits, controls and rituals that make killing a quasi-religious experience. For example, a Dutch manufacturer of slaughter equipment names it "Walhalla", after the promised afterlife of Norse warriors, and Grandin (1975) described the "Stairway to Heaven" system at the Swift Fresh Meats plant in Tolleson, Arizona.

These three approaches to working in a slaughterhouse are remarkably similar to the three approaches to hunting described by Kellert. Utilitarian hunters are practical and matter-of-fact about what they do, and appear to be very similar to the "mechanical" slaughterhouse workers in this regard. Kellert's Naturalistic hunters have made a kind of a nature-oriented ritual of their activity, treating it as part of the great chain of life in a way that resembles the slaughterhouse workers who make a "sacred ritual" of their work. Dominionistic hunters appear to be like Grandin's sadistic workers, concerned with "machismo" and acts of dominance over animals. These three approaches to killing animals may have rather general significance.

MOTIVES FOR PURE, SADISTIC CRUELTY

Kellert & Felthous (1985), on the basis of interviewing 152 criminals and non-criminals regarding animal cruelty, were able to classify nine principal motives for such behavior.

(1) To control behavior of an animal. Flogging a dray horse that could not pull its load was a common observance when farming and transportation depended on animals. Nowadays pet owners often use punishment when their dogs or cats disobey them, or eliminate in inappropriate spots. Domination of animals appears important.

(2) To retaliate for some provocation by an animal, but revenge rather than training by punishment appeared to be involved.

(3) To express a prejudice against a particular species. Kellert and Felthous found that cats were commonly disliked, and likely to be tortured. One man reported putting a cat in a microwave oven because he simply hated cats.

(4) To express free-floating hostility by re-directing it toward animals. The animals became "scapegoats" in the original, ancient use of the word.

(5) To enhance a reputation for aggressiveness or toughness (machismo). Bullfighting, or rodeo events such as "bronco-busting" and wrestling steers to the ground require physical courage that most people lack. Frontier sports such as "gander-pulling", or some of the bloody variations described earlier, merely require an ability to overcome revulsion in the presence of gore.

(6) To shock others for personal thrills. One respondant had stuffed several cats in a pillow case, doused it in lighter fluid, lit it and threw it into a crowded bar.

(7) To get back at a person for past wrongs. In Mario Puzo's "The Godfather" a man discovers his racehorse in his bed - dead, bloody, and dismembered. One respondant hung the testes of a raccoon on the door of a woman who had wronged him. Revenge is directed toward a person rather than the animal.

(8) To displace aggression from a person to an animal. Children may be frustrated in expressing aggression toward parents or teachers, and may express their impulses toward helpless creatures. This was particularly likely in physically abused children.

(9) To express non-specific sadism. These people had nothing against the animals, had experienced little or no provocation, and were not particularly hostile. Extinguishing life appeared to be the primary motive.

Particularly with children there may well be additional motives behind animal cruelty which are more difficult to discover. Casual observation of children interacting with pets or domestic animals suggests that simple curiosity, fear, or ignorance can result in unintended torment and injury of the animals even when there is no sadistic intent. Attempting to bend a dog's leg in particular directions, for example, will hurt or injure the dog. A curious young child is unlikely to know this. Unfamiliarity may thus cause apparently aggressive behavior, in the absence of intention.

INTENTION TO INJURE

Technically, most definitions of aggression require that injury inflicted by one participant on the other must be intentional (Zillmann, 1979). Predatory interactions pose a different problem since injury to the victim is intentional, although the major outcome intended by the predator is ingestion, and not simply the injury or death of the prey (Baenninger, 1978). Moyer (1968) included predation as a kind of aggression. But there are still more definitional problems in examining violence and aggression toward animal targets. The farmers to whom Henry Wadsworth Longfellow addressed his poem *Birds of Killingworth* were not killing the birds to eat, nor for "sport", nor out of simple cruelty. They were protecting the value of their crops against avian competitors, and the slaughter was certainly intentional. Sheep ranchers do intend to kill coyotes, because their economic livelihood is at stake; if non-harmful means of removing coyotes and safeguarding lambs could be found most sheep ranchers would probably adopt them willingly. But there are also many forms of unintentional killing of animals. Commercial tuna fishermen do not intend to injure, or kill, the marine mammals that are caught in their nets. Motorists who collide with wild animals such as deer do not intend to kill them, and may suffer personal injury and a large financial outlay for repairs.

Intent is difficult to ascertain, objectively. A motorist may miss a deer in his path; if he then stops, backs up, and tries again unsuccessfully, and then jumps out of his car and shoots his rifle but misses the deer, and then drives across fields in pursuit of the fleeing animal we would surely conclude that he intended to injure or kill the deer. The point is that the occurrence of several responses directed toward the same goal, which cease when the goal is achieved, is what convinces us that there is an intent to achieve that goal or outcome. Unless there is a pattern, a single response that succeeds in injuring an animal is not clear evidence of aggressive intent; it is only when responses are repeated, or when changes and corrections in responding occur that we infer intent to achieve the goal toward which the different responses lead. Merely hitting a deer while driving is inconclusive evidence for aggressive intentions of the motorist. The inept deer hunter who stops attempting to kill his victim before any injury to it occurs may, of course, simply be giving up; his failure to achieve the victim's death does not prove the absence of intent to kill.

DIMENSIONS OF HARMING ANIMALS

Defining aggression is always difficult; defining it with respect to animals is especially complex and multifaceted since we routinely kill or injure them intentionally, for the things they provide us with, for self-protection, or because they are an economic threat. Those who harm members of other species may or may not believe that the animals share human feelings such as the experience of pain. These two dimensions of (1) intentionality and (2) anthropomorphism may be relatively independent. Aggressive, harmful acts toward members of other species may be intentional (or not); the perpetrator of the acts may (or may not) believe that other species resemble us.

When animals are intentionally harmed by a person who believes that they experience feelings like ours I believe we can speak of cruelty. If the harm is unintentional, or if the person believes that they do not have feelings like those of humans, then we cannot really infer a motive to behave cruelly.

The scientist whose experiments intentionally injure animal subjects, and who believes that they are suffering, is being cruel to them even when important benefits for animals or humans result from the injuries of the animals. The scientist normally believes that the knowledge gained for humanity necessitates and outweighs the harm done to the experimental subjects. Some scientists may rationalize the injuries to their animal subjects by coming to believe that animals are unlike humans; others may come to believe that the benefits to humanity do not outweigh the suffering caused to their animal subjects.

None of the motives for animal cruelty listed by Kellert & Felthous involved any legitimate benefits to humanity. Animals were injured for idiosyncratic, psychological reasons, not for food, clothing, work, protection of self or loved ones, or defense of personal property. The bulldozer driver who crushes field mice and moles while destroying their habitat during the construction of a housing development may be totally unaware of the unintended havoc created in the little lives beneath the treads, or may find it psychologically necessary to deny that the fieldmice have feelings of terror, pain, or grief. But driving the bulldozer eventually benefits people by providing shelter for them. Ultimately, it is the willingness to place benefits to humanity above those of other species that permits sane people to perform cruel acts toward animals, whatever the rationalizations or defense mechanisms to which they resort. Denial or repression, whether by scientists, bulldozer operators, slaughterhouse workers or hunters, may be necessary; for example, "utilitarian" hunters and "mechanical" slaughter house employees surely think of their victims as objects rather than sentient beings.

BENEFITS TO HUMANITY

Deciding what sort of benefits to humanity can justify doing violence to members of other species is obviously fraught with ambiguities, and requires Solomonic wisdom. At the very least I would exclude "psychological" benefits. We can speak of cruelty when injury or death of animals is required only to provide entertainment, fashion, or psychological well-being.

Are there evolutionary benefits from the human violence and aggression toward other species that have occurred for millennia? I have discussed some of the proximal ontogenetic, motivational aspects of violence and aggression toward other species, the behavioral causes during lifetimes of individuals. What of phylogenetic aspects, the ultimate causes of behavior? Are there benefits for our species?

According to sociobiological theory, the basic duty of every individual organism is to maximize its inclusive fitness, i.e. the extent to which its own and similar genotypes appear in the next generation. Actions that increase representation in the next generation are beneficial. Thus, individuals have a primary duty to promote their own welfare and reproduction, and that of their kin. Since human genotypes are necessarily more similar to each other than they are to those of any other species, it follows that humans (and members of every other species) have a secondary duty to promote the welfare of their own species. This should take precedence over any concern for other species, and from an evolutionary perspective aggression toward other species may be more likely than kindness. Given the modern problems of overpopulation and the resulting environmental degradation that have resulted from our reproductive success as a species, it may be difficult to accept such an implication. But if the sociobiologists are right we have no choice; to do otherwise would be to engage in a form of "speciesism" directed against our own species. Putting the needs of other species ahead of legitimate human needs cannot be justified in evolutionary terms.

It does not follow from this reasoning that human *cruelty* to other species is a phylogenetic imperative, although threatening, injuring, or killing them may be if legitimate benefits to humanity result. Our use of other species for furthering our own ends (whether for food, clothing, work, or some other function that contributes to human success) is sociobiologically appropriate. Human needs for resources must come first, not because we have a God-given right to do so but because every species has a duty to promote itself. The needs of the tigers of Ranthambore cannot be placed ahead of the needs of Indian villagers for the arable land they need to survive and reproduce. Even those people who support their families by killing endangered wildlife to provide the wealthy with fashionable coats, dagger handles, or aphrodisiacs are not necessarily behaving cruelly (if they kill their prey quickly). But we may certainly condemn those who provide the demand for such trinkets because they are responsible for such a travesty of predation. (Similarly, users of illegal drugs are responsible for the travesty of agriculture when farmers grow coca or marijuana plants or opium poppies instead of food crops). It is possible to put human needs first, while treating other species with the respect that they deserve. Mistreatment of animals for frivolous, perverted, imaginary, or sociobiologically unnecessary reasons has never had any ethical justification.

CONCLUSIONS

From an ecological or sociobiological perspective human predation, competition, or parasitism cannot be considered cruel unless these interactions do not benefit humans or humanity. But our many, varied, and symbolic interactions with other species have made possible varieties of violence that eventually produced restraining legislation in modern, industrial societies. The determinants of cruelty to animals, defined as intentional injury by an aggressor who believes animals share some human experiences, and who derives no benefit from the aggression, have not been studied very much. We know little about children's reactions to animals, the processes by which their adult attitudes are formed, the ways in which they generalize from animals to people, and the extent to which adults perceive animals as similar to people. Our human relationships with members of other species, including violence, aggression, and cruelty, have not been studied by psychology as a dimension of adult personality. Scientifically, and morally, it is time that they were.

REFERENCES

Ascione, F. (1984). *Bless the Beasts and the Children.* Paper presented at Southwestern Society for Research in Human Development meeting, Denver, CO, April 17, 1984.

Baenninger, R. (1978). Some aspects of predatory behavior. *Aggressive Behavior, 4,* 287-311.

Baenninger, R. (1987). Hunting: predation and interspecies aggression. In Caprara, G.V. & Renzi, P. (Eds.) *L'Aggressivita Animale.* Rome: Bulzoni Editore.

Baenninger, R. (1988). Animals in art: some trends across three millennia. *Journal of Psychology, 122,* 109-112.

Baenninger, R. (1990, in press). Consciousness and comparative psychology. In Johnson, M.G. &. Henley, T.B. (Eds). *The Principles of Psychology at 100: William James after a Century.* Hillsdale, NJ: L. Erlbaum.

Barloy, J.J. (1978). *Man and Animals.* London: Gordon & Cremonesi.

Bathurst, J.E. (1933). A study of sympathy and resistance (negativism). among children. *Psychological Bulletin. 30,* 625-626.

Beach, F.A. (1950). Beasts before the bar. *Natural History*.

Bettelheim, B. (1976). *The Uses of Enchantment.* New York: Alfred A. Knopf.

Braudel, F. (1981). *The Structures of Everyday Life.* New York, Harper & Row.

Bryant, B.K. (1987). In N. Eisenberg and J. Strayer (Eds.) *Empathy and its Development.* New York: Cambridge University Press.

Campbell, J. (1983). *The Way of the Animal Powers.* London: Summerfield Press.

Campbell, J.R. and Lasley, J.F. (1985). *The Science of Animals that Serve Humanity.* New York: McGraw-Hill.

Caras, R.A. (1964). *Dangerous to Man.* New York: Holt, Rinehart & Winston.

Carr, W.G. (1965). *Man and Animal: Man Through his Art (vol.3).* Greenwich, Conn: NY Graphic Society.

Climent, C.E., Hyg, M.S. & Ervin, F.R. (1972). Historical data in the evaluation of violent subjects. *Archives of General Psychiatry, 27,* 621-624.

Dart, R.A. (1953). The predatory transition from ape to man. *International Anthropological and Linguistic Review, 1.*

Dickens, C. (1866). *Inhumane Humanity.* All the Year Round, 15, 238-240.

Dutile, F.N. and Foust, C.H. (1987). *The Prediction of Criminal Violence.* Springfield: C.C.Thomas.

Edwards, P. (1986). In Fogel, A. and Melson, G.F. (Eds.) *Origins of Nurturance: Developmental, Biological and Cultural Perspectives on Caregiving.* Hillsdale, NJ,: L. Erlbaum.

Eisenberg, N. and Mussen, P. (1989). *The Roots of Prosocial Behavior in Children.* New York: Cambridge University Press

Evans, M.P. (1904). *Criminal Prosecution and Capital Punishment of Animals.* London: William Heinemann.

Felthous, A.R. (1980). Aggression against cats, dogs, and people. *Child Psychiatry and Human Development, 10,* 169-177.

Felthous, A.R. & Kellert, S.R. (1986). Violence against animals and people: is aggression against living creatures generalized? *Bulletin of American Academy of Psychiatry and Law, 14,* 55-69.

Felthous, A.R. & Kellert, S.R. (1987). Childhood cruelty to animals and later aggression against people: a review. *American Journal of Psychiatry, 144,* 710-717.

Fisher, J. (1967). *Zoos of the World.* Garden City NY: Natural History Press.

Grandin, T. (1975). Stairway to heaven. *National Humane Review.*

Grandin, T. (1988). Behavior of slaughter plant and auction employees toward the animals. *Anthrozoos, 1,* 205-213.

Griffin, D.R. (1984). Animal thinking. *American Scientist. 72,* 456-464.

Hellman, D.S. and Blackman, N. (1966). Enuresis, firesetting and cruelty to animals: a triad predictive of adult crime. *American Journal of Psychiatry, 122,* 1431-1435.

Herzog, H.A. and McGee, S. (1983). Psychological aspects of slaughter reactions of college students to killing and butchering cattle and hogs. *International Journal for the Study of Animal Problems, 4,* 124-132.

Hoffman, M.L. (1977). Empathy, its development and prosocial implications. In C.B. Keasey (Ed.) *Nebraska Symposium on Motivation.* Lincoln: University of Nebraska Press, 169-217

Holden, C. (1988). Experts ponder simian well-being. *Science, 241,* 1753-1755.

Hyams, E. (1972). *Animals in the Service of Man.* Philadelphia: J.B. Lippincott.

Katcher, A. & Beck, A. (Eds.) (1984). *New Perspectives on our Lives with Companion Animals.* Philadelphia: University of Pennsylvania Press.

Kellert, S.R. (1978). Characteristics and attitudes of hunters and anti-hunters. *Transactions of North American Wildlife and Natural Resources Conference, 43,* 412-423.

Kellert, S.R. & Felthous, A.R. (1985). Childhood cruelty toward animals among criminals and noncriminals. *Human Relations, 38,* 1113-1129.

Kellert, S.R. and Westervelt, M.O. (1983). Children's attitudes, knowledge and behavior toward animals. *U.S. Fish and Wildlife Service. U.S. Govt. Printing Office, Document #024-010-00641-2.*

Langdon, J. (1986). *Horses, Oxen, and Technological Innovation: The Use of Draught Animals In English Farming from 1066-1500.* Cambridge: Cambridge University Press.

Lansbury, C. (1985). *The Old Brown Dog: Women, Workers, and Vivisection in Edwardian England.* Madison: U. of Wisconsin Press.

Lester, D. (1988). Attitudes toward animals and personal violence. *Psychological Reports, 63,* 810.

Levinson, B.M. (1969). *Pet-Oriented Psychotherapy.* Springfield: Charles Thomas.

Levinson, B.M. (1983). The future of research into relationships between people and their companion animals. In Katcher, A.H. and Beck, A.M. (Eds.) *New Perspectives on our Lives with Companion Animals.* (pp. 536-550). Philadelphia: University of Pennsylvania Press.

Lillie, H.R. (1954). Man - A biological failure. *UFAW Courier, 10,* 10.

Lonsdale, S. (1981). *Animals and the Origins of Dance.* New York: Thames and Hudson.

Lorenz, K. (1966). *On Aggression.* London: Methuen.

McCrea, R. (1910). *The Humane Movement.* New York: Columbia University Press.

Midgley, M. (1983). *Animals and Why They Matter.* Athens: University of Georgia Press.

Montague, A. (1982). Of man, animals, and morals. In S.R. Westerland (Ed.) *Humane Education and Realms of Humaneness.* Washington, D.C.: University Press of America.

Moyer, K.E. (1968). Kinds of aggression and their physiological basis. *Communications in Behavioral Biology, 2,* 65-87.

Muckerman, H. (1906). *The Humanizing of the Brute.* St. Louis and Freiburg (Baden).: B. Herder.

Nitecki, M.H. and Nitecki, D.V. (1987). *The Evolution of Human Hunting.* New York: Plenum.

Niven, C.D. (1967). *History of the Humane Movement.* New York: Transatlantic Arts.

Ortega y Gasset, J. (1972). *Meditations on Hunting.* New York: Scribner's.

Radke-Yarrow, M. (1983). Children's prosocial dispositions and behavior. In Hetherington, M. (Ed.) *Socialization, Personality, and Social Development. Volume 4 in Mussen's Handbook of Child Psychology.* New York: Wiley.

Rheingold H.L. and Emery, G.N. (1986). The nurturant acts of very young children. In D. Olweus, J.B. Block and M.Radke- Yarrow (Eds.) *Development of Antisocial and Prosocial Behavior.* New York: Academic Press.

Ritvo, H. (1987). *The Animal Estate: The English and Other Creatures in the Victorian Age.* Cambridge, Mass: Harvard University Press.

Ruspoli, M. (1987). *The Cave of Lascaux.* London: Thames and Hudson.

Shepard, P. (1978). *Thinking Animals.* New York: Viking.

Sinclair, U. (1906). *The Jungle.* New York: Doubleday, Page.

Thorndike, E.L. (1898). Animal intelligence; an experimental study of the associative processes in animals. *Psychological Review, Vol II of Monograph Supplement,* pg. 46.

Waddell, H. (1934). *Beasts and Saints*. London: Constable & Co.

Warden, C.J., Jenkins, T.N., and Warner, L.H. (1935). *Comparative Psychology (Vol. 1). Principles and Methods*. New York: Ronald Press.

Wax, D.E. & Haddox, V.G. (1974). Enuresis, fire setting, and animal cruelty: a useful danger signal in predicting vulnerability of adolescent males to assaultive behavior. *Child Psychiatry and Human Development, 4*, 151-156.

Winthrop, J. (1853). In James Savage (Ed.) *History of New England from 1630-1649*. Boston.

Zillmann, D. (1979). *Hostility and Aggression*. Hillsdale, NJ: Lawrence Erlbaum Associates.

3

Victimization Among School Children
Dan Olweus[1]

Bully/victim problems among school children ("mobbing") have been an issue of great concern in Scandinavia for almost two decades (Olweus, 1973a, 1978, 1986). A strong societal interest in bully/victim problems was first aroused in Sweden in the late 1960s and early 1970s (Heinemann, 1972; Olweus, 1973a), but it was quickly spread to the other Scandinavian countries.

In Norway, bully/victim problems were an issue of general concern in the mass media and among teachers and parents for a number of years, but the school authorities did not engage

---

[1]*The research reported was supported in various periods by grants from the William T. Grant Foundation, the Norwegian Ministry of Education, the Norwegian Research Council for the Humanities and the Social Sciences, and the Swedish Delegation for Social Research (DSF). Several of the ideas presented were developed while the author was a Fellow at the Center for Advanced Study in the Behavioral Sciences, Stanford, USA. He is indebted to the University of Bergen, the Spencer Foundation, the Norwegian Research Council for the Humanities and the Social Sciences, and the Center for Advanced Study in the Behavioral Sciences for financial support of his year at the Center in 1986-87.*

themselves officially with the phenomenon. A few years ago, a marked change took place.

In late 1982, a newspaper reported that three 10-14 year old boys from the northern part of Norway had committed suicide, in all probability as a consequence of severe bullying by peers. This event aroused a lot of uneasiness and tension in the mass media and the general public. It triggered a chain of reactions the end result of which was a nationwide campaign against bully/victim problems in Norwegian comprehensive schools (grades 1-9), launched by the Ministry of Education in the fall of 1983.

In the latter part of this chapter I will report some main results of the intervention program developed in connection with the campaign, as evaluated in 42 schools in Bergen. I will also briefly describe the content of the program and some of the principles on which it was based. First, I will give an overview of some basic research findings on bully/victim problems among schoolchildren. I will mainly confine myself to results of the two recent large-scale studies I was commissioned by the Ministry of Education to conduct in that context.

A number of findings concerning developmental antecedents of bullying problems, characteristics of typical bullies and victims, and the veracity of some popular conceptions of the causes of these problems will be presented only briefly in this chapter, since these results have been described in detail in previous publications (e.g., Olweus, 1973a, 1978, 1980, 1981, 1983, 1984, 1986). It should be mentioned, however, that the findings from this earlier research have generally been replicated in several different samples and were obtained with a number of different methods, including peer ratings, teacher nominations, self-reports, grades, projective techniques, hormonal assays, and mother/father interviews about child-rearing practices. Most of these results were derived from my

Swedish longitudinal project, which started in the early 1970s and is still continuing (see Table 1, below).

BASIC INFORMATION
What is Meant by Bullying?

The word used in Scandinavia for bully/victim problems is "mobbing" (Norway, Denmark) or "mobbning" (Sweden, Finland). This word has been used with several different meanings and connotations. The original English word stem "mob" implies that it is a (usually large and anonymous) group of people who are engaged in harassment (Heinemann, 1972; Olweus, 1973a). But the term has also often been used when one person picks on, harasses, or pesters another. Even if the usage is not quite adequate from a linguistic point of view, I believe it is important to include in the concept of "mobbing" or bullying both situations in which a single individual harasses another and those in which a group is responsible for the harassment. In many cases, it may not make much difference for the victim whether he or she is bullied by one or by several tormentors. Recent data collected in the large-scale study in Bergen (Olweus, 1985a, 1986; below) showed that a substantial portion of victimized students were bullied primarily by a single student. Acordingly, it is natural to regard bullying from a single student and from a group as closely related phenomena - even if there may be some differences between them. In particular, it is reasonable to expect that bullying by several peers is more unpleasant and possibly detrimental to the victim.

Bullying can be defined in the following general way: A person is being bullied when he or she is exposed, repeatedly and over time, to negative actions on the part of one or more other persons.

Table 1.
Overview of Studies

	Nationwide study in Norway (1983)	Intensive Study in Bergen, Norway (1983-1985)	Study in Greater Stockholm, Sweden (1970 –)
Units of Study:	715 Schools, Grades 2-9 (130.000 Boys and Girls)	4 Cohorts of 2500 Boys and Girls in Grades 4-7 (1983) 3-400 Teachers, 1000 Parents	3 Cohorts of Boys (900 Boys in all), Originally in Grades 6-8 (1973)
Measurement Occasions:	One	Several	Several
Measures Include:	Inventory on Bullying (Aggregated to Grade and School Level), Data on Recruitment Area of School Population Density, Socio-economic Conditions, Percent Immigrants	Self-Reports on Bully/Victim Problems, Aggression, Antisocial Behavior, Anxiety, Self-Esteem, Attachment to Parents and Peers, etc. Grades, Some Peer Ratings	Self-Reports and Reports by Mothers on a number of Dimensions, Peer Ratings, Teacher Nominations, Official Records on Criminal Offences, Drug Abuse
	School Size, Average Class Size, Composition of Staff	Teacher Data on Characteristics of Class, Group Climate, Staff Relations	For Subgroups: Interviews on Early Child Rearing, Hormonal Data, Psychophysiological Data

The meaning of the expression negative actions must be specified further. It is a negative action when someone intentionally inflicts, or attempts to inflict, injury or discomfort upon another - basically what is implied in the definition of aggressive behavior (Olweus, 1973b). Negative actions can be carried out by physical contact, by words, or in other ways, such as by making faces or dirty gestures or by refusing to comply with another person's wishes.

Even if a single instance of more serious harassment can be regarded as bullying under certain circumstances, the definition given above emphasizes negative actions that are carried out "repeatedly and over time.: The intent is to exclude occasional nonserious negative actions that are directed against one person at one time and against another on a different occasion.

It must be stressed that the term bullying is not (or should not be) used when two persons of approximately the same strength (physical or psychological) are fighting or quarreling. In order to use the term bullying, there should be a certain *imbalance in the strength relations:* The person who is exposed to the negative actions has difficulty in defending him/herself and is somewhat helpless against the person or persons who harass.

It is useful to distinguish between *direct bullying* - with open attacks on the victim - and *indirect bullying* in the form of social isolation and exclusion from a group. It is important to pay attention also to the second, less visible form of bullying. In the present chapter the expressions bullying problems and bully/victim problems are used synonymously.

Some Information About the Recent Studies

The basic method of data collection in the recent large-scale studies in Norway and Sweden[2] has been an inventory that I developed in connection with the nationwide campaign against bullying. The inventory, which can be administered by teachers, differs from several previous inventories on bully/victim problems in a number of respects, including the following:

- o It provides a "definition" of bullying so as to give the students a clear understanding of what they are to respond to.
- o It refers to a specific time period.
- o Several of the response alternatives are quite specific, such as "about once a week" and "several times a day," in contrast to alternatives like "often" and "very often," which lend themselves to more subjective interpretation.
- o It includes questions about the environment's reactions to bullying as perceived by the respondents, that is, the reactions and attitudes of peers, teachers, and parents.

In connection with the nationwide campaign all primary and junior high schools in Norway were invited to take the inventory. We estimate that approximately 85% actually participated. For closer analyses I selected representative samples of some 830 schools and obtained valid data from 715 of them, comprising

---

[2]*There is now an expanded English version of this inventory (one version for grades 1-4, and another for grades 5-9 and higher grades). This inventory as well as other materials related to the intervention program (see footnote 2, below) are copyrighted which implies certain restrictions on their use. For more details, please write to Dan Olweus, University of Bergen, Oysteinsgate 3, N-5007 Bergen, Norway (phone: (5) 21 23 27).*

approximately 130,000 students from all over Norway. These samples constitute almost a fourth of the whole student population in the relevant age range (roughly 8 to 16; first-grade students did not participate, since they did not have sufficient reading and writing ability to answer the inventory). This set of data gives good estimates of the frequency of bully/victim problems in different school grades, in boys as compared with girls, etc. In addition, it provides information on how differences between schools in these regards relate to the characteristics of the schools themselves and of the surrounding communities in terms of population density, degree of urbanization, economic resources, percentage of immigrants, and similar parameters. I will report here on some main findings from this study, but a number of more refined analyses remain to be done.

Roughly at the same time, a similar set of data was collected from approximately 17,000 Swedish students in grades 3-9, from 60 schools in the communities of Goteborg, Malmo, and Vasteras. These three communities were selected to "match" in size as closely as possible the three largest cities in Norway: Oslo, Bergen, and Trondheim.

To get more detailed information on some of the mechanisms involved in bully/victim problems and on the possible effects of the campaign, I also conducted a longitudinal project in Bergen. This study comprises some 2500 boys and girls in four adjacent cohorts, originally in grades 4 through 7, from 28 primary and 14 junior high schools. In addition, we obtained data from 300-400 teachers and principals as well as some 1000 parents. We collected data from these subjects at several points in time.

An overview of my main projects on bullying and related problems (not including the recent Swedish study mentioned above) is given in Table 1.

One Student out of Seven

I will now report some figures on the frequency of bully/victim problems in Norwegian and Swedish schools. It should be emphasized, however, that the percentages presented are dependent on the method and the definition of bullying that have been used. This fact may make it difficult to compare directly these percentages with other results obtained with different methods and other definitions or maybe no definitions at all.

One can roughly estimate that some 83,000 students, or 15% of the total in the Norwegian comprehensive schools (568,000 in 1983-84), were involved in bully/victim problems "now and then" or more frequently (autumn 1983) - as bullies or victims. This percentage represents one student out of seven. Approximately 9% or 53,000 students "now and then" or more frequently . Some 9,000 students were both victims and bullies.

Assuming that we can generalize to Sweden as a whole from the three Swedish cities studied (in combination with the Norwegian data) we get the following rough estimates for Sweden: Approximately 145,000 students were involved as bullies or victims; some 100,000 were victims, 63,000 were bullies, and 18,000 were both bullies and victims.

In calculating the percentages above, I have drawn the line at "now and then" or more frequently: For a student to be considered bullied or bullying others, he or she must have responded that it happened "now and then" or more frequently (i.e., from "about once a week" to "several times a day").

Analyses from the Bergen study indicate that there are good grounds for placing a cutting point just here. But it can also be useful to estimate the number of students who are involved in more serious bully/victim problems. We find then that slightly more than 3% or 18,000 students in Norway, were bullied "about once a week" or more frequently, and somewhat less than 2%, or 10,000 students, bullied others at that rate. Using this cutting point, only 1,000 students were both bullies and victims. A total of approximately 27,000 students (5%) in Norwegian comprehensive schools were involved in more serious bullying problems as victims or bullies - about 1 student out of 20.

It is natural to wonder if the reported results give an exaggerated picture of the frequency of bullying problems. This question can be examined by means of some findings from the Bergen study (Olweus, 1985a). Each of some 90 form masters and mistresses was asked to assess which of the students in his or her class were bullied or bullied other students. The teachers used exactly the same response categories as in the students' inventory. The agreement between the percentages obtained from the teachers' assessments and from the responses of the approximately 2000 students (in grades 4-7) was striking: There were differences on the order of only 1% to 2%. In short, the results indicated that "outside observers" of the relations among the students gave estimates that corresponded closely to what the students themselves reported.

In general, these findings suggest that the percentages reported were not inflated. Considering that the student (as well as the teacher) inventory refers only to the autumn term, it is even likely that the figures underestimate the number of students who were involved in such problems during a whole year.

Against this background, it can be stated that *bullying is a considerable problem in Norwegian and Swedish comprehensive schools*, a problem that affects a very large number of students.

Bully/Victim Problems in Different Grades

If one draws a graph of the percentage of students in different grades who are bullied at school a fairly smoothly declining curve is obtained for both boys and girls (see Figure 1). The decline is most marked in the primary school grades. Thus the percentage of students who are bullied decreases with higher grades. *It is the younger and weaker students who reported being most exposed.*

In Junior high school (grades 7-9) the curves decline less steeply. The average percentage of students (boys and girls combined) who were bullied in grades 2-6 (11.6%) was approximately twice as high as that in grades 7-9 (5.4%). With regard to the way in which the bullying is carried out, there is a clear trend towards less use of physical means in the higher grades.

From the Bergen study it can also be reported that *a considerable part of the bullying was carried out by older students.* This is particularly marked in the lower grades: More than 50% of the bullied children in the lowest grades (2 and 3) reported that they were bullied by older students. It is natural to invoke the latter finding at least as a partial explanation of the form of the curves in Figure 1. The younger the students are, the more potential bullies they have above them; accordingly, the inverse relationship between percentage of victims and grade level seems reasonable. This is only a preliminary interpretation, however, and a more detailed analysis of the factors affecting the shape of the curves will be undertaken later.

As regards the tendency to bully other students, depicted in Figure 2 (question 12 in the Inventory), the changes with grades are not so clear and systematic as in Figure 1. The average percentage for the junior high school boys was slightly higher (11.3%) then for the boys in the lower grades (10.7%), whereas the opposite was true for the girls (2.5% in junior high vs. 4.0% in the lower grades). The relatively marked drop in the curves for grade 7, in particular for the boys, is probably a reflection of the fact that these students were

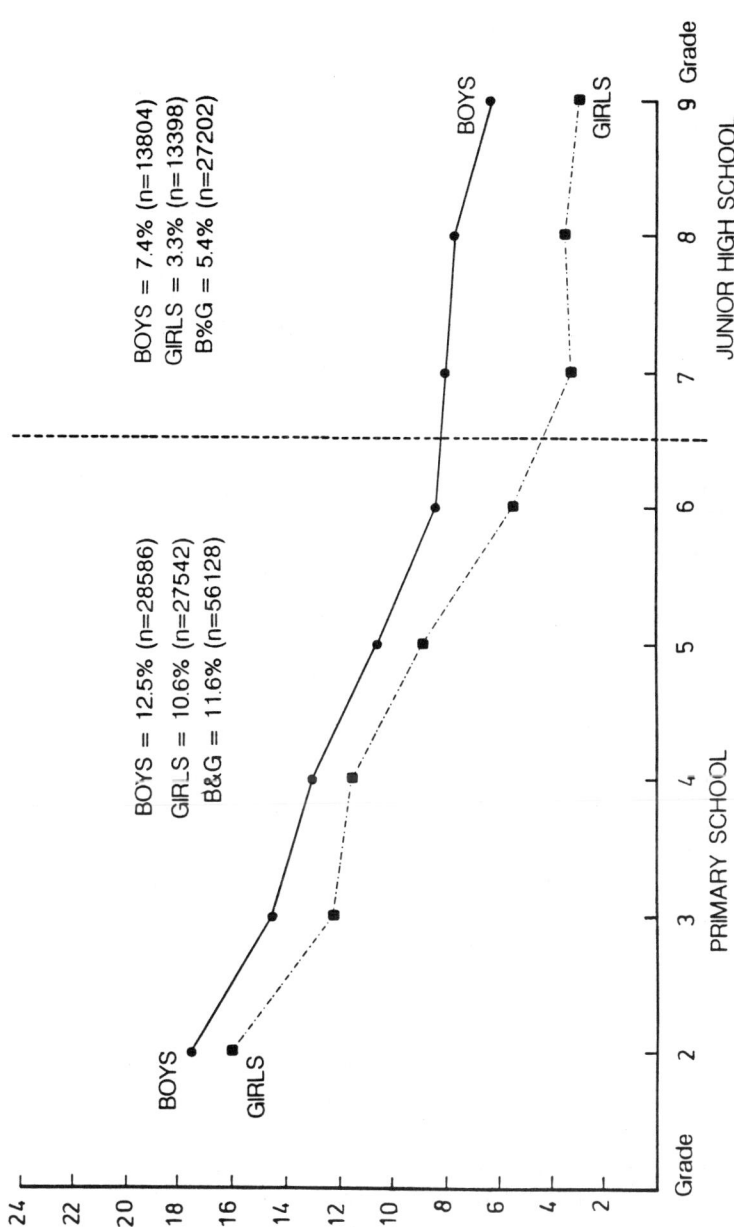

Figure 1. Percentage of students in different grades who reported being bullied (being exposed to direct bullying)

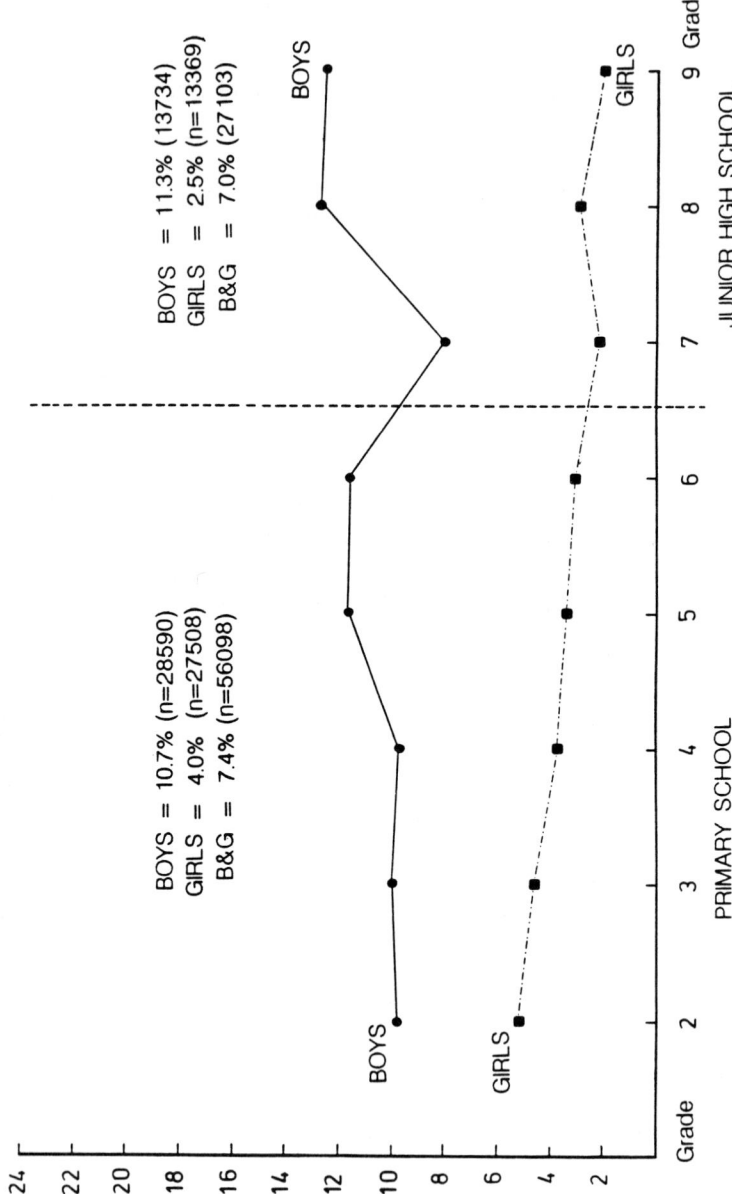

Figure 2. Percentage of students in different grades who reported having bullied other students.

the youngest ones in junior high school and accordingly did not have "access to suitable victims" in lower grades to the same extent.

The trends demonstrated in the Norwegian material confirmed in all essentials the corresponding Swedish analyses.

The analyses above concern the distributions of victims and bullies across grades. The most remarkabled result is that *bully/victim problems in primary schools were considerbly more marked than previously assumed.*

Have Bully/Victim Problems Increased?

Several different methods, including inventories (for overviews in Scandinavian languages, see Raundalen & Raundalen, 1979; Roland, 1983; Pikas, 1975), teacher nominations (Olweus, 1973a, 1978), and peer ratings (Largerspetz, Bjorkqvist, Berts, & King, 1982), have been used in previous Scandinavian studies of the frequency of bully/victim problems. The samples have mainly consisted of students in grades 6 through 9. In summary, it can be stated that the percentages of bullied and bullying students, respectively, were found to be in the vicinity of 5-10%. By and large, the figures in these studies conducted chiefly in the 1970s are somewhat lower than the percentages obtained in the surveys reported on above. Whether this discrepancy reflects differences in methods, definitions, and the composition of the samples, or whether it shows that the frequency of bullying has actually increased in recent years, is difficult to know with certainty. There are no good data available to directly assess whether bully/victim problems have become more or less frequent in the 1980s. Several indirect signs, however, suggest that bullying both takes more serious forms and is more prevalent nowadays than 10-15 years ago.

Whatever method of measurement used, there is little doubt that bullying is a considerable problem in Norwegian and Swedish comprehensive schools, one which must be taken seriously. At the same time, it is important to recognize that some 60-70% of the students (in a given semester) are not involved in bullying at all either as targets or as perpetrators. It is essential to make use of this group of students in efforts to counteract bully/victim problems at school.

Bullying Among Boys and Girls

As is evident from Figure 1, there is a trend for boys to be more exposed to bullying than girls. This tendency is particularly marked in the junior high school grades.

These results concern what was called direct bullying, with relatively open attacks on the victim. It is natural to ask whether girls were more often exposed to indirect bullying in the form of social isolation and exclusion from the peer group. One of the inventory questions makes it possible to examine this issue ("How often does it happen that other students don't want to spend recess with you and you end up being alone?"). The responses confirm that girls were more exposed to indirect and more subtle forms of bullying than to bullying with open attacks. At the same time, however, the percentge of boys who were bullied in this indirect way was approximately the same as that for girls. In addition, a somewhat larger percentage of boys was exposed to direct bullying, as mentioned above. (It may also be of interest that there was a fairly strong relationship between being a victim of direct and of indirect bullying.)

It should be emphasized that these results reflect main trends. There are of course a number of schools and classes in which there are more girls, or as many girls as boys, who are exposed to direct bullying, also in junior high school.

An additional result from the Bergen study is relevant in this context. Here it was found that *boys carried out a large part of the bullying that girls were subjected to.* More than 60% of bullied girls in grades 5-7 reported being bullied mainly by boys. An additional 15-20% said they were bullied by both boys and girls. The great majority of boys, on the other hand - more than 80% - were bullied chiefly by boys.

These results lead in a natural way to Figure 2, which shows the percentage of students who had taken part in bullying other students. It is evident here that a considerably larger percentage of boys than girls had participated in bullying. In junior high school, more than four times as many boys as girls reported having bullied other students.

In summary, *boys were more often victims and in particular perpetrators of direct bullying.* This conclusion is in good agreement with what can be expected from research on sex differences in aggressive behavior (Ekblad & Olweus, 1986; Hyde, 1984; Maccoby & Jacklin, 1980). It is well documented that relations among boys are by and large harder, tougher, and more aggressive than among girls (Maccoby, 1986). These differences have certainly both biological and social/environmental roots.

The results presented here should definitely not be construed as implying that we need not pay attention to bullying problems among girls. As a matter of course, such problems must be acknowledged and counteracted, whether girls are the victims of bullying or they themselves perpetrate such behavior. It should be recalled in this connection that girls were exposed to indirect bullying to about the same extent as boys. In addition, it *may* be the case that girls use such subtle methods of bullying that we have not been able to tap them in this version of the inventory.

How Much Do the Teachers Do and How Much Do the Parents Know?

The students responses to one of the inventory questions give information on how often the teachers try to interfere when a student is being bullied at school. Roughly 40% of bullied students in the primary grades and almost 60% in junior high school reported that the teachers tried to "put a stop to it" only "once in a while or almost never." And about 65% of bullied students in elementary school said that the form master/mistress had *not* talked with them about the bullying. The corresponding figure for junior high school students was as high as 85%. Almost the same results were obtained for students who bullied others. It can thus be established that *the teachers do relatively little to put a stop to bullying at school* according to both the bullied and bullying students. They also make only limited contact with the students involved in order to talk about the problems. This is particularly true in junior high school.

Once again, it should be stressed that these are main trends in the data. The results should not hide the fact that there were great individual differences among schools (and teachers): There were individual schools in which the teachers interfered with bullying and talked with the students involved much more often than the average. The other side of the coin is of course that there were also schools where the teachers did so considerably less than the average.

About 55% of bullied students in the primary grades reported that "somebody at home" had talked with them about the bullying. In junior high school this percentage was reduced to approximately 35%. For students who reported having bullied others the figures were considerably lower. The conclusion can be drawn that *parents of students who are bullied and, in particular, who bully others, are relatively unaware of the problem and talk with their children about it only to a limited extent.*

Although these results do not speak directly to the issue of the frequency or causes of bully/victim problems, they are important pieces of information to consider when countermeasures are planned.

Bullying at School and on the Way to and from School

It is fairly often asserted that bullying chiefly takes place on the way to and from school rather than at school. The results from the recent studies in Norway and Sweden clearly show that this view is not valid. There were almost twice (in junior high school, three times) as many students who were bullied at school as on the way to and from school. (There is a farily strong association here, however: Students who were bullied on their way to and from school tended to be bullied at school, too.) *The school is, no doubt, where most of the bullying occurs.*

The students reported, however, that they got considerably less help from others if they were bullied on their way to and from school. Accordingly, it is important to take effective measures against bullying there as well.

Comparison Between Norway and Sweden

It is possible and meaningful to compare the responses of the 17,000 students from the three Swedish communities of Goteborg, Malmo, and Vasteras, with the results from approximately 32,000 Norwegian students drawn from Oslo, Bergen, and Trondheim. The main impression is that there are great similarities. But there are also interesting differences, and I choose to focus briefly on the discrepancies here.

One marked finding is that the Swedish students were more exposed to indirect bullying in the form of social isolation and exclusion from the group. Eighteen percent of the Swedish primary school students (grades 3-6) as compared with scarcely 13% of students in corresponding grades in the Norwegian schools reported that "other students didn't want to spend recess with them and that they ended up being alone." There seems to be more loneliness and isolation among the Swedish youngsters.

The Swedish students were also to a greater extent victims of direct bullying (with open attacks) than the Norwegian students, in particular in junior high school. Furthermore, the Swedish junior high school students bullied other students slightly more. With regard to the more serious form of bullying ("once a week" or more frequently), a larger percentage of Swedish junior high school students bullied others or were bullied by others, respectively. The Swedish junior high school students also bullied tachers more often than the Norwegian students (13% as contrasted with 9%).

By and large, then, bully/victim problems were somewhat greater and more serious in the Swedish schools than the Norwegian schools. This conclusion applies in particular to junior high school students and, as regards indirect bullying, to primary school students.

Other results worth mention are that the Norwegian teachers interfered to stop bullying slightly more often (junior high school) but that the Swedish teachers talked with bullied and bullying students somewhat more frequently than the Norwegian teachers (in both primary and junior high schools). The Swedish parents also talked with their bullied or bullying children slightly more often. The students' responses suggest that Swedish teachers and parents were somewhat more aware of bully/victim problems. Both the

Swedish and Norwegian results, however, must be considered clearly unsatisfactory in this regard.

Is Bullying Primarily a Big-City Problem?

It has been commonly assumed that bullying occurs primarily in big-city schools. Results from the nationwide Norwegian surveys show that this is a myth. The percentage of students in Oslo, Bergen, and Trondheim (with populations varying from 150,000 to 450,000 inhabitants) who were bullied or who bullied others were approximately the same as or somewhat lower than corresponding figures from the rest of the country. The "big-city" children and youth were thus better than their reputation in this respect. It was also found that teachers as well as parents in the three cities talked more often with students involved in bullying problems than was done in other parts of the country. These results point to a somewhat greater awareness of the problems in the cities.

In this context it is also of interest to consider the results from a comparison of 307 "ordinary" primary schools (with at least one class at each grade level) and some 90 one-room (in Norwegian: *faadelte*) schools (with students from more than one graded level in the same class). The one-room schools, which constitute approximately 50% of the number of the primary schools in Norway but only 15% of the student population in that age range, are for the most part situated in the country. The average number of students who took the inventory was 43 in the one-room schools and 184 in the ordinary schools.

The basic finding from this comparison was that the percentage of bullied students in the small one-room schools was almost the same as in the larger, ordinary primary schools. The percentage of students who bully others was even slightly higher in the one-room schools. This finding certainly runs counter to the popular conception of the one-room school as an idyllic and conflict-free place.

The Size of the School and the Class

Another common view, popular in particular among teachers, is that bully/victim problems increase in proportion to the size of the school and the class. The data from 10 schools in greater Stockholm that I presented in the beginning of the 1970s (Olweus, 1973a, 1978) gave no support at all to these hypotheses. Data from three schools in Finland also failed to show any relationship between percentage of bullied or bullying students on one hand and school or class size on the other (Ekman, 1977; Lagerspetz, Bjorkqvist, Berts, & King, 1982).

The recent Norwegian and Swedish surveys give new and considerably extended possibilites of testing the validity of these hypotheses. With the available data one can make comparisons among more than 700 schools and several thousand classes. It should be noted, however, that such comparisons must be carried out within the same kind or type of school (e.g., primary schools or junior high schools) in order to be meaningful.

The variations in school and class size among the units compared were quite substantial. For example, the smallest ordinary grade 1-6 school had only 43 students, whereas the largest had 930. With regard to averge class size, the range was from approximately 7 to 27 students per class for schools of this kind.

The results were clear-cut: There were no positive relationships between level of bully/victim problems (the percentage of bullied and/or bullying students) and school or average class size.

The international research on the "effects" of class and school size agrees in suggesting that these factors are of no great significance, at least within the ranges of size variation typically found (e.g., Rutter, 1983). We can thus conclude that *the size of the class or school appears to be of negligible importance for the relative frequency or level of bully/victim problems in the class or the school.* Accordingly, one must look for other factors to find the origins of these problems.

It is nevertheless a fact that the *absolute number* of bullied and bullying students is greater on average in big schools and in big classes. It is therefore possible that it is somewhat easier to *do* something with the problems in a small school or a small class. This possibility will be examined more closely in the Bergen study.

Supervision during Recess

In the Bergen study we have been able to explore the relationship between certain aspects of the supervision system during recess and the level of bully/victim problems in school. For the approximately 40 schools participating in this research, we found a negative correlation of the order of -.50 between relative "teacher density" during recess time and the amount of bully/victim problems. That is: The greater the number of teachers (e.g., per 100 students) supervising during recess, the lower the level of bully/victim problems in the school. This result indicates that it is of great importance to have a sufficient number of adults present among the students during recess time (probably on condition that the adults are willing and prepared to interfere with incipient bullying episodes).

At a more general level, this finding suggests that the attitudes of the teachers towards bully/victim problems and their behavior in bullying situations are of major significance for the extent of bully/victim problems in the school or the class. In the Bergen study, we will attempt to specify in more detail which components of the teachers' attitudes and behaviors are particularly important.

On Analyses at Different Levels

A good deal of what has been reported in this chapter is descriptive information about the distribution of bully/victim problems across various conditions. However, we have also briefly considered some possible causes of bully/victim problems, such as the size of the school or class and the way supervision during recess time is organized. In the latter cases, we examined characteristics of the environment or the system that can possibly influence the extent or level of bully/victim problems for a whole group of students such as the school or the class (*the group*, or aggregated data, is the *unit of analysis*). This is certainly an important set of issues to study, for example, in order to get more knowledge and ideas about what kind of measures at the school or class level can reduce bully/victim problems.

Another set of issues is directed to the study of characteristics of different kinds of students, those who are bullies, victims, or neither (*the individual* is the basic *unit of analysis*). In these analyses, it is important to consider external characteristics and personality attributes of these kinds of students as well as whether there are differences in their situations or environments, for instance, as regards school and family conditions. Examples of questions to be examined are: Do external deviations such as fatness or red hair contribute to a student's becoming more easily victimized? Have bullied or bullying youngsters experienced a type of child-rearing which differs from what is characteristic of youngsters in general?

It is essential to address both these sets of issues, which are complementary, in order to get a more complete understanding of the mechanisms involved in bully/victim problems and for the design of good programs of countermeasures.

As I stated in the beginning of the chapter, I will not go into detail here on the extensive findings related to the second set of issues. However, I will touch briefly on a couple of popular hypotheses about the causes of bully/victim problems that have not been supported by empirical data. I will also draw a thumbnail sketch of the characteristics of typical bullies and victims.

Two Nonsupported Hypotheses

In the general debate it has been commonly maintained that bullying is a direct consequence of competition and striving for grades in school. More specifically, it has been argued that the aggressive behavior of the bullies toward their environment can be explained as a reaction to failures and frustrations in school. A detailed causal analysis of data on 444 boys from greater Stockholm, who were followed from grade 6 to grade 9, gave no support at all for this hypothesis. Though there was an association between poor grades in school and aggressive behavior, there was nothing in the results to suggest that the behavior of the aggressive boys was a consequence of poor grades and failure in school (Olweus, 1983).

Further, a widely held view explains victimization as caused by external deviations. It is argued that students who are fat, are red-haired, use glasses, or speak in unusual dialect, etc., are particularly likely to be the targets of bullying. This explanation seems to be quite common among students.

Also this hypothesis received no support from empirical data. In two samples of boys, victims of bullying were by and large found to be no more externally deviant (with regard to 14 external characteristics assessed by means of teacher ratings) than a control group of boys who were not exposed to bullying (Olweus, 1973a,

1978). The only "external deviation" that differentiated the groups was physical strength: The victims were physically weaker than boys in general, whereas the bullies were stronger than the average, and in particular stronger than the victims. This characteristic, however, has generally not been implicated in the hypothesis discussed. In spite of the lack of empirical support for this hypothesis, it seems still to enjoy considerable popularity. Some probable reasons why this is so have been advanced, and the interested reader is referred to this discussion (Olweus, 1978, 1986).

A Sketch of the Typical Victim

The picture of the typical victim emerging from the research literature is relatively unambiguous (see Olweus, 1978, 1986; Olweus & Roland, 1983). Victims of bullying are more anxious and insecure than students in general. They are often cautious, sensitive, and quiet. When attacked by other students, they commonly react with crying (at least in the lower grades) and withdrawal. They have a negative view of themselves and their situation. They often look upon themselves as failures and feel stupid, ashamed, and unattractive.

Further, the victims are lonely and abandoned at school. As a rule, they don't have a single good friend in their class. They are not aggressive or teasing in their behavior; accordingly, one cannot explain the bullying as a consequence of the victims themselves being provocative to their peers (see below). If they are boys, they are likely to be physically weaker than boys in general.

In summary, the behavior and attitude of the victims seem to signal to others that they are insecure and worthless individuals who will not retaliate if they are attacked or insulted. A slightly different way of describing the typical victims is to say that they are characterized by *an anxious personality pattern combined* (at least in the case of boys) *with physical weakness.*

Detailed interviews with parents of victimized boys (unpublished) indicate that these boys were cautious and sensitive already at a young age. Boys with such characteristics (and maybe physical weakness in addition) are likely to have had difficulty in asserting themselves in the peer group. There are thus good reasons to believe that these characteristics directly contributed to their becoming victims of other children's aggression. At the same time it is obvious that the repeated harassment by peers must have considerably increased their anxiety, insecurity, and generally negative evaluation of themselves.

Data from the same interviews suggest that victimized boys have a closer contact and more positive relations with their parents, in particular their mothers, than boys in general. Sometimes teachers interpret this fact as overprotection on the part of the mothers. It is reasonable to assume that such tendencies toward overprotection are both a cause and consequence of the bullying.

This is a sketch of the most common type of victim, who I have called *the passive victim*. There is also another, much smaller group of victims, *the provocative victims*, who are characterized by a combination of both anxious and aggressive behavior patterns. See Olweus (1973a, 1978) for more information about this kind of victim.

The Bullies

A distinctive characteristic of the typical bullies is their aggression toward peers; this is implied in the definition of a bully. They are, however, often also aggressive toward others, teachers, parents, and siblings. Generally, they have a more positive attitude to violence and use of violent means than students in general. They are often characterized by impulsivity and strong needs to dominate others. They seem to have little empathy with victims of bullying.

In contrast to a fairly common assumption among psychologists and psychiatrists, we have found no indications that the aggressive bullies (boys) are anxious and insecure under a tough surface. Data based on several samples and using both direct and indirect methods such as projective techniques and hormonal assays all pointed in the same direction: The bullies had unusually little anxiety and insecurity or were roughly average on such dimensions (Olseus, 1981, 1984). And they did not suffer from poor self-esteem.

These conclusions apply to the bullies regarded as a group. The results certainly do not imply that there may not be (a certain, relatively small proportion of) bullies who are both aggressive and anxious.

It should also be emphasized that there are students who sometimes participate in bullying but who usually do not take the initiative - they may be called *passive bullies, followers, or henchmen.* The group of passive bullies is likely to be fairly heterogeneous and can certainly also contain insecure and anxious students.

In summary, the *typical bullies* can be described as having *an aggressive personality pattern combined* (at least in the case of boys) *with physical strength.*

Bullying can also be viewed as a *component of a more generally antisocial and rule-breaking behavior pattern.* From this perspective, it is natural to predict that youngsters who are aggressive and bully others in school run a clearly increased risk of later engaging in other problem behaviors such as criminality and alcohol abuse. Several recent studies confirm this general prediction (Loeber & Dishion, 1983; Magnusson, Stattin, & Duner, 1983).

In my own follow-up studies we have also strong support for this assumption. Approximately 60% of boys who were characterized as bullies in grades 6-9 had at least one court conviction at the age of 24. Even more dramatically, as much as 35-40% of the former bullies had three or more court convictions at this age while this was true of only 10% of the control boys (those who were neither bullies nor victims in grades 6-9). Thus, as young adults the former school bullies had a fourfold increase in the level of relatively serious, recidivist criminality.

It may be mentioned that the former victims had an average or somewhat below average level of criminality in young adulthood.

Development of an Aggressive Personality Pattern

In light of the characterization of the bullies as having an aggressive personality pattern, it becomes important to examine the question: What kind of rearing and other conditions are conducive to the development of an aggressive personality pattern? Very briefly, the following four factors have turned out to be particularly important (based chiefly on research with boys; for details, see Olweus, 1980):

1. The basic emotional attitude of the primary caretaker(s) toward the child. A negative emotional attitude, characterized by lack of warmth and involvement, increases the risk that the child will later become aggressive and hostile toward others.

2. Permissiveness for aggressive behavior by the child. If the primary caretaker is generally permissive and "tolerant" without setting clear limits to aggressive behavior toward peers, siblings, and adults, the child's aggression level is likely to increase.

3. Use of power-assertive child-rearing methods such as physical punishment and violent emotional outbursts. Children of parents who make frequent use of these methods are likely to become more aggressive than the average child.

We can summarize these results by stating that *too little love and care and too much "freedom" in childhood are conditions that contribute strongly to the development of an aggressive personality pattern.*

4. Finally, the temperment of the child. A child with an active and hot-headed temperament is more likely to develop into an aggressive youngster than a child with an ordinary or more quiet temperment. The effect of this factor is smaller than those of the two first-mentioned conditions.

The factors listed above can be assumed to be important for both younger and somewhat older children. It can be added that, for adolescents, it is also of great significance that the parents supervise the children's activities outside the school reasonably well (Patterson & Stouthamer-Loeber, 1984)--what they are doing and with whom.

It should also be pointed out that the aggression levels of the boys participating in the analyses above (Olweus, 1980) were not related to the socio-economic conditions of their families, measured in several different ways. Similarly, there were no (or very weak) relationships between the four childhood factors discussed and the socio-economic conditions of the family.

Some Group Mechanisms

When several students jointly engage in the bullying of another student, some group mechanisms are likely to be at work.

Several such mechanisms have been discussed in detail in Olweus (1973a, 1978). Because of space limitations, they will only be listed here: 1) Social "contagion," 2) weakening of the control or inhibitions against aggressive tendencies, 3) distribution of responsibility, and 4) gradual cognitive changes in the perception of bullying and of the victim.

A Wider Perspective on Bully/Victim Problems

In the nationwide survey we have found great differences in the extent of bully/victim problems among schools. In some schools the risk of being bullied was up to 4 or 5 times greater then in other schools within the same community.

More generally, such differences between schools or areas in the extent of bully/victim problems can be viewed as a reflection of the interplay between two sets of countervailing factors: Some conditions tend to create or enhance bully/victim problems, whereas other factors have controlling or mitigating effects.

Among the bullying- or aggression-generating factors, poor childhood conditions in general and certain forms of child-rearing and family problems in particular are important. It is natural to postulate that schools with high levels of bullying are situated in areas where a relatively large proportion of children receive a "less satisfactory upbringing" and there are many family problems. A less satisfactory upbringing implies among other things that the child gets too little love, care, and supervision, and that the caretakers do not set clear limits to the child's behavior (above). Family problems can be conflict-filled interpersonal relationships between the parents, divorce, psychiatric illness, alcohol problems, etc.

The degree to which a school will manifest bully/victim problems is not only dependent on the amount of aggression-generating factors in the areas, however. It is also largely contingent on the strength of the countervailing forces. The attitudes, routines, and behaviors of the school personnel, in particular the teachers, are certainly decisive factors in preventing and controlling bullying activities and in redirecting such behaviors into more socially acceptable channels. This generalization is supported, for example, by the clear negative correlation between teacher density during recess and amount of bully/victim problems in the Bergen schools, reported above. In addition, the attitudes and behaviors of the students themselves, as well as of their parents, can in important ways reduce the probability or extent of bully/victim problems in the school. And in a situation where bullying problems already exist, it is obvious that the reactions of students who do not participate in bullying can have a major influence both on the short-term and long-term outcome of the situation (see more on appropriate countermeasures below).

A Question of Fundamental Democratic Rights

The reported results demonstrate convincingly that bullying is a considerable problem in Scandinavian elementary and junior high schools, that the teachers (in 1983) did relatively little to counteract it, and that the parents knew too little about what their children were exposed to or engaged in. The *victims* of bullying are a large group of students who are to a great extent neglected by the school. We know that many of these youngsters are the targets of harassment for long periods of time, often for many years (Olweus, 1977, 1978). It does not require much imagination to understand what it is to go through the school years in *a state of more or less permanent anxiety and insecurity and with poor self-esteem*. It is not surprising that the victims' devaluation of themselves sometimes becomes so overwhelming that they see suicide as the only possible solution.

Bully/victim problems have even broader implications than those suggested in the previous paragraph. They really concern some of our *fundamental democratic principles: Every individual should have the right to be spared oppression and repeated, intentional humiliation, in school as in society at large.* No student should be afraid of going to school for fear of being harassed or degraded, and no parent should need to worry about such things happenings to his or her child.

Bully/victim problems also relate to a society's general attitude to violence and oppression. What kind of view of societal values will a student acquire who is repeatedly bullied by other students without interference from adults? The same question can be asked with regard to students who, for long periods of time, are allowed to harass others without hindrance from adults. *To refrain from actively counteracting bully/victim problems in school implies a tacit acceptance.*

In this context, it should be emphasized that it is also of great importance to counteract these problems for the sake of the aggressive students. As reported above, school bullies are much more likely than other students to follow an antisocial path. Accordingly, it is essential to try to redirect their activities into more socially acceptable channels. And there is no evidence to suggest that a generally "tolerant" and permissive attitude on the part of adults will help bullies outgrow their antisocial behavior pattern.

INTERVENTION
Main Goals and Components of Intervention Program

Up to this point, an overview of what is known about bully/victim problems has been presented, based primarily on my own research. Against this background it is now natural to briefly describe the effects of the intervention program that we developed in connection with the nationwide campaign against bully/victim problems in Norwegian schools. The program was offered to all comprehensive schools (grades 1 through 9) via the ordinary administrative channels of the Ministry of Education.

The *major goals of the program* were to reduce as much as possible existing bully/victim problems and to prevent the development of new problems.

The *main components* of the program[3], which was aimed at teachers and parents as well as students, were the following:

1) A 32-page booklet for school personnel describing what is known about bully/victim problems (or rather: what is know about bully/victim problems (or rather: what was known in 1983) and giving detailed suggestions about what teachers and the school can do to counteract and prevent the problems (Olweus & Roland, 1983). Efforts were also made to dispel common myths about the nature and causes of bully/victim problems which might interfere with an adequate handling of them. This booklet was distributed free of charge to all comprehensive schools in Norway.

2) A 4-page folder with information and advice to parents of victims and bullies as well as "ordinary" children. This folder was distributed by the schools to all families in Norway with school-age children.

---

[3]*The "package" related to the intervention program against bully/victim problems consists of the inventory for the measurement of bully/victim problems (above and footnote 1), a copy of a small book <u>Bullying - what we know and what we can do</u> (Olweus, in press[c]) aiming at teachers and parents, and a parent folder. (Additional materials are being developed). These materials are copyrighted which implies certain restrictions on their use. For more information please write to the author at the address given in footnote 1.*

3) A 25-minute video cassette showing episodes from the everyday lives of two bullied children, a 10-year old boy and a 14-year old girl. This cassette could be brought or rented at a highly subsidized price.

4) A short inventory of questions (questionnaire) designed to obtain information about different aspects of bully/victim programs in the school, including frequency and the readiness of teachers and students to interfere with the problems. The inventory was completed by the students individually (in class) and anonymously. Registration of the level and nature of bully/victim problems in the school was thought to serve as a basis and starting point for active interventions on the part of the school and the parents. - A number of the results presented earlier in this chapter were based on information collected with this inventory.

Another "component" was added to the program as used in Bergen, the city in which the evaluation of the effects of the intervention program took place. Approximately 15 months after the program was first offered to the schools (in early October, 1983) we gave, in a 2-hour meeting with the staff, individual feedback information to each of the 42 schools participating in the study (Manger & Olweus, 1985). This information, derived from the students' responses to the inventory in 1983, focused on the level of problems and the social environment's reactions to the problems in the particular schools related to data from comparable schools obtained in the nationwide survey (October, 1983). At the same time, the main principles of the program and the major procedures suggested for intervention were presented and discussed with the staff. Since we know from experience that many (Norwegian) teachers have somewhat distorted views of the characteristics of bullying students, particular emphasis was placed on a discussion of this topic and on appropriate ways of handling bullying behavior. Finally, the teachers rated different aspects of the program, in particular its feasibility and potential efficacy. Generally, this addition to the program as well as the program itself were quite favorably received by the teachers, as expressed in their ratings.

Subjects and Design

Space limitations prevent detailed presentation of methodological information including sampling scheme, definition of measuring instruments and variables, and significance tests. Only summary descriptions and main results will be provided in this context.

Evaluation of the effects of the intervention program is based on data from approximately 2500 students originally belonging to 112 grade 4-7 classes in 42 primary and junior high schools in Bergen (modal ages at Time 1 were 11, 12, 13 and 14 years respectively). Each of the four grade/age cohorts consisted of 600-700 subjects with a roughly equal distribution of boys and girls. The first time of data collection (Time 1) was in late May (and early June), 1983, approximately four months before the initiation of the campaign. New measurements were taken in May 1984 (Time 2) and May 1985 (Time 3).

Since the campaign was nationwide, it was not possible to set up a strictly experimental study with random allocation of schools or classes to treatment and control conditions. Instead, a quasi-experimental design was chosen, making use of "time-lagged contrasts between age-equivalent groups". In particular, for three of the cohorts data collected at Time 1 (see Figure 3) were used as a base line with which data for age-equivalent cohorts at Time 2 could be compared. The latter groups had then been exposed to the intervention program for about 8 months. To exemplify, the data

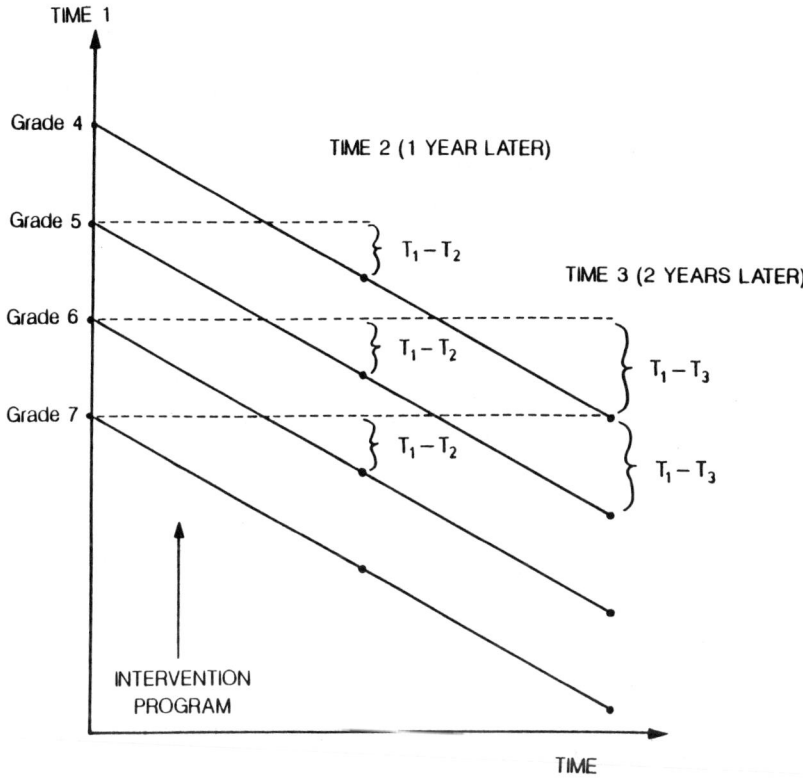

Figure 3. Design for evaluation of effects of intervention program, Fictitious data (which to some extent reflect the general trend of the empirical findings).

for the grade-5 cohort at Time 1 (modal age 12 years) were compared with the Time 2 data for the grade-4 cohort which at that time had reached approximately the same age as the base line group. The same kind of comparisons were made between the grade-6 cohort at Time 1 and the grade-5 cohort at Time 2, and between the grade-7 cohort at Time 1 and the grade-6 cohort at Time 2.

Comparisons of data collected at Time 1 and Time 3 permit an assessment of the persistence or possible decline or enhancement of the effects over a longer time span. For these comparisons data for only two of the cohorts could be used as a base line, those of the grade-6 and grade-7 cohorts, which were contrasted with data collected at Time 3 on the grade-4 and grade-5 cohorts respectively. The latter groups had been exposed to the intervention program during approximately 20 months at that time.

An attractive feature of the design is the fact that two of the cohorts serve as a base line group in one set of comparisons and as a treatment group in another. This is the case with the grade-5 cohort at Time 1 the data for which are used as a base line in comparison with the grade-4 cohort data collected at Time 2 (after 8 months of intervention). In addition, the grade-5 cohort data obtained at Time 2 serve to evaluate the possible effects of 8 months of intervention when they are compared with the data for the grade-6 cohort at Time 1. The same situation applies to the grade-6 cohort in comparisons with the grade-5 and grade-7 cohorts respectively.

The advantage of this aspect of the design is that a possible bias in the sampling of the cohorts would operate in opposite directions in the two sets of comparisons, thus making it more "difficult" to obtain consistent "intervention effects" across cohorts as a consequence of such bias. There are, however, no grounds for expecting such bias since the classes/schools were distributed on the different cohorts by a basically random procedure. Accordingly, the cohorts should be essentially equivalent in important respects at Time 1. For certain variables, this assumption can and will be empirically tested. This aspect of the design would provide the same kind of protection against faulty conclusions in case the base line data for one or both of these cohorts were unusually high or low simply as a function of chance.

To avoid erroneous conclusions due to possible selective attrition (more extreme or deviant individuals may be more likely to drop out in longitudinal studies) analyses were restricted to students for whom there were valid data at both time points in a particular comparison (both for the base line and the intervention groups). In the present research, however, the results were basically the same whether we controlled or did not control for attrition.

It should also be noted that since selection of the subjects was not based on some kind of "extreme score" criterion, the problem with "regression toward the mean" which looms large in many evaluation studies, is not at issue in the present research. By the present design the common and serious problem of attempting to statistically adjust for initial differences between nonequivalent groups is also avoided.

Outcome Variables

The main variables on which possible effects of the intervention could be expected to show up, are of course related to different aspects of bully/victim problems. In the present context only data for the key individual items reflecting these problems will be reported. In later publications analyses of more reliable composites of items will be presented.

The three key items were worded as follows:
 a) How often have you been bullied in school? (Being exposed to direct bullying or victimization, with

relatively open attacks on the victim.)
b) How often have you taken part in bullying other students in school? (Bullying or victimizing other students.)
c) How often does it happen that other students don't want to spend recess with you and you end up being along? (Being exposed to indirect bullying or victimization by means of social isolation, exclusion from the group.)

As mentioned in the beginning of the chapter, to avoid idiosyncratic interpretations the students were provided with detailed but simple "definition" of bullying before answering question a). And in both the written and the oral instructions, it was repeatedly emphasized that their answers should refer to the situation "this spring", i.e., the period "from Christmas until now". All three questions had the same seven response alternatives, ranging from "it hasn't happened this spring" (scored o) over "now and then" (scored 2) and "about once a week" (scored 3) to "several times a day" (scored 6).

Other items referred to being bullied or bullying others respectively on the way to and from school. Several items also concerned the individual's attitude toward victims of bullying (e.g., "how do you usually feel when you see a student being bullied in school?") and bullying students (e.g., "What do you think of students who bully others?").

With regard to the validity of self-reports on variables related to bully/victim problems, it may be mentioned that in my early Swedish studies (Olweus, 1978) composites of 3-5 self-report items on being bullied or bullying and attacking others respectively correlated in the range .40-.60 (unpublished) with reliable peer ratings on related dimensions (Olweus, 1977). Similarly, Perry,

Kusel, and Perry (1988) have reported a correlation of .42 between a self-report scale of three victimization items and a reliable measure of peer nominations of victimization in elementary schoolchildren.

In the present study we also obtained a kind of peer rating in that each student had to estimate the number of students in his or her class who were bullied or bullied others during the reference period. These data were aggregated for each class and the resulting class means correlated with the means derived from the students' own reports of being victimized or victimizing others. The two sets of class means were quite substantially corrrelated, the average correlations across the grade 5-7 cohorts being .61 for the victimization dimension and .58 for the bullying variable (Time 1). Corresponding coefficients for estimated average *proportion* of students in the class being bullied or bullying others (which measure corrects for differing number of students in the classes) were even somewhat higher, .62 and .68 respectively. There was thus considerable agreement across classes between class estimates derived from self-reports and from this form of peer ratings. *The results presented above certainly attest to the validity of the self-report data employed.*

Since a link has been established between bullying behavior and antisocial/criminal activities, it was hypothesized that the intervention program against bullying *might* also lead to a reduction in antisocial behavior. To measure different aspects of antisocial behavior in relatively young people, preadolescents and adolescents, a new self-report instrument was developed (Olweus & Endresen, in preparation; Olweus, in press[a]). This inventory shows many similarities with the instruments recently developed by Elliott & Ageton (1980) and by Hindelang, Hirschi, and Weis (1981) but our inventory contained fewer items on serious crimes and more items related to school problems.

The 23 core items of the inventory were selected from two broad conceptual domains. One concerned disciplinary problems and other rule-breaking behavior in school, while the second covered more general and non-school related antisocial acts such as vandalism, theft, burglary, and fraud. Though it was possible and meaningful to divide the times into two separate scales roughly corresponding to the two conceptual domains, the results to be presented in this context only concern the Total Scale of Antisocial Behavior (TAS) consisting of all 23 items. Psychometric analyses of the inventory have given quite encouraging results indicating that the scales have satisfactory or good reliability, stability, and validity as well as theoretical relevance.

Finally, it was thought important to assess possible effects on student satisfaction with school life, in particular during recess time. (In Norwegian comprehensive schools, students usually have a break of approximately ten minutes every 45 minutes. In addition, they have a lunch break of 20-30 minutes in the middle of the day.) Since most of the bullying takes place at school (during recess and on the way to and from clsses, and not on the way to and from school, see above) the following question was considered relevant: "How do you like recess time?"

Statistical Analyses

Since classes rather than students were the basic sampling units (with students nested within clsses), it was considered important to choose a data analytic strategy that reflected the basic features of the design. Accordingly, data were analyzed with ANOVA (analysis of variance) with students nested within classes nested within schools nested within times/occasions (Time 1 versus

Time 2, Time 1 versus Time 3). Sex of the subjects was crossed with times, schools (within times), and classes (within schools). Since several of the cohorts figured in two comparisons, the analyses had to be conducted separately for each combination of cohorts (for further information, see Olweus, in press[b]).

For several of the variables (or derivatives of them such as percentages), less refined (and in some respects, less informative) analyses with t-tests and chi square were also carried out. The findings from these analyses were in general agreement with those obtained in the ANOVAs.

Results

The results for some of the variables discusseed above are presented separately for boys and girls in Figures 4-9. Since the design of the study is relatively complex, a few words about how to read the figures are in order.

The panel to the left shows the effects after 8 months of intervention, while the one to the right displays the results after 20 months. The upper curves (designated Before) show the base line data (Time 1) for the relevant cohorts (the grade-5), grade-6, and grade-7 cohorts in the left panel and the grade-6 and grade-7 cohorts in the right). The lower curves (designated After) display data collected at Time 2 (after 8 months of intervention) in the panel to the left and at Time 3 (after 20 months of intervention) in the right-hand panel for the age-equivalent cohorts (the grade-4, grade-5, and grade-6 cohorts at Time 2 and the grade-4 and grade-5 cohorts at Time 3).

It should be noted that in some of the figures there are more differences in base line data (Before) for the grade-6 and grade-7 cohorts when presented in the left hand right panels respectively. This is a consequence of the restriction of the analyses to subjects

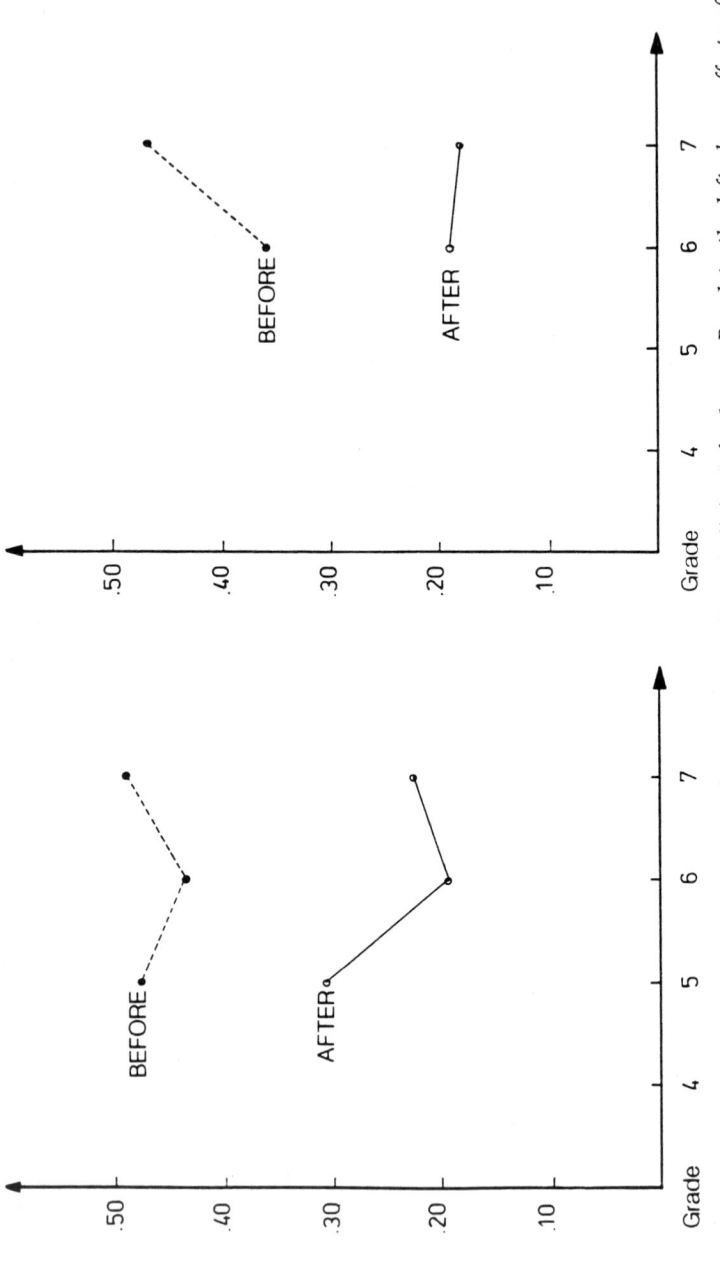

Figure 4. Effects of intervention program on "Being exposed to direct bullying" for boys. Panel to the left shows effects after 8 months of intervention, and panel to the right displays results after 20 months of intervention. Upper curves (designated Before) show base line data (Time 1), and the lower curves (designated After) display data collected at Time 2 in the left panel and at Time 3 in the panel to the right.

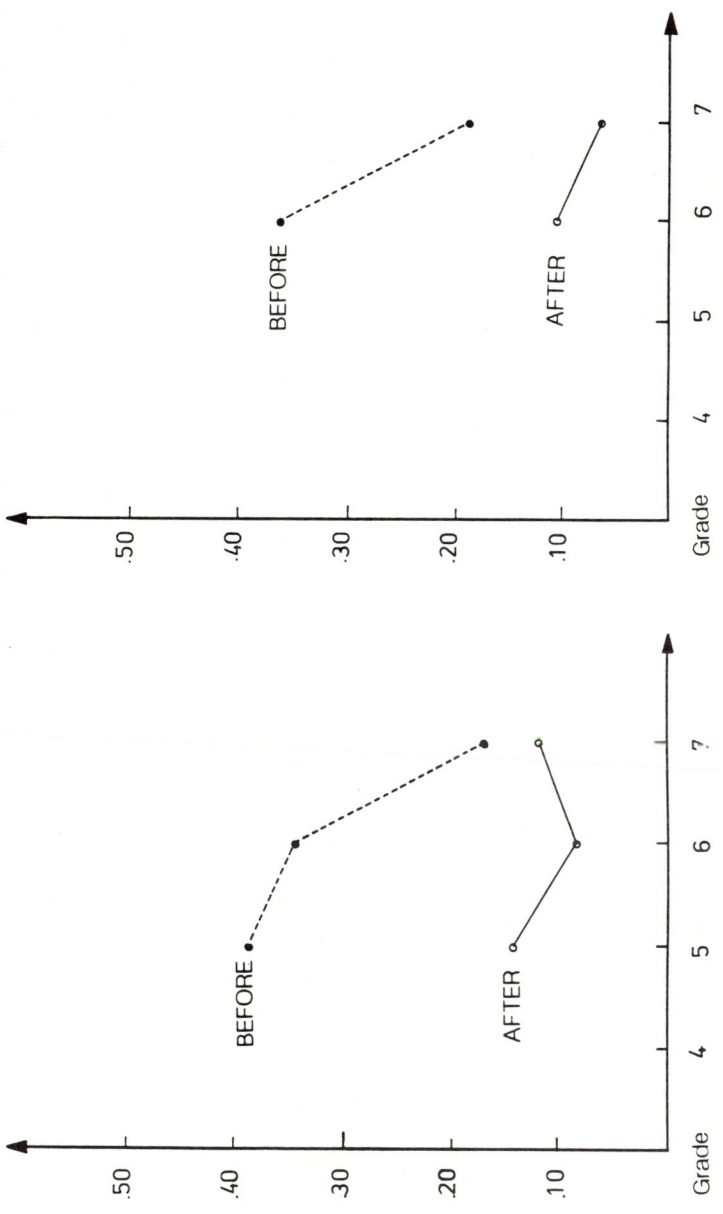

Figure 5. Effects of intervention program on "Being exposed to direct bullying" for girls. See Figure 4 for explanation of the figure.

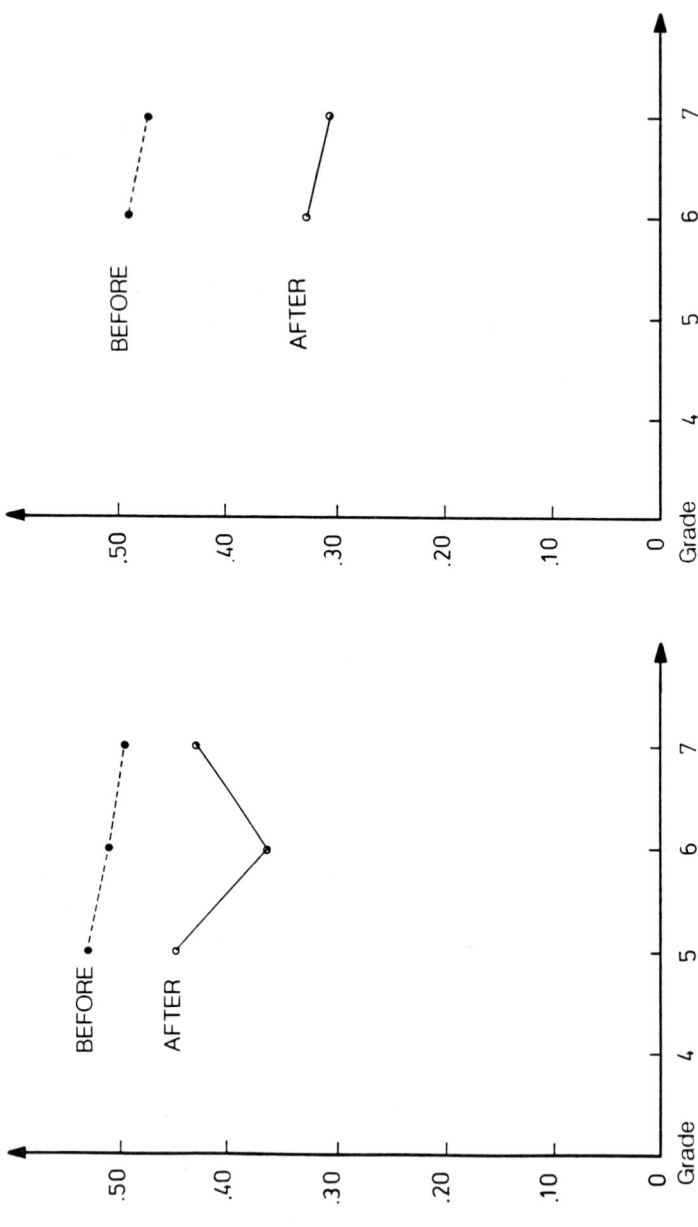

Figure 6. Effects of intervention program on "Bullying other students" for boys. See Figure 4 for explanation of the figure.

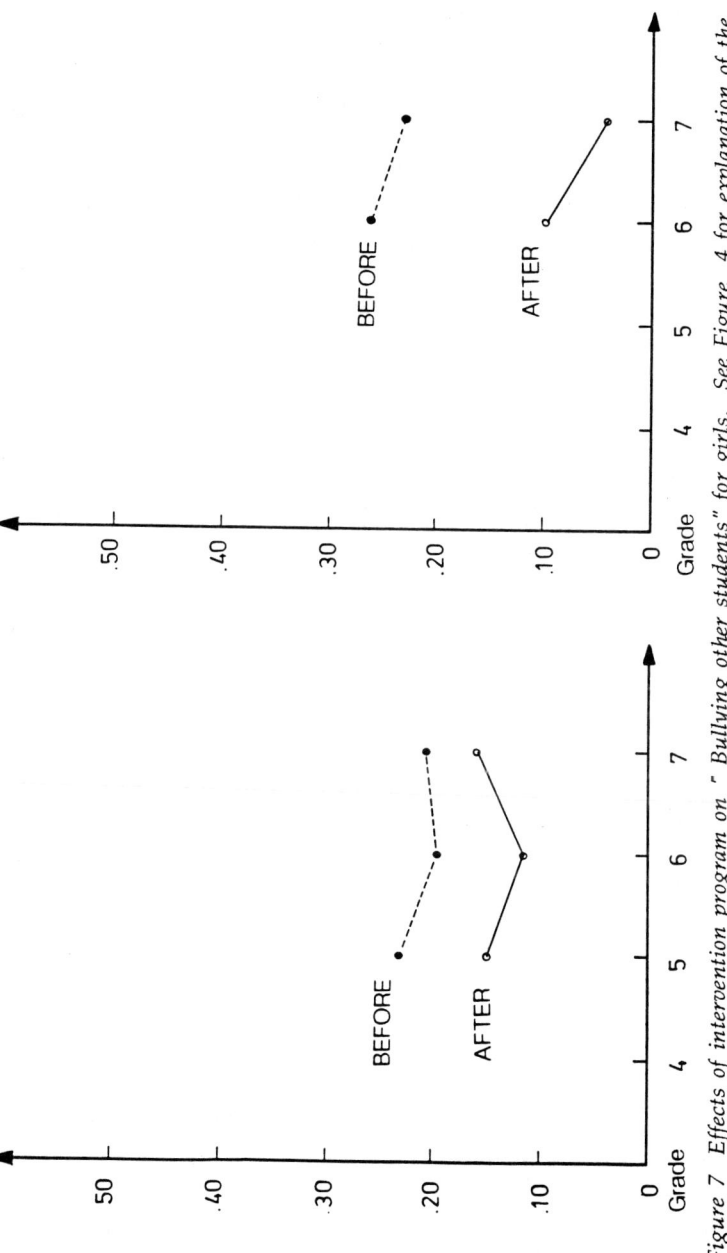

Figure 7 Effects of intervention program on "Bullying other students" for girls. See Figure 4 for explanation of the figure.

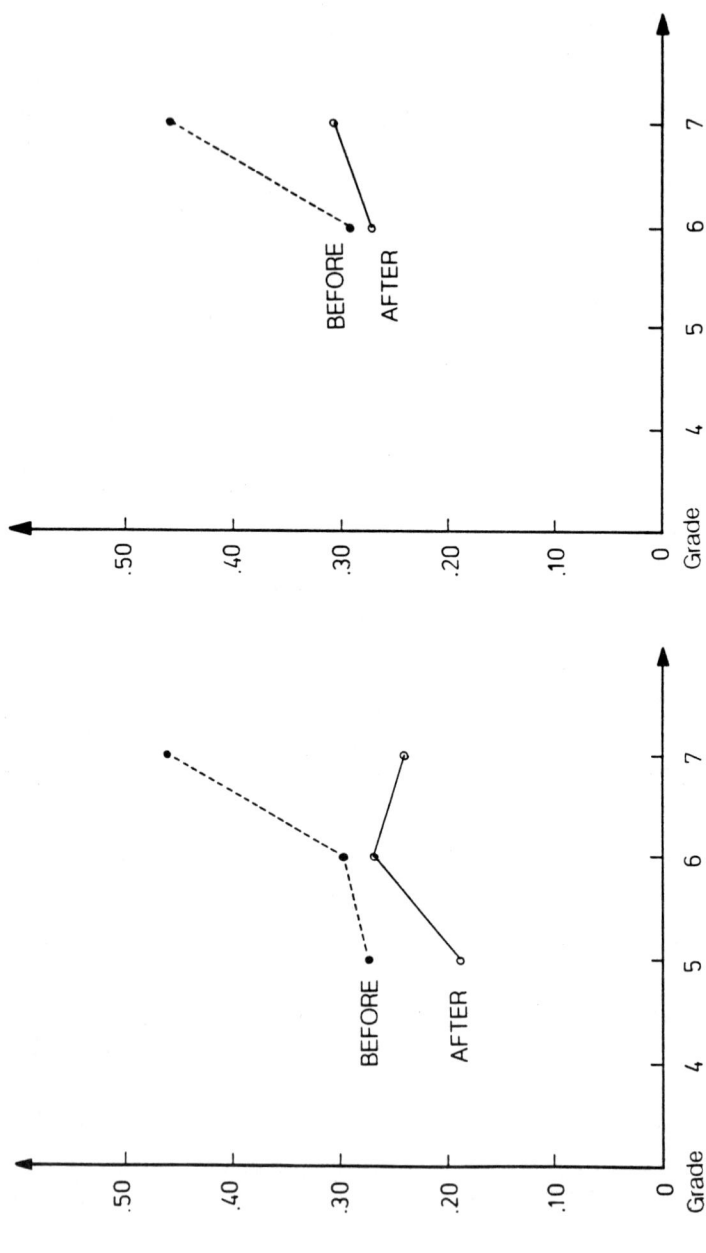

Figure 8. Effects of intervention program on "Total Scale of Antisocial Behavior" (TAS) for boys. See Figure 4 for explanation of the figure.

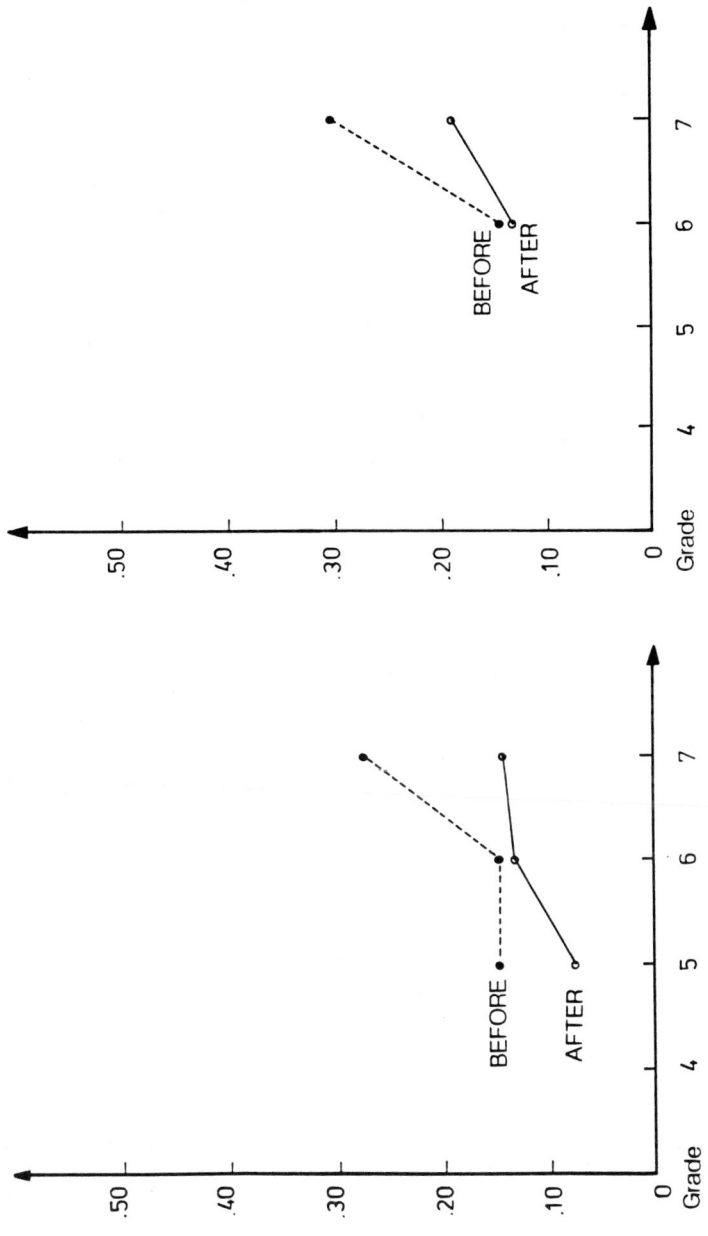

Figure 9. Effects of intervention program on "Total Scale of Antisocial Behavior" (TAS) for girls. See Figure 4 for explanation of the figure.

who had valid data at both time points; according, it is not exactly the same subjects who entered the two sets of analyses. The scales on the Y-axis are in some sense arbitrary simply reflecting the system used in scoring the variables.

The *main findings* of the analyses can be summarized as follows:

1. There were marked reductions in the levels of bully/victim problems for the periods studied, 8 and 20 months of intervention respectively (Figures 4-7). By and large, reductions were obtained for both boys and girls and across all cohorts compared. For the longer time period the effects persisted in the case of "Being exposed to direct bullying" and "Being exposed to indirect bullying" and were strengthened for the variable "Bullying others".
2. Similar reductions were obtained for the aggregated "peer rating" variables "Number of students being bullied in the class" and "Number of students in the class bullying others". There was thus consensual agreement in the classes that bully/victim problems had decreased during the periods studied.
3. In terms of percentages of students reporting being bullied or bullying others "now and then" or more frequently, the reductions amounted to approximately 50% or more in most comparisons (time 1 - Time 3 for "Bullying others".)
4. There was no displacement of bullying from the school to the way to and from school. There were reductions or no changes on the items measuring bully/victim problems on the way to and from school.

5. There was also a reduction in general antisocial behavior (Figurs 8 and 9) such as vandalism, theft, and truancy. (For the grade-6 comparisons the effects were marginal for both time periods.)
6. At the same time, there was an increase in student satisfaction with school life as reflected in "liking recess time."
7. There were weak and inconsistent changes for the questions concerning attitudes to different aspects of bully/victim problems.

In the majority of comparisons for which reductions were reported above, the differences between base line and intervention groups were highly significant or significant (in spite of the fact that many of them were based on single items).

Quality of Data and Possible Alternative Interpretations

It is beyond the scope of this chapter to discuss in detail the quality of the data collected and the possibility of alternative interpretations of the findings. An extensive discussion of these matters can be found elsewhere (Olweus, in press[c]). Here I limit myself to summarizing the conclusions in the following "point statements":

1. Self-reports, which were implicated in most of the analyses conducted so far, are in fact the best data source for the purposes of this study.
2. It is very difficult to explain the results obtained as a consequence of (a) underreporting by the students; (b) gradual changes in the students' attitudes to bully/victim problems; (c) repeated measurement; and (d) concomitant changes in other factors. All in all, it is *concluded that the reductions in bully/victim*

> and associated problems described above are likely to be mainly a consequence of the intervention program and not of some other "irrelevant" factor.

In addition, a clear "dosage-response" relationship ($r=.51$, $n=80$) has been established in preliminary analyses at the class level (which is the natural unit of analysis in this case): Those classes that showed larger reductions in bully/victim problems had implemented three presumably essential components of the intervention program (including establishment of class rules against bullying and use of role playing of such problems) to a greater extent than those with smaller changes (additional information on these analyses can be found in Olweus, in press[b]). This finding certainly provides corroborating evidence for the effects of the intervention program. It will be followed up with more systematic and comprehensive analyses.

BASIC PRINCIPLES

Having reported the main goals and components of the intervention program as well as some of its effects it is now natural to present its underlying principles and major subgoals.

The intervention program is build around *a limited set of key principles* derived chiefly from research on the development and modification of the implicated problem behaviors, in particular aggressive behavior. It is considered important to try to create a school (and ideally, also home) environment characterized by *warmth, positive interest, and involvement from adults* on one hand and *firm limits to unacceptable behavior* on the other. Third, in cases of violations of limits and rules, *nonhostile, nonphysical sanctions* should be consistently applied. Implied in the latter two principles is also a certain degree of *monitoring and surveillance* of the students' activities in and out of school (Patterson, 1986).

Finally, *adults* are supposed to *act as authorities at least in some respects*.

It can be seen that the first three of these principles largely represent the opposite of the child rearing dimensions found to be important in the development of an aggressive personality pattern discussed above: negativism on the part of the primary caretaker, permissiveness and lack of clear limits, and use of poor-assertive methods (Olweus, 1980). In a sense, the present intervention program represents an *authoritative adult-child interaction, or child rearing, model (cf. e.g., Baumrind, 1967) as applied to the school setting*.

The principles listed above can be translated into a number of specific measures to be used at the *school*, *class*, and *individual levels*. It is considered very important to work on all of these levels, if possible. Figure 10 lists a number of such measures which were recommended in the intervention program (Olweus & Roland, 1983; a few of the measures in Figure 10 including cooperative learning were not included in the original program). Spaced limitations prevent detailed description of the various measures suggested but such an account can be found in a small book designed for teachers and parents (Olweus, 1986, in press[c])

With regard to implementation and execution, the program is mainly based on a *utilization of the existing social environment*: teachers and other school personnel, students, and parents. Non-experts thus play a major role in the desired *restructuring of the social environment*. Experts such as school psychologists and social workers may also serve important functions as planners and coordinators and in counseling teacher and parent groups and in handling more serious cases.

COMPONENTS TO PROGRAM PACKAGE AGAINST BULLYING

GENERAL PREREQUISITES: AWARENESS + INVOLVEMENT

SCHOOL LEVEL	CLASS LEVEL	INDIVIDUAL LEVEL
• Better supervision of recess	• Class rules against bullying: clarification, praise, and sanctions	• Serious talks with bullies and victims
• More attractive school playground	• Regular class meetings	• Serious talks with parents of involved children
• Contact telephone	• Cooperative learning	• Teacher use of imagination
• Meeting staff--parents	• Meeting teacher--parents/children	• Help from "neutral" students
• Teacher groups for the development of the "school climate"	• Common positive activities	• Advice to parents (parent brochure)
• Parent circles (study and discussion groups)	• Role playing	• "Discussion" groups with parents of bullies and victims
	• Literature	• Change of class or school

Figure 10. *Overview of measures at the school, class, and individual levels presented in the intervention program.*

Additional Characteristics

Further understanding of the program and its way of working can be gained from a brief description of its four major subgoals (this entails some repetition of earlier material):

1) *To increase awareness of the bully/victim problem and advance knowledge about it* including to dispel some of the myths about it and its causes. Use of the inventory is an important step in obtaining more specific knowledge about the frequency and nature of the problems in the particular school.

2) *To achieve active involvement on the part of teachers and parents.* This implies among other things that the adults must recognize that it is their responsibility to control to a certain degree what goes on among the children at school. One way of doing this is to provide adequate supervision during recess time. Further, the teachers are encouraged to intervene in possible bullying situations and give a clear message to the students: Bullying is not accepted in our school. Teachers are also strongly advised to initiate serious talks with victims and bullies, and their parents, if a bully/victim problem has been identified in the class. Again, the basic message should be: We will not tolerate bullying in our school and will see to it that it comes to an end. Such an intervention on the part of the school must be regularly followed up and closely supervised; otherwise the situation may easily become worse for the victim than before the intervention.

3) *To develop clear rules against bullying behavior* such as: (a) We shall not bully others. (b) We shall try to help students who are bullied. (c) We shall make a point to include students who become easily left out. Such a set of rules may

serve as a basis for class discussions about what is meant by bullying behavior in concrete situations and what kind of sanctions should be used for students who break the rules. The behavior of the students in the class should be regularly related to these rules in class meetings ("social hour"), and it is important that the teacher make consistent use of sanctions (some form of nonhostile, nonphysical punishment) in cases of rule violations and also give generous praise when the rules have been followed.

4) *To provide support and protection for the victims.* If followed, class rules against bullying certainly support children who tend to be victimized. In addition, the teacher may enlist the help of "neutral" or well-adjusted students to alleviate the situation of the victims in various ways. Also, teachers are encouraged to use their imagination to help victimized students to assert themselves in the class, to make them valuable in the eyes of their classmates. Parents of victims are exhorted to help their children develop new peer contacts and to teach them in detail how to make new acquaintances and to maintain a friendship relation.

It may be added that the present intervention program has been evaluated by more than 1000 Norwegian and Swedish teachers. In short, their reactions have generally been quite favorable, indicating among other things that the teachers see the proposed principles and measures as useful and realistic.

CONCLUDING WORDS

Though what has been presented in this chapter about the effects of the intervention program only represents the first stages of analysis, the basic message of our findings is clear: *It is definitely possible to reduce substantially bully/victim problems in school and related problem behaviors with a suitable intervention program.* Thus, whether these problems will be tackled or not no longer depends on whether we have the knowledge necessary to achieve desirable changes. It is much more a matter of our willingness to involve ourselves and to use the existing knowledge to counteract these problems.

REFERENCES

Baumrind, D. (1967). Child care practices anteceding three patterns of preschool behavior. *Genetic Psychology Monographs, 75,* 43-88.

Cook, T. D., & Campbell, D. T. (1979). *Quasi-Experimentation.* Chicago: Rand McNally.

Ekblad, S. & Olweus, D. (1986). Applicability of Olweus'aggression inventory in a sample of chinese primary school children. *Aggressive Behavior, 12,* 315-325.

Ekman, K. (1977). *Skolmobbning.* Pro gradu-arbete. Abo, Finland: Abo Akademi.

Elliott, D. S., & Ageton, S. S. (1980). Reconciling race and class differences in self-reported and official estimates of delinquency. *American Sociological Review, 45,* 95-110.

Heinemann, P. P. (1972). *Mobbning - Gruppvald Bland Barn Och Vuxna.* Natur och Kultur.

Hindelang, M. J., Hirschi, T., & Weis, J. G. (1981). *Measuring Delinquency.* Beverly Hills, CA: Sage.

Hyde, J. S. (1984). How large are gender differences in aggression? A developmental meta-analysis. *Developmental Psychology, 20,* 722-736.

Lagerspetz, K. M., Bjorkqvist, K., Berts, M., & King, E. (1982). Group aggression among school children in three schools. *Scandinavian Journal of Psychology, 23,* 45-52.

Loeber, R., & Dishion, T. (1983). Early predictors of male delinquency: A review. *Psychological Bulletin*, *94*, 69-99.

Maccoby, E. E. (1986). Social groupings in childhood: Their relationships to prosocial and antisocial behavior in boys and girls. In D. Olweus, J. Block, & M. Radke-Yarrow (Eds.) *Development of Antisocial and Prosocial Behavior*. New York: Academic Press.

Maccoby, E. E., & Jacklin, C. N. (1980). Sex differences in aggression: A rejoinder and a reprise. *Child Development*, *52*, 964-980.

Magnusson, D., Stattin, H. & Duner, A. (1983). Aggression and criminality in a longitudinal perspective. In K. T. Van Dusen & S. A. Mednick (Eds.) *Prospective Studies of Crime and Delinquency*. Boston: Kluwer-Nijhoff.

Manger, T. & Olweus, D. (1985). Tilbakemelding til skulane. *Norsk Skoleblad* (Oslo, Norway), *35*, 20-22.

Olweus, D. (1973a). *Hackkycklingar Och Oversittare: Forskning om Skol-Mobbning*. Stockholm: Almqvist & Wiksell.

Olweus, D. (1973b). Personality and aggression. In J. K. Cole & D. D. Jensen (Eds.) *Nebraska Symposium on Motivation, 1972* (Vol. 20). Lincoln: University of Nebraska Press.

Olweus, D. (1977). Aggression and per acceptance in adolescent boys: Two short-term longitudinal studies of ratings. *Child Development*, *48*, 1301-1313.

Olweus, D. (1978). *Aggression in the Schools: Bullies and Whipping Boys*. Washington, D.C.: Hemisphere (Wiley).

Olweus, D. (1979). Stability of aggressive reaction patterns in males: A review. *Psychological Bulletin*, *86*, 852-875.

Olweus, D. (1980). Familial and temperamental determinants of aggressive behavior in adolescent boys: A causal analysis. *Developmental Psychology*, *16*, 644-660.

Olweus, D. (1981). Bullying among school boys. In N. Cantwell (Ed.) *Children and Violence*. Stockholm: Akademilitteratur.

Olweus, D. (1983). Low school achievement and aggressive behavior in adolescent boys. In D. Magnusson & V. Allen (Eds.) *Human Development. An Interactional Perspective*. New York: Academic Press.

Olweus, D. (1984). Aggressors and their victims: Bullying at school. In N. Frude & H. Gault (Eds.) *Disruptive Behavior in Schools*. New York: Wiley.

Olweus, D. (1985). 80 000 barn er innblandet i mobbing. *Norsk Skoleblad* (Oslo, Norway), *35*, 18-23.

Olweus, D. (1986). *Mobbning - Vad Vi Vet Och Vad Vi Kan Gora*. Stockholm: Liber.

Olweus, D. (1987). Bully/victim problems among schoolchildren. In J. P. Myklebust & R. Ommundsen (Eds.) *Psykologprofesjonen Mot Ar 2000*. Oslo: Universitetsforlaget.

Olweus, D. (in press[a]). Prevalence and incidence in the study of antisocial behavior: Definitions and measurement. In M. Klein (Ed.) *Cross-National Research in Self-Reported Crime and Delinquency*. Dordrecht, The Netherlands: Kluwer.

Olweus, D. (in press[b]). Assessing change in a cohort-longitudinal study with hierarchical data. In D. Magnusson, L. Bergman, G. Rudinger, & B. Torestad (Eds.) *Matching Problems and Methods in Longitudinal Research*. New York: Cambridge University Press.

Olweus, D. (in press[c]). *Bully/victim problems among school children: Basic facts and effects of a school based intervention program*. Hillsdale, N.J.: Erlbaum.

Olweus, D. & Endresen, J. (in preparation). *Assessment of Antisocial Behavior in Preadolescence and Adolescence.* Manuscript.

Olweus, D. & Roland, E. (1983). *Mobbing - bakgrunn oq tiltak.* Oslo, Norway: Kirke-og undevisningsdepartementet.

Patterson, G. R. (1986). Performance models for antisocial boys. *American Psychologist, 41,* 432-444.

Patterson, G. R. & Stouthamer-Loeber, M. (1984). The correlation of family management practices and delinquency. *Child Development, 55,* 1299-1307.

Perry, D. G., Kusel, S. J., & Perry, L. C. (1988). Victims of peer aggression. *Developmental Psychology, 24,* 807-814.

Pikas, A. (1975). *Sa Stoppar Vi Mobbning.* Stockholm: Prisma.

Raundalen, T. S. & Raundalen, M. (1979). *Er Du Pa Var Side?* Oslo: Universitetsforlaget.

Roland, E. (1983). *Strategi Mot Mobbing.* Oslo: Universitetsforlaget.

Rutter, M. (1983). School effects on pupil progress: Research findings and policy implications. *Child Development, 54,* 1-19.

4

Victim Risk Factors in the Physical Abuse of Children
John F. Knutson, Helen A. Schartz, and Lisa Y. Zaidi

The abuse of children by parents and caretakers is a topic of relatively recent interest in both behavioral research and clinical service. Indeed, the topic has been addressed for only slightly less than three decades. During that time, however, it has moved from a topic of modest interest to one of great interest with burgeoning research, public policy changes, and media attention (Nelson, 1984). It is, perhaps, not surprising that there has been a substantial increase in estimates of incidence and prevalence of abuse since the early work in this area (e.g., Kempe, Silverman, Steele, Droegemueller & Silver, 1962), because of increasing professional and public awareness, statutory requirements for mandatory reporting of suspected abuse, and increased vigilance by service agencies.

In a society where the word "family" is treated as a term of approbation child abuse is often viewed with dismay. When children are thought to be highly valued, the prevalence of child abuse is thought to be extremely low. In such a context, attempts to understand child abuse tend to focus on the attributes of perpetrators, with particular attention to the role of their assumed psychopathology and extreme behavioral deviance. Yet, as reviews of research on parent characteristics and abuse have routinely noted (e.g.,Berger, 1985; Parke & Collmer, 1975), extreme psychopathology has not been identified as a critical factor in the emergence and maintenance of the physical abuse of children. Moreover, while deviant and maladaptive behaviors of parents outside the domain of diagnosable psychopathology have been identified, the understanding of child abuse by focusing exclusively on parents has not been as fruitful as early investigators had hoped (Knutson, 1988). As a result, attempts to understand the emergence of themal treatment of children have broadened and current conceptual frame works have attempted to integrate information about caretakers, information about victims, and information about environmental variables that provide support for the abusive behavior. Models, such as those offered by Kempe and Helfer (1972) or Cicchetti and colleagues (e.g., Cicchetti, Taraldson & Egeland, 1978; Cicchetti & Toth, 1987), suggest that abuse occurs when sets of parent characteristics and child characteristics are coupled with environmental stressors that occasion the abusive parenting.

Within such interactive models, the putative role of the child as a contributor to the abuse has resulted in some controversy. Indeed, from many quarters, to suggest that the victim contributed to the occurrence of abuse is seen as unconscionable scapegoating of the victim. While such concerns are often more directly expressed in the context of sexual abuse than physical abuse (e.g., Brossard & Wagner, 1988), it is an issue raised in physical abuse as well. Because of such controversy and the fact that focusing on the role of victims in child abuse could be misunderstood as placing blame or responsibility on the victim, it is important to note at the outset that the present chapter considers victim characteristerics to be potential *risk-factors*. That is, this chapter attempts to contribute to the understanding of the physical abuse of children by a consideration of child attributes that may be associated with an increased risk for abuse. As Belsky (1984) has argued, a consideration of victim attributes should be placed in a context to determine whether the child characteristics mesh with the features of the abusive parent and the environment. If there are child-based risk factors in the occurrence of abuse, it is incumbent upon investigators, clinicians, and formulators of public policy to consider such risks factors.

It is also important to note that the focus of the present chapter is on the physical abuse of children. The literature tends to distinguish among physical abuse, sexual abuse, and neglect as three differentiable types of maltreatment. Therefore, there is clear precedent for confining consideration of victims to only physical abuse. It is, however, also clear from clinical and research evidence that the three types of maltreatment are not entirely independent. For example, much sexual abuse, especially that involving penetration, can be sufficiently injurious or coercive to be considered a physically abusive event. Additionally, there is a growing literature (e.g., Herrenkohl & Herrenkohl, 1981) demonstrating that there can be a strong association between abuse and neglect. If neglect is considered maltreatment associated with acts of omission by child caretakers and abuse is considered acts of commission by caretakers, then the major focus of the present chapter is on victim characteristics as they contribute to risks for abusive acts of commission by parents, exclusive of sexual exploitation.

Methodological Issues

Research with clinical samples often poses particular difficulties for investigators. Research on child abuse is certainly no exception. Indeed, research on child abuse in general and victim risk factors in particular provide a formidable challenge. As a result of the challenging circumstances under which abuse research may be conducted, research on physical abuse has, to some extent, produced a literature that is methodologically compromised and more ambiguous than some other areas of aggression research. Reviews that have called attention to methodological difficulties (e.g., Knutson, 1988; Plotkin, Azar, Twentyman, & Perri, 1981) have noted the relative absence of original data and the inadequacies of selected control groups. In studies of victim characteristics as risk factors in abuse, limitations on control groups seriously compromise the development of firm conclusions from many available data sets.One of the foremost problems in understanding the contribution of the role of the victim in the emergence of abusive parenting is the relative absence of longitudinal studies. While prospective studies are represented in the child abuse literature (e.g., Egeland & Brunnquell, 1979; Elmer, 1977, 1978; Farber & Egeland, 1987), such studies are quite rare. Farber and Egeland (1987) have noted that retrospective analyses of abused groups are greatly compromised by potential subject selection biases that preclude the unequivocal determination of causal variables. Of course, the problems with such follow-back studies are not limited to investigations of risk factors in abuse, but are also present in studies of psychopathology and psychotherapy (e.g., Kohlberg, LaCrosse, & Ricks, 1972). Braucht, Loya, and Jamieson (1980) noted that the same problem arises in studies of victims of violent death as well. At the present time, attempts to understand victim contributions to physical abuse must consider retrospective analyses in spite of their interpretive limitations. It is important to note that, although it is difficult to ascertain whether a specific event is an antecedent to abuse, it is no less difficult to determine whether a specific event is a consequence of abuse. Thus conclusions regarding behavioral, intellectual, cognitive, and psychopathological consequences of abuse may be based on data actually reflecting antecedent events (e.g., Ammerman, Cassisi, Hersen & Van Hasselt, 1986; Elmer & Gregg, 1967; Sandgrund, Gaines, & Green, 1974). Another problem with the available research on abuse is the over-representation of persons from economically disadvantaged groups and previously identified clinical samples. Thus, when one attempts to understand the possible contribution of victims to abuse, the available data are often limited in some fashion.

In the absence of suitable longitudinal studies, considerations of victim risk factors tend to be confined to cross-sectional studies attempting to contrast the attributes of abused children with attributes of nonabused children from suitable comparison groups. Comparison groups are often selected on the basis of neglect or matched on the basis of socioeconomic status. Yet, those matching variables are almost certainly not sufficient for an understanding of risk factors in abuse (Herrenkohl & Herrenkohl, 1981). Another critical problem relates to the difficulty in distinguishing between those victim characteristics existing prior to abuse and those victim attributes that might be sequelae of the abusive experiences. For example, recent studies (e.g., Farber & Egeland, 1987; Downey & Walker, 1989) suggest that the maltreatment of children is an extremely potent variable in the ontogeny of behavioral deviance. Thus, when indices of behavioral deviance are identified as an attribute of the victim, it is important to recognize that the child's characteristic may not have preceded the emergence of abuse. Consequently, although the possible contribution of the child to abuse has been considered for many years (e.g., Friedrich & Boriskin, 1976; Friedrich & Einbender, 1983; Knutson, 1988), it continues to be extremely difficult to assert with confidence that many specific child attributes were antecedents to the abusive event. Indeed, virtually all of the identified characteristics of abused children could be either consequences or antecedents of abuse.

Although it has been recognized that the characteristics of abused children could be either antecedents or consequences, many contemporary models of abuse implicate the victim as a possible contributing force almost without regard to which of the child characteristics are antecedent events. This approach to the role of the victim is prevalent regardless of the theoretical orientation of the model. Thus, models which draw heavily on a psychoanalytic approach (e.g., Steele & Pollack, 1968), as well as more behavioral or empirically based approaches (e.g., Friedrich & Boriskin, 1976; Lynch, 1976; Green, Gaines, & Sandgrund, 1974; Cohn, 1982) implicate child characteristics as contributing factors. Theoretical models of abuse and other coercive interactions, have the potential to provide some guidance in identifying victim attributes that could contribute to abusive exchanges and those that are more likely to be consequences. That is, various theoretical models of abuse should implicate specific and general child characteristics as abuse risk factors, either as evokers of abuse or sustainers of abusive interactions.

One could also look for parallels between the abuse literature and the aggression literature for cues regarding victim attributes as factors in abuse. For example, if physical abuse were conceptualized as an area of aggression research (e.g., Knutson, 1978), then target characteristics known to influence the emergence of aggressive behavior might be examined as variables in abuse research. The contribution of victim characteristics and target characteristics has been recognized in aggression research for many years. In both human (e.g., Baron, 1977; Buss, 1973) and nonhuman studies(e.g., Alberts & Galef, 1973; File & Pope, 1974; Hynan, 1976; Knutson, 1973), evidence strongly suggests that the behavioral characteristics of targets play an important role in intraspecific aggression. These may be either general aggression-evoking target attributes or they may reflect an associative process (e.g., Berkowitz, 1974) in which conditioning histories make aggressors particularly vulnerable to specific target cues. Within physical abuse research, such a possibility would not be inconsistent with early observations of Fontana (1971), implicating the victim's role in abuse, or the conditioning treatment strategy of Sandford and Tustin (1973) to reduce abusive responses towards a child victim. Other related research that implicates potential victim variables as risk factors in abuse extends from studies documenting that the child can contribute importantly to parent-child interactions (e.g., Bell, 1968; Lamb, 1981; Patterson, 1982). Thus, both contemporary research on aggression and contemporary research on parent-child interactions implicates the child as a contributing factor in many aspects of interactions between adults and children, including maltreatment.

It should be apparent to the reader that the present section serves as an introductory caveat regarding the conclusions that can be drawn regarding victim risk factors in physical abuse. Those victim characteristics that are considered in this chapter were selected because they have a theoretical basis for consideration or a data base sufficient to evaluate their inclusion. Nevertheless, the current state of the literature makes some hypothesizing inevitable.

Demographic Variables as Victim Characteristics

With mandatory reporting laws and various central registry data banks, one might expect that clear and unequivocal data regarding basic demographic characteristics of victims of abuse would be readily available. Unfortunately, the central registry data are compromised to some extent by reporting biases and limited information from populations who do not use public service agencies. Nevertheless, analyses of reports of abuse in central abuse registries have been conducted (e.g., Rosenthal, 1988; U.S. Department of Health and Human Services, 1988; Wilson, Daly & Weghorst, 1981). From central registry and national probability samples, both the age and sex of victims have been considered. In general, incidents of physical abuse increase with age. More importantly, there appears to be an inverse relationship between the age of the child and the severity of the abuse. That is, fatalities are more prevalent among younger children, whereas moderate injurious consequences of physical abuse are associated with older children. Interestingly, Jason and Andereck (1983) suggest that younger children with younger parents are at the greatest risk for fatal abuse. While girls are at greater risk for sexual abuse and this gender-related risk increases as a function of age, there are gender-determined age relationships in injurious physical abuse as well. In children 12 years old and under, a majority of victims experiencing serious or minor injury are male, whereas a majority of serious or minor injury recipients 13 years old and above are female. It was suggested by Rosenthal (1988) that the declining risk for serious injury to male adolescents reflects their greater capacity to reciprocate, especially with regard to female perpetrators. Consistent with that hypothesis, there is a steady increase in the proportion of physically abusive perpetrators who are male as the age of the victim increases. This pattern accurately reflects the uncommon event of female perpetrators against male adolescent victims. Such a pattern is also reflected in the data described by Wilson et al. (1981), with more males represented among victims of physical abuse under age 11 and more females represented among victims over the age of 12, exclusive of sexual abuse.

Although it is clear that physical abuse of children occurs in all socioeconomic strata, the notion of the classlessness of abuse has occasioned considerable controversy (e.g., Pelton, 1978). While it is the case that abuse does occur in all socioeconomic strata, increasing evidence (e.g., Pelton, 1978 U.S. Department of Health and Human Services, 1988) suggests that low income is a significant risk factor for injury, impairment, and reported frequencies of abuse. It is, however, important to note (e.g., Farber & Egeland 1987) that large segments of economically disadvantaged children are not physically abused and that disadvantaged groups may be over-represented in abuse statistics because of their reliance on public service agencies. These agencies are more likely to report suspicions of abuse than are private healthcare and service agencies. Additionally, as Hampton and Newberger (1985) noted, reporting of suspected abuse is most likely when the alleged perpetrator is nonwhite and from a lower social class. These reporting tendencies probably reduce the representation of more affluent and white groups in central registry data and probably result in a systematic social class bias in existing data sets. Studies that assert that minorities are over-represented in the abuse statistics, even when controlling for social class (e.g., Spearly & Lauderdale, 1983), are questionable because of their reliance on central registry data. The probable bias between reported and unreported cases strongly suggests that our existing data sets regarding social class and ethnicity as risk factors in abuse require further study.

Many models of abuse (e.g., Straus, 1980) implicate stressors as contributors to the emergence of abuse. Membership in lower socioeconomic classes can be considered a significant stressor. While currently available data are, perhaps, compromised by the bias noted above, Pelton (1978) argues that a significant disservice is done to disadvantaged children by suggesting they are at the same risk for maltreatment as more advantaged children. In support of Pelton, prevalence differences among socioeconomic groups incross cultural studies (e.g., Nakau, Adam, Stathacopoulou, & Agathonos,1982), as well as differences in prevalence estimates among socioeconomic groups that exceed the expected values attributable to reporting bias, suggest that economic disadvantage is worthy of continuing consideration as a child risk factor in the emergence of abuse.

Early Childhood and Developmental Antecedents to Abuse

In attempting to identify child characteristics that are antecedent risk factors rather than consequences of maltreatment, one tactic has been to consider only congenital or early neonatal factors. Such an approach is used to establish causal relationships through temporal associations. Two early childhood characteristics that have attracted considerable attention are prematurity and low birth-weight full-term infants. There is a relatively large literature (e.g., Faranoff, Kennell, & Klaus, 1972; Frodi, 1981; Goldberg,1979; Herrenkohl & Herrenkohl, 1979, 1981; Klein & Stern, 1971; Martin, 1976; Smith, 1976) that provides support for the position that low birth-weight or premature infants are at greater risk for physical abuse. While this literature has had considerable impact in areas of clinical practice and on assumptions underlying some abuse prevention programs, the evidence regarding these neonatal characteristics and abuse is not unequivocal. Leventhal (1981) has reviewed the prematurity and low birth-weight literature and has identified methodological inadequacies that raise serious questions about the validity of the assertion that prematurity and low birthweight are importantly related to physical abuse. Additionally, studies by Egeland and Brunnquell (1979), Egeland and Vaughn (1981) and Gaines, Sandgrund, Green, and Power (1978) could not establish a linkage between the premature status of the child and abusive parenting.

It is clear that there is some continuing controversy about the possible association between prematurity or low birth-weight and physical abuse. Those who support the position that prematurity or low birth-weight are risk factors in abuse typically invoke the likely attachment difficulties that could exist between the abusive mother and her child. That is, the premature or low birth-weight child is considered to be a child with whom a complementary relationship between the child and the caretaker may be impaired (Goldberg, 1979). This impairment of the relationship is thought to be exacerbated by the mother-infant separation required by some intensive pediatric interventions. Additionally, Herrenkohl and Herrenkohl (1979) have suggested that the premature birth could be the result of maternal prenatal emotional stress coupled with a negative attitude toward the pregnancy. Thus, they speculate that the parent of the premature infant may have a negative predisposition toward parenting as well as a difficult-to-rear child.

Other data that have been introduced to support the prematurity link with abuse is the work of Frodi and her colleagues (e.g., Frodi, Lamb, Leavitt, Donvoan, Neff, & Sherry, 1978; Frodi, Lamb, Wille, 1981). This research demonstrated that premature infants display vocalizations and crying that are more irritating to listeners than those of full-term infants. Additionally, Frodi and Lamb (1980) have demonstrated that these irritating vocalizations evoke different responses by abusive and nonabusive parents. Such work suggests that there could be an interaction between at risk parents and the behaviors of premature infants that would increase abuse risk.

The impact of many early childhood characteristics that may occasion abusive interactions with a child are often thought to be mediated through the disruption of the attachment process between the child and the mother. Consistent with this hypothesis, Egeland, Breitenbucher, and Rosenberg (1980) noted that not all at-risk mothers become abusive; therefore, they suggest an interaction between mother attributes and child characteristics that impair attachment and increase risk for abuse. From their work, it appears that both the unresponsive child and the inappropriately responsive child are at greater risk for abuse when the at-risk mother has been exposed to other life stressors that contribute to her anxiety or emotional lability.

Such a possible role of impaired attachment in the occurrence of the abuse has remained controversial because some studies of attachment and maltreatment have identified some apparently securely attached infants who were maltreated. Recently, however, Carlson, Barnett, Cicchetti, and Braunwald (1989) provided data suggesting that the controversy regarding attachment and maltreatment may be due, in part, to the limitations of the widely used three-category classification system for assessing attachment in the strange situation test of Ainsworth, Blehar, Waters, and Wall (1978). A more recent four-category classification system permits a fuller assessment of attachment disruption, by adding a disorganized-disoriented category to the original taxonomy of anxious-avoidant, anxious-ambivalent, and securely attached infants. Carlson et al.(1989) identified the disorganized-disoriented infant attachment pattern among maltreated infants; these infants would not have been categorized as either anxious-avoidant or anxious ambivalent in the three-category systemand would have been misclassified as "securely attached." Thus, it is possible that the apparently securely attached infants who were maltreated in some studies could have been infants manifesting disorganized-disoriented attachment patterns.

Lyons-Ruth, Connell, Zoll, and Stahl (1987) identified resistant- avoidance patterns of infant attachment by those infants who were maltreated. Of course, in this and other studies, it is impossible to unequivocally distinguish among the child contributions to disrupted attachment, the mother's contribution, and the interaction of the two. There are, however, recent studies (e.g., Lewis & Feiring, 1989) identifying avoidance and irritable infant patterns in an attachment test as young as three months. While these early infant behaviors could reflect maternal influences, the possibility of some genetic contribution to temperament (e.g., Plomin, 1983) supports the position that early temperamental characteristics interact with maternal attributes to determine attachment, an hypothesis proposed by Egeland et al. (1980). Additionally, the recent work by El-Sheikh, Cummings, and Goetsch (1989) identified temperamental and physiological differences among children in response to angry behavior by adults. These data are consistent with a child vulnerability hypothesis or a hypothesis of greater reactivity by some at-risk children. While all of these attachment and temperamental difficulties may not effectively account for the emergence of the original abuse and maltreatment, they do suggest a possible vector for continuing abuse and sustained negative interactions between children and parents. That is, if the mother-child attachment interactions become increasingly disrupted and if the child becomes increasingly avoidant, reactive, or disoriented in attachment, then the risks for continuing abuse would be expected to increase.

There are other areas of research related to naturally occurring difficulties faced by parents that could be contributors to the emergence of physical abuse. For example, Lynch (1975) speculated about childhood illness as a factor that could be a contributor to abuse. Again, the illness is conceptualized as a stressor in the parenting relationship. The speculation was based largely on the high base-rate of illness among abused children and the parenting difficulties that can occur in attempting to meet the needs of unhealthy children. A prospective study by Sherrod, O'Connor, Vietze, and Altemeier (1984) assessed a range of child characteristics in abused, neglected, failure-to-thrive, or comparison children. The Sherrod et al. (1984) study suggests that during the first three years of life abused youngsters were more likely to have patterns of illness and accidental injuries prior to the occurrence of abuse. The differences among groups in terms of illnesses diminished as the children aged, suggesting that frequent illness could be a risk factor in abuse primarily during the early childhood years. Interestingly, the greater frequency of accidents among the abused children relative to the neglected and failure-to-thrive children implicate behavioral factors as well as health factors in abuse risk. That is, there is some evidence that there are behavioral risk factors in accidental injuries (e.g., Pless & Stulginskas, 1982), including aggressiveness, suggesting that the greater prevalence of accidents in the abused group could reflect a set of behavioral antecedents to abuse.

In addition to temperamental and health characteristics of children, appearance has also been considered as a factor in the emergence of maltreatment. Although early data (e.g., Dion, 1974) has suggested that attractiveness may affect punitive interactions, recent work (e.g., Herrenkohl & Herrenkohl, 1981; Starr, Dietrich, Fischhoff, Ceresnie, & Zweier, 1984) has failed to support the assertion that physical anomalies contribute significantly to abuse. There are, however, data that implicate unattractive physical appearance as an additional factor in the disruption of attachment that may indirectly increase a risk for abuse. Research by Barden, Ford, Jensen, Rogers-Salyer, and Salyer (1989) demonstrated that craniofacial deformity in infants was associated with consistently less nurturant behavior by their mothers when compared to the mothers of children without such deformities. Interestingly, Barden et al.(1989) observed that the mothers of the children with deformities were quite unaware of their less nurturant responses. Moreover, in spite of their actual behavior, the less nurturant mothers of deformed infants rated their interactions more positively than did the mothers of normal children. The Barden et al. (1989) data strongly suggest the possibility that initial unattractiveness and appearance-related deformities could contribute to greater risk for physical abuse through disrupted attachment.

Another interacting variable contributing to the physical abuse of the difficult-to-rear infant is the age of the parent. Although young parents are thought to be at greater risk for abusive behavior (e.g., Bolton, Laner, Kane, 1980; Lynch & Roberts, 1982), some evidence suggests that the association between youthful parenthood and abuse may be a function of the added stress induced by unplanned pregnancies (e.g., Furstemberg, 1976; Russell, 1980). Zuravin (1987) observed that unplanned pregnancies in the absence of contraception were more likely to be associated with neglect while unplanned pregnancies which occurred in spite of contraceptive efforts were associated with abuse. Economic disadvantage and disturbed relationships in the families of origin(e.g., Earp & Ory, 1980; Kinard & Klerman, 1980) are also thought to contribute to the occurrence of abuse by young mothers of difficult infants. Recent research by Crockenberg (1987) suggests that the irritable and difficult to rear infant who has an irritable adolescent mother is likely to become increasingly noncompliant. Taken together the Crockenberg (1987) and the Zuravin (1987) data suggest there would be an interaction between the irritability of the child and the irritability of the reluctant adolescent mother that would increase the risk of excessively punitive parenting.

Another interactional aspect of physical abuse that could relate to victim characteristics concerns the developmental status of the child coupled with the perceptions and expectations of the care providers. There is a growing literature suggesting that abused children evidence developmental delays in language (e.g., Fox, Long, & Langlois, 1988), social-cognitive development (e.g., Barahal, Waterman, Martin, 1981; Daniel, Hampton, & Newberger, 1983), and social-emotional interactions (e.g., Kaufman & Cicchetti, 1989). While all of the cognitive and social-cognitive victim characteristics could easily be consequences of abuse, Fox et al. (1988) suggest that some language delays could contribute to increased difficulty in parenting and thus contribute to abusive child care. It seems likely that language delays and social-cognitive limitations could impair the acquisition of knowledge of proscribed behaviors and contingent consequences and thereby increase the risk for more severe and potentially injurious disciplinary tactics. Additionally, studies by Twentyman and Plotkin (1982) and Larrance and Twentyman (1983) indicate that abusive parents can have distorted perceptions of child behavior. As a possible factor in abuse, unrealistic expectations regarding developmental milestones was implicated by research of Azar, Robinson, Hekimian, and Twentyman, (1984). This work suggests that language and cognitive delays could contribute to the development of abuse, or the sustaining of excessively punitive punishment, when parents are confronted with children who fail to meet their expectations. Similarly, a study by Weston (1974), regarding single episode abuse events, also suggests that developmental delays in areas such as compliance and toilet training could be proximal evokers of physical abuse.

In addition to early childhood developmental delays or unrealistic expectations by parents, problems can arise in later years. For example, Doueck, Ishisaka, and Greenaway (1988) suggest the possibility that a misunderstanding of the transition from childhood to adolescence could contribute to the emergence of abuse at that stage of development. These authors also implicate external stressors and personal difficulties of the parents, but the proximal evoker of abuse is conceptualized as the child's transition to adolescence.

Handicapping Conditions

A factor that could contribute directly to difficulty in child care and perhaps increased risk for abuse is the presence of a handicapping condition. Handicapping conditions can result in children who are behaviorally difficult to manage, who evidence significant intellectual and cognitive impairment, who are communicatively handicapped, or who are orthopedically impaired. Any of these problems could be conceptualized as acute or chronic stressors for child care providers as well as disruptors of the attachment process. Thus, there is some basis to suspect handicapping conditions could contribute to physical abuse. Additionally, virtually all of the handicapping conditions, such as celebral palsy, retardation, deafness, or blindness that can not be demonstrated to have a genetic or congenital basis have also been identified as possible consequences of maltreatment (e.g., Solomon, 1979; Sandgrund, et al., 1974; Jaudes & Diamond, 1985).

While the presence of a handicapping condition has been implicated as an important contributor to abuse by several authors (e.g., Gil, 1975; Gillespie, Seaberg, & Berline, 1977; Morse, Sahler, & Friedman, 1970; Friedrich, & Boriskin, 1976) support for that positions has been questioned in recent reviews (e.g., Starr, et al., 1984) and studies of handicapped children (e.g., Coon, Beck, & Coon, 1980). The major criticism of the hypotheses regarding handicapping conditions inducing abuse is based on the relative absence of convincing evidence that handicapped conditions are associated with increased prevalence of abuse. Unfortunately, epidemiological data regarding handicapping conditions are not available in the abuse central registries of close to half of the states (e.g., Camblin, 1982). Consequently, the lack of solid epidemiological data on handicapping conditions among abused groups, as well as problems identifying cause and effect relationships in retrospective studies, greatly compromise the capability to assess the contribution of handicaps to abuse.

There are, however, some studies and some indirect lines of evidence that suggest children, adolescents, and adults with disabilities may be at increased risk for physical abuse (e.g., Garbarino, Brookhouser, & Authier, 1987). This indirect evidence and morerecent studies have caused some reviewers (e.g., Ammerman, Van Hasselt, & Hersen, 1988) to take issue with the Starr et al. (1984) conclusion regarding the absence of evidence demonstrating that handicapping conditions contribute to abuse. For example, Ammerman et.al. (1988) suggest such a conclusion is premature because of the lack of specificity in the definition and analysis of handicapping conditions, as well as methodological inadequacies in the research.

One of the studies that might be used to argue that it is premature to disregard handicap as a potentiator of physical abuse is a recent study by Ammerman, Van Hasselt, Hersen, McGonigle, and Lubetsky (1989). In their recent assessment of multihandicapped children hospitalized in a psychiatric facility, Ammerman et al. (1989) established a 19% physical abuse prevalence rate. The absence of appropriate comparison groups makes unequivocal conclusions regarding an association between handicaps and abuse impossible, but the authors stated the base rate is much greater than would be expected if handicaps did not play a role. However, with abuse rates of approximately 24% obtained in other inpatient psychiatric samples (e.g., Zaidi, Knutson, & Mehm, 1989), it is hard to argue that handicaps increase abuse risk beyond that identified in inpatient recipients of child psychiatric services.

It is important to note that many handicaps severely impair communication, and communicatively impaired persons may not be effective in disclosing the occurrence of abuse. Additionally, many practitioners are not prepared to evaluate handicapped persons, especially in the area of abuse-related evaluations. Thus, there is the strong possibility that the abuse of severely or profoundly handicapped persons is greatly under-identified or under-reported. Consistent with that possiblity is the dramatic increase in referrals to the Center for Abused Handicapped Children at the Boys Town National Research Hospital as publicity and awareness of the abuse of the handicapped increases
(P. Sullivan, personal communication, July 18, 1989).

Although the handicapping conditions typically considered in the context of abuse risk include intellectual, sensory, or orthopedic impairment, the Ammerman et al. (1989) study and other studies (e.g., Zaidi, et.al., 1988) suggest that children with psychiatric diagnoses could be at increased risk for abuse. In particular, attention deficit hyperactivity disorder (ADHD; DSMIII-R, 1988) has been noted as a likely abuse-evoking psychiatric disorder. For example, Johnson and Morse (1968) suggested that a child presenting with ADHD from an abusive family was the child most likely to have been physically abused and that the ADHD condition was likely to have preceded the abuse. Available data suggesting that parents are more physically intense and controlling in their interactions with ADHD boys (e.g., Whalen, Henker, & Dotemoto, 1981), as well as less positive in their interactions with ADHD children (e.g., Campbell, 1975; Cunningham & Barkley, 1979), further implicates ADHD as a possible risk factor in abuse. A recent study from this laboratory (Whitmore, Kramer, & Knutson, 1989), however, failed to establish a relationship between ADHD and physical abuse. In this research, young adult males who had been diagnosed as ADHD at a tertiary care psychiatric facility, their biological brothers who did not show evidence of ADHD, and control subjects identified from the classroom of the probands at the time of original diagnosis, participated in a longitudinal study of ADHD and punitive childhood histories. Results suggest the disciplinary experiences of ADHD youth were not appreciably different from those of their siblings and their peers. Such data certainly caution against a conclusion that ADHD per se is an important contributor to physical abuse.

Other suggestive evidence of the possibility that handicapping conditions occasion physical abuse emerges in the context of abuse in residential programs (e.g., Brookhouser, 1987). Severely or profoundly communicatively and sensorily impaired youngsters often reside in out-of-home placements because of their handicapping conditions. Recent media reports of the occurrence of abuse by caretakers in residential facilities for the deaf suggest the possibility that the handicapping condition could increase risk for abuse in out-of-home placements. Evidence does exist that parents and child careworkers involved in the care of deaf children are more punitive and tend to use more corporal punishment (e.g., Schlesinger & Meadow, 1972) and such data certainly implicate communication difficulties as a contributing factor in physical abuse by child care workers. Whittaker (1987) has also argued that handicapped children in residential facilities might be at considerable risk for abuse because of the unique demands of the handicap coupled with the out-of-home placement.

Much of the work on handicapping conditions and physical abuse implicates the behavioral concomitants of the handicapping condition as the important factor in the emergence of abuse. That is, authors typically invoke the behavioral challenges that the handicap produces rather than the handicap itself. Thus, it seems likely that behavioral attributes of handicapped youngsters are the critical issues to consider in the context of victim attributes as evokers of physical abuse.

Behavioral Risk Factors in Physical Abuse

Early theoretical conceptualizations of child abuse promoted the idea that one child in a family was singled out for maltreatment. Much like *Cinderella*, one of the children was perceived as different and that child functioned as the family scapegoat (e.g., Fontana, 1971). Though some research has lent support to the scapegoat hypothesis (Friedrich & Boriskin, 1976), other studies have reported that a significant proportion of abusive families have more than one target of maltreatment. Herrenkohl and Herrenkohl (1981) reported that 46.5 percent of the abusive families that they studied had more than one target of maltreatment.

Though there may be multiple targets of abuse, studies have suggested that abusive parents describe the maltreated child or children as the most difficult and demanding of their children

(Coombes, 1980; Green, et al., 1974; Herrenkohl & Herrenkohl, 1981). In a comparison of 146 infants who were injured (Gregg & Elmer, 1969), physicians were unable to discern any differences between the children who were abused and those who sustained accidental injuries. However, the reports by the mothers of the abused children suggested that they perceived their children as very different and more difficult to rear. Similarly, Martin and Kourany (1980) reported on cases of abusive adolescent babysitters who often described the children that they abused as being clingy, fearful, manipulative and oppositional.

Although maltreated children have been described as difficult and demanding, the fact that the source of the report is often involved as a perpetrator in the abusive interactions confounds the validity of the reports. Consistent with attributional research of Brock and Pallak (1969), reports of child behavior by abusive parents may, in fact, reflect merely a rationalization and justification for the abusive act rather than a veridical description of the child. A number of studies have suggested that abusive parents view the abused child more negatively and feel less able to influence that child's behavior compared to nonabused children from the same family (Herrenkohl & Herrenkohl, 1979). Others have failed to replicate these distorted perceptions (e.g., Halperin, 1983). Moreover, when abusive mothers were compared to mothers who were experiencing "parenting difficulties", perceptions by abusive mothers of the children were no more negative than the nonabusive mothers (Rosenberg & Repucci, 1983). It may be that parents who are having difficulty controlling their children, regardless of the extent of their physically coercive acts, perceive their children more negatively.

Though abusive parents seem to describe the abused child as different and difficult to manage, these descriptions are often not supported by parental reports on standardized inventories of child behavior problems when compared with appropriate control groups (e.g., Rohrbeck & Twentyman, 1986). Using standardized behavior rating measures, parents of maltreated children have been reported to describe their children differently than do parents of control children, but only when the control children come from nondistressed families who are not seeking psychological services (e.g., Hoffman-Plotkin & Twentyman, 1984; Perry, Doran, & Wells, 1983; Wolfe & Mosk, 1983). In contrast, such standardized parental reports of children's behavior from samples of children referred to service agencies have not been found to discriminate between abused and nonabused children. For example, Wolfe and Mosk (1983) compared parental reports on the Achenbach Child Behavior Checklist (Achenbach & Edelbrock, 1982) for 35 physically abused children, 36 nonabused children referred to a child welfare agency and 35 nonabused children recruited from the local community. The two groups of children referred to the child welfare agency were described by their mothers as exhibiting more behavior management problems than children from the community sample. Agency children were described as more anxious/obsessive, depressed/withdrawn, hyperactive, delinquent and aggressive. Importantly, the abused and nonabused groups of agency children did not differ significantly on any of the behavioral measurement scales.

Salzinger, Kaplan, Pelcovitz, Samit, and Krieger (1984) found significant differences between behavior ratings of a group of children from abusive families and children from nonabusive control families. All of the children were being seen at the same hospital but in different clinics. Children from abusive families were rated by their parents as being less socially competent and exhibiting more problem behaviors than children from control families. When children from abusive families who were actually abused were compared to children from abusive families who had not been the targets of abuse, nosignificant differences were found for parent ratings. Unfortunately, the sample of children from abusive families in the Salzinger et al. (1984) study contained physically abused, sexually abused, emotionally abused and neglected children, limiting any conclusions that might be drawn regarding characteristics of victims of physical abuse alone. The Salzinger et al.(1984) study and the Wolf and Mosk (1983) study raise questions regarding the selection of appropriate control children for comparisons with abused children.

Another source of information about behavioral characteristics of maltreated children has been derived from reports by teachers. In a comparison of teacher ratings of abused, neglected and control children, Reidy (1977) found that abused and neglected children were reported to exhibit more behavior problems in the school setting than did control children. Teacher ratings, however, did not differentiate between those children that were abused and those that were neglected. In contrast Salzinger, et al. (1984) reported that children from abusive families were rated by their teachers as displaying more negative behaviors than control children. Implicating a victim role within the sample of children from abusive families, teacher ratings made significant distinctions between the behavior of children who were the targets of abuse and children who were not targets of abuse from the same home. Specifically, target children were reported to exhibit more conduct problems, more hyperactivity, more attention problems, and more tension and anxiety than nontarget children. In addition to this range of negative behaviors displayed by target children, teachers reported that nontarget children displayed more positive behaviors than the target children.

The finding that teacher ratings differentiated between children who were the targets of abuse and children who were not is intriguing given that parental ratings did not differentiate between these two groups of children. Salzinger, et al.(1984) hypothesize that the different scales completed by parents and by teachers may account for some of the discrepancy, with one or the other scale being more sensitive to the types of child behaviors that may be involved in abusive interactions. They also suggest that abusive parents may have a lower threshold for considering certain child behaviors as disturbing. The failure to assess positive child behaviors in most studies and the teachers ratings of nonabused children as more positive suggests the possibility that abusive parents are reacting to the lower rate of positive child behaviors as well as negative ones. Furthermore, children may differentially display behaviors based on situational stimuli. Therefore, all children from abusive families may display more disturbing behavior at home. At school, nontarget children may be better able to monitor or control their behavior than target children. Further studies of teacher ratings of children from abusive families and distressed families seem warranted.

In contrast with the standardized rating scale information, observational data has tended to support the hypothesis that abused children or children from abusive homes are often more aggressive than children from nonabusive distressed homes. George and Main (1979) reported that abused toddlers were more physically and verbally aggressive with peers and caregivers and more avoidant of other children when compared to matched control toddlers from families experiencing stress. Burgess and Conger (1977) reported that children in abusive families displayed more aggressive behaviors than children in either neglectful or control families.

Several studies from the Oregon Social Learning Center support the position that abused children are more aggressive or oppositional. Reid, Taplin and Lorber (1981) contrasted home observational data involving children from three types of families: those referred for child management problems together with evidence of child abuse; those referred for child management problems but with no evidence of abuse; those recruited from the community as distressed families. The children from the abusive families displayed significantly higher levels of aversive behaviors than either of the comparison groups. Furthermore, Reid (1984) reported significant correlations between the rates of aversive and oppositional acts by children and aversive behaviors by their parents. Suggesting a pattern of reciprocity, Patterson (1980) notes that the rate of aversive acts by children on a given day is significantly related to aversive acts by their mothers. Moreover, Reid, Patterson, and Loeber (1982) argue that the probability that a parent will abuse, hit or threaten a child is, in part, influenced by the behavioral problems that the child presents. Given that children often behave poorly in the presence of their parents, the authors suggest that most children are at a serious risk of instigating their own physical abuse.

The fact that abused children are more aggressive than their nonabused peers is consistent with social learning models of aggressive behavior (e.g., Bandura, 1973; Patterson, 1982). It is often assumed that the aggressive behavior is a consequence of their physical abuse. It is, however, just as plausible that aggressive behavior in abused children is a consequence of the interaction of a difficult child with parents who lack the skills to reduce the child's coercive behaviors. Burgess (1985) implies that abused children are doubly handicapped becausethey do not receive the necessary exposure to socially competent models at home and they do not receive consistent and contingent reinforcement for prosocial behavior. Parents of abused children have been reported to lack certain parenting skills. In the absence of the requisite skills, they are poor observers of children's behaviors (Burgess, Anderson, Schellenbach, & Conger, 1981), they respond noncontingently to children's behaviors, and they are less likely to reinforce positive behaviors (Dumas & Wahler, 1985),and more likely to punish negative behaviors than are nonabusive parents (Burgess & Conger, 1978; Reid, Taplin, & Lorber, 1981). Therefore, it is quite conceivable that abusive parents are less skilled and less able to monitor and modify their children's behavior and thus may be especially taxed by a difficult or aggressive child. Therefore, children who present as difficult to rear children contribute to their victimization when they have the misfortune of having unskilled parents.

In addition to aggression, abused children are often described as noncompliant, especially to parental requests. Observations of mother-child interactions between physically abusive mothers and their children and nonabusive mothers with their children have demonstrated that the abused children complied significantly less often to requests by mothers than the control children (George & Main, 1979; Schindler & Arkowitz, 1986). This pattern of a lack of appropriate responsivity to social overtures has been noted in studies of peer interactions of abused children as well. For example, in observational research by Jacobsen and Straker (1982), triads of abused children and control children, aged 5 to 10, were videotaped while they interacted. Though the children did not differ on measures of hostility and aggression, abused children were found to be less socially interactive than the nonabused peers. Impaired peer interactions have been noted in other studies of abused children (e.g., Herrenkohl & Herrenkohl, 1981; Johnson & Morse, 1968; Young, 1964).

The unresponsiveness and lack of social interaction by abused children may in fact be a result of the elevated aggressiveness of the maltreated children. The work of Dodge and his colleagues (Dodge, Pettit, McClaskey & Brown, 1986) on the formation of friendships in children suggest that children who are inappropriately aggressive in the early stages of peer interaction tend to be rejected by their peers. Coie and Kupersmidt (1983) have found that peer status based on classroom ratings of children is a stable phenomenon, while others (e.g., Dodge, 1982; Dodge & Frame, 1982; Dodge & Newman, 1981) have noted that rejected children are more likely to take offense and to draw hostile inferences from their interactions with peers. Considering the aggressiveness and problems with peer interactions that abused children tend to exhibit, abused children appear to be at an elevated risk for problems throughout their lives. Not only may they be at a heightened risk for abuse, but they may be at a greater risk for later adult adjustment problems, including social deviance and aggressive behavior and later criminal behavior (cf. Robins, 1966).

Due to the lack of prospective studies of victim attributes, as well as the methodological difficulties associated with retrospective analyses, the role of child behavioral characteristics in the emergence of physical abuse cannot be unequivocally determined. Unlike investigations of some neonatal characteristics, studies of many behavioral characteristics as risk factors for physical abuse have not been able to establish the presence of the necessary characteristics prior to the occurrence of abuse. Though the role of behavioral characteristics in the emergence of physical abuse is often the primary issue, it is just as important to consider child behaviors that could be associated with the maintenance, rather than the initiation, of physical abuse. Indeed, the role of child behaviors has been substantiated in the coercive family interactions of families with antisocial children (cf. Patterson, 1986). Patterson (1986) hypothesizes that deficient parental management skills interact with common irritating child behaviors and together they initiate interactional sequences which typically escalate to physical assault. Moreover, these interactional sequences of family members exchanging aversive behaviors are initially reinforcing through processes of negative reinforcement. As these coercive exchanges endure and escalate induration and severity, the risk for physical assault increases (Reid, 1984). Patterson (1986) argues that the aggressiveness of a child is the result of learned behavior patterns, progressing from noncompliance to physical assault. These coercive behavior patterns then place aggressive children at an elevated risk for physical abuse during coercive exchanges with their parents. This role of behavior patterns in physically coercive parent-child interactions is also consistent with theory and research on the coercive patterns of abusive marital dyads as proposed by Jacobson and Margolin (1982). Though actual evidence concerning child behaviors as risk factors in the emergence of physical abuse is limited, theoretical and experimental evidence certainly implicate behavioral characteristics as risk factors in the maintenance of coercive, and perhaps assaultive, parent-child interactions.

An Analog Test of the Role of Victim Behavior

While there is considerable indirect evidence that victim attributes may contribute to the occurrence of abusive parenting, the amount of direct evidence is limited. Even in prospective studies, the unequivocal assessment of the child's contribution to the emergence of abuse cannot be made, because the shared contributions of the parent and the child in their continuing interactions have not been disentangled. One research tactic that seems promising inexperimentally assessing the role of the child in abusive parenting is the use of laboratory analog tasks. The use of analog tasks in studies of clinical problems has occasioned some criticism, primarily related to the "artificial nature" of analog research. Kazdin (1978), however, has asserted that virtually all experimental psychological research with humans is an analog in so far as the imposition of experimental, or even observational procedures, always results in circumstances that only approximate the nonexperimental conditions to which investigators might hope to generalize. Moreover, Kazdin (1978) argues that analog tests of hypotheses in the clinical domain are not necessarily less stringent tests of hypothesized relationships. Rather, because of opportunities for experimental control, subject selection, and manipulations on dimensions related to generalizability, analogs can provide critical tests of hypothesized relationships in the clinical domain. Because of the probable advantages of analog research and the difficulties inherent in conducting prospective studies of child abuse, as well as the interpretive problems with retrospective studies, it might be expected that analog research would be a widely used tactic for attempting to understand physical abuse in general and victim factors in particular.

In spite of the apparent utility of the analog strategy in physical abuse research, there are relatively few analog studies of abuse and abuse-related phenomena. The work of Larrance and Twentyman (1983), which involved parental reactions to photographs of children, could be conceptualized as an analog of abuse which attempted to assess distorted perceptions of child behavior by deviant parents. Two other examples of laboratory analogs designed to assess variables that could contribute to punitive reactions by child caretakers are studies by Vasta and Copitch (1981) and Passman and Mulhern (1977). The former demonstrated the lack of awareness of their behavior by persons who evidenced escalated patterns of punitive reactions to children. The latter indicated that child-dependent interruptions can result in more punitive reactions by mothers in an analog setting. The Passman and Mulhern (1977) study also supports the utility of analog tests of child behaviors as a potential risk factor in the occurrence of abuse.

In the laboratory of the present authors, analog parenting tasks have been used to attempt to assess the possible consequences of punitive childhood histories in studies of the transgenerational hypothesis of abuse (Berger, 1981; Zaidi, Knutson & Mehm, 1989). In this research, young adults of child rearing age drawn from auniversity population were selected on the basis of their response to a questionnaire that assesses childhood disciplinary experiences. Selected subjects then react to depictions of child behaviors that could induce disciplinary responses. One analog task to which selected subjects responded (See Zaidi et al., 1989) consisted of twenty slides projected on a screen, each depicting a different childhood behavior. The depicted behaviors included activities that are within the normal range of childbehaviors but are probably irritating to parents, as well as activities that are unequivocally deviant. Subjects were instructed to imagine that they were responsible for the care of the child depicted in the slide. They were asked to indicate their reaction to the child's behavior and to select disciplinary responses that they would use to alter that child's behavior. The Zaidi et al. (1989) study indicated that young adults from highly punitive backgrounds were more likely to endorse physical discipline as a tactic for changing the undesirable behaviors of the children. The analog task data, together with abuse data from families seen at a child psychiatric clinic, provided support for a restricted version of the transgenerational hypothesis of abuse.

Namely, that persons from more punitive backgrounds have a lower threshold for selecting a physical disciplinary response to proscribed or provocative child behaviors and that this lowered threshold contributes to some transgenerational patterns of abuse.

Since the Zaidi et al. (1989) analog study was designed to assess the consequences of childhood histories rather than victim attributes as evokers of abuse, the analog task did not assess a full complement of childhood behaviors. Thus, the task did not permit an analog analysis of victim characteristics. During the course of that analog study, however, the investigators became aware that some types of child behaviors seemed to be more likely to result in more physically punitive disciplinary choices. Because of the impression that classes of children's behavior could influence disciplinary choices, Zaidi (1988) developed a modification of the analog parenting task described in Zaidi et al. (1989).

In the new version of the analog task, seven different scenes were prepared to depict each of three transgression classes of child behaviors. The three transgression classes were: (1) acts which are potentially injurious or dangerous to the child; (2) destructive behaviors; (3) socially inappropriate and rule violating activities. Examples of the potentially dangerous activities included: sitting on the edge of a roof, hanging out of the window of a moving car, loading a revolver while unsupervised. Examples of destructive acts included: bending a television antenna, stepping on a calculator, and drawing on a wall with crayons. The socially inappropriate scenes included: lighting a cigarette, drinking beer, and viewing a sexually explicit magazine. To assess the impact of these classes of misbehavior on the disciplinary choices of adults, a study similar to that of Zaidi et al. (1989) was conducted.

Subjects for the study were selected as a function of their responses to the Physical Punishment scale of the *Assessing*

Environments III (AEIII), a questionnaire designed to assess punitive childhood experiences and abuse-related aspects of the childhood home of the respondent (see Berger, Knutson, Mehm & Perkins, 1988; Knutson & Mehm, 1988). The AEIII was administered to 1053 undergraduate students volunteering to participate in this research as one of many possible research opportunities that the laboratory experience requirement of an introductory course in psychology. Each student who completed the AEIII was instructed *not* to put any name or personal identification numbers on their AEIII answer sheet. To permit *anonymous* follow-up contact with participants selected for the analog sessions, each answer sheet was precoded with an *idiosyncratic* identification number; attached to the answer sheet was a 2 inch by 2 inch card with this idiosyncratic identification number. Persons completing the AEIII were requested to retain this numbered card, which was then used to confirm eligibility for participation in the analog parenting sessions. Since these numbers were not associated with any identifying information, the use of the number did not compromise the anonymity of the subjects and, therefore, facilitated candid responding. Thus, each questionnaire was coded to an individual subject so that childhood histories for the questionnaire could be related to responses on the analog task without using identifying information.

Based on the Zaidi et al. (1989) study and the Berger et al. (1988) demonstration that a score of four on the Physical Punishment scale effectively discriminated between abused and nonabused adolescents, persons responding affirmatively to four or more items of the Physical Punishment scale of the AEIII were selected as members of a Severe Physical Punishment History (SPP) group. Respondents whose scores on the Physical Punishment scale were 1-3 were considered to be members of a Mild Physical

Punishment History (MPP) group. Additionally, subjects who endorsed no items on the Physical Punishment scale were identified as members of a No Physical Punishment History (NPP) group. All of the members of the SPP and NPP groups were considered to be eligible for participation in the analog study; fifty percent of the MPP group were randomly selected by computer to be eligible for participation in the analog sessions. Twenty-two men and 22 women from the SPP group chose to participate in the analog parenting session. Forty-two men and 49 women from the MPP group chose to participate, while 13 men and 44 women from the NPP group volunteered for the analog sessions. Analyses of subject characteristics indicated that the eligible subjects who volunteered to participate in the analog task were indistinguishable from eligible subject who did not participate. Subjects completed the analog task in small groups; the administration of the analog task was conducted by an experimenter who was uninformed with respect to the group membership of the subjects. All subjects were informed that all of their responses were anonymous. Each subject responded individually to the analog parenting task by selecting a disciplinary choice from among verbal, physical, and nonphysical but not verbal disciplinary techniques for each depicted child behavior.

The endorsement of physical disciplinary responses by subjects as a function of disciplinary history and class of child transgression was assessed in a 3 X 3 mixed analysis of variance with punishment history as the between subjects factor and type of child transgression as the within subjects factor. The results of this analysis identified a statistically significant punishment history by transgression class interaction, $F(2,370) = 6.38$, $p<.001$. This statistically significant interaction compromises the interpretability of the statistically significant influence of the effect of the transgression type, $F(2,370) =45.33$, $p<.001$. This interaction is shown in Figure 1. While there was a statistically significant linear trend $F(1,185) = 11.198$, $p<.001$, for an increasing use of physical discipline as a function of the severity of childhood punishment histories it is apparent that the disciplinary choices were clearly influenced by the class of child misbehavior as well. Within the SPP and MPP groups, the destructive depictions evoked the greatest amount of physical discipline. Within the NPP group, physical discipline was rarely selected and its occurrence was not differentially influenced by the class of childhood transgression. The data from this experiment suggests that the persons who might be at risk to use more punitive disciplinary responses because of their own disciplinary histories are most reactive to child behaviors that are destructive. It is interesting that depictions of socially inappropriate or rule violating acts and depictions of acts that are potentially dangerous to the child are relatively unlikely to educe an initial reaction involving physical discipline.

Abusive disciplinary actions by parents are often embedded in extended exchanges. Extended aversive exchanges often result in an escalation to more potentially injurious interactions (e.g., Patterson, 1982; Patterson & Reid, 1970). To assess the possibility of disciplinary escalation in exchanges involving different classes of child behaviors, the analog parenting task requests subjects to indicate how many times they would permit a child to continue the depicted behavior before changing their disciplinary response. If the respondent changes from a nonphysical disciplinary response to a physical disciplinary response, or if they shift from a mild physical disciplinary response to a potentially injurious one, their response is considered to be an escalation. In the present study, most of the depictions of child behavior did not evoke an escalation response. When escalation occurred, the SPP group was most likely to escalate and the NPP group was least likely to escalate. Escalation

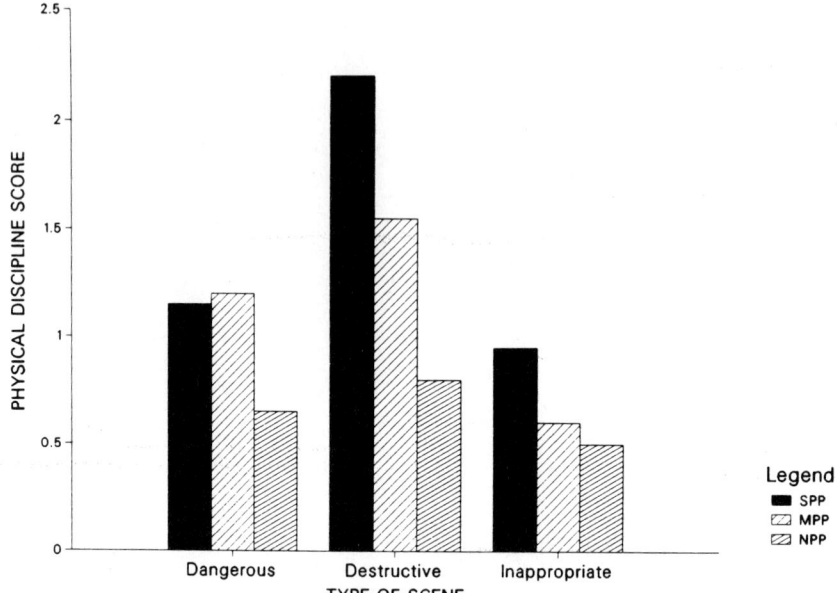

was also a function of the type of depiction. Figure 2 shows escalation as a function of the class of transgression. Depictions of destructive acts were most likely to evoke an escalated physical disciplinary response and depictions of dangerous acts were more likely than rule violations to induce an escalated response. There is considerable clinical evidence that injurious physical abuse occurs in response to parental perceptions of child misbehavior. The present data suggest the occurrence of specific classes of child behavior in conjunction with childhood histories of parents could play a role in establishing a pattern of interaction that places a child at risk for physical abuse. Thus, these and other analog data (e.g., Passman & Mulhern, 1977) implicate a role for child victim behaviors as contributors to the emergence of abuse.

Summary and Conclusion

Theoretical models of aggression (e.g., Patterson, 1982) and abuse (e.g., Cicchetti et al., 1978) that recognize the dyadic nature of physical coercion typically invoke some role for the victim in the occurrence of extreme aggression and violence. Thus, there is some considerable theoretical support for the notion that victims of physical abuse actually play some role in the emergence of abuse. Moreover, evidence that abused children are distinguishable from nonabused children on many dimensions is consistent with the position that children's behavior could contribute to the emergence of abuse or the persistence of abuse in physically abusive households. That is, although there are ambiguities in the evidence and discerning the difference between causes and consequences of abuse is not always clear, many available retrospective, prospective, and analog studies support the possibility that a child's behavior could be a risk factor in evoking potentially injurious disciplinary acts by caretakers. This is not to suggest that children who are

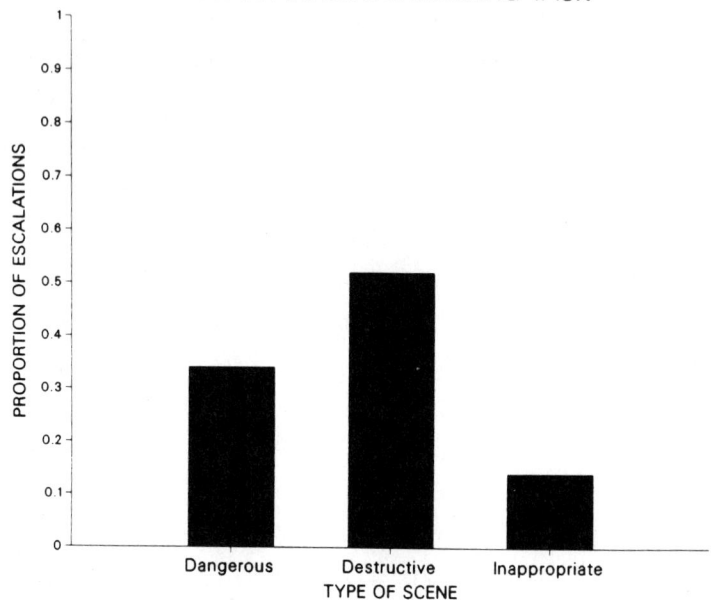

maltreated by excessively punitive disciplinary acts somehow deserve that treatment. Rather, the data do suggest that investigators of variables involved in the physical abuse of children and persons attempting to provide clinical service carefully consider the possibility that attributes of the child, especially difficult or stress-inducing behaviors, could be an important contributor to abuse. While the available evidence is not without some severe limitations, it would be decidedly premature to disregard child characteristics as potentially critical factors in the emergence of the physical abuse of children at the present time. It is also important that investigators recognize and avoid the methodological inadequacies that so limit the understanding of the role of the child in abuse and thereby compromise the development of research-based interventions and prophylaxis in the physical abuse of at-risk children.

REFERENCES

Achenbach, T.M., & Edelbrock, C.S. (1982). *Manual for the Child Behavior Checklist and Child Behavior Profile.* Burlington, VT: Child Psychiatry, University of Vermont.

Alberts, J.R,. & Galef, B.G. (1973). Olfactory cues and movement: Stimuli mediating intraspecific aggression in the wild norway rat. *Journal of Comparative and Physiological Psychology, 85,* 233-242.

Ainsworth, M.D.S., Blehar, M.C., Waters, E., & Wall, S. (1978). *Patterns of attachment: A psychological study of the strange situation.* Hillsdale, NJ: Erlbaum.

Ammerman, R.T., Cassisi, J.E., Hersen, M., & Van Hasselt, V.B. (1986). Consequences of physical abuse and neglect in children. *Clinical Psychology Review, 6,* 291-310.

Ammerman, R.T., Van Hasselt, V.B., & Hersen, M. (1988). Maltreatment of handicapped children: A critical review. *Journal of Family Violence, 3,* 53-72.

Ammerman, R.T., Van Hasselt, V.B., Herson, M., McGonigle, J.J., & Lubetsky, M.J. (1989). Abuse and neglect in psychiatrically hospitalized multihandicapped children. *Child Abuse & Neglect, 13,* 335-343.

Azar, S.T., Robinson, D.R., Hekimian, E., & Twentyman, C.T. (1974). Unrealistic expectations and problem-solving ability in maltreating and comparison mothers. *Journal of Consulting and Clinical Psychology, 52,* 687-691.

Barden, R.C., Ford, M.E., Jensen, A.G., Rogers-Salyer, M., & Salyer, K.E. (1989). Effects of craniofacial deformity in infancy on the quality of mother-infant interactions. *Child Development, 60,* 819-824.

Bandura, A. (1973). *Aggression: A social learning analysis.* Englewood Cliffs, NJ: Prentice-Hall.

Barahal, R.M., Waterman, J., & Martin, H.P. (1981). The social cognitive development of abused children. *Journal of Consulting and Clinical Psychology, 49,* 508-516.

Baron, R.A. (1977). *Human aggression.* New York: Plenum Press.

Bell, R.C. (1968). A reinterpretation of the direction of effect in studies of socialization. *Psychology Review, 75,* 81-95.

Belsky, J. (1984). The determinants of parenting: A process model. *Child Development, 55,* 83-96.

Berger, A.M. (1981). *An examination of the relationship between harsh discipline in childhood, later punitiveness toward children and later ratings of adjustment.* Unpublished doctoral dissertation, University of Iowa, Iowa City.

Berger, A.M. (1985). Characteristics of child abusing families. In L. L'Abate (Ed.) *Handbook of Family Psychology and Therapy (Vol. 2)*. Homewood, IL: Dorsey Press.

Berger, A.M., Knutson, J.F., Mehm, J.G., & Perkins, K.A. (1988). The self-report of punitive childhood experiences of young adults and adolescents. *Child Abuse & Neglect, 12,* 251-262.

Berkowitz, L. (1974). Some determinants of impulsive aggression: Role of mediated associations with reinforcements for aggression. *Psychological Review, 81,* 165-176.

Bolton, F.G., Laner, R.H., & Kane, S. (1980). Child maltreatment risk among adolescent mothers: A study of reported cases. *American Journal of Orthopsychiatry, 50,* 489-504.

Braucht, G.N., Loya, F., & Jamieson, K.J. (1980). Victims of Violent Death: A critical review. *Psychological Bulletin, 87,* 309-333.

Brock, T.C., & Pallak, M.S. (1969). The consequences of choosing to be aggressive: An analysis of the dissonance model and review of relevant research. In P.G. Zimbardo (Ed.) *The Cognitive Control of Motivation*. Glenview, IL: Scott, Foresman and Company.

Brookhouser, P.E. (1987). Ensuring the safety of deaf children in residential schools. *Otolaryngology Head and Neck Surgery, 97,* 361-368.

Brossard, S.D., & Wagner, W.G. (1988). Child sexual abuse: Who is to blame? *Child Abuse & Neglect, 12,* 563-569.

Burgess, R. (1985). Social incompetence as a precipitant to and consequence of child maltreatment. *Victimology, 10,* 72-86.

Burgess, R.L., Anderson, E.A., Schellenbach, C.J., & Conger, R. (1981). A social interactional approach to the study of abusive families. In J.P. Vincent (Ed.) *Advances in Family Intervention, Assessment, & Theory: An Annual Compilation of Research (Vol. 2)*, (pp. 1-46). Greenwich, CT: JAI Press, Inc.

Burgess, R.S., & Conger, R.D. (1977). Family interaction patterns related to child abuse and neglect: Some preliminary findings. *Child Abuse & Neglect, 1,* 269-277.

Buss, A.H. (1973). Aggression pays. In J.L. Singer (Ed.) *The Control of Aggression and Violence* (pp. 7-18). New York: Academic Press.

Camblin, L.D., Jr. (1982). A survey of state efforts in gathering information on child abuse and neglect in handicapping populations. *Child Abuse & Neglect, 6,* 465-472.

Campbell, S.B. (1975). Mother-child interactions: A comparison of hyperactive, learing disabled, and normal boys. *American Journal of Orthopsychiatry, 45,* 51-57.

Carlson, V., Barnett, D. Cicchetti, D. & Braunwald, K. (1989). Disorganized/disoriented attachment relationships in maltreated infants. *Developmental Psychology, 25,* 525-531.

Cicchetti, D., Taraldson, B., & Egeland, B. (1978). Perspectives in the treatment and understanding of child abuse. In A. Goldstein (Ed.) *Perspectives for Child Mental Health and Education.* New York: Plenum.

Cicchetti, D., & Toth, S.L. (1987). The application of a transactional risk model to intervention with multi-risk maltreating families. *Zero to Three, 7(5),* 1-40.

Cohn, A.H. (1982). Stopping abuse before it occurs: Different solutions for different population groups. *Child Abuse & Neglect, 6,* 473-483.

Coie, J.D., & Kupersmidt, J.B.(1983). A behavioral analysis of emerging social status in boys' groups. *Child Development, 54,* 1400-1416.

Coombes, P. (1980). Are we protecting children? An approach to measuring impact in protection services. *Child Abuse & Neglect, 4,* 105-113.

Coon, K.B., Beck, F.W., & Coon, R.C. (1980). Implications for evaluating abused children: An independent study of the frequency of abused children referred to and enrolled in special education classes in a major southeastern United States Metropolitan area. *Child Abuse & Neglect, 4,* 153-156.

Crockenberg, S. (1987). Predictors and correlates of anger toward and punitive control of toddlers by adolescent mothers. *Child Development, 58,* 964-975.

Cunningham, C.E., & Barkley, R.A. (1979). The interactions of normal and hyperactive children with their mothers in free play and structured tasks. *Child Development, 50,* 217-224.

Daniel, J.H., Hampton, R.L., & Newberger, E.H. (1983). Child abuse and accidents in black families: A controlled comparative study. *American Journal of Orthopsychiatry, 53,* 645-653.

Diagnostic and statistical manual of mental disorders (rev. ed.). (1987). Washington DC: American Psychiatric Association.

Dion, K.K. (1974). Children's physical attractiveness and sex as determinants of adult punitiveness. *Developmental Psychology, 10,* 722-778.

Dodge, K.A. (1980). Social cognition and children's aggressive behavior. *Child Development, 51,* 162-170.

Dodge, K.A., & Frame, C.L. (1982). Social cognitive biases and deficits in aggressive boys. *Child Development, 53,* 620-635.

Dodge, K.A., & Newman, J.P. (1981). Biased decision-making processes in aggressive boys. *Journal of Abnormal Psychology, 90,* 375-379.

Dodge, K.A., Pettit, G.S., McClaskey, C.L., Brown, M.M. (1986). Social competence in children. *Monographs of the Society for Research in Child Development, 51(2),* Serial No. 213.

Doueck, H.J., Ishisaka, A.H., Greenaway, K.D. (1988). The role of normative development in adolescent abuse and neglect. *Family Relations, 37,* 135-139.

Downey, G., & Walker E. (1989). Social cognition and adjustment in children at risk for psychopathology. *Developmental Psychology, 25,* 835-845.

Dumas, J.E., & Wahler, R.G. (1985). Indiscriminant mothering as a contextual factor in aggressive-oppositional child behavior. *Journal of Abnormal Child Psychology, 13,* 1-17.

Earp, J.A., & Ory, M.G. (1980). The influence of early parenting on child maltreatment. *Child Abuse & Neglect, 4,* 237-245.

Egeland, B., Breitenbucher, M., & Rosenberg, D. (1980). Prospective study of the significance of life stress in the etiology of child abuse. *Journal of Consulting and Clinical Psychology, 48,* 195-205.

Egeland, B., & Brunnquell, D. (1979). An at-risk approach to the study of child abuse. *Journal of Child Psychiatry, 18,* 219-235.

Egeland, B., & Vaughn, B. (1981). Failure of "bond formation" as a cause of abuse, neglect, and maltreatment. *American Journal of Orthopsychiatry, 51,* 78-84.

El-Sheikh, M., Cummings, M., & Goetsch, V.L. (1989). Coping with adults' angry behavior: Behavioral, physiological, and verbal responses in preschoolers. *Developmental Psychology, 25,* 490-498.

Elmer, E. (1977). *Fragile Families, Troubled Children: The Aftermath of Infant Trauma.* Pittsburgh, PA: The University of Pittsburgh Press.

Elmer, E. (1978). Effects of early neglect and abuse on latency aged children. *Journal of Pediatric Psychology, 3,* 14-19.

Elmer, E., & Gregg, G.S. (1967). Developmental characteristics of abused children. *Pediatrics, 40,* 596-604.

Faranoff, A., Kennell, J., & Klaus, M. (1972). Follow-up of low birth weight infants - the predictive value of maternal visting patterns. *Pediatrics, 49,* 287-290.

Farber, E.A., & Egeland, B. (1987). Invulnerability among abused and neglected children. In E.J. Anthony & B.J. Cohler (Ed.) *The Invulnerable Child* (pp. 253-288). New York: The Guilford Press.

File, S.E., & Pope, J.H. (1974). Social interaction between drugged and undrugged rats. *Animal Learning & Behavior, 2,* 161-164.

Fontana, V. J. (1971). *The Maltreated Child* (2nd ed.). Springfield, Illinois: Thomas.

Fox, L., Long, S.H., & Langlois, A. (1988). Patterns of language comprehension deficit in abused and neglected children. *Journal of Speech and Hearing Disorders, 53,* 239-244.

Friedrich, W.N., & Boriskin, J.A. (1976). The role of the child in abuse: A review of the literature. *American Journal of Orthopsychiatry, 46,* 580-590.

Friedrich, W.N., & Einbender, A.J. (1983). The abused child: A psychological review. *Journal of Clinical Child Psychology, 12,* 244-256.

Frodi, A.M. (1981). Contributions of infant characteristics to child abuse. *American Journal of Mental Deficiency, 85,* 341-349.

Frodi, A.M. & Lamb, M.E. (1980). Child abusers' responses to infant smiles and cries. *Child Development, 51,* 238-241.

Frodi, A.M., Lamb, M.E., Leavitt, L.A., Donovan, W.L., Neff, C., & Sherry, D. (1978). Fathers' and mothers' responses to the faces and cries of normal and premature infants. *Developmental Psychology, 14,* 490-498.

Frodi, A.M., Lamb, M.E., & Wille, D. (1981). Mothers' responses to the cries of normal and premature infants as a function of the birth status of their own child. *Journal of Research and Personality, 15,* 122-133.

Furstenberg, F.F., Jr. (1976). Premarital pregnancy and marital instability. *Journal of Social Issues, 40,* 580-590.

Gaines, R., Sandgrund, A., Green, A.H., & Power, E. (1978). Etiological factors in child maltreatment: A multivariate study of abusing, neglecting and normal mothers. *Journal of Abnormal Psychology, 87,* 531-540.

Garbarino, J., Brookhouser, P.E., & Authier, K.J., (1987). *Special Children Special Risk: The Maltreatment of Children with Disabilities.* New York: Aldine De Gruyter.

George, C., & Main, M. (1979). Social interactions of young abused children: Approach, avoidance and aggression. *Child Development, 50,* 306-318.

Gil, E. (1975). Unraveling child abuse. *American Journal of Orthopsychiatry, 45,* 346-456.

Gillespie, D., Seaberg, J., & Berline, S. (1977). Observed causes of child abuse. *Victimology, 2,* 342-349.

Golberg, S. (1979). Premature birth: Consequences for the parent-infant relationship. *American Scientist, 67,* 214-220.

Green, A.H., Gaines, R.W., & Sandgrund, D. (1974). Child abuse: Pathological syndrome of family interaction. *American Journal of Psychiatry, 131,* 882-886.

Gregg, G.S. & Elmer, E. (1969). Infant injuries: Accident or abuse? *Pediatrics, 44,* 434-439.

Halperin, S.M. (1983). Family perceptions of abused children and their siblings. *Child Abuse & Neglect, 7,* 107-115.

Hampton, R.L., & Newberger, E.H. (1985). Child abuse incidence and reporting by hospitals: Significance of severity, class, and race. *American Journal of Public Health, 75,* 56-60.

Herrenkohl, E.C., & Herrenkohl, R.C. (1979). A comparison of abused children and the nonabused siblings. *Journal of Child Psychiatry, 18,* 260-269.

Herrenkohl, R.C., & Herrenkohl, E.C. (1981). Some antecendents and developmental consequences of child maltreatment. *New Directions for Child Development, 11,* 57-76.

Hoffman-Plotkin, D., & Twentyman, C.T. (1984). A multimodal assessment of behavioral and cognitive deficits in abused and neglected preschoolers. *Child Development, 55,* 794-802.

Hynan, M.T. (1976). The influence of the victim on shock: Induced aggression in rats. *Journal of the Experimental Analysis of Behavior, 25,* 401-409.

Jacobsen, R.S., & Straker, G. (1982). Peer group interaction of physically abused children. *Child Abuse & Neglect, 6,* 321-327.

Jacobson, N.S., & Margolin, G. (1979). *Marital Therapy: Strategies Based on Social Learning and Behavior Exchange Principle.* New York: Brunner/Mazel, Inc.

Jason, J., & Andereck, N.D. (1983). Fatal child abuse in Georgia: The epidemiology of severe physical child abuse. *Child Abuse & Neglect, 7,* 1-9.

Jaudes, P.K., & Diamond, L.J. (1985). The handicapped child and child abuse. *Child Abuse & Neglect, 9,* 341-347.

Johnson, B., & Morse, H.A. (1968). Injured children and their parents. *Children, 15,* 147-152.

Kaufman, J., & Cicchetti, D. (1989). Effects of maltreatment on school-age children's socioemotional development: Assessments in a day-camp setting. *Developmental Psychology, 25,* 516-524.

Kazdin, A.E. (1978). Evaluating the generality of findings in analogue therapy research. *Journal of Consulting and Clinical Psychology, 46,* 673-686.

Kempe, C.H., & Helfer, R.E. (1972). *Helping the Battered Child and His Family.* Philadelphia: J.B. Lippincott.

Kempe, C.H., Silverman, F.N., Steele, B.F., Droegemueller, W. & Silver, H.K. (1962). The battered child syndrome. *Journal of the American Medical Association, 181,* 17-24.

Kinard, E.M., & Klerman, L.V. (1980). Teenage parenting and child abuse: Are they related? *American Journal of Orthopsychiatry, 50,* 481-488.

Klein, M., & Stern, L. (1971). Low birth weight and the battered child syndrome. *American Journal of Diseases of Children, 122,* 15-18.

Knutson, J.F. (1973). Aggression as manipulatable behavior. In J.F. Knutson (Eds.) *Control of Aggression: Implications From Basic Research* (pp. 253-295). Chicago: Aldine-Atherton.

Knutson, J.F. 1978). Child abuse as an area of aggression research. *Journal of Pediatric Psychology, 3*, 20-27.

Knutson, J.F. (1988). Physical abuse and sexual abuse of children. In D.K. Routh (Ed.) *Handbook of Pediatric Psychology*. New York: Guilford Press.

Knutson, J. F., & Mehm, J. G. (1988). Transgenerational patterns of coercion in families and intimate relationships. In Gordon W. Russell (Ed.) *Violence in Intimate Relationships*. New York: PMA Publishing.

Kohlberg, L., LaCrosse, J., & Ricks, D. (1972). The predictability of adult mental health from childhood behavior. In B.B. Wolman (Ed.) *Manual of Child Psychopathology* (pp. 1217-1284). New York: McGraw-Hill.

Lamb, M.E. (Ed.). (1981). *The Role of the Father in Child Development*. New York: John Wiley and Sons.

Larrance, D.T., & Twentyman, C.T. (1983). Maternal attributions and child abuse. *Journal of Abnormal Psychology, 92,* 449-457.

Leventhal, J.M. (1981). Risk factors for child abuse: Methodologic standards in case-control studies. *Pediatrics, 68,* 684-690.

Lewis, M., & Feiring, C. (1989). Infant, mother, and mother-infant interaction behavior and subsequent attachment. *Child Development, 60,* 831-837.

Lynch, M.A. (1975). Ill-health and child abuse. *Lancet, 2,* 317-319.

Lynch, M.A. (1976). Risk factors in the child: A study of abused children and their siblings. In H.P. Martin (Ed.) *The Abused Child: A Multidisciplinary Approach to Developmental Issues and Treatment* (pp. 43-56). Cambridge, MA: Ballinger Publishing Co.

Lynch, M.A., & Roberts, J. (1982). *Consequences of Child Abuse.* New York: Academic Press.

Lyons-Ruth, K., Connell, D.B., Zoll, D., & Stahl, J. (1987). Infants of social risk: Relations among infant maltreatment, maternal bahavior, and infant attachment behavior. *Developmental Psychology, 23,* 223-232.

Martin, H.P. (1976). Which children get abused: High risk factors in the child. In H.P. Martin (Ed.) *The Abused Child: A Multidisciplinary Approach to Developmental Issues and Treatment* (pp. 27-41). Cambridge, MA: Ballinger Press.

Martin, J.E., & Kourany, R.F.C. (1980). Child abuse by adolescent babysitters. *Child Abuse & Neglect, 4,* 15-22.

Morse, C., Sahler, O., & Friedman, S. (1970). A three-year follow-up of abused and neglected children. *American Journal of Diseases of Children, 120,* 439-446.

Nakau, S., Adam, H., Stathacopoulou, N., & Agathonos, H. (1982). Health status of abused and neglected children and their siblings. *Child Abuse & Neglect, 6,* 279-284.

Nelson, B.J. (1974). *Making an Issue of Child Abuse: Political Agenda Setting for Social Problems.* Chicago: University of Chicago Press.

Parke, R.D., & Collmer, C.W. (1975). Child abuse: An interdisciplinary analysis. In E.M. Hetherington (Ed.) *Review of Child Development Research.* Volume 5. Chicago, IL: University of Chicago Press.

Passman, R.H., & Mulhern, R.K., Jr. (1977). Maternal punitiveness as affected by situational stress: An experimental analogue of child abuse. *Journal of Abnormal Psychology, 86,* 565-569.

Patterson, G.R., (1980). Mothers: The unackowledged victims. *Monographs of the Society for Research in Child Development, 45 (4, Serial No. 186).*

Patterson, G.R. (1982). *Coercive Family Process.* Eugene, OR: Castalia Publishing Company.

Patterson, G.R. (1986). Performance models for antisocial boys. *American Psychologist, 41,* 432-443.

Patterson, G.R., & Reid, J.B. (1970). Reciprocity and coercion: Two facets of social systems. In. C. Neuringer & J.L. Michael (Eds.) *Behavior Modification in Clinical Psychology* (pp. 133-177). New York: Meredity Corporation.

Pelton, L.H. (1978). Child abuse and neglect: The myth of classlessness. *American Journal of Orthopsychiatry, 48,* 608-617.

Perry, M., Doran, L., & Wells, E. (1983). Developmental and behavioral characteristics of physically abused children. *Journal of Clinical Child Psychology, 12,* 320-324.

Pless, I.B., & Stulginskas, J. (1982). Accidents and violence as a cause of morbidity and mortality in childhood. In L.A. Barness (Ed.) *Advances in Pediatrics, 29* (pp. 471-495). Chicago: Year Book.

Plomin, R. (1983). Childhood temperament. In B. Lahey & A. Kazdin (Eds.) *Advances in Clinical Child Psychology, Vol. 6* (pp. 45-92). New York: Plenum.

Plotkin, R.C., Azar, S., Twentyman, C.T., & Perri, M.G. (1981). A critical evaluation of the research methodology employed in the investigation of causative factors of child abuse and neglect. *Child Abuse & Neglect, 5,* 449-455.

Reid, J.B. (1984). Social-interactional patterns in families of abused and nonabused children. In C. Zahn-Waxler, M. Cummings, & M. Radke-Yarrow (Eds.) *Social and Biological Origins of Altruism and Aggression.* Cambridge Press.

Reid, J.B., Patterson, G.R., & Loeber, R. (1982). The abused child: Victim, instigator, or innocent bystander. In D. Berstein (Ed.) *Response Structure and Organization.* Lincoln, NE: University of Nebraska Press.

Reid, J.B., Taplin, P.S., & Lorber, R. (1981). A social interactional approach to the treatment of abusive families. In R.B. Stewart (Ed.) *Violent Behavior: Social Learning Approaches to Prediction, Management, and Treatment* (pp. 135-180). New York: Bruner/Mazel.

Reidy, T.J. (1977). The aggressive characteristics of abused and neglected children. *Journal of Clinical Psychology, 33,* 1140-1145.

Robins, L.N. (1966). *Deviant Children Grown-Up: A Sociological and Psychiatric Study of Sociopathic Personality.* Baltimore, MD: Williams & Wilkins.

Rohrbeck, C.A., & Twentyman, C.T. (1986). Multimodal assessment of impulsiveness in abusing, neglecting, and normal treating mothers and their preschool children. *Journal of Consulting and Clinical Psychology, 54,* 231-236.

Rosenberg, M.S., & Repucci, N.D. (1983). Abusive mothers: Perceptions of their own and their children's behavior. *Journal of Consulting and Clinical Psychology, 51,* 674-682.

Rosenthal, J.A. (1988). Patterns of reported child abuse and neglect. *Child Abuse & Neglect, 12*, 263-271.

Russell, C.S. (1980). Unscheduled parenthood: Transition to "parent" for the teenager. *Journal of Social Issues, 36*, 45-63.

Salzinger, S., Kaplan, S., Pelcovitz, D., Samit, C., & Krieger, R. (1984). Parent and teacher assessment of children's behavior in child maltreating families. *Journal of the American Academy of Child Psychiatry, 23*, 458-464.

Sandford, D.A., & Tustin, R.D. (1974). Behavioral treatment of parental assault on a child. *The New Zealand Psychologist, 2*, 76-82.

Sandgrund, A., Gaines, R.W., & Green, A.H. (1974). Child abuse and mental retardation: A problem of cause and effect. *American Journal of Mental Deficiency, 79*, 327-330.

Schindler, F., & Arkowitz, H. (1986). The assessment of mother-child interactions in physically abusive and nonabusive families. *Journal of Family Violence, 1*, 247-257.

Schlesinger, H., & Meadow, K. (1972). *Sound and Sign: Child Deafness and Mental Health*. Berkeley: University of California Press.

Sherrod, K.B., O'Connor, S., Vietze, P.M., & Altemeier, W.A., III (1984). Child health and maltreatment. *Child Development, 55*, 1174-1183.

Smith, S.M. (1976). *The Battered Child Syndrome*. London: Butterworths.

Solomon, G. (1979). Child abuse and developmental disabilities. *Developmental Medicine in Child Neurology, 21*, 101-108.

Spearly, J.L. & Lauderdale, M. (1983). Community characteristics and ethnicity in the prediction of child maltreatment rates. *Child Abuse & Neglect, 7,* 91-105.

Starr, R.H., Dietrich, K.N., Fischhoff, J., Ceresnie, S., Zweier, D. (1984). The contribution of handicapping condictions to child abuse. *Topics in Early Childhood Special Education, 4,* 55-69.

Steele, B.F., & Pollack, C.G. (1968). A psychiatric study of parents who abuse infants and small children. In R.E. Helfer and C.H. Kempe (Eds.) *The Battered Child* (1st ed.). Chicago: The University of Chicago Press.

Straus, M.A. (1980). Stress and physical child abuse. *Child Abuse & Neglect, 4,* 75-88.

Twentyman, C.T., & Plotkin, R. (1982). Unrealistic expectations of parents who maltreat their children: An educational deficit that pertains to child maltreatment. *Journal of Clinical Psychology, 38,* 497-503.

U.S. Department of Health and Human Services (1988). *Executive Summary: Study of National Incidence and Prevalence of Child Abuse and Neglect: 1988.* Washington DC: National Center on Child Abuse and Neglect.

Vasta, R., & Copitch, P. (1981). Simulating conditions of child abuse in the laboratory. *Child Development, 52,* 164-170.

Weston, J.T. (1974). A summary of neglect and traumatic cases. In. R.E. Helfer & C.H. Kempe (Eds.) *The Battered Child.* (2nd. ed.). Chicago: University of Chicago Press.

Whalen, C.K., Henker, B., & Dotemoto, S. (1981). Teacher response to methylphenidate versus placebo status of hyperactive boys in the classroom. *Child Development, 52,* 1005-1014.

Whitmore, E., Kramer, J., & Knutson, J.F. (1989). *The Association Between Child Abuse, Hyperactivity, and Aggressive Behavior.* Unpublished manuscript, University of Iowa, Iowa City.

Wilson, M.I., Daly, M., & Weghorst, S.J. (1981). Differential maltreatment of girls and boys. *Victimology, 6,* 1-4.

Whittaker, J.K. (1987). The role of residential institutions. In J. Garbarino, P.E. Brookhouser, & K.J. Authier (Eds.) *Special Children Special Risk: The Maltreatment of Children With Disabilities* (pp. 83-100). New York: Aldine De Gruyter.

Wolfe, D.A., & Mosk, M.D. (1983). Behavioral comparisons of children from abusive and distressed families. *Journal of Consulting and Clinical Psychology, 51,* 702-708.

Young, L. (1964). *Wednesday's Children: A Study of Child Neglect and Abuse.* New York: McGraw-Hill.

Zaidi, L.Y. (1988). *The Influence of Personal Disciplinary Experiences and Children's Behavior on Disciplinary Choices in an Analog Parenting Task.* Unpublished doctoral dissertation, University of Iowa, Iowa City.

Zaidi, L.Y., Knutson, J.F., & Mehm, J.B. (1989). Transgenerational patterns of abusive parenting: Analog and clinical tests. *Aggressive Behavior, 15,* 137-152.

Zuravin, S.J. (1987). Unplanned pregnancies, family planning problems, and child maltreatment. *Family Relations, 36,* 135-139.

5

Institutional Violence Directed Toward Children: The Case of Corporal Punishment in Schools

Irwin A. Hyman and Jacqueline Clarke

History is replete with accounts of sanctioned violence against children in Western societies. The efforts of Charles Dickens were seminal and enduring in arousing public sensitivity to the plight of children subjected to institutionalized brutality. There is little question that, since the days of Dickens, institutionally approved aggression against children in post-industrial societies has greatly diminished. Yet, in America, hardly a decade passes without shocking accounts of child victimization in a variety of institutions, including the public schools. Economic hardships, lack of staff training, legal sanctions, religious ideology, discipline imperatives, burnout and instinctual aggressiveness are some of the factors used to describe and/or justify the aggression of adult caretakers against children. By far, one of the most frequent explanations for the use of pain-inflicting aggression is for the purposes of discipline.

Corporal punishment is widely accepted in America as a useful, and often necessary, procedure for disciplining children. Over 85% of Americans indicate that it is appropriate to spank or otherwise physically discipline their children if they have misbehaved (Hyman, 1989). However, a Harris poll conducted in 1989 (Hyman, 1989) indicated that 54% of parents were against educators paddling children in schools. But a Gallup poll (Hyman, 1989), conducted in the same year, indicated that only 38% of teachers disapproved. Most respondents to these and other polls do not consider corporal punishment as an act of violence. Yet, it is clear that the intent of corporal punishment is to inflict pain.

There is an inherent connection between child abuse and corporal punishment, since at some point the infliction of pain crosses a boundary where the act becomes abusive. While guidelines for the definition of abuse vary, we would suggest that the presence of bruises which result from hitting are prima facie evidence that violence has occurred. For instance, the state of Florida maintains a registry to prevent abusers from working with children. According to their definition, abuse occurs when bruises on the bodies of children are visible for at least two days.

Florida's definition of abuse caused little trouble for state authorities until they decided to include educators in the registry if the paddling in schools caused bruises (Hyman, in press). The ensuing media attention reflects several levels of contradiction and confusion in thinking regarding children as victims of violence when abuse is defined not by the act, but by the setting in which it occurs.

There is a great deal of theory and research concerning violence against children in the home, yet relatively little about violence in institutions where children are subject to disciplinary procedures defined and meted out by authorities (Straus, 1989). In general, society recognizes the vulnerability of children in closed institutions, such as correctional and mental health facilities, yet seems less concerned about the violence which occurs in relatively "open" institutions, such as public schools. The purpose of this chapter is to present some explanations for the sanctioned use of overly severe disciplinary procedures in public schools. These procedures fall under the general rubric of corporal punishment which is considered by many educators as a necessary method to maintain discipline. This example serves as a paradigm for understanding the problem of the institutionalized violence toward children.

This chapter examines the ideology of the continued acceptance and practice of violence against children in school settings. The general premise is that institutionalized corporal punishment can be explained by religious ideology and social learning theory as conceptualized in terms of modeling. This is not to leave out the incidents which involve educators who are pathologically violent. They may remain in their positions because school authorities are often reluctant to file the lengthy and difficult due process procedures involved in removing an educator from public employment.

This chapter offers (1) a definition for corporal punishment as it applies to schools, (2) a brief historical overview, (3) the influence of religion, (4) Anglo-Saxon traditions, and (5) modeling theory to explain the continued use of the infliction of pain as a disciplinary procedure in American schools. The last section is devoted to the demographics of abusive corporal punishment in American education.

DEFINING CORPORAL PUNISHMENT

Corporal punishment in the schools is the purposeful infliction of pain or confinement as a penalty for an offense committed by a student.

The use of a wooden paddle is the most frequent method of administration. These are often manufactured by potential victims in school woodworking shops. Some school boards decree official specifications as to thickness, width, and length.

In states where corporal punishment is forbidden, the use of force is allowed in specific situations (with the incidental and unintentional infliction of pain), to quell a disturbance or to protect oneself, property, or another person. Teachers also may use force to protect a student from self-injury. All states and all school districts which forbid corporal punishment recognize teachers' rights to protect themselves against student assaults.

Confinement for long periods has increasingly become a problem, especially with handicapped children. Too frequently, this approach to discipline is a distortion of "time out" procedures.

ANGLO-SAXON TRADITION

The more recent history of brutal floggings and denigration of children in seventeenth-century English schools and in Colonial America are well documented (Hyman & Wise, 1979). One only has to read the novels of Dickens to understand the relationship between education and child abuse as a part of the historical English mindset.

In 1669, and in 1698, the children of England unsuccessfully petitioned Parliament for redress from beatings and sadism. Freeman (1979) recounts the story of brutal floggings in seventeenth-century English schools. The petition itself was not only a plea for relief against corporal punishment, but against the sadistic school masters who sought "punishment for its own sake". The petition is written on behalf of "the children of the land" and complained that knowledge of Latin and Greek should not automatically qualify one to be a teacher. They plead for teachers to have some knowledge of children and childhood. This was a precursor to contemporary requirements that certified teachers must have training in child development, psychology, and teaching methods.

Contemporary efforts by the petitioner's decendents were finally successful. In the summer of 1987, English law finally banned corporal punishment in the schools. Yet, while all of Continental Europe, Ireland, Israel, Japan, Communist and Socialist societies have banned corporal punishment, the majority of the original English speaking colonies have not.

RELIGIOUS IDEOLOGY

The use of corporal punishment in child rearing and education appears early in the recorded history of western cultures. Its roots in the Old Testament trace to Proverbs (13:24), where Solomon urges that "he that spareth the rod hateth his son, he that loveth him, chasteneth him". Other Old Testament pronouncements include: Proverbs (23:13-14) "Withold not correction from the child: for if thou beatest him with the rod, he shall not die. Thou shalt beat him with the rod, and shall deliver him from hell". Or Proverbs (22:15) "Foolishness is bound in the heart of a child; but the rod of correction shall drive it from him".

By far, the most common justification for the use of corporal punishment is Biblical. The term "spare the rod and spoil the child" is part of the fabric of beliefs about the child rearing, yet this often quoted phrase does not explicitly appear in the Bible.

In his book *The English Vice* (1978), Ian Gibson points out that the Victorians attributed the expression, "spare the rod and spoil the child" to Solomon, the supposed author of Proverbs. This well-known defense of corporal punishment was first used by the English author Samuel Butler in a satirical poem, "Hudibras", published in 1664 (Gibson, 1978). In actuality, this poem was meant to ridicule the practice of corporal punishment.

A critic, Henry Salt, in 1916 pointed to an obvious irony in the poem: "It is significant that a witty writer, who frankly treats the subject of whipping for what it is - an indecent subject - should have provided many generations with a supposed precept from the Bible (Gibson, 1978, p.49)."

In Christian theology, the use of corporal punishment is historically related to concepts of original sin and the need to combat Satan by "beating the devil" out of children. This belief was, and still is, an important element of evangelical and fundamental Protestant belief (Greven, 1977). The concept of "possession" by some sort of evil spirit is a common explanation of deviant behavior in ancient and primitive cultures. It is therefore not unusual that the ancient Hebrews used this explanation to account for mental illness, misbehavior and even hereditary diseases.

The "demon" theory of deviance was carried from Catholic theology to Protestantism by, among others, Martin Luther who in "sixteenth-century Europe ordered mentally defective children drowned because he was convinced they were instruments of the devil" (Radbill, 1974).

Contemporary concern with the devil's effect on children is still an important part of fundamentalist theology. Like their sixteenth-century forbearers, educators in so called "Christian Schools" which preach fundamentalist doctrine believe that corporal punishment instills character, obedience and humility, traits needed to ward off the devil (Hyman & Wise, 1979).

There is some evidence that belief in the devil may possibly underlie American support for corporal punishment if one accepts the "beat the devil out of them" approach to disciplining children. A Gallup poll reported in the December, 1988 issue of *Psychology*

Today reveals some startling information. Unfortunately, the article did not report the methodology for the data collection.

People in 14 countries were asked if they believed in the devil. The results of percentages of respondents who said," I believe in the devil" were as follows: United States-66%; Northern Ireland-66%; Republic of Ireland-57%; Spain-33%; Italy- 30%; Great Britain-30%; Finland-29%; Norway-28%; Belgium-20%; Netherlands-20%;WestGermany-18%;France-17%;-Denmark-12%; and Sweden-12%. With 66% of Americans believing in the devil, it is not hard to understand why it is so difficult to eliminate corporal punishment in schools.

Pokalo (1986) studied the relationship between religious orientation and modeling theory in an attempt to explain the level of punitiveness of child care workers in institutions for mentally retarded children. In her study, she asked how severely the respondents would punish a variety of misbehaviors.

The frequency of punishment in their own childhoods was the best predictor of how severely they would punish the retarded children in their care. Those who described themselves as Baptists with a fundamentalist orientation were by far the most punitive group. That is, they would use much more severe punishments for almost all misbehaviors than would Catholics, Jews, and other Protestants who said they were either Methodists, Lutherans, or Presbyterians. Those who said they were evangelical in orientation were the second most punitive, but were closer to the other groups.

A study by Wiehe (1989) focused on religion and attitudes toward corporal punishment. In his survey research, he found that respondents who belonged to church groups which claimed *literal* belief in the Bible valued the use of hitting as a disciplinary tool more than those whose religious beliefs were not based on literalism.

In summary, this brief description of religious ideology suggests that Old Testament precepts of punishment still have an important role in the way contemporary people view child rearing. While many adults may not subscribe to literal interpretation of Biblical passages prescribing physical punishment, traditions inexplicably are bound in those beliefs. Clearly those traditions are perpetuated most strongly in areas, such as the "Bible belt", where religious beliefs are closely intertwined with social practices (Hyman, 1989).

Corporal punishment of school children had firm roots in Colonial America. The spirit of the times was exemplified in a schoolhouse built in Sunderland, Massachusetts in 1793. Built into the floor was a sturdy whipping post to which miscreant children were tied. This method assured no escape from the vigorous birchings by the school master.

In those "good old days" teachers like Master Todd, described in the *Annals of Philadelphia and Pennsylvania* published in 1870, reigned supreme, as long as they were stronger than their students. Master Todd didn't need a whipping post as this account attests (Manning, 1979, p.50):

> Wanting elbow room, the chair would be quickly thrust on one side, and Master John Todd was to be seen dragging his stuggling suppliant to the flogging ground in the center of the room. Having placed his left foot upon the end of the bench, with a patent jerk peculiar to himself, he would have the boy completely horsed across his knee, with his left elbow on the back of his neck to keep him securely on . . . . Having his victim thus completely at his command. . . . once more to the staring crew would would be exhibited the dexterity of the master and strap. . . .moving in quick time, the fifteen inches of bridle rein would be seen. . . leaving on the "place beneath" a fiery streak at every slash.
> "Does it hurt?"
> "Oh yes, Master! Oh don't Master!"
> "Then I'll make it hurt three more...Thou shan't

want a warming pan tonight."

The above is one of many memoirs and stories of floggings, beatings, and humiliations in Colonial American education.

Even as late as 1850, school reports from Boston indicated that it took "sixty-five beatings a day to operate a school of four hundred" (Hyman & Wise, 1979). In the school year ending in 1876, before the New Jersey ban on flogging had been fully implemented, Newark, New Jersey recorded 9,408 beatings in a system of 10,000 students. The birch rod was synonymous with education until secular philosophies proposed by people like Rousseau, Pestalozzi, and Horace Mann began to effect reforms. Not all of society thought whippings were needed for education. In 1853 the Indiana Supreme Court (Hentoff, 1979, p. xi) suggested:

> The public seems to cling to the despotism in the government of schools that has been discarded everywhere else. . .The husband can no longer moderately chastise his wife: nor. . .the master his servant or his apprentice. Even the degrading cruelties of the naval service have been arrested. Why the person of the schoolboy. . . should be less sacred in the eyes of the law than that of the apprentice or the sailor, is not easily explained.

The first major change occurred in 1867, when the New Jersey legislature banned the use of corporal punishment in schools. However, local control prevailed and it was not until the twentieth-century that the ban was taken seriously.

MODELING THEORY

In a classic experiment, Bandura and Huston (1961) exposed nursery school children to aggressive and nonaggressive behavior, using adults as models. Children observed situations in which aggressive adults hit an inflatable plastic "Bobo" doll with a mallet. In addition to hitting it, the adult model yelled at the doll, sat on it, punched it, kicked it, and tossed it in the air. Another group of children watched nonaggressive play with the Bobo doll, while a third group did not view play with the doll at all. When the three groups were placed in play rooms with the Bobo dolls, only those who viewed the aggression against the doll became aggressive themselves.

Bandura and associates went on to do other similar studies, as have other researchers. Strauss (1989); Strauss, Gelles and Steinmetz (1980); and Gelles and Strauss (1979); and Gil (1970) have demonstrated that parents who use excessive corporal punishment to the point of abuse were themselves abused. Aggression towards misbehaving children is learned in childhood because of adult models (Zaidi, Knutson, & Mehm, 1989). Actual abuse may be triggered by a variety of factors such as parental stress, isolation, alcoholism, etc. However, because society sanctions the actual hitting of children, the mechanism for abuse is in place early in life when children are hit themselves or observe their siblings being hit.

Eron, Walder, and Lefkowitz (1971) studied 870 eight year olds in rural New York. They studied how severely punished they were. The indicators ranged from no physical punishment at all to slaps and spankings. They then asked other children to judge how aggressive the children in the sample were. The more aggressively children were punished, the more aggressive they were with other children. Twenty years later, Eron (Kohn, 1988) again studied the aggressive children as adults. It was no surprise that they had become aggressive adults with aggressive children.

Lennox (1982) devised a questionnaire which was administered to teachers in Pennsylvania, New York, Florida, Tennessee, and Mississippi. Teachers were asked a variety of questions about their training, their years of experience and their own childhood. Other significant questions were asked, including how often they paddled their own students. The study clearly showed that the most significant reason why teachers paddled was how often they were spanked as children, and/or paddled in school. Teachers who were spanked rarely or never in their own childhoods almost never paddled children. Most of those who were paddled or spanked did the same as teachers. A small group of those who were paddled or spanked, (which has appeared in all of our studies) did not use punitive techniques as teachers. The reasons why modeling theory did not hold with this group will be explained later.

Sofer (1983) developed a questionnaire to study the effects of modeling on psychologists' recommendations for the use of corporal punishment. It was reasoned that if the education and training of teachers did not significantly influence their use of corporal punishment, then it could be because they lacked specific in-depth training in the use of positive methods of discipline. Surely psychologists, who are highly trained regarding the use of rewards and punishments, would reflect that training in their recommendations about the use of corporal punishment. A questionnaire was sent to psychologists all over the country. The questionnaire was similar to the one developed by Lennox but included additional items. Sofer asked the respondents to indicate what research or theory they would use to support whether or not they would recommend the use of corporal punishment. The results were surprising. While 49% of the respondents said they would never recommend the use of corporal punishment and accurately cited the research and theory supporting that belief, 51% said that in certain instances they might recommend its use. Its use might be suggested in situations that were dangerous to the child or where the misbehavior was severe and occurred repeatedly. 30% said they would recommend its use in the school.

It was surprising that so many psychologists considered it appropriate to use corporal punishment. Even more surprising were the explanations given for recommending it. The largest group of psychologists who would recommend the use of corporal punishment cited the research of B.F. Skinner, which falls under the general category of behaviorism. This rationale was absolutely incorrect, since B.F. Skinner himself has repeatedly spoken and published articles about the ineffectiveness and inadvisability of the use of corporal punishment with children (Hyman & Wise, 1979)

THOSE WHO WERE HIT BUT DON'T HIT AS PARENTS

Mishkin (1987) developed a questionnaire similar to the others described. However, she asked more detailed questions relating to experiences which might convince one that hitting is a bad idea. As with the other studies, modeling theory explained most of the adult's (in this case parents) disciplining of children. However, Mishkin examined the group who were hit as children, but who rarely or never hit their own children. The following refers to that group.

The parents who were hit as children and rarely or never hit their own children, as compared to others, tended to have their children later in life. That is, they were more mature when they became parents. In addition, on a general scale of temperament and anger level, they tended to become frustrated less readily.

An interesting finding about those who were hit and did not hit is that in general they had a much higher education level than the general population. This group and the parents who were not hit and don't hit both had educations beyond the college level. As a group they had gone to graduate and professional schools. Many reported that courses in child development and psychology had made them think about alternatives to spanking. Many had taken workshops in parenting. Another important factor was who hit them as children.

Many in the hit-no-hit group said that they were only hit by their mothers. Apparently being hit by your father or by both parents increases the chances you will become a swatting parent yourself.

Finally, the hit-no-hit parents said that a major factor in their conversions was the experience of seeing the bad effects of hitting on other children. They tended to view a swatting parent as more out of control than the misbehaving child. Obviously, this group, for a variety of reasons, had developed empathy for children.

THE DEMOGRAPHICS OF SCHOOL CORPORAL PUNISHMENT
Regionalism and Socioeconomic Explanations

Farley (1983) conducted a national survey of 400 junior high schools from across the United States to identify and describe the characteristics associated with the use and non-use of corporal punishment as a disciplinary technique. A 19-item questionnaire which included items on student, school and respondent characteristics was sent to the principal of each school, asking that the person most responsible for discipline respond. Analyses were completed on 219 questionnaires (58% return), with 67% of the respondents being principals, 26% vice principals and 7% with titles such as counselor. Findings indicate that schools reporting high use of corporal punishment had the poorest student population, the largest average class size and the most severe disciplinary practices. They were also concentrated in the Southeast region of the United States (38%). Schools which did not use corporal punishment had larger student enrollments, more white students and were concentrated in the Northeast region (48%). No significant differences were found for perceived effectiveness in maintaining a climate suitable for learning. The decision to use corporal punishment appeared to be based in part on an orientation towards physical punishment by school personnel, which may have been supported by local values and/or traditional beliefs.

Research over a thirteen year period (Hyman, 1989) clearly indicates that poor children are more frequently paddled and/or are more frequently the recipients of severe corporal punishment than are children from affluent families. Data from the Office of Civil Rights suggest that minority children are more frequently paddled than are White children. However, studies (Rose, 1984) which have controlled for SES have indicated that SES is a much better predictor than race. A more plausible explanation which accounts for racial factors is that a larger *proportion* of minority children are poor than are White children. Therefore, if you are Black or Hispanic, it is more likely that you are poor and more likely that you will live in an inner city or rural Southern community. As a result, you are at greater risk of being hit than if you were White. Also, while data are not available concerning the rates of Black educators hitting Black children, Hyman (1989) indicates that a random sample of 1250 adults, 7% of Whites responded that they were hit very often as children by their parents. But 25% of Black respondents and 11% of Hispanic respondents that they were hit frequently as children in the home. Based on modeling theory, it is probable that poor Black children are being hit at an equivalent or greater frequency than they are hit by White teachers.

In summary, there is strong evidence that school children from low SES families are at risk as acceptable targets for violence by educators. Teachers often comment that poor children "only understand the use of force". In truth, the evidence suggests that poor children are more frequently hit at home and more frequently learn that the use of force is an appropriate way to solve problems.

It may be true that teachers, therefore, are more likely to evoke force in school. Also, a self-fulfilling prophesy may operate in the repeated use of violence against children who continue to engage in misbehavior. However, despite the mythology concerning the discipline of lower SES children, there is overwhelming evidence that these children can be taught more appropriate and less violent alternatives to solving problems (Hyman & Lally, 1982).

The following section of this chapter is devoted to an explication of the types of overly severe disciplinary procedures which result in the victimization of school children.

NEWSPAPER REPORTS OF CORPORAL PUNISHMENT INCIDENTS IN SCHOOLS

Types of Punishment

Punishments may be viewed as severe when the detailed accounts of the cases are investigated. In several districts which sanction the use of corporal punishment, the administration has issued "regulation" instruments to be utilized by its staff. For example, in some districts the educators may be given paddles (Atteberry, 1980), leather straps (Smith, 1982), or a "thin rattan" (Rule & Zoeckler, 1977). There are incidents of staff personnel who have modified these implements. Some have wrapped the paddles with masking tape (Hudgins, 1982). Others had holes drilled in the paddle so the air would not be able to "work as a cushion" ("The Paddling," 1977). One case involved the teacher's name being drilled across the paddle ("15-year-old," 1977).

In contrast to many people's belief that corporal punishment is meted out by a standarized or authorized implement, there are many reported accounts which show that other instruments have been used instead of the recommended paddle, strap, or rattan. Besides a wooden paddle, children have been hit with various objects which are readily available and/or easily accessible to an educator. This runs counter to the myth that there are certain standardizations set which attempt to govern this form of punishment in our nation's schools.

Children throughout the United States have been hit with a: hand ("Suit Filed," 1977), "doubled-over" belt ("Who is," 1982), lacrosse stick (Blaker, 1977), Jai Alai stick (Blaker, 1977), tennis shoe (Ruble, 1977), fist (Eyre, 1979), clipboard ("Teacher Gets," 1979), baseball bat which was "shaved down into a ceremonial" paddle (Titone, 1977), arrow (Howard, 1978), electrical cord (Hale, 1981), bamboo stick (Hamilton, 1982), a rubber (Reid, 1981) or leather ("Teacher Sentenced," 1978) strap, pencil ("Parents File," 1983), yardstick ("Suit Claims Coach," 1983), ping-pong paddle ("Youth Home," 1979), "one by four board" ("Parents Say," 1981), stick which "was used to point out things on a bulletin board" ("Teacher Faces," 1982), broomstick (Bracey, 1981), "ten foot piece of wood" (Hoffman, 1982), hammer ("Charges Teacher," 1982), rattan (Rule & Zoeckler, 1977), wooden (Woodhams, 1981) or plastic (Haynes, 1979) ruler, rubber paddle (Row, 1980), metal ("Teacher Charged," 1983) or steel pipe (Rollins, 1980), Jocari game paddle ("Angry Parents," 1983), and a wooden drawer divider (Riley, 1983).

In addition they have been subjected to the cutting off of their hair; they have been put in a storeroom, box, cloak room, closet, and/or school vault; thrown against a wall, desk, and/or concrete pillar; forced to run the "gauntlet" or "belt line"; forced to perform punishment push-ups; stuck with a pin; had their mouth, hands, and/or body taped; disrobed in private or before peers; made to stand on their toes for long periods of time; punched; dragged by the arm and/or hair; had meals withheld; choked; forced to lie on a wet floor in their clothing; forced to eat cigarettes; tied to a chair with rope; as well as forced to sit at a desk in a coat room with constant criticism (Clarke, et al., 1980).

Some children also have been disciplined with a metal cattle prod ("Teacher Charged in," 1981) and an electrostatic generator ("Hispanics Accept," 1979) as devices of punishments. A nine-year-old learning disabled pupil had a "three and a half-inch rubber-tipped stick" applied to the muscles of his body which reportedly left "dark red marks 'about the size of a dime up and down his back'" (Goodrich, 1982). An investigator who underwent the "pressure technique" found it was "excruciatingly painful."

Paddling Injuries

Although most (if not all) regulations on the use of corporal punishment emphatically state that the administration should not be "excessive" nor meted out "in anger or malice," this has not been found to be entirely true in many cases. Most believe that corporal punishment only leaves transient bruises which last for a few hours. In the case of the paddling of a seven-year-old (Atrent, 1979), the bruises lasted two weeks. Another child was hospitalized with head injuries for 10 days (Nihen, 1976).

Paddling cases have included students who have developed "red welts" on their buttocks ("Principal Cleared," 1977) or over their back "from his belt (line) to his shoulders" (Dagley, 1983). In other incidences, children have suffered "blistering welts" (Kalwary, 1979) or "blood blisters" (Caltabiano, 1982). Some of these bruises and welts range from a four-inch by six- to eight-inch welt ("Parents Bring," 1981), an eight-inch bruise ("Teacher's Appeal," 1976), or "identical three- to four-inch hematomas on each buttock" (Jones, 1977) after being paddled. Some have developed blood clots ("School Paddling," 1977) or broken veins (Davis, 1982) and/or blood vessels were broken ("District Attorney's," 1982) in the area which was struck by the educator. Another child developed "large purplish-red blotches" on her legs and on her arm which reportedly caused the child "great pain" (Ewing, 1979) after being spanked.

Many of us are likely to underestimate the extent of injury incurred in a paddling. A fifth grader suffered "sciatic nerve damage" (Markley, 1980) after a paddling. Children had their legs (Pekarski, 1978) become numb and "lost use of (their) arm" (McGonigle, 1978) after the paddling. Some have required treatment for "skin and muscle injuries" (Row, 1980). After a six-year-old boy was paddled "from just below the beltline to the tops of his legs," a physician determined that "the first inch or so of his flesh (had) been damaged" (Howard, 1977). Another boy was taken to a hospital thirty minutes after his paddling to undergo "emergency surgery for 'a rupture'" due to an injury to his testicles (Razler, 1980). Some have sustained "possible permanent damage" to the buttocks and legs (Colvin, 1982).

Other Injuries

Usually corporal punishment is perceived to be administered to only the buttocks area of the child. The following is a list of body parts injured in corporal punishment cases reported in the press. Students in our nation's schools have sustained injuries on their ribs (Seigel, 1981), chest (Colter, 1978), back (Harrison, 1981), jaw ("Pupil's Jaw," 1978), ear (Kiesling, 1980), hip (Hudgins, 1982), skull (Rollins, 1980), scalp (Chira, 1982), shoulder (Witherspoon, 1981), elbow ("Teacher Summons," 1977), back of hand ("Teacher Retires," 1981), palm of hand (Haynes, 1979), knuckles ("Parents File," 1983), arms ("Charges Teacher," 1982), legs ("Teacher 'Sentenced'," 1978), thighs (Fister, 1979), knee ("Suit Claims Boy," 1978), stomach (Hernandez, 1982), neck ("Mahopac School," 1980), forehead (Haynes, 1979), cheek (Hernandez, 1982), lip (Kraft, 1979), mouth (Smith, 1980), hair (Sullivan, 1980), eyebrow (Barrineau, 1981), nose ("Chester County," 1983), eye (Eichenberger, 1978), facial bone (Eichenberger, 1978), esophagus (Smith, 1980), spine ("High School," 1983), coccyx bone ("Spanking Issue," 1978), collarbone (Richardson, 1982), and teeth ("Youth Injured," 1983).

When the infliction of the physical punishment is not focused in the buttocks area, other injuries tend to occur with similarly devastating effects on the child's body. Some have sustained headaches from being hit on the head (Jochimsen, 1982) or felt dizzy when hit over the head by a piece of wood (Hoffmann, 1982); sustained a cerebral concussion and sprained neck (Gibbs, 1977); left with "impaired hearing" after being thrown against a wall and struck ("Boy Sues," Undated); suffered a perforated eardrum after being struck on the side of the head ("Parents Sue," 1979); sustained a "sprained arm and facial abrasions" when the child's arm was twisted behind her back and she was wrestled to the ground ("Teacher Pleads," 1979); vomited blood after being kicked (Hunt, 1982); had bloody (Brush, 1982) and fractured noses ("Chester County," 1983); had a "two-inch patch of hair" pulled out the head (Sullivan, 1980); left with "a five-inch cut" on the side of the face after a spanking (Birkland, 1981); required six stitches to close the wound on the mouth when hit with a paddle ("Erie Teacher," 1981); "suffered a gash in (the) eye that required seven stitches" and a "possible hairline fracture of the bones beneath the damaged eye" (Eichenberger, 1978); had "blurred vision" after being thrown against a wall ("Mahopac School," 1980); and a "tail bone (which) was deeply bruised" after being kicked (Schoppenhorst, 1982). An eighth grade boy had two teeth chipped and had the "ligaments in his mouth" torn when his teacher struck him in the mouth with his lunch bag which contained a twelve-ounce bottle of pop ("Youth Injured," 1983).

The force of an educator's blow may be considered excessive if various body parts were damaged in the process. These include a fractured nose ("Chester County," 1983), fractured skull (Rollins, 1980), hairline fracture of the spine (Callaway, 1982), fractured arm ("Parents Seek," 1979), fractured shoulder ("Court Rules," 1980), fractured bone in the hand ("Child Service," 1978), broken knee cap ("Suit Claims Boy," 1978), a broken jaw ("Pupil's Jaw," 1978), and an injured coccyx bone ("Spanking Issue," 1978). In other cases, parts were separated by the force of the punishment. A girl's hip was "knocked out of joint" after a paddling (Hudgins, 1982) and a seventh grade boy suffered a "separated cartilage in his shoulder" after being grabbed and dragged by his teacher (Deller, 1979).

Devised Punishments

There are some educators who devise their own form of punishment, at times, with unexpected results. A fifth grade teacher of the deaf disciplined a student by sticking a straight pin in the child's leg for "goofing off." The child later "developed blood poisoning" (Smith, R., 1978). A twelve-year-old boy suffered second degree burns when he was disciplined by the teacher "holding a cup of hot water over the boy when the water spilled" ("Teacher Suspended," 1982). A metal-shop teacher put a "student's hands into the shop vise as a disciplinary measure" (Hinch, 1982). Two children had their noses pinched by their teacher causing severe nose bleeding ("Shelby Teacher," 1983). Pupils have also been subjected to being tied to their chair ("Two Teachers," 1982) and desk ("Hand Tying," 1982) causing limbs to become numb.

A second grader suffered an "irritated mouth and esophagus" after her teacher "forced her to rinse her mouth out with liquid hand soap containing lye" (Smith, M., 1980). A physician stated that the child's "mouth was blistered and her esophagus (also) was blistered." Children have had pepper (Drake, 1980) and Tabasco sauce (Butterfield, 1983) put into the mouth; another was forced to drink water from an aquarium (Urban, 1982). A sixth grader sustained a concussion after falling down steps at school. He was forced to "carry the entire locker's contents around with him the rest of the day" as a penalty for forgetting his books ("Telford Woman," 1979). After a teacher took crutches away, a child was forced to walk on an injured leg which later required additonal medical treatment (Bracey, 1981).

Some punishments centered around problems which occurred in the school cafeteria. A child had her lunch thrown out because she misbehaved (Dieter, 1978). Some children were required to eat lunch facing a wall while holding their tray as a form of punishment (Briseno, 1980). A nine-year-old boy was physically restrained and force-fed broccoli because he did not finish eating his school lunch. The boy, who later vomited, was treated for strained ligaments in his right arm at a hospital. According to the report of the incident, a rule of the school "is that a child bring his lunch from home or eat the lunch he purchases at school." The child had bought two lunches that day which consisted of pizza, macaroni, and broccoli (Benedict, 1983).

Other problems were incurred as a result of the imposition of punishment drills. Seventh to ninth graders were forced to crawl on hot concrete around a "pool three times on hands and knees" causing blistering on both the hands and legs ("Gym Class," 1977). Football drills have resulted in a knee injury requiring a cast (Koonse, 1976) and a fractured leg (Kelly, 1979). A nine-year-old girl was forced to do three hundred push-ups by her teacher. After completing one hundred, the child collapsed. She later developed swollen arms that night (Schabath, 1979).

Deaths

Some deaths have been associated with punishment drills imposed during school activities. An eighteen-year-old football player was required to complete "a mammoth series of punishment drills" which included: ten 50-yard dashes, ten 100-yard dashes, two 100-yard bear crawls, 50 situps, 50 pushups, four 100-yard drills, and finally had to run the entire field both ways before his death ("Player's Punishment," 1978). A seven-year-old girl was forced to run a lap of about 170 yards around the exercise area. The 47-pound youngster collapsed and died after completing the lap (Richardson, 1981). After a twelve-year-old boy was spanked twice "with a wooden 'paddle-like object'" on the leg, he died later from "cardio-respiratory arrest due to intracerebral hemotoma and right occipital cerebral vascular accident" (Ellison, 1981). The parents alleged that the spanking caused "emotional and mental stress" which, in turn, "caused the blood vessel to burst."

Special Education Students

Special education students do not appear to be protected against such practices. Many of these exceptional children are vulnerable (both physically and emotionally) due to their handicaps. Not only have emotionally disturbed (Woodhams, 1981), deaf (Smith, R., 1978), mentally retarded (Bliss, 1982), children with cerebral palsy (Bliss, 1982) or "kidney illness" ("Parents Upset," 1977), and/or learning disabled (Goodrich, 1982) students been subjected to physical punishment at the hands of an educator, the files are replete with other exceptionalities.

For example, an "arthritic and rheumatic" third grade boy was spanked (with a wooden drawer divider) even after the parent indicated that she did not want her child spanked (Riley, 1983). Due to the stress of being spanked, a seven-year-old child had an epileptic seizure. This was the first convulsion she had in over a year (Copeland, 1978). An asthmatic ten-year-old girl was "struck across the chest" because she mispronounced a word during reading class (Cisneros, 1983).

A kindergarten girl, whose chest "begins to hurt when she gets excited" because of recent open heart surgery, had her mouth taped shut (Stein, 1978) and a seven-year-old boy with a heart murmur was paddled (Zamarr, 1983). A blind four-year-old boy received a paddling from his elementary principal ("Corporal Punishment," 1979). It was related that the child's blindness was "the result of his being beaten as an infant by his natural parents." A boy with muscular dystrophy was treated "for abrasions and contusions" after being hit "about the left and right knees and thighs with a ruler" ("Did Lie," 1983).

Analysis of Corporal Punishment Cases in Schools

Clarke, Erdlen, and Hyman (1984) and Hyman, Clarke, and Erdlen (1987) conducted extensive studies of overly severe disciplinary procedures used by school personnel. The data was derived from press clippings of cases.

Subjects

The sample population only involved newspaper reports of those children who were of school age (5 - 20 years of age) and who were enrolled in a traditional school setting (either public or nonpublic). Staff (teachers, principles, bus drivers, etc.) comprised those personnel from kindergarten level through twelfth grade. Cases which involved pre-school, vocational, and/or higher education were not analyzed.

Materials

This compilation of divergent corporal punishment cases was obtained from the newspaper clipping library at the National Center for the Study of Corporal Punishment and Alternatives in Schools, Temple University. The authors recognize that the sample cases may be inherently biased. A later study by Clarke (1986) found that the people who pressed their cases to the point that they were reported in newspapers may be different than those parents who did not persevere in seeking redress. Also, newspapers may only report the extreme cases. Additionally, only those children whose parents were willing to advocate on their behalf may have been included. The majority of the cases mentioned in this chapter encompass those articles purchased from the Luce Press Clipping service. The clipping service receives approximately 1800 dailies and over 7000 weeklies from across the nation. Additionally, the service scans over 4000 consumer and trade magazines. The representation includes large city and small town newspapers whose editorial opinions range from liberal to conservative. This service conducted a study, in 1978, to determine the percentage of newspaper articles located by their employees on a particular subject. The results of this study indicated that 80% of such articles were detected (Richard Behnke, personal communication, March 28, 1984).

Procedure

From a total of 846 reported cases in the nationwide newspapers in the Center's collection, a sample population of 212 cases was extracted. This sample was chosen on the basis of those which contained the six selected variables (i.e., the sex of the educator, the sex of the pupil, the nature of the infraction, the severity of the punishment, the job position of the staff member, and the age of the student) within the obtained newspaper account(s).

The infractions were divided into two categories: violent and nonviolent. Violent acts were those which caused harm to other persons or damage to property. Examples of a violent infraction included: fighting with another at school and/or on the school bus, pulling a chair out from under another student, kicking rocks against the school building. Nonviolent acts included such violations as: playing hooky from school and/or class, possessing cigarettes, getting poor grades, staying in the bathroom too long, incorrectly pronouncing words in a kindergarten phonics class (Clarke, Lieberman-Lascoe, & Hyman, 1980).

The severity of the punishment was subdivided into three categories. The first contained those cases which required some kind of medical attention for the student as a result of the punishment. The second category included those cases which resulted in some type of physical manifestation which did not receive medical treatment, e.g., blistering, bruises, welts, etc. Lastly, the remaining group contained those incidents which were thought by the parent(s) to be improperly administered, unnecessary, and/or excessive.

Analysis of Data

The purpose of the analysis was to determine the extent to which certain variables are associated when a punishment is administered to students. A content analysis of corporal punishment cases was performed to reveal the extent of its effects on children.

A crosstabulation procedure was selected to analyze the data. Initially a chi square test was completed on pairs of variables to determine the probability that the observed relationship may have occurred by mere chance. Then an appropriate measure of association was performed to determine the degree to which the two variables under investigation were related.

Sex of Educator vs. Sex of Student

The crosstabulation of sex of educator vs sex of student (see Table 1) yielded a significant chi square ($p<.01$), but there was not a strong association between the two variables ($phi=.24$). The Office of Civil Rights survey (Stewart, 1983) found an even higher ratio (25:1) in favor of males being paddled. Roughly four out of five students punished were male. Male educators inflicted the consequences more than three times as often as female staff. This finding is partially related to the disproportionate number (over 80%) of males in administrative positions within the schools (*Statistical Abstracts of the United States*, 1982). When males physically punished students, nearly 85% of the pupils were also male; when females meted out the punishment only 62% of the offenders were male. Generally, male and female educators tend to use corporal punishment with opposite-sex students in equal proportion and at a low frequency relative to the entire sample.

Table 1
Relationship of Sex of Student to Sex of Educator

Sex of student	Sex of educator	
	Male	Female
Male	64.8%	14.6%
	(n = 138)	(n = 31)
Female	11.7%	8.9%
	(n = 25)	(n = 19)

Chi-square = 10.65, phi = .24

These findings seem to corroborate and quantify common sex-role assumptions present in our schools. First, it may be believed necessary and acceptable to control boys' behavior with physical force. The social taboo against males hitting females lends girls relative immunity from corporal punishment. Further, Duker felt that girls may model more passive behavior (Stewart, 1983) and, therefore, may not warrant such extreme discipline. Perhaps girls' misbehaviors tend to be more covert. Secondly, the application of punishment (and resultant bodily harm) falls within the province of manly prerogatives. Just as naughty children must "wait for their father to come home," students wait until male staff are available to enforce the rules. Also, the recalcitrant student may be perceived by male staff as a threat to his authority and sex role identity (Gelles, 1973). Invoking social learning theory, male students observe people being controlled by valued adults (those with prestige, authority, high salary, etc.) through violent means. Over generations, the persistence of corporal punishment is not difficult to understand.

Sex of Educator vs. Age of Student

The crosstabulation of sex of educator vs age of student yielded a significant chi square (87.2, $p<.01$, $df = 14$). In a follow-up test of association, the eta coefficient (.57 with age as the dependent variable) indicated a high positive relationship between these two variables. A later study (Gerak, Nacik, and Hyman, 1988) investigated clippings from 1984 to 1987. This study essentially confirmed the aforementioned results.

This relationship is graphically represented in Figure 1. From the obtained sample, a low frequency of primary grade students was involved in corporal punishment. As student's age increased, the frequency rose sharply, peaked in the junior high school years,

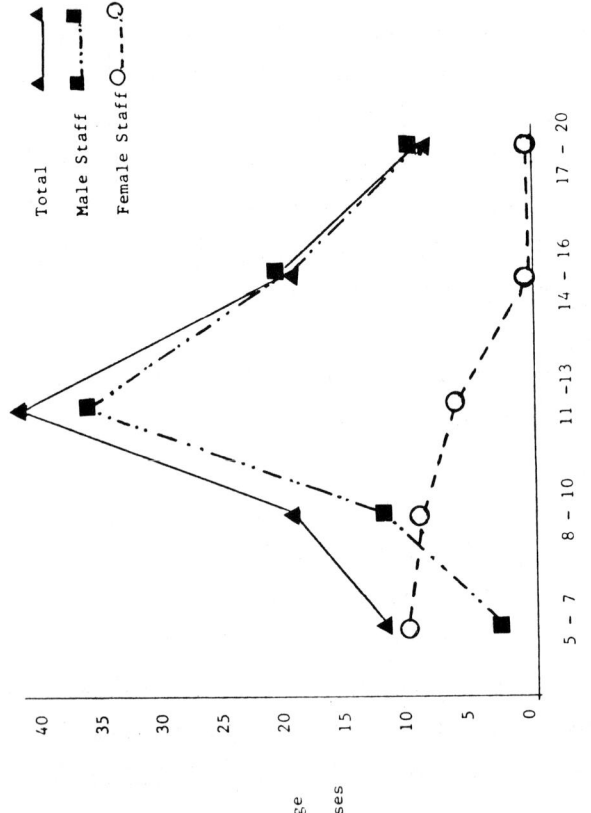

Fig. 1. Percentage of total cases of corporal punishment for each age group.

then dropped off dramatically for older students. The major contribution to this trend, as reported previously, was the participation of the males. The curve for the male staff mirrored the overall results. In the cases studied, a greater proportion of corporal punishment in the primary grades was administered by females than by males. The frequency of female staff involved in corporal punishment declined as student age increased. No student aged thirteen or older was physically punished by a female teacher.

These patterns reflect our everyday observations. A higher percentage of primary grade teachers are female (*Statistical Abstracts in the United States*, 1982). Female staff who strike young children are less likely to have a student retaliate in kind. As the student age (and size) increases, the chances of a female teacher being at risk in a corporal punishment situation becomes greater (Eyre, 1979).

The high incidence of corporal punishment cases among junior high school students may be related to the relative frequency of their misbehavior. As Toby (Cordes, 1984) noted,"junior high schools are more violent than senior high schools because junior high schools have a high proportion of students who would rather not be there." Viewing the overall curve, there appears to be several reasons for the low incidence of older students (14-20) involved in corporal punishment. Using physical punishment with this age group would make the educator more vulnerable to a hostile student's reaction ("School Shooting," 1978; "Student Hits," 1979). The student drop-out rate and school policies which "push-out" disruptive students may tend to distort that portion of the curve. Lastly, even proponents of corporal punishment may feel that it is inappropriate with this older age group.

Severity of Punishment vs. Age of Student

When comparing the variables for severity of punishment with age of child, the data suggest that the degree of the severity of the punishment may not be considered when meted out to children of different ages. The chi square results (chi-square=21.17, p=.818, df=28) did not approach statistical significance; the outcome could have occurred by chance more than 80% of the time. Additionally, these two variables were not closely associated (eta=.069 with age as the dependent variable). Therefore, it appears that severity of corporal punishment is unrelated to the vulnerability of the child. The younger child tends to be more susceptible to physical damage. An older pupil may be perceived as being better able to withstand more intense punishment. This is especially pertinent when the punishment is administered by an adult male who tends to be physically larger.

There are many examples of very young children who received corporal punishment. A three-year-old Illinois boy was paddled in a Christian academy for taking another child's lollipop and subsequently lying about the incident (O'Brien, 1975). A day care center used the following standards for the administration of "swats" to children: eighteen months to two and a half years, one hit; two and a half to four years, two hits; and four to six years, three hits. It was also suggested that the infliction of this punishment should not take place more than twice a day (Maurer, 1979).

According to the law in many states, an 18-year-old is usually considered an adult. These young adults may drink alcoholic beverages, be drafted to fight for their country, marry, engage in work, register to vote, be prosecuted in court as an adult, etc. In contrast, our schools treat these young adults in a demeaning manner by continuing to physically discipline them as if they did not have rights. As can be seen from Figure 1, these 18-year-olds (and older) students also have received corporal punishment.

A 15-year-old boy with "emotional problems" had been paddled repeatedly while in eighth grade. The adolescent was paddled by a school official 56 times during a two month period at the junior high school he attended (Dell, 1980). Another 14-year-old boy was paddled 96 times by a teacher's aide who was six-foot four-inches tall and weighed about 300 pounds. Another pupil in the same class had previously received 150 "licks" at one time from this same employee (Riley, 1982).

Sex of Student vs. Severity of Punishment

Although the distribution of the data for the comparison of sex of student with severity of punishment was significant (chi-square=6.39, df=2, $p<.04$), the degree to which these two variables were associated was relatively low (Cramer's V=.17). The data suggest that males tend to receive corporal punishment more than females, as reported earlier (with 79.3% and 20.7% respectively). The results show that males also tend to receive all degrees of severity of corporal punishment more frequently than females. Although females appear to receive all levels of severity of punishment in comparable proportion, cases of corporal punishment with male students involve twice as many which required medical attention compared to those which were felt to be less severe (wherein only the parent felt the punishment was excessive, improper, and/or unnecessary).

When the sex of the pupil is ignored, the results showed that overall 43.7% (n=93) of the sample population received medical attention after the punishment, 31.9% (n=68) sustained some type of physical manifestation on the body, and 24.4% (n=53) of the student's parent(s) felt that the punishment was improperly administered, excessive, and/or unnecessary. It appears that the addition of the female cases to the overall analysis did not essentially alter the trend already evidenced with the male sample. As noted earlier, these results may be attributed to a reporting bias of the sample population.

Severity of Punishment vs. Nature of Offense

When the severity of the punishment was crosstabulated with the nature of the offense, the results (see Table 2) did not approach statistical significance (p=.54); the data could occur by chance about 50% of the time. Additionally, there seems to be little (if any) association between the two variables (Cramer's V=.077). The results show that most of the offenses committed by the students were nonviolent (80.3%) rather than violent offenses (19.7%). These results essentially are consistent with a previous study (Clarke et al., 1980) which obtained 94.5% for nonviolent cases as compared to 5.5% for violent cases. The data also suggest that although there were more nonviolent offenses committed, there was little (if any) difference in the degree of severity which would be administered to the offender. The degree of severity for the punishment seemed to be meted out in an inconsistent manner by the staff involved. Apparently, the punishment does not match the offense committed, e.g., violent reprimands are not administered for violent infractions.

Many who deal (either directly or indirectly) with our youth tend to minimize the devastating effects of the use of corporal punishment. Some superintendents of schools state that "some children just bruise easily" (Burney, 1979; Throne, 1983). A teacher who witnessed a paddling stated later that she felt the punishment "was reasonable" and that the principal "was not aware that he was bruising them at the time or he would not have continued" with the punishment ("Boone Principal," 1977). A physician who examined a child after a paddling concluded that the bruises on the child's body were the result of "a normal paddling" ("Educators Freed," 1977). There are cases in which a judge remarked that "some will bruise easier than others...If you get struck by a paddle, you expect to have marks" (Gilhooly, 1978). Interestingly, the court decided in the Gasperjohn case that bruises were not a sign of unreasonable force despite medical testimony indicating that the student was not easily susceptible to bruising. An appeal court ruling of a paddling incident stated that the punishment "was reasonable" and that minor bruises "are to be expected" ("Appeal Court," 1979).

Table 2

Comparison of Severity of Punishment with Nature of Offense

Severity of Punishment	Nature of Offense		
	Violent	Nonviolent	Total
Medical attention sought	8.5% (n = 18)	35.2% (n = 75)	43.7% (n = 93)
Physical injury evidenced	7.5% (n = 16)	24.4% (n = 52)	31.9% (n = 68)
Parent(s) felt punishment excessive	3.8% (n = 8)	20.7% (n = 44)	24.4% (n = 52)

Chi-square = 1.25, Cramer's V = .077

FINAL CONCERNS

The wealth of case evidence summarized here and by others (Clarke et al., 1980) clearly suggests American children are targets of violence and are at risk in those schools which allow corporal punishment. Understanding why children can be legally is an important step in eliminating this practice. The evidence suggests that modeling theory accounts for the major variance in predicting which educators will use corporal punishment and how frequently they will use it. Frequency and the amount of force used in the administration of corporal punishment appear to be mediated by religious belief and community traditions. In essence, a potent combination of societal factors and individual experiences account for the use of this ritualized form of violence.

Political agendas, constitutional interpretations, and other factors not discussed mitigate against change. However, advocacy research and efforts by citizen and professional groups have moved the country away from acceptance of allowing educators to inflict pain upon school children (Hyman, 1989). Research on behavorial change (Skinner, 1976; Hyman & Wise, 1979; Hyman & Lally, 1982) clearly demonstrates that positive reinforcement is more effective than punishment. Furthermore, Van Houten (1983) summarized punishment research to report that incremental increases of punishment over time diminishes its effectiveness.

Unfortunately, corporal punishment is likely to remain an embarrassment to our educational system until several objectives are accomplished. In addition to realizing the ineffectiveness (and often the harm) of physical punishment, educators must realize the vulnerable position they put themselves in whenever they strike a student. The authors concede that only a small proportion of corporal punishment cases result in civil suits or criminal charges ("Teacher Charged With," 1977) and few of those cases actually find the educator culpable. The convicted educator however has paid a heavy financial penalty ("Mahopac School," 1980; "School Board, Employee," 1982) and jeopardized a career (Eyre, 1979). As more cases are brought before the courts, individual teachers and their professional organizations must weigh the risk of using physical discipline.

Many advocates for the use of corporal punishment recommend that the practice is needed to "maintain discipline or to enable teachers to defend themselves" (Hechinger, 1980). But this often is not the case as can be seen in the following example. A second grader was paddled so severely that his buttocks were found to be "raw and bleeding" when he arrived home. The boy had screamed due to another child kicking him during class and was paddled twenty times by his teacher. After the child found it too difficult to sit down, he was sent to the principal who also paddled him twenty more times (Hechinger, 1980).

Legal Issues

Previous research (Clarke et al., 1980) found that parents were more likely to receive favorable resolution from their local school board than from the courts in corporal punishment complaints. Despite this, in many cases the offending educator has been sued on the basis of the violation of the child's and/or the parent(s)' constitutional rights under the Fourteenth Amendment which forbids the imposition of cruel and unusual punishment and/or the Eighth Amendment, which guarantees due process (Jones, 1977). This approach frequently has proven unproductive and unsuccessful. A West Virginia Circuit Court ruled that the "parents' due process rights had not been violated, because the general application of corporal punishment is consistent legally with the schools' interest in keeping order" (Row, 1980). When a New York child's parents took their son's paddling to court (Hechinger, 1980), the judge threw out the case because no law had been violated, since educators are acting under the guise and sanctioning of "in loco parentis" protection of the law. Additionally, in many states, the plaintiff (parents/child) must substantiate that the educator imposed the reprimand with malice in addition to proving that irreparable injury had occurred as a direct result of the punishment (Duffey, 1979; Miller, 1983).

There have been a limited number of cases in which parents have pressed charges of assault (or assault and battery) on the part of the staff member (Cote, 1979). *Black's Law Dictionary* (Black, 1951) defines assault as "an intentional, unlawful offer of corporal injury to another by force, or force unlawfully directed toward the person of another, under such circumstances as create well-founded fear of imminent peril, coupled with apparent present ability to execute attempt, if not prevented." Battery is defined as "an unlawful beating, or other wrongful physical violence or constraint, inflicted on a human being without his consent...the slightest touching of another, or of his clothes or anything else attached to his person, if done in a rude, insolent, or angry manner." Another suggestion made by the Supreme Court in the *Ingraham vs. Wright* (1976) case implicated the Fourteenth Amendment which encompasses equal rights for all citizens. Many cases involving police brutality had selected this amendment as the basis for their appeal (Maurer, 1981). If these prove to be a more viable course of action for parents to pursue, then administrators and educators as well as school boards are encouraged to take the necessary steps to redefine their present stance on the use of corporal punishment, in addition to formulating guidelines for its use to help allay future law suits which might prove costly (both monetarily and personally).

This viewpoint may be seen in this illustration. A juror who served on the panel of a paddling (of a three-year-old) case related that the jury would have convicted the adult of child abuse if that had been the charge. A second juror on the same trial stated that he thought the defendent was guilty, but found him innocent with reference to the specific allegations (O'Brien, 1975).

Not only are individuals held accountable for administering punishment, the school districts are frequently included in the lawsuit ("School Board," 1982). There is no guarantee that the district will be able to afford judgments on behalf of the plaintiff. This brings the individual taxpayer (interested or not) squarely within the field of battle.

RECOMMENDATIONS

To prevent disasters and tragedies from occurring, the need for extensive teacher training is essential. Not only should teachers be thoroughly versed in the approved disciplinary techniques of their districts, they need to study the successful discipline alternatives elsewhere. The impetus for such an investment of time, effort, and money is the proper responsibility of the school administration (as representatives of school boards) and the teacher's association whose primary function is the protection of its members.

Present guidelines governing the administration of corporal punishment have not protected school children. Guidelines and procedures cannot readily legislate tempers and often do not include a monitoring component nor impose specific consequences for violators. The difficulty of operationalizing the terms "excessive" and "reasonable force" is obvious in the inadequacy of adopted codes. Any proposed guidelines which do not document parental consent, use of less intrusive alternatives, due process procedures, and an independent review by a human rights committee are clearly insufficient. It is precisely because guidelines have not served their intended purpose that corporal punishment becomes excessive.

In 1976, when the senior author first began to collect data on corporal punishment in schools, only two states and a scattering of school districts forebade its use. As a result of massive public education based on research, the efforts of state legislatures, parent pressure, professional urging and litigation, as of October, 1989, nineteen states, most major cities, and many affluent suburban school disticts have abolished corporal punishment in schools. While individual pathology among teachers cannot be eliminated completely, the climate for dismissal of those teachers is ripe when hitting of children is considered illegal. In essence, the available evidence suggests that education concerning alternates to corporal punishment, and sanctions against its use in schools have clear dampening effects on its use. Research by Mishkin (1987) clearly supports high levels of education and parent training in reducing the use of corporal punishment at home, despite the strength of the modeling effect. Most educators receive little (or no) training in theory, research, and/or practice of non-aggressive problem-solving techniques for dealing with and preventing misbehavior.

REFERENCES

Appeal court upholds school paddling. (1979, November 13). *Advocate* (Louisiana).

Atrent, J. (1979, April 28). Principal convicted in paddling of boy. *Gazette-Telegraph* (Colorado).

Atteberry, M. (1980, April 15). Police called to investigate pupil's alleged mistreatment. *Indianapolis Star* (Indiana).

Bandura, A. & Huston, A. (1961). Identification as a process of incidental learning. *Journal of Abnormal and Clinical Psychology, 63,* 311-318.

Barrineau, M. (1981, April 18). Police probe 12-year-old's charge gym teacher beat him with paddle. *Times-Herald* (Texas).

Benedict, D. (1983, January 14). Teacher, aide charged in force-feeding. *Houston Chronicle* (Texas).

Birkland, D. (1981, January 30). Mother attacks principal who spanked her daughter.

Black, H. (1951). *Black's Law Dictionary* (4th ed.). St. Paul, Minnesota: West Publishing Co.

Blaker, H. (1977, September 8). Teacher hearings continue. *Breeze* (Pennsylvania).

Bliss, M. (1982, October 27). Mother claims handicapped child mistreated at school. *Southeast Missourian* (Missouri).

Boone principal 'sorry' about paddling 3 pupils. (1977, December 3). *Gazette* (West Virginia).

Boy sues La Crosse principal. (Undated; Wisconsin).

Bracey, L. (1981, March 12). Tooth pulling incident leads to battery charge. *Times* (Florida).

Briseno, O. (1980, March 25). Discipline nets objection. *Times* (Indiana).

Brush, M. (1982, July 15). Teacher sued for striking boy. *Courier Times* (Pennsylvania).

Burney, A. (1979, January 19). Johnson resolves paddling complaint at southside. *Register* (Virginia).

Butterfield, K. (1983, May 19). Bartonville police studying charges of physical abuse. *Peoria Journal Star* (Illinois).

Callaway, W. (1982, December 10). Mother files complaint against local teacher. *Chronicle* (Texas).

Caltabiano, M. (1982, February 25). Suit filed over paddling at school. *Valley Monitor* (Texas).

Charges teacher beat him, sues schools for $30,000. (1982, July 11). *Post-Dispatch* (Missiouri).

Chester county youth sues, saying teacher attacked him. (1983, October 12). *Inquirer* (Pennsylvania).

Child service probes paddling by teacher. (1978, October 4). *News* (Pennsylvania).

Chira, S. (1982, March 13). School officials investigating case of teacher charged with assault. *Times* (New York).

Cisneros, J. (1983, April 19). Teacher is censored for slapping student. *Oakland Press* (Michigan).

Clarke, J. (1986). *Some effects of corporal punishment and psychological abuse on school students and their parents.* Unpublished doctoral dissertation, Temple University.

Clarke, J., Erdlen, R., & Hyman, I.A. (April, 1984). *Analysis of recent corporal punishment cases reported in national newspapers.* Paper presented at the annual convention of the National Association of School Psychologists, Philadelphia, PA.

Clarke, J., Lieberman-Lascoe, R., & Hyman, I. (1980, April). *An analysis of corporal punishment cases as reported in nationwide newspapers: Types, incidents, and outcomes.* Paper presented at the National Association of School Psychologists Convention, Washington, D.C.

Colter, S. (1978, April 25). No rules to deal with 'yardstick' teachers. *Afro-American* (Washington, D.C.).

Colvin, L. (1982, April 13). Spanking may prompt legal action by parent. *Commercial-Pine Bluff* (Arkansas).

Cooke, G. (Producer; 1984, February 12). "Are they really bankrupt? *Sixty Minutes.* New York: CBS.

Copeland, S. (1978, February 24). Parents await spanking report. *Observer* (North Carolina).

Cordes, C. (1984, March). Researchers flunk Reagan on discipline theme. *APA Monitor,* pp. 12-13.

Corporal punishment policy 'unacceptable'. (1979, September 6). *Courier* (Texas).

Cote, W. (1979, July 18). Teacher, principal to pay for hitting boy with stick. *Journal* (Michigan).

Court rules school spanking OK. (1980, March 18). *Sentinel* (Pennsylvania).

Dagley, J. (1983, January 8). Father takes out warrant against teacher. *Enquirer & Ledger* (Georgia).

Davis, M. (1982, May 21). Elkhorn parents protest violent paddlings. *News* (West Virginia).

Decision due on classroom incident. (1977, April 28). *Commercial Appeal* (Tennessee).

Dell, A. (1980, November 26). The system has failed my son. *Journal* (Florida).

Deller, M. (1979, April 11). Storm clouds gather over incidents. *Citizen Journal* (Texas).

Did lie test prove teacher innocent? (1983, January 21). *Journal* (Georgia).

Dieter, M. (1978, November 4). Teacher suspended in discipline probe. *Register-Star* (Illinois).

District attorney's office probes Sequoyah paddling incident. (1982, December 12). *Progress* (Oklahoma).

Drake, A. (1980, September 18). Teacher returns to classroom after suspensons for discipline. *Star* (Indiana).

Duffey, D. (1979, December 18). Teacher cleared in child child spanking case. *Herald* (North Carolina).

Educators freed in child abuse case. (1977, February 11). *Banner* (Texas).

Eichenberger, B. (1978, October 27). Drill comes under probe. *Telegraph* (Georgia).

Ellison, E. (1981, September 4). Parents say son's death caused by school beating. *Constitution* (Georgia).

Erie teacher sued for striking student. (1981, April 21). *Journal* (Pennsylvania).

Eron, L., Walder,L. & Lefkowitz, M. (1971). *Learning Aggression in Children*. Boston: Little, Brown, & Co.

Ewing, J. (1979, March 9). High school construction quiet. *Post-A-Thenian* (Tennessee).

Eyre, R. (1979, April 25). Teacher firing. *Times-Herald* (Texas).

Farley, A. (1983). *National survey of the use and non-use of corporal punishment as a discipinary technique in U. S. public schools*. Unpublished Doctoral Dissertation, Temple University (A summary article is available at NCSCPAS).

15-year-old gives details on paddling. (1977, January 31). *Chronicle* (Washington).

Fister, G. (1979, May 1). Watson chapel teacher suspended for using strap on 8-year-old. *Commercial* (Arkansas).

Freeman, C.D. (1979). The children's petition of 1669 and its sequel. In I. Hyman and J. Wise (Eds.) *Corporal Punishment in American Education*. Philadelphia: Temple University Press.

Gelles, R. (1973,). Child abuse as psychopathology: A sociological critique and reformulation. *American Journal of Orthopsychiatry, 43*, pp. 611-621.

Gelles, R. & Strauss, M. (1979). Violence in the American family. *Journal of Social Issues, 35* 15-39.

Gerak, J., Nacik, E.M., and Hyman, I.A. (1988). *An analysis of corporal punishment from 1984 to 1987*. Unpublished paper (NCSCPAS).

Gibbs, G. (1977, September 7). Hospitalized boy says PE teacher beat him up. *News* (Florida).

Gibson, I. (1978). *The English Vice*. London: Duckworth.

Gil, D.(1970). *Violence Against Children.* Boston: Harvard University Press.

Gilhooly, B. (1978, April 24). McGowan is acquitted. *Maryland Gazette* (Maryland).

Goodrich, T. (1982, April 8). School told to stop 'pressure-stick' use. *Morning American Statesman* (Texas).

Greven, P. (1977). *The Proteton Temperament.* New York: Alfred Knopf, Inc.

Gym class forced to crawl on hot concrete in Mesa. (1977, September 23). *Republic* (Arizona).

Hale, M. (1981, February 26). School officials say they can't substantiate children's claims that teacher hit them with cord. *Times* (Florida).

Hamilton, E. (1982, January 22). Paddling: It's controversial elsewhere, but Martin students take their licks. *News* (Florida).

Hand-tying nets teacher suspension. (1982, October 21). *Enquirer* (Georgia).

Harrison, D. (1981, July 7). Parents protest excessive spanking. *Herald* (Georgia).

Haynes, D. (1979, April 26). Teacher represented by lawyer at meeting. *Home* (Alabama).

Hechinger. F. (1980, Febrary 5). Limits sought on discipline of students. *New York Times* (New York).

Hentoff, N. (1979). Preface. In I. Hyman and J. Wise, (Eds.) *Corporal Punishment in American Education.* Philadelphia: Temple University Press.

Hernandez, M. (1982, June 12). Parents win but no one rejoices. *Times* (California).

High school settles suit in student's spanking. (1983, Febrary 24). *Journal* (Pennsylvania).

Hinch, R. (1982, April 10). Vise not corporal punishment, teacher says. *Independent Press Telegram* (California).

Hispanics accept regrets expressed by teacher. (1979, July 19). *Herald* (Connecticut).

Hoffman, E. (1982, May 19). Fatima board hands reprimand to both student, teacher. *Unterrified Democrat* (Missiouri).

Howard, A. (1977, November 24). Fellowship school principal acquitted in child beating. *Herald* (North Carolina).

Howard, S. (1978, October 20). Teacher had been warned about disciplining students. *Tribune* (Florida).

Hudgins, B. (1982, Febrary 12). Paddling probe closed; no policy violations. *Cleveland Daily Banner* (Tennessee).

Hunt, D. (1982, November 9). Panel recommends firing coach in paddling incident. *Houston Chronicle* (Texas).

Hyman, I.A. (in press). *Reading, Writing, and the Hickory Stick: Apalling Story of Physical and Psychological Abuse of American School Children.* Lexington, MA: Lexington Book Company.

Hyman, I.A. (1989). *Using Advocacy Research to Change Public Policy: The Case of Corporal Punishment in the School.* Paper presented at the Annual Convention of the American Psychological Association, New Orleans.

Hyman, I.A., Clarke, J. & Erdlen, R. (1987). An analysis of physical abuse in American schools. *Aggressive Behavior, 13,* 1-7.

Hyman, I.A. and Lally, D. (1982). The effectiveness of staff development programs to improve school discipline. *Urban Review, 14,* 181-196.

Hyman, I.A. and Wise, J. (1979). *Corporal Punishment in American Education.* Philadelphia: Temple University Press.

Jochimsen, D. (1982, October 6). Parent claims daughter was struck by teacher. *Messenger & Chronicle* (Iowa).

Jones, St. (1977, September 22). Paddling right upheld. *News-Ledger* (Virginia).

Kalwary, K., & Howard, S. (1979, February 3). Police probe paddling of Tampa 7th grader. *Tribune* (Florida).

Kelly, B. (1979, December 4). Lansing: Intraclass discipline policy not needed. *Leader-Telegram* (Wisconsin).

Kiesling, M. (1980, June 14). '149' teacher charged with abusing student. *Sun Journal* (Illinois).

Kohn, A. (1988, April). You know what they say... *Psychology Today*, p. 36-41.

Koonse, A. (1976, October 28). No reprimand for coaches after two players hurt in drill. *Register* (Iowa).

Kraft, R. (1979, November 7). ASD mishap hurts boy, irks parents and officials. *Chronicle* (Pennsylvania).

Lennox, N. (1982). *Teacher Use of Corporal Punishment as a Function of Modeling Behavior*. Unpublished doctoral dissertation, Temple University.

Mahopac school 7th grader suing teacher for $100,000. (1980, March 28). *Citizen-Register* (New York).

Manning, J. (1979). Discipline in the good old days. In I. Hyman & J.Wise, (Eds.) *Corporal Punishment in American Education*. Philadelphia: Temple University Press.

Markley, M. (1980, March 18). Spanking irks child's father. *Brazosport Facts* (Texas).

Maurer, A. (1979). It does happen here. In I. Hyman & J. Wise (Eds.) *Corporal Punishment in American Education* (pp. 219-236). Philadelphia, Pennsylvania: Temple University Press.

Maurer, A. (1981). *Paddles Away: A Psychological Study of Physical Punishment in Schools*. Palo Alto, California: R & E Research Associates.

McGonigle, St. (1978, May 24). G-P hears charge of teacher brutality. *Caller* (Texas).

Miller, F. (1983, March 19). Teacher aide found not guilty in paddling. *Greensboro Daily News* (North Carolina).

Mishkin, A. (1987). *Corporal Punishment: Why Some Parents Use Less Severe Discipline Practices Than They Experienced as Children*. Unpublished doctoral dissertation, Temple University.

Nihen, B. (1976, December 3). Pre-trial unit offers help. *Herald-News* (New Jersey).

O'Brien, J. (1975, May 17). The print of paddle on son, mother says. *Tribune* (Illinois).

Parents bring paddling case before board. (1981, February 18). *Benton County Democrat* (Arkansas).

Parents file $450,000 suit against school. (1983, May 12). *Arkansan Democrat* (Arkansas).

Parents say their son hit by M.R. teacher. (1981, March 24). *Enterprise* (Louisiana).

Parents seek compensation in student discipline case. (1979, February 14). *Journal* (Pennsylvania).

Parents sue for $10,000, say school aide injured son. (1979, June 23). *Inquirer* (Pennsylvania).

Parents upset over incident at school. (1977, February 14). *Press* (New York).

Pekarski, M. (1978, February 23). Father considering legal action after punishment of son. *Times-Herald* (New York).

Pesce, C. (1983, April 11). USA gives spankings bad marks. *U.S.A. Today* (Washington, D.C.).

Player's punishment reported by witnesses. (1978, March 27). *Tribune* (California).

Pokalo, M. (1986). *Caregivers' Attitudes Toward the Severity of Punishment for Forty-Four Misbehaviors in Mental Retardation Institutions.* Unpublished doctoral dissertation, Temple University.

Principal cleared of paddling charges. (1977, March 10). *News-Sentinel* (Tennessee).

Pupil's jaw broken by teacher. (1978, October 12). *Sentinel-Star* (Florida).

Radbill, S., (1974). A history of child abuse and infanticide. In R. Helford & C. Kempe (Eds.) *The Battered Child,* Chicago: University of Chicago Press.

Razler, D. (1980, April 11). Police ask state attorney to probe school paddling. *Herald* (Florida).

Reid, D. (1981, October 3). Rubber strap threatens student's weak kidneys. *Democrat* (Arkansas).

Richardson, L. (1981, October 1). The last day of Stephanie Halbert. *Times-Herald* (Texas).

Riley, R. (1982, December 19). City case arouses concern over school paddling. *Greensboro Daily News and Record* (North Carolina).

Riley, R. (1983, June 12). School spanking no federal case. *Greensboro Daily News* (North Carolina).

Rollins, N. (1980, March/April). Why do we permit beatings in our schools? (New York).

Rose, T. (1984). Current uses of corporal punishment in American public schools. *Journal of Educational Psychology, 76,* 427-441.

Row, S. (1980, May 13). Due process keys paddling appeal. *News-Leader* (Virginia).

Ruble, W. (1977, November 13). Harrisburg debates show-swatting. *Oregonian* (Oregon).
Rule, S., & Zoeckler, E. (1977, April 20). Rod is used... Sparingly in many schools in area. *Post-Dispatch* (Misssiouri).
Schabath, G. (1979, December 11). Pupil-abuse allegations stir up town. *News* (Michigan).
School board develops new corporal punishment policy. (1979, March 10). *News* (Mississippi).
School paddling reported. (1977, September 21). *Sun* (North Carolina).
School shooting spree. (1978, October 18). *Gazette* (Missouri).
Schoppenhorst, C. (1982, October 28). Teacher suspended for kicking student. *Journal* (Georgia).
Seigel, C. (1981, September 24). Beating of teammate leaves player uninterested in game. *Rocky Mountain News* (Colorado).
Shelby teacher fired for alleged pinching of noses (1983, July 1). *The Birmingham News* (Alabama).
Simmons, J. (1980, March 26). Coosa school board hears paddling complaint. *Home* (Alabama).
Skinner, B.F. (1976, August). *Corporal Punishment*. Paper presented at the annual convention of the American Psychological Association, Washington, D.C.
Smith, M. (1980, October 29). Mom says teacher forced daughter to wash mouth with soap. *Journal* (Georgia).
Smith, R. (1978, December 8). Teacher reprimanded in pin incident. *Evening American Statesman* (Texas).
Smith, R. (1982, April 23). Mother says son 'beaten', not whipped, by principal. *Gazette* (Missiouri).

Sofer, B. (1983). *Psychologist's Attitude Toward Corporal Punishment*. Unpublished doctoral dissertation, Temple University.

Spanking issue angers parents. (1978, March 27). *Standard* (New York).

Statistical Abstract of the United States (1982; Document No. 003024050102) Washington, D.C.: U.S. Government Printing Office.

Stein, G. (1978, May 12). Board probes reports teacher taped children's hands. *News* (North Carolina).

Stewart, V. (1983, April 17). Corporal punishment: Guidelines don't exist. *The Clarion-Ledger* (Mississippi).

Straus, M. (1989). *Corporal Punishment and Crime: A Theoretical Model and Some Empirical Data*. Unpublished paper presented at the Department of Criminal Justice, Indiana University.

Publication of the Family Violence Research Program of the Family Research Laboratory, University of New Hampshire, Durham, N.H.

Straus, M., Gelles, R. & Steinmetz, S. (1980). *Behind Closed Doors: Violence in the American Family*. New York: Doubleday/Anchor.

Student hits Idabel principal. (1979, February 15). *Daily Gazette* (Oklahoma).

Suit claims coach hit teenager. (1983, June 13). *Times* (Alabama).

Suit claims boy maimed. (1978, February 11). *Caller* (Texas).

Suit filed in paddling of student. (1977, April 14). *Sun-Sentinel* (Florida).

Sullivan, P. (1980, July 5). County teacher is sued over lost lock of hair. *Free Lance-Star* (Virginia).

Teacher's appeal sustained. (1976, December 31). *Patriot* (Pennsylvania).
Teacher charged at Dudley. (1983, February 1). *The Greensboro Record* (North Carolina).
Teacher charged in assault. (1981, March 13). *Register* (Virginia).
Teacher charged with assault in paddling. (1977, May 13; California).
Teacher faces assault charge. (1982, April 26). *Free Press* (North Carolina).
Teacher gets suspended jail term. (1979, May 17). *News-Leader* (Virginia).
Teacher pleads innocent to assault charge. (1979, October 5). *Rock Island* (Illinois).
Teacher retires after reprimand. (1981, February 14). *Call & Post* (Ohio).
Teacher 'sentenced' in whipping. (1978, January 6). *Chieftain* (Colorado).
Teacher summons issued. (1977, December 5). *News* (New York).
Teacher suspended for scalding. (1982, June 14). *Record-Eagle* (Michigan).
Telford woman files suit against Pennridge district. (1979, August 22). *News-Herald* (Pennsylvania).
The paddling kings. (1977, April 28). *News & Record* (Virginia).
Throne, G. (1983, February 5). Paddling bruises son, mon charges. *Sentinel* (Florida).
Titone, J. (1977, February 2). Corporal punishment: Maybe they should've used a ruler. *Highline Times* (Washington).
Two teacher suspended after allegedly tying second-graders to chairs. (1982, September 24; Texas).

Urban, J. (1982, March 25). Teacher fired in aquarium incident. *Herald* (Texas).

Van Houten, R. (1983). Punishment: From the animal laboratory to the applied setting. In S. Axelrod & J. Apsche (Eds). *The Effects of Punishment on Human Behavior.* New York: Academic Press.

We believe in the devil (1988, December). *Psychology Today,* p. 8.

Who is speaking for the children? (1982, February 22). *Telegraph* (Georgia).

Wiehe, E. (1989). *Religious Influence of Parental Attitudes Toward the Use of Corporal Punishment.* Unpublished manuscript, Department of Social Work, University of Kentucky, Lexington, KY.

Witherspoon, T. (1981, May 22). Parents file suit about alleged beating. *Sun* (Texas).

Woodhams, M. (1981, December 10). Jury finds teacher innocent of excessive pupil discipline. *Sun-Sentinel* (Florida).

Youth home closed for its discipline policies. (1979, September 19). *Union* (Kansas).

Youth injured when teacher hits student. (1983, May 27). *News* (Minnesota).

Zamarr, H. (1983, September 30). Eula student's parents protest paddling. *Reporter News* (Texas).

Zaidi, L.Y., Knutson, JF., and Mehm, J.G. (1989). Transgenerational patterns of abusive parenting: Analog and clinical tests. *Aggressive Behavior, 15,* 137-152.

6

Athletes as Targets of Aggression
Gordon Russell[1]

INTRODUCTION

This chapter highlights athletes, specifically aspects of their role in serving as targets for the aggression of others. Throughout the discussion, targets is used in a wider-than-usual sense to describe athletes who stand to be harmed either at the hands of others or by hazards present in the sport's setting. Of course, being a target is often a transitory role. Targets typically retaliate and themselves become aggressors, attacking the instigator either in an exchange or at some future point in the competition. The portrayal of athletes as targets dictates an emphasis on those sports that tolerate or condone interpersonal aggression. Sports differ widely in this regard. The sanctions for on-site violence are usually codified and imposed at the discretion of the sport's governing body. Rarely is the legal system involved. In this vein, it appears that among sports the

---

[1]The writer wishes to thank Shelley A. Russell for her comments on an earlier version of the manuscript and George M. Yeoman for the use of his hockey tapes.

severity of sanctions for aggression is negatively related to the levels of violence displayed by athletes. In violent sports, e.g., boxing, football, ice hockey, relatively mild punishments are meted out for excesses, e.g., warnings, nominal fines, temporary or permanent expulsion from the contest. Conversely, one can predict with certainty that were assaultive behavior to occur in the more genteel sports, e.g., curling, golf, tennis, it would almost certainly result in career-ending suspensions.

AN OVERVIEW

Any comprehensive discussion of the role of targets in sports that pose personal risks must begin by addressing what is being risked. What exactly are the stakes for those who would make themselves available as targets? In partial answer to this question, a highly selective and circumscribed set of findings from the sports medicine and neurological literatures is presented, highlighting the potentially harmful consequences of participation in certain sports.

Considering costs also provides one with a fuller appreciation of the strength and often overriding influence of the motivational pressures that guide some people toward hazardous sporting activities.

Just as the weight of factors that might favor one's participation or persistence in a sport, e.g., larger purses, greater recognition, can change over time, so the weight of factors that might discourage an individual's participation can also change, e.g., an increased likelihood of harm, decreased satisfactions. The second section suggests that the one term in the athlete's personal equation whose value is most likely to be misjudged is the level of risk he or she will assume by engaging in an activity. More generally, the section asks whether sports are becoming more or less violent as settings for the expression of competitive motives. Alternately, do today's sports present the athlete with an increased or decreased likelihood of becoming embroiled in conflict, with the attendant risk of injury compared to such probabilities in earlier decades? Until recently, "opinion" has provided the only answers. However, historical evidence from at least one sport is described.

The following section examines the motivations of those who knowingly risk injury. What factors might account for the willingness of some people to endanger life and limb in pursuit of sporting activities perceived to carry a high degree of risk? Two theoretical models providing important insights into the motives of those who expose themselves to possible harm are outlined.

A further question asks where on the field of play athletes are most likely to be victimized. A preliminary answer to that question is provided by some previously unpublished data. A concluding section identifies a variety of sources from which attacks on athletes are launched. The sources are schematically diagrammed, highlighting their major features and interrelationships.

THE COSTS OF BEING A TARGET

People in all sports stand to realize important benefits from their participation. Those involved at a recreational level may experience an increased sense of well-being and an enriched social life, or derive intrinsic satisfactions from their chosen activity. Elite athletes may also receive abundant extrinsic satisfactions including money, acclaim and status. However, there is a darker and less publicized side to everyone's participation: the prospect of injuries.

I would estimate that the frequency of accidents and injury in the majority of sports and recreational activities is only slightly greater than that occurring in the home or workplace. However, a small number of combatant and high risk sports present the athlete with a sharply elevated chance of injury. While the media and promoters tend to minimize or ignore altogether the risks associated with sport, athletes frequently pay a price for their participation; in particular sports, they can pay a terrible price. To be sure, many injuries are inflicted deliberately by opponents, usually in violation of the accepted rules. Of course, boxing and its variants are exceptions in that the sanctioned and unabashed purpose of the enterprise is to inflict injury.

The risk and types of injuries that athletes sustain vary widely from sport to sport and with the level of competition. Injuries also vary temporally across sports, from injuries producing short-term effects to ones plaguing athletes long after their playing days are over. A sample of studies from the extensive sports medicine and neurological literatures will illustrate some of the extreme costs. Spectators and millions of television viewers of a National Hockey League game were horrified by the sight of Buffalo Sabres' goalie Clint Malarchuk collapsing to the ice with blood spurting from a severed jugular vein, the result of an errant skate blade ("Scared Malarchuk," 1989). Prompt medical attention fortunately averted a tragedy. In the days following, the media kept the story alive for a fascinated public through televised replays of the incident. In this and other instances, the media's interest in injuries appears stimulated primarily by the presence of dramatic elements, e.g., uncertainty, the unusual; more commonplace but equally serious injuries go largely unreported. Simply put, injuries in themselves are not especially newsworthy. The few injuries that are deemed newsworthy typically involve "star" players or injuries that could affect adversely a team's fortunes. News of even severe injuries to the legions of unheralded individuals also taking part in violent sports is at best reported only locally. One result is that, unless governing bodies or researchers have established injury-reporting networks, annual tallies in a sport are often unavailable or fragmentary. The public and would-be participants, in turn, remain poorly informed of the incidence of injuries nationwide. Left largely to their own devices, people estimate the likelihood of injury upon the basis of information supplied by spokespersons for a sport and/or selective media accounts.

An example of an annual injury toll that year after year had passed largely unnoticed was reported in an early medical investigation (Pashby, Pashby, Chisholm & Crawford, 1975). A questionnaire mailed to members of the Canadian Opthalmology Society and medical schools with departments of opthalmology sought detailed information on reported eye injuries during the 1974-75 ice-hockey season. A surprising and troubling finding was the number of youngsters who had been legally blinded in one eye. During a single season of organized hockey, 37 young players lost the sight of an eye, an injury most often inflicted by sticks. Of course, because the Pashby et al. (1975) data were based solely on those questionnaires returned, the number of youngsters blinded was undoubtedly a conservative estimate.

The potential costs to athletes for participating in contact sports can also be assessed from a neurological perspective. Head injuries provide a case in point. Sometimes referred to as the "silent epidemic," postconcussion syndrome involves any of a number of cognitive deficits experienced by people who have suffered mild head injuries. Among the symptoms that may be experienced in the aftermath of a head injury are memory loss, headaches, irritability, an intolerance to frustration, depression, tinnitus, attentional deficits, lowered sexual drive and intolerance to alcohol (Barth, Alves, Ryan, Macciocchi, Rimel, Jane & Nelson, 1989; Benton, 1989). However, the injury may or may not be accompanied by a loss of consciousness.

Not surprisingly, most postconcussion syndrome cases are the result of motor vehicle accidents. A recent study of California's hospital admissions for mild head injury revealed that 42% resulted from vehicular collisions. A further 23% resulted from falls while 14% were attributed to assaults; 6%, to bicycle accidents; and 6%, to recreational and sporting activities. In sports, young males are especially at risk; the incidence of head injuries to boys between the ages of 10 and 14 far outstrips that to girls in the same age group (Kraus & Nourjah, 1989).

Although head trauma has been studied in a variety of sports, e.g., equestrian events (Foster, Tilley & Leiguarda, 1976), football (Harbaugh & Saunders, 1984) and rugby (Roy, 1974), boxing has provided the major focus of studies of both mild and severe head injuries. The popular label "punch drunk" or, more formally, "dementia pugilistica" (Lampert & Hardman, 1984) have come to characterize a behavioral syndrome involving an unsteady gait, speech and motor loss, and upper body tremors, all the result of damage sustained in the ring. The possible long-term consequences for those participating in combatant sports are seen in the conclusion of a neurological study of Finnish boxers. Kaste, Vilkki, Sainio, Kuurne, Katevuo and Meurala (1982) concluded "...that the effects of repeated concussions are cumulative, and for each individual there is a limit beyond which recovery is not complete" (p. 1188).

A study of 10 professional boxers (Casson, Sham, Campbell, Tarlau & DiDomenico, 1982) shortly after they had been knocked out revealed that all had suffered mild head injuries. All but two of the boxers exhibited further neurological deficits: five had abnormal computer tomography (CT) scans, two had abnormal electroencephalography (EEG) readings and a neurological examination revealed abnormalities in another. Moreover, the damage sustained by these boxers was unrelated to their boxing skills; rather, it was related to the number of fights in which they had participated. Inasmuch as each of these men had been knocked out fewer than three times, the authors suggested that the etiology of the boxers' conditions was the "...cumulative effect of multiple subconcussive head blows" (p. 174).

Finally, more recent evidence ("Ex-boxers face," 1989) suggests a link between boxing and later symptoms of Alzheimer's disease. Of eight former fighters who underwent thorough neurological assessments, all were diagnosed with Alzheimer's, three of whom also presented symptoms of Parkinson's disease.

Interestingly, the sequelae of mild head injury described in recent investigations may be foreshortened. Lawrence Marshall, a neurosurgeon attending a conference in Vail, Colorado, fell and struck his head while skiing and sustained a head injury. His account of the accident (Marshall & Ruff, 1989) and his recovery provide an important "patient" perspective and raise serious questions about the time generally thought necessary for recovery. Current testing procedures indicate that full recovery usually takes three months. Yet Dr. Marshall continued to experience difficulties in several areas, e.g., memory of recent events, for up to 18 months. Apparently, recovery from mild head injuries may be gradual and, in some cases, never complete.

The potential costs of engaging in sports that call for participants to present themselves as targets of physical attacks range from bruises to death. While the severity of an injury can obviously be judged by the degree to which that injury is life-threatening, a temporal dimension is also important. For example, the life of the Buffalo goalie whose jugular vein was slashed was jeopardized for a short time. Still, a week later, he had made a full recovery and was back in the nets. Other equally serious injuries, although not life-threatening prove disabling for prolonged periods of time. Such injuries are chronic insofar as the individual's physical, emotional or cognitive capabilities are impaired for years, perhaps for a lifetime.

Still other serious injuries e.g., brain damage, are seldom recognized as such and go unrecorded in the injury column. Their effects are insidious, a loss of function often passing unnoticed, even by the victim. As a consequence, the public consistently underestimates the risks associated with combatant sports.

Fortunately, some types of injuries have been reduced or even eliminated by innovations in safety equipment, e.g., facial visors and/or regulations to curb interpersonal aggression. However, from the standpoint of overall levels of safety, one might ask whether such reductions in the frequency and/or severity of injuries are not offset by the increased frequency of injury-producing acts of aggression in sports generally. It is to this question that we now turn.

ARE THE RISKS INCREASING OR DECREASING?

While the attendant costs of being a target of aggression are often high, one might question whether the likelihood of athletes incurring those costs has changed in recent decades. In effect, have sports become more violent? Certainly, expressions of concern about gratuitous violence have not been restricted to the twentieth century (e.g., Guttmann, 1986). But the question of whether the actual play of athletes has recently become more or perhaps less fractious is difficult to answer. Speculation notwithstanding, only a few studies cast light on this important issue [see Smith (1983, pp. 138-141) for a discussion of recent trends in fan misbehavior].

Conveniently, the public record has provided the means to

address the question in the case of ice hockey. Summaries of penalties have been routinely reported in North American newspapers for virtually all games played in the National Hockey League since its inception. Beginning with the 1930-31 season, all aggressive infractions were tallied with nonaggressive penalties, e.g., "too many men on the ice" screened from the calculations (Russell, 1985). The procedure was repeated thereafter at five year intervals, to the present[2]. The updated results are presented in Figure 1.

Mean annual levels of on-ice aggression declined gradually from 1930, through World War II, until shortly after 1945. Thereafter, they climbed steeply to the present, reaching a level more than twice that of 1930 and more than four times that of the immediate postwar years. Since World War II, hockey has presented each successive generation of players with a significantly increased risk of being targeted for aggression. Moreover, a tracking of annual levels of interpersonal aggression for over half a century reveals a fundamental change in the nature of the game. What was earlier a sport played with relatively few aggressive incidents has been transformed into a sport that explicitly features violence.

The question of levels of violence in sports is, of course, distinct from the extent to which violent and/or combatant sports are present in a society. Perhaps the most dramatic recent change has been the upsurge of interest in the martial arts. Scarcely known to earlier generations of North Americans, diverse forms of the sport have appeared and grown rapidly in popularity since World War II (Back & Kim, 1984). A glance at the telephone directory of any North American city reveals literally dozens of studios offering

---

[2]*During the 1987-88 season, game officials were instructed to call more penalties as a means of controlling on-ice violence.*

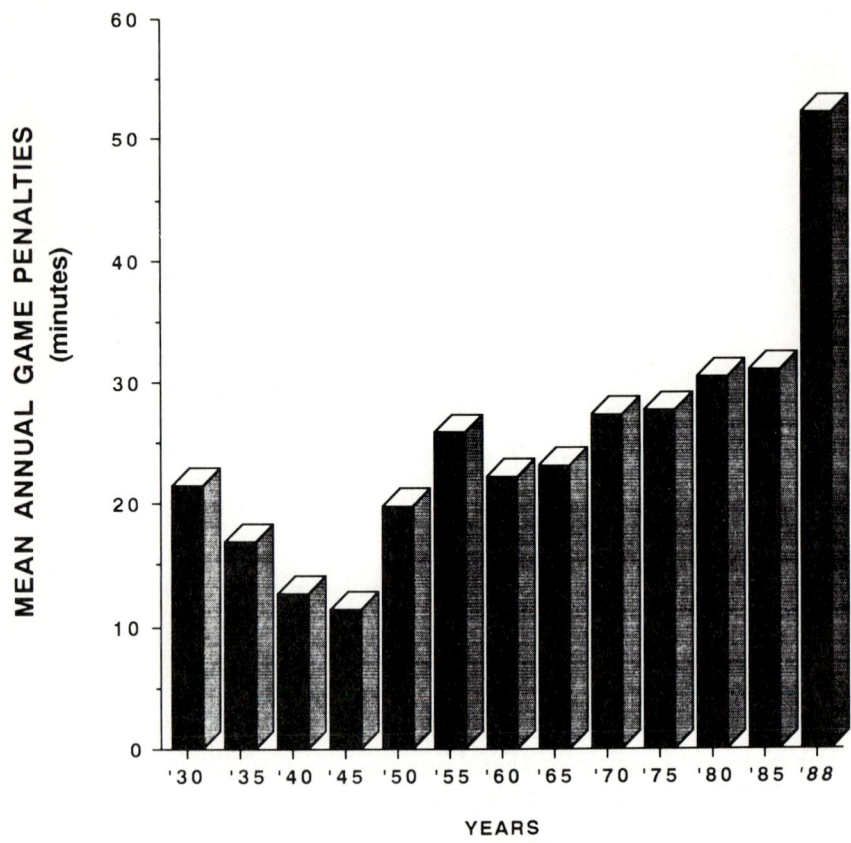

Figure 1. NHL Aggression 1930-'88

training in various martial arts. The most troubling aspect of this development lies in the fundamental changes to the training regimens that have accompanied the arts' introduction to North American markets. The "philosophical" component stressing meditation and the inculcation of Zen values has, in many instances, been de-emphasized or eliminated (Back & Kim, 1984). In short, lethal skills are being taught without benefit of a nonviolent rationale.

The critical importance of the context in which martial arts skills are acquired has been demonstrated by Trulson (1986). His subjects were young delinquents who learned Tae Kwon Do either in the traditional form or in a "modified" version that ignored philosophical elements. Compared to physically active controls, those boys assigned to the traditional regimen became progressively less aggressive over the six months of training; in contrast, those assigned to the modified regimen became more aggressive and more delinquent in their daily activities[3].

Combative skills, then, can be acquired without the learner's becoming more aggressive. However, the philosophical perspective that has traditionally accompanied instruction appears essential to a positive outcome. In general, traditional training results in less aggressive students; conversely, curricula lacking a peaceable component may produce violent practitioners (Nosanchuk & MacNeil, 1989; Trulson, 1986).

Thus, the available evidence, sparse as it is, suggests that the likelihood of being victimized in sports may be greater today than in the recent past. Indeed, the contemporary sports menu may

---

[3]*Trulson does not indicate that subjects were randomly assigned to the conditions of his experiment.*

include more activities capable of yielding anti-social consequences than previous generations. What, then, might account for the apparent growth in popularity of such activities?

THE MOTIVATIONS FOR BEING A TARGET

Traditional theories of motivation have generally accounted adequately for the processes through which people are initially attracted to sports and have also explained why one athlete might persist, and another, retire from a sport. However, for a subset of sporting and leisure time activities, the explanations provided by traditional theories fall short of the mark. Such activities include those in which the athlete assumes a higher than usual risk of injury either at the hands of other competitors or through physical features of the activity's setting. One might ask why some people jeopardize life and limb in deliberately seeking out the dangerous experiences provided by certain sports. Surely, such individuals can just as easily satisfy achievement needs (McClelland, 1987), growth needs (Alderfer, 1972), or intrinsic/extrinsic motivations (Deci & Ryan, 1985) in the vast majority of sports that pose only a nominal degree of danger.

Answers to why some athletes willingly expose themselves to attack or otherwise place themselves in harm's way are partially provided through an individual differences approach. Two models of personality that have provided especially insightful explanations for the attraction to high risk activities are outlined below. The first resulted from the recent efforts of Mosher and Sirkin (1984) to develop a profile of the Macho personality. The second model originated from a more lengthy tradition of theory and research on stress-seeking, well represented by the work of Klausner (1968).

The Macho Personality

Machismo or variants of the original Spanish concept have become a pervasive theme in many contemporary sports. A dominant and culturally-prized trait in Hispanic cultures, machismo has become increasingly emphasized in North American sporting and recreational activities. Examples of macho themes are plentiful. Turnbull and Brown (1977) took pains to describe the "super-males" of Western Canada: "There seems to be a sense of pride involved in living under adverse weather conditions, manifested by the often grossly inappropriate (under)dress for those conditions worn by Saskatchewan males" (p. 77). The authors see these hypermasculine males as a natural outgrowth of the "pioneer/farmer tradition," a tradition in which contact sports are popular and promoted vigorously. The Australian counterpart to the Macho male is the ocker. Everett (1988) captures the essence of the ocker stereotype in describing it as "The pot-bellied, singlet-clad, can-in-hand Australian male" (p. 138).

Hypermasculinity has also served as the subject of several books by contemporary writers, notably Real Men Like Violence (Lewis, 1983) and The Male Machine (Fasteau, 1975). In his book, Fasteau eloquently describes the idealized image of masculinity to which most American men aspire. The importance he ascribes to sport is evident in a chapter being devoted to an analysis of the forces operating specifically within sports to foster and sustain the development of stereotypical male behavior. Sports, then, are seen by popular and academic writers alike as a major proving ground for the development of hypermasculinity.

Perhaps at no time have macho themes found greater cultural expression than in the duelling practice of Mensur that flourished at German universities during the late nineteenth and early twentieth centuries. Swordsmanship and the ritual were rehearsed by young boys in the gymnasium and even by children at play in the nursery. The duel itself was believed to instill coolness and courage in German youth although at least one witness to the Mensur deemed it a brutalizing experience. What follows are excerpts from a particularly lurid, eyewitness account provided by the British playwright and journalist Jerome K. Jerome (1900): "The setting is squalid. The room is bare and sordid; its walls splashed with mixed stains of beer, blood, and candle-grease; its ceiling, smokey; its floor, sawdust covered. The combatants are marionettes. Quaint and rigid, with their goggle-covered eyes, their necks tied up in comforters, their bodies smothered in what looks like dirty bed quilts, their padded arms stretched straight above their heads, they might be a pair of ungainly clock-work figures. During the duel, the whole interest is centered in watching the wounds. They come always in one of two places - on the top of the head or the left side of the face. Sometimes a portion of hairy scalp or section of cheek flies up into the air, to be carefully preserved in an envelope by its proud possessor, and shown round on convivial evenings; and from every wound, of course, flows a plentiful stream of blood. It splashes doctors, seconds, and spectators; it sprinkles ceiling and walls; it saturates the fighters, and makes pools for itself in the sawdust. Doctors--actually medical students--rush in and make deliberately clumsy efforts to repair the wounds. The duel continues: Now and then you see a man's teeth laid bare almost to the ear, so that for the rest of the duel he appears to be grinning at one half of the spectators, his other side remaining serious; and sometimes a man's nose get slit, which gives to him as he fights a singularly supercilious air.

Who emerges as the victor? Paradoxically, he is invariably the fighter with the most extensive and severe wounds. Indeed, the hope of the mutilated victor is that his scars will last a lifetime, a hope likely to be realized thanks to the inept work of the "doctors" attending his wounds. For the victor, social prospects soar as he becomes "...the envy of German youth" and attracts "...the admiration of the German maiden. He who obtains only a few unimportant wounds retires sulky and disappointed" (pp. 153-154). Nor are the financial implications of a gaping wound inconsequential. A purely monetary motive for participating in the Mensur is implicit in Jerome's observation: "Such a wound, judiciously mauled and interfered with during the week afterwards, can generally be reckoned on to secure its fortunate possessor a wife with a dowry of five figures at the least" (p. 154).

The behavior of individuals in freely choosing activities that invite pain and injury has, predictably, drawn a psychoanalytic interpretation. In analyzing adolescent masochism, Sarnoff (1988) describes a tendency among young adolescents to brag about those occasions during which they have experienced pain or extreme discomfort. Exhibiting what Sarnoff refers to as a "Heidelberg-scar mentality" (p. 210), these youths enthusiastically relate anecdotes designed to invite heroic interpretations of what the youths have endured. To be held in awe is reward enough. Sarnoff also sees fraternity pins as a modern day equivalent of duelling scars in that the pins, too, proudly proclaim suffering successfully endured, i.e., hazing!

It was however, Mosher and Sirkin (1984) who first gave formal theoretical expression to the constellation of values and attitudes underlying the behavior of the macho male. The authors proposed a ground-breaking model that identifies three basic components of the macho personality. First, the macho male holds sexually calloused attitudes toward women whereby "...sexual intercourse with women establishes masculine power and female submission, and is to be achieved without empathic concern for the female's subjective experience" (Mosher & Sirkin, 1984, p. 152). This aspect of the macho personality is predictive of several unwanted social behaviors. The macho male is especially likely to be tolerant of rape, sexually coercive (Mosher & Anderson, 1986) and involved in familial violence (Everett, 1988; Lewis, 1983). Second, he believes that verbal and physical aggression is manly behavior and the preferred means of expressing his dominance over other men. This component ensures his easy willingness to target others for aggression and to run the concomitant risk of his being targeted in retaliation. Third, danger is perceived as exciting. The macho man assumes that his masculinity will be reaffirmed or enhanced through demonstrations of survival in a dangerous environment. He tends, among other things, to be impulsive, reckless, fearless, and adventuresome, seeking out new, often risky experiences that allow him to tempt fate. Thus, the conflict endemic to certain sports holds a strong attraction for the macho man, an attraction undiminished by the attendant personal risks.

While Mosher and his colleagues (Mosher & Sirkin, 1984; Mosher & Tomkins, 1988) attribute the origins of hypermasculinity to influences embedded in early parental socialization experiences, later involvement in sports and other peer group activities, e.g., delinquency, can reinforce and further guide the male adolescent in specific ways toward a macho ideal. All-male sports containing elements of physical danger provide an ideal training environment in which the lessons of machismo can be mastered effectively.

To be sure, other theoretical perspectives offer equally valid and insightful explanations of the motivations underlying individuals' participation in sporting activities that expose them to conflict or risk. One of several such perspectives is found in the work of Klausner (1968) on stress-seeking.

Stress Seekers

The topic of stress has proven popular with researchers since World War II. Typically, stress has been characterized as an unpleasant, negative state, the ideal human condition being one that lacks stress, anxiety, or tension. The "natural" and optimum state for people is one of peace and tranquility, with departures from that state setting in motion processes that act to restore the former equilibrium. Klausner (1968), among others, has observed that some individuals do not appear to behave in accord with this homeostatic model. On the contrary, these people often act to increase rather than to decrease the stress in their lives. These stress-seeking initiatives, then, he defines as "...behavior designed to increase the intensity of emotion or level of activation of the organism" (Klausner, 1968, 139). In practice, certain individuals quite deliberately seek out situations in sports as elsewhere, that create tension producing conflicts with others or increase the risk of personal harm.

Sport is but one of several spheres of activity in which people can experience increased arousal. Contemporary sporting activities offer individuals a wide range of often demanding and threatening experiences. The stress-seeker can accept the challenge of rafting a perilous stretch of white water or ascending a peak by a new route. Still others may experience high levels of negatively toned arousal in deliberately provoking others to acts of interpersonal aggression.

Curiously, the critical feature of the model is not arousal per se. That is, the attraction for the stress-seeker lies not in the heightened arousal such experiences provide but in the "drop" that follows the conclusion of the activity. It is this arousal jag (Berlyne, 1960, pp. 197-200), i.e., a jump in arousal followed by a quick return to the former level, that is pleasurable for the stress-seeker. The pre-eminent role of relief rather than heightened arousal is illustrated by Berlyne (1960): "If mountaineers were habitually suspended over abysses for days on end instead of for a few minutes at a time, their number might well be smaller than it is..." (pp. 198-199). Thus, while the activity or interpersonal conflict itself may be aversive, it is the relief that accompanies the termination of the unpleasant emotional state that has a strong appeal for the stress-seeker.

What characteristics set the stress-seeker apart from his or her less adventuresome, less conflict-prone peers? Klausner (1968) offers a profile of the stress-seeker's personality, highlighting three basic features: rationality, egocentricity, and repetitiveness. First and foremost, the stress-seeker is rational and, despite appearances, does not deliberately tempt fate. He does not leap into his sport with reckless abandon; stress-seekers spend an inordinate amount of time in checking the safety of their equipment and rehearsing sport-relevant skills. Egocentricity also defines their behavior. In Klausner's words, they "...may demand center stage" (p. 144). Just as duellists sport their scars and fraternity members, their pins for all who stand to be impressed, so stress-seekers revel in the attention of others. Finally, there is an obsessive quality to their behavior. They return again and again to the stress-producing activity, each time undertaking incrementally greater levels of risk. Are women excluded from the model? Apparently not. The pursuit of risk and interpersonal conflict is not solely a male pasttime; it is also the prerogative of females, although a relatively small percentage of women participate in sports that appeal to stress-seekers. One writer has suggested that the number of stress-seeking outlets is generally limited for women, and, as a consequence "...excitement has to be sought in different channels". She concludes: "There is, then, no reason to believe that women are naturally any less stress-seeking than men, or even, perhaps, less violent" (Bernard, 1968, p. 39).

A Digression

A characteristic common to macho and stress-seeking individuals deserves a few digressive comments. Sportspeople with strong macho and stress-seeking tendencies share an active concern with impression or image-management. Duellists wear their scars with pride, setting hearts aflutter, while skydivers enjoy being photographed in flight. It might be argued that this attraction to the spotlight is sufficiently strong that for some it alone can serve as a motivation to take up sports generally perceived to contain elements of risk and conflict. This assumes, of course, that the spotlight of public acclaim shines more brightly on athletes in these sports, than on those in the more benign sports.

But are there stronger incentives for adolescents to leave their mark in sports than in other spheres of achievement? Does successful participation in violent or hazardous sports earn an added measure of respect? The results of two large scale surveys of U.S. high school students (Coleman, 1961; Thirer & Wright, 1985) provide an ordering of teenagers' priorities. Coleman asked students what they would most like to be remembered for from their high school days. Among boys, the top ranked basis of popularity was "being an athlete." Girls chose "being in the leading crowd," being a "leader in activities," and "being a cheerleader," all well ahead of "high grades, honor role," and "being an athlete." A 25-year replication of Coleman's work (Thirer & Wright, 1985) revealed that females chose "brilliant student" and "most popular" ahead of athletic achievements. Males, however, continue to choose "athletic star" as what they would like remembered in their adult years. Incidentally, these findings are consistent with the earlier observation of Bernard (1968) that females find excitement in non-sporting channels.

Sports containing elements of personal danger may appeal particularly to males whose self-images rely heavily on the admiration of others. A degree of fame may be achieved in any sport. However, success in a contact or otherwise risky sport draws an added measure of admiration. Any potentially negative consequences seem a chance well worth taking. Given a culture favoring risk-taking and news media providing extensive coverage of risky activities, the athlete is guaranteed a quicker, greater and more enduring reputation than might be realized in other less dramatic sports.

The importance of image management was brought home to the writer in the course of collecting data from a high school-age hockey team. Although the league had recently mandated the use of helmets in all games, none was being worn during the pre-game warmup. My question to the team's coach was answered by a nod in the direction of a bevy of giggling girls in the stands. The answer, of course, was that helmets would obscure the players' carefully groomed hairstyles from the sight of their adoring fans.

A GEOGRAPHY OF AGGRESSION

For those involved in aggressive sports, it would be advantageous from several standpoints to know where the risk of attacks is greatest. Are some locations on the playing surface more likely than others to witness attacks between players? If aggression is distributed in a nonrandom fashion, how might that aggression be explained? While the answers to such questions are essential to a comprehensive understanding of the role of situational factors in violent exchanges, there is also a practical side to this line of inquiry. Researchers in sports medicine have demonstrated a continuing interest in not just the "how", "when", and "why" of athletic injuries but also the "where." Two studies, one in football (Garrick, Collins, & Requa, 1977) and the other in ice hockey (Hastings, Cameron, Parker & Evans, 1974), illustrate the importance of identifying the areas of risk for athletes. Garrick et al. (1977) were interested in injuries to football players who ran or were knocked out of bounds during play. Based on analyses of game films, collisions with sideline obstacles were found to occur more frequently in the area of the 50-yard line than in other areas although the distances of player excursions did not vary with field location. The authors' recommendation that a buffer zone be established along the sidelines has been quietly ignored.

In hockey, Hastings et al. (1974) attempted to identify areas of the playing surface that present an increased risk of injury to players. Reports of serious injuries to youngsters playing in organized competition were classified according to three playing zones, i.e., between the blue-lines (center ice), inside the blue-lines and behind the goal keeper's net. An analysis that controlled for the area of each zone revealed that by far the greatest number of injuries occurred behind the net[4]. In contrast, the area between the blue lines was relatively free of injuries. While it is important to pinpoint the location of accidents, one cannot conclude in the absence of estimates of playing time in each zone that the zone behind the net is necessarily more dangerous. That zone may simply see more traffic.

Whether for reasons of injury-reduction and/or controlling

---

[4] $X2(2) = 216.28$, *p. <.001, calculated from tabled data.*

aggression, it is important to athletes, fans and officials in many sports to know where violence occurs. In hockey, fan excesses are confined to the arena (Lewis, 1982) while virtually all player violence takes place on the ice surface. Seldom are players found brawling in the corridors to the dressing rooms or entering the stands to do battle with spectators. Notwithstanding these exceptions, an exploratory study was undertaken in an attempt to determine where on the playing surface interpersonal aggression is most likely to occur.

Senior students were initially instructed in the criteria for judging encounters as provocative and/or aggressive, as well as in the procedures for recording the locations of those encounters. Two judges were assigned to observe play from opposite sides of the arena at each of ten home games of the Lethbridge franchise in the Western Hockey League. A hostile exchange was judged to have occurred if play was stopped because of an actual or impending fight. Thus, confrontations that involved only threats or shoving were recorded: they need not have resulted in a penalty being awarded. The location of each exchange was recorded on a diagram of the rink drawn to scale.

Inasmuch as comparisons of the frequency of aggressive events are made relative to the amount of time play occurs in the areas being compared, the collection of independent baseline data was undertaken. Three league games were videotaped and re-run in a frame by frame analysis of puck location. As there were no between period or between game differences in play location, the amount of time that the puck was in each of four zones was averaged over games.

The results of the analysis of confrontations across four zones is shown in Figure 2. Aggressive interactions are heavily concentrated in the corners (zone # 1) and in front of the net (zone # 2). [$X2 (3)$

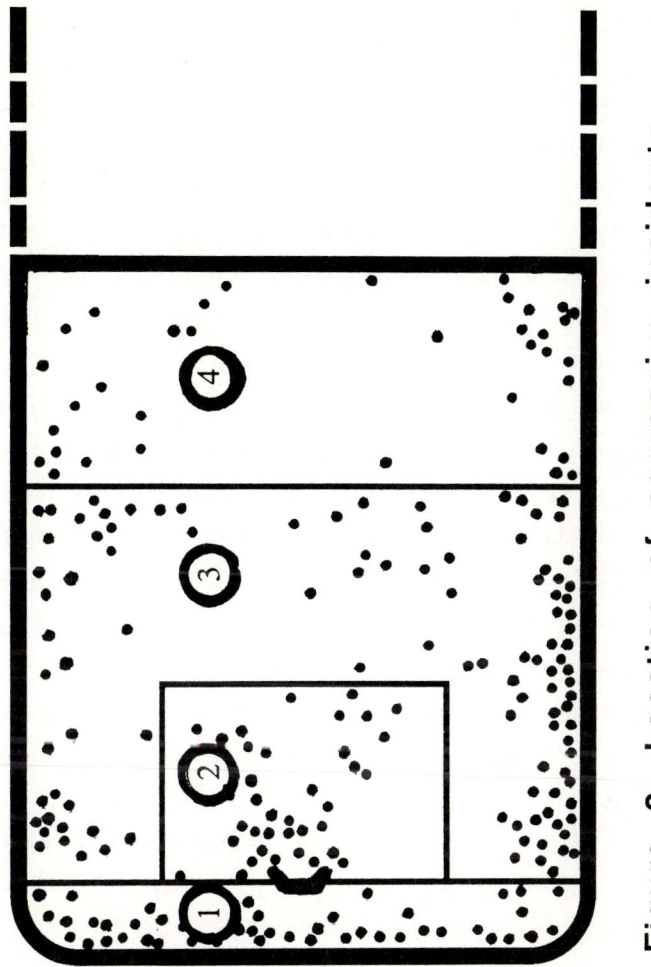

Figure 2. Location of aggressive incidents

= 18.41, p<.001]. Typically, the flow of play is relatively slow along the boards and in the corners, a situation that favors would-be attackers. Not only do slow moving players present an easy target but they can also be hit with great effect in this area of the playing surface. The effects of body checking players against the boards are at least twofold. Starting with the initial check that drives the target on a collision course with the boards, the target sometimes bounces back from the boards to be hit yet again. Thus, it is generally recognized that hits administered in these areas can benefit from a multiplier effect.

The preponderance of aggressive acts occuring in front of the net lends itself to an interpretation based upon the frustrations inherent in goal-mouth scrambles. While the possibility of frustration is removed for the team scoring, continued high arousal and sudden frustration are the lot of the defenders. Conversely, a successful defense of the goal creates frustrations for players on the attacking team.

The location of attacks in other sports will obviously vary with the physical setting and structure of those sports. The boxing fraternity, for example, has long recognized the importance of location in relation to injuries. An old adage admonishes fighters to stay off the ropes and especially out of the corners when they find themselves in difficulty. A slow moving target is all too easy to hit. Lacrosse, water polo and basketball are among a number of sports sharing some of the physical features of ice hockey. It might be predicted that interpersonal aggression in such sports is more likely to occur close to the goal or under the basket, where players are congested, less mobile, and frequently thwarted in their play.

The previous sections have dealt with several questions associated with aggression by opposing players, e.g., the frequency, location and harmful consequences of their attacks. Obviously, participation in many sports exposes the athlete to attacks from additional sources. These attacks may assume a variety of forms, including physical and verbal aggression, threats, intimidation, and character assassination. For athlete-targets, there is the potential for physical, psychological, or even economic harm.

THE ATTACKERS

Given the diverse sources from which attacks on athletes are launched, a schematic diagram may prove useful as a means of facilitating comparisons and for representing several hypothesized relationships. Figure 3 depicts six major sectors from which attacks originate, viz., opposing players, rival fans, the media, home town fans, and two lesser sources - the coaching staff and teammates. Examples of attacks are introduced sparingly, to illustrate each source. Not based on empirical sources, the schematic itself is speculative on my part. It is intended to provide a general overview of sources of attack across a number of major sports. The examples representing the sources emphasize those sports in which violent expressions are lightly regarded, condoned, or considered normative behavior. Beyond that, the diagram will hopefully guide the discussion that follows.

In addition to identifying six sources of attack, the schematic also distinguishes between the major categories of physical and verbal aggression. The intensity of attacks is represented by hypothetical values on the ordinate, the triangular form indicating that the most intense attacks occur toward the apex and are also less common. The area of each triangle represents an estimate of the relative frequencies with which physical or verbal aggression generally arises from each source.

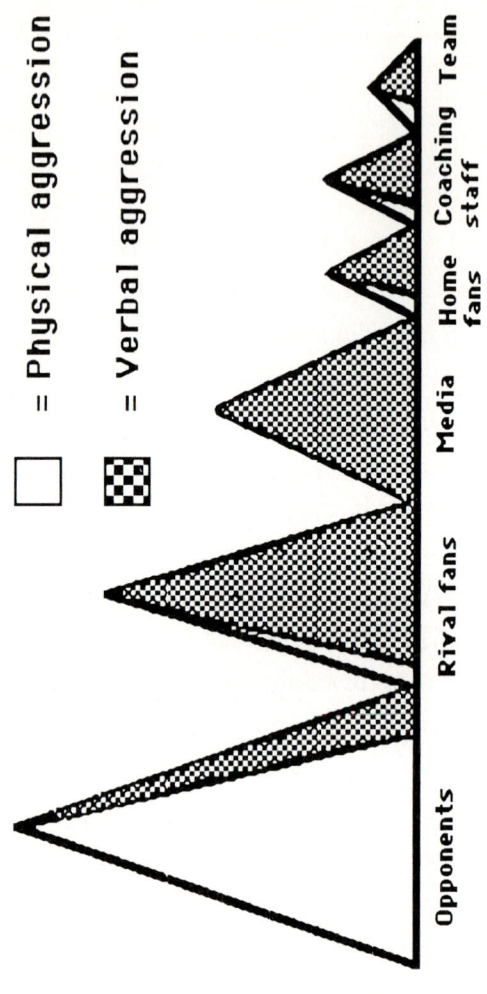

Figure 3. Sources of Attacks

It is proposed, then, that four dimensions characterize attacks on athletes in contact sports: (1) source, (2) type, i.e., physical-verbal, (3) intensity and (4) frequency of aggression. The schematic itself describes the key elements of sports settings in which athletes are open to the aggressive actions of interested others who react negatively to aspects of those athletes' performance.

Opponents

As suggested in Figure 3, the preponderance of physical attacks on athletes originates with opposing players. Moreover, considering the physical conditioning of opponents and the numerous opportunities they have to attack on terms favorable to themselves, the intensity of their assaults is generally greater than those launched from the remaining sources. Consequently, injuries inflicted by rivals during the heat of competition are also among the most severe and debilitating.

Not noted as a violent sport, auto racing provides an interesting example that from a frustration-aggression perspective includes the ideal combination of antecedent conditions for aggression (Baron, 1977; Berkowitz, 1989). Donny Allison was leading Cale Yarborough on the last lap of the 1979 Daytona 500. The lead was relinquished to Richard Petty when the two front runners collided and spun into the infield. When their cars came to rest, Allison and Yarborough immediately began fighting ("Road hog," 1979). In retrospect, both drivers undoubtedly had realistic expectations of victory, however, each was severely thwarted close to the finish line and saw the accident as having been caused needlessly by the other. As some writers have proposed (e.g., Baron, 1977, pp. 87-92), frustration is most likely to facilitate aggression under conditions in which it is severe and arbitrary or unjustified. From a frustration-aggression perspective, the resulting exchange of blows could hardly have been otherwise.

Parenthetically, willful assaults occurring in virtually any sphere of human activity other than warfare generally result in court appearances. Yet sport enjoys an anomalous status whereby aggressors are dealt with far less harshly than allowed under provisions of the Criminal Code. Specifically, the voluntary aspect of the athlete's participation can make the successful prosecution of assault charges and injury suits problematic (Barnes, 1983; Yasser, 1985).

While the majority of attacks by opposing players is physical, opponents also engage in a substantial amount of verbal aggression. Prize fighters frequently taunt each other in the weeks before and during a match; players in many team sports exchange barbs from the bench and at close range during play. Such remarks serve as a tactic intended to anger and/or disrupt the concentration of rivals.

Support for the effectiveness of such tactics is seen in an experiment by Silva (1979). Subjects were required to play a modified three-on-three basketball game with five confederate co-performers. Subjects assigned to a condition in which the confederates exhibited provocative behavior designed to elicit hostility experienced a loss in concentration and lower shooting percentages than subjects in a neutral control condition.

There is, however, another sense in which words can hurt, viz., when words turn to blows. Verbal insults often act as strong provocations for physical aggression. As an instigator of interpersonal aggression, insults may be more effective than some common sources of frustration (Geen, 1968). Thus, what may begin as an exchange of derogatory comments can quickly escalate to physical violence. Once the process is underway, neither party is able to extricate himself easily from the upward spiral of aggressive exchanges (Goldstein, Davis, Kernis & Cohn, 1981).

Rival fans: The fans of one's rival team represent for the athlete a further major source of aggression. Such aggression, however, is overwhelmingly verbal. Threats, jeers, and derision are hurled at the visiting team in a number of mass spectator sports. In some sports, e.g., baseball, basketball, football, soccer, verbal hostility by spectators has long been established as normative behavior and in some cases is openly encouraged by cheerleaders and electronic displays. These activities are promoted as a means of showing support for the home team or as part of an "entertainment package". In such settings, expressions of support for one's team are frequently interpreted by fans to mean hostile actions aimed at visiting athletes. Cheering for the home team then, is often subordinated to abusive behaviors directed at the visiting team.

Athletes are not immune to these attempts to impair their performance (e.g., Greer, 1983; Laird, 1923; Russell, 1983a). An early experiment by Laird (1923) clearly demonstrated the disruptive effects of abusive spectators on performance. Fraternity pledges were engaged in a motor task in the presence of observers who either subjected them to "razzing" or remained passive. Subjects were angered and performed less well in the presence of the abusive audience.

Similar results have been found beyond the laboratory among spectators at hockey and basketball games. Russell (1983a) reported that increases in the size of partisan hockey crowds were associated with corresponding decreases in the performance of visiting players. A similar result has been reported by Greer (1983). The play of visiting basketball teams was found to deteriorate immediately after periods of sustained spectator booing. As common wisdom would have it, a large turnout of supportive and boisterous hometown fans can spur the home team to victory. However, any advantage those fans provide is probably realized not through their encouragement of the locals but through their successful efforts to disrupt the performance of visitors.

Although not commonplace, fans sometimes become physically embroiled with visiting players. Just as spectators can influence the aggression of players (e.g., Borden & Taylor, 1973), so players can influence the aggression of those in the stands (Russell, 1983b). Smith (1983, pp. 168-170) has drawn attention to the reciprocal nature of spectator-athlete influence, noting that 74% of all violent outbursts by hockey fans are preceded by on-ice fights among players. Thus, on those few occasions when angry and abusive fans riot or physically attack players, the targets of the fans' wrath may have unwittingly contributed to the attack through their own aggressive actions.

Attacks can also be premeditated and deferred until an opportune moment. A severe head injury prematurely ended the career of Toronto Maple Leaf hockey star, Ace Bailey in 1933 when he was assaulted in a game by Boston's Eddie Shore ("Fists fly," 1933). Fans arriving for a subsequent benefit match came armed with cans of nuts and bolts!

Media

For many skilled athletes, participation in high level competitions in which the public has a strong interest opens them to the possibility of attacks by the media. Whereas an outstanding performance may receive generous praise, a series of poor results is often met with harsh, sometimes savage criticism. Unrealistic expectations of consistently above average performances by individual athletes or teams are predictably dashed with some regularity. Seldom do the media recognize that below average performances will occur about as often as above average performances. Rather, the athlete's abilities, motivation or character is frequently called into question in the aftermath of an inferior performance. Just such a fate was suffered by golfer Nick Faldo. Acknowledged for many years as one of Britain's finest golfers, he had nonetheless failed to win a major title although he came close in several tournaments. A critical British press dubbed him Nick Foldo. As a footnote, Faldo successfully weathered this and other attacks, recently winning the British Open and the 1989 and 1990 Masters championship at Augusta.

Just as the composer, playright and actor must face the often stinging comments of the critic, so the athlete is a target for the press corps. Obviously, individual performers of any stripe can be personally devastated by attacks that run to the heart of their abilities. These disruptive states run the gamut from anger, anxiety or depression to withdrawal from the sport following severe and/or protracted criticism. Moreover, verbal attacks by the media may be more damaging in their effects than similar attacks by either opposing players or rival fans. Disparaging remarks from the latter sources are seen for what they are, i.e., a tactic intended to hinder the athlete's performance. Virtually no one would regard comments from these sources as a candid or valid appraisal of his abilities. On the other hand, some athletes may perceive sportswriters and certainly their coaching staff as "experts" in their roles as critics. Tactless and unfeeling comments from these sources may be especially hurtful.

There is, however, a further sense in which the media critic may unwittingly foster the inferior performance of his target.

Self-efficacy stands to be undermined by negative feedback from various sources (Bandura, 1982). Failure or a series of failures may weaken feelings of self-efficacy, particularly for those athletes who are already less self-assured. Their situation is worsened by media attacks in cases in which they perceive the media's evaluations as valid. The result is that destructive criticism or outright attacks may, among other things, further undermine self-efficacy and increase the likelihood that sub-standard performances will be perpetuated.

The media, then, are an important source of attacks, albeit exclusively verbal. The harm dealt targets through such verbal attacks is usually not apparent. For the majority of athletes, personal attacks are not taken seriously and have few, if any effects. However, for others, harsh personal criticism may produce a variety of negative effects, some of which are transitory, others may result in long-term emotional scarring. While some among those who have weathered attacks by the media have ultimately proven their detractors wrong, others have withdrawn from their sport. Their numbers are a matter for speculation. However, other Gretskys, Grieses, Hershisers and Jordans are undoubtedly out there; they have just taken other paths. Sports are the poorer for their absence.

Home Town Fans

Like the media, home town fans are often impatient with "their" team or local athletes who turn in losing or substandard performances for any length of time. The fans' impatience easily gives way to hostility: boos, insults and sometimes debris rain on the targets of their anger. While disaffected fans traditionally have distanced themselves physically from a losing effort by absenting themselves from the next home game (Russell, 1986), a modern variation sees fans wearing paper bag hoods as a means of symbolically distancing themselves from failure. In either case, the message is clear.

Although aggression toward their own players tends to be overwhelmingly verbal, there are rare occasions when the wrath of local fans finds physical expression. One such occasion occurred when the Italian national soccer team was eliminated from World Cup play after gaining only a tie in its match against North Korea. Upon returning home, the team members were met at the Genoa airport by 700 of their "supporters". The reception included insults and a barrage of tomatoes ("Italians return," 1966). Angry questions were asked in the Italian parliament in the wake of this "national humiliation". For those fans who choose to show their exasperation through symbolic or aggressive means, the ignoble sentiments implied by their actions are clear. Neither a good effort nor even a respectable showing is an acceptable substitute for winning.

Coaching Staff

Not infrequently, athletes are subjected to verbal and even physical attacks by their own coaching staff. For example, a hockey coach was convicted of assault causing bodily harm after twice punching his 17-year old player in the face. The youth had refused to hang up his sweater in the dressing room ("Coach receives," 1980).

However, there is another sense in which athletes become targets for the aggression of coaches. In several sports, e.g., basketball (Yasser, 1985, p. 22) and hockey, coaches commonly designate one or more players whose principal role calls for them to defend weaker teammates and/or to attack opposing players. The order to attack may be given openly by the coach or understood by the player as operative in certain situations. A traditional coaching tactic has been to set the enforcer on the opposition's star player either to impair the star's performance or to have both players serve penalties. The loss of the less skillful goon leaves his team with a relative talent advantage.

The unquestioning obedience of players to the orders of their coaches invites a comparison with the Milgram (1974) paradigm. The resemblance, however, is at best superficial. The authority of a coach is vastly greater than that represented in the Milgram experiments. Failure to obey the coach can and has ended careers. Also, unlike the passive Milgram learner, the target of an attack can and usually does retaliate. Who, then, is the aggressor in these circumstances, the goon or his coach? I think both. The player commits an act of instrumental aggression; the coach also aggresses instrumentally, albeit indirectly. It can also be argued that the enforcer is a target of his coach's aggression. In ordering his player into battle, the coach intentionally exposes him to the inevitable counterattacks of his victim. While the coach may not relish giving the order, he is nonetheless inflicting certain harm on his player through a willing agent, e.g., the other team's enforcer.

Instrumental attacks notwithstanding, the regnant form of coaches' aggression is verbal. The public perception of coaches in many sports sees them haranguing, bullying and verbally berating their charges. However, the actual extent of locker room aggression by coaches remains an open question. In what is probably an exception, it is heartening to note that Curtis, Smith and Smoll (1979) found punitive coaching practices in only 3% of the Little League baseball teams they observed in the Seattle area.

Teammates

A final, significant source of attack is teammates. For example, Paul Brown, a football coach with 40 years' experience at various levels, has commented that "flare-up" fighting occurred frequently at his practices (Yasser, 1985, p. 14). Other sports may be no different. Consider, for example, the following: during the 1978 season the dressing room of the Los Angeles Dodgers was the scene of a fight between two of baseball's most celebrated and, I would add, immature performers. Teammates Steve Garvey and Don Sutton were attempting to settle their respective claims that they were the better player. History did not think it necessary to record the winner.

There is a sense in which some attacks in this source category might be classified more accurately under "opponents" than under "teammates". Cognitively, teammates may become opponents temporarily when there is competition to make the team or to hold their positions. Players may perceive teammates as opponents until positions are secure; thereafter, they may become teammates.

Fights at hockey practices are also not unknown. The bemused coaching staff see fighting as a means for players to "let off steam"; at the same time those coaches note who gets the best of the scrap. While their cathartic interpretation lacks empirical support (Russell, 1983b), the fact remains that a threatening learning environment is not conducive to developing or refining an athlete's playing skills (e.g., Peters, 1987). The public's perception of teammates striving harmoniously with a common purpose may in some sports be largely illusory.

SUMMARY

The foregoing discussion adopted an approach to sports violence that cast athletes in the role of targets for the aggression of others. An initial section highlighted several studies from the sports medicine and neurological injury literatures that focused on the potentially serious consequences for those who are physically attacked. It was also noted that the media seldom feature the topic of sport-related injuries or medical evidence of the serious long-term costs often incurred by participants in high risk sports. A further question asked whether the potential for injuries arising from interpersonal conflicts in sports has generally increased or decreased in recent decades. The limited evidence on trends suggests that aggression in sports has risen steadily to new heights since the 1940's.

Two theoretical perspectives were examined that account for the motivational forces that prompt some individuals to participate in or continue playing sports that entail an elevated likelihood of pain and injury. Models of the macho personality and stress-seekers were offered as examples of frameworks that account for the attraction of dangerous sports more adequately than conventional theories of motivation.

The practical question of where on the hockey surface athletes are likely to be attacked by other competitors was investigated. A mapping of player confrontations revealed that they are concentrated in the corners and immediately in front of the net. An identification of the sources from which attacks on athletes generally originate was undertaken in a concluding section. A schematic was proposed in which six attack sources were roughly ordered along a frequency continuum ranging from opposing players to teammates. To conclude, diverse elements within the sports world are at liberty to single out athletes as targets for physical and/or verbal aggression with virtual impunity. The harm inflicted by all such sources may be short-lived or have serious life-long consequences for the athlete-target. For a handful of our more violent/popular sports, the full potential costs to participants and to society are excessive and would be unacceptable to people engaged in almost any other area of human endeavor. A Candidesque view of sport persists, a societal view that uncritically equates participation with physical and psychological well-being. A view that more faithfully reflects reality is to be hoped for in the future.

REFERENCES

Alderfer, C. P. (1972). *Existence, Relatedness, and Growth.* New York: Free Press.

Back, G., & Kim, D. (1984). The future course of the eastern martial arts. *Quest, 36,* 7-14.

Bandura, A. (1982). Self-efficacy mechanism in human agency. *American Psychologist, 37,* 122-147.

Barnes, J. (1983). *Sports and the Law in Canada.* Toronto: Butterworths.

Baron, R. A. (1977). *Human Aggression.* New York: Plenum Press.

Barth, J. T., Alves, W. M., Ryan, T. V., Macciocchi, S. N., Rimel, R. W., Jane, J. A., & Nelson, W. E. (1989). Mild head injury in sports: Neuropsychological sequelae and recovery of function. In H. S. Levin, H. M. Eisenberg & A. L. Benton (Eds.) *Mild Head Injury* (pp. 257-275). New York: Oxford University Press.

Benton, A. L. (1989). Historical notes on the postconcussion syndrome. In H. S. Levin, H. M. Eisenberg & A. L. Benton (Eds.) *Mild Head Injury* (pp. 3-7). New York: Oxford University Press.

Berkowitz, L. (1989). Frustration-aggression hypothesis: Examination and reformulation. *Psychological Bulletin, 105,* 59-73.

Berlyne, D. E. (1960). *Conflict, Arousal and Curiosity.* New York: McGraw-Hill.

Bernard, J. (1968). The eudaemonists. In S. Z. Klausner (Ed.) *Why Men Take Chances* (pp. 6-47). Garden City, NY: Anchor Books.

Borden, R. J., & Taylor, S. P. (1973). The social instigation and control of physical aggression. *Journal of Applied Social Psychology, 3,* 354-361.

Casson, I. R., Sham, R., Campbell, E. A., Tarlau, M., & DiDomenico, A. (1982). Neurological and CT evaluation of knocked-out boxers. *Journal of Neurology, Neurosurgery, and Psychiatry, 45,* 170-174.

Coach receives penalty for punch. (1980, July 18). *Winnipeg Free Press,* p. 1

Coleman, J. S. (1961). *The Adolescent Society.* New York: Free Press.

Curtis, B., Smith, R. E., & Smoll, F. L. (1979). Scrutinizing the skipper: A study of leadership behaviors in the dugout. *Journal of Applied Psychology, 64,* 391-400.

Deci, E. L., & Ryan, R. M. (1985). *Intrinsic Motivation and Self-Determination in Human Behavior.* New York: Plenum Press.

Everett, A. (1988). The role of personality in violent relationships. In G. W. Russell (Ed.) *Violence in Intimate Relationships* (pp. 135-148). Great Neck, NY: PMA Publishing.

Ex-boxers face Alzheimer risk, study finds. (1989, April 17). *The Toronto Star,* p. A19.

Fasteau, M. F. (1975). *The Male Machine.* New York: Dell.

Fists fly when Toronto Maple Leafs defeat Boston. (1933, December 13). *Winnipeg Free Press,* p. 16.

Foster, J. B., Tilley, P. J. B., & Leiguarda, R. (1976). Brain damage in national hunt jockeys. *Lancet, 1,* 23-29.

Garrick, J. G., Collins, G. S., & Requa, R. K. (1977). Out of bounds in football: Player exposure to probability of collision injury. *Journal of Safety Research, 9,* 34-38.

Geen, R. G. (1968). Effects of frustration, attack, and prior training in aggressiveness upon aggressive behavior. *Journal of Personality and Social Psychology, 12,* 87-94.

Goldstein, J. H., Davis, R. W., Kernis, M., & Cohn, E. S. (1981). Retarding the escalation of aggression. *Social Behavior and Personality, 9,* 65-70.

Greer, D. K. (1983). Spectator booing and the home advantage: A study of social influence in the basketball arena. *Social Psychology Quarterly, 46,* 252-261.

Guttmann, A. (1986). *Sports Spectators.* New York: Columbia University Press.

Harbaugh, R. E., & Saunders, R. L. (1984). The second impact in catastrophic contact-sports head trauma. *Journal of The American Medical Association, 252,* 538-539.

Hastings, D. E., Cameron, J., Parker, S. M., & Evans, J. (1974). A study of hockey injuries in Ontario. *Ontario Medical Review, November,* 686-698.

Italians return home to a tomato welcome. (1966, July 23). *New York Times,* p. 18.

Jerome, J. K. (1900). *Three Men on the Bummel.* Bristol, England: Arrowsmith.

Kaste, M., Vilkki, J., Sainio, K., Kuurne, T., Katevuo, K., & Meurala, H. (1982). Is chronic brain damage in boxing a hazard of the past? *Lancet, November,* 1186-1188.

Klausner, S. Z. (Ed.). (1968). *Why Men Take Chances.* Garden City, NY: Anchor Books.

Kraus, J. F., & Nourjah, P. (1989). The epidemiology of mild head injury. In H. S. Levin, H. M. Eisenberg & A. L. Benton (Eds.) *Mild Head Injury* (pp. 8-22). New York: Oxford University Press.

Laird, D. A. (1923). Changes in motor control under the influence of razzing. *Journal of Experimental Psychology, 6,* 236-246.

Lampert, P. W., & Hardman, J. M. (1984). Morphological changes in brains of boxers. *Journal of The American Medical Association, 251,* 2676-2679.

Lewis, G. (1983). *Real Men Like Violence.* Kenthurst, Australia: Kangaroo Press.

Lewis, J. M. (1982). Fan violence: An American social problem. *Research in Social Problems and Public Policy, 2,* 175-206.

Marshall, L. F., & Ruff, R. M. (1989). Neurosurgeon as victim. In H. S. Levin, H. M. Eisenberg & A. L. Benton (Eds.) *Mild Head Injury* (pp. 276-280). New York: Oxford University Press.

McClelland, D. C. (1987). *Human Motivation.* New York: Cambridge University Press.

Milgram, S. (1974). *Obedience to Authority.* New York: Cambridge University Press.

Mosher, D. L., & Anderson, R. D. (1986). Macho personality, sexual aggression, and reactions to guided imagery of realistic rape. *Journal of Research in Personality, 20,* 77-94.

Mosher, D. L., & Sirkin, M. (1984). Measuring a macho personality constellation. *Journal of Research in Personality, 18,* 150-163.

Mosher, D. L., & Tomkins, S. S. (1988). Scripting the macho man: Hypermasculine socialization and enculturation. *The Journal of Sex Research, 25,* 60-84.

Nosanchuk, T. A., & MacNeil, M. L. (1989). Examination of the effects of traditional and modern martial arts training on aggressiveness. *Aggressive Behavior, 15,* 153-159.

Pashby, T. J., Pashby, R. C., Chisholm, L. D. J., & Crawford, J.S. (1975). Eye injuries in Canadian hockey. *Canadian Medical Association Journal, 119,* 663-666.

Peters, D. P. (1987). Eyewitness memory and arousal in a natural setting. In M. M. Gruneberg, P. E. Morris & R. N. Sykes (Eds.) *Practical Aspects of Memory: Current Research and Issues* (Vol. 1, pp. 89-94). London: John Wiley & Sons.

Road hog charge causes wild saloon-style brawl after race. (1979, February 19). *The Edmonton Journal,* p. C5.

Roy, S. P. (1974). The nature and frequency of rugby injuries: A pilot study of 300 injuries at Stellenbosch. *South African Medical Journal, 2,* 2321-2327.

Russell, G. W. (1983a). Crowd size and density in relation to athletic aggression and performance. *Social Behavior and Personality, 11,* 9-15.

Russell, G. W. (1983b). Psychological issues in sports aggression. In J. H. Goldstein (Ed.) *Sports Violence* (pp. 157-181). New York: Springer-Verlag.

Russell, G. W. (1985, September). *A History of Professional Hockey Violence.* Paper presented at the meeting of the International Society for Research on Aggression, Parma, Italy.

Russell, G. W. (1986). Does sports violence increase box office receipts? *International Journal of Sports Psychology, 17,* 173-183.

Sarnoff, C. A. (1988). Adolescent masochism. In R. A. Glick & D.I. Meyers (Eds.) *Masochism: Current Psychoanalytic Perspectives* (pp. 205-224). Hillsdale, NJ: The Analytic Press.

Scared Malarchuk expected to die after grisly accident. (1989, March 25). *The Edmonton Journal*, p. G2.

Silva, J. M. (1979). Behavioral and situational factors affecting concentration and skill performance. *Journal of Sport Psychology, 1,* 221-227.

Smith, M. D. (1983). *Violence and Sport.* Toronto: Butterworths.

Thirer, J., & Wright, S. D. (1985). Sport and social status for adolescent males and females. *Sociology of Sport Journal, 2,* 164-171.

Trulson, M. E. (1986). Martial arts training: A novel "cure" for juvenile delinquency. *Human Relations, 39,* 1131-1140.

Turnbull, D., & Brown, M. (1977). Attitudes towards homosexuality and male and female reactions to homosexual and heterosexual slides. *Canadian Journal of Behavioural Science, 9,* 68-80.

Yasser, R. L. (1985). *Torts and Sports: Legal Liability in Professional and Amateur Athletics.* Westport, CT: Quorum Books.

7

Aggression on Roadways
Raymond W. Novaco[1]

Virtually all drivers know the experience of provocation behind the wheel, but our sense of risk and destructiveness associated with driving is, for the most part, restricted to the occurrence of accidents. This is, of course, actuarily sound. Yet in the social consciousness of those living in metropolitan areas, there is some inclination to think of automobile driving on congested roadways as resembling what Thomas Hobbes in the 17th century described as the state of nature, a "war of every man against every man." Although this is hyperbole, there are many indications that aggressive behavior on roadways occurs with sufficient prevalence and in various forms to merit attention as a condition of risk for individuals and communities. In this regard, the roadway aggression

---

[1] *Portions of the manuscript were presented at the meeting of the International society for Research on Aggression, Szombatheley, Hungary, June, 1989. This project was supported by a grant from the Drivetime Foundation, administered through the Institute of Transportation Studies, and by the Public Policy Research Organization at the University of California, Irvine. The author thanks Lion Jacobs and Emily Eggleston for their assistance.*

concept can serve an organizing function as a rubric for otherwise disparate forms of harm-doing behavior that occur in driving situations, all of which have escaped the attention of systematic research.

Studies of human aggression and violence curiously have ignored the roadway context, despite the abundance of research on these general subjects and despite the recurrent association of aggressivity and the automobile. The symbolization of the automobile has commonly incorporated aggressive themes, reflected in car names and marketing images. Both cars and trucks are often used by their drivers as instruments of dominance, and the road serves as an arena for competition and control. Moreover, roadways in metropolitan areas have become contexts where aggressive scripts (mental programming of antagonistic behavior) are activated by driving circumstances. The disposition for aggression, otherwise subdued by the restraining contingencies, palliatives, and gentilities of societal living, becomes engaged behind the wheel, being easily provoked by traffic and the behavior of other drivers. The roadway, whether freeway or surface street, whether urban or rural, is a context where aggressive behavior is potentiated precisely because of multiple disinhibitory influences[2] which will be discussed in the latter section of this chapter.

Regarding the concept of aggression, let it be clear at the outset that I am referring to harm-doing behavior, intended to be so. This is to distinguish occurrences of aggression from other forms of activated behavior in driving. Various types of ritualized

---

[2]*Physiological arousal, anger provocation due to travel impedance, anonymity, opportunity for escape, the automobiles symbolization, cognitive scripts for aggression, and community contagion mechanisms convergently operate to lower restraints on aggression.*

dueling, from hot rod drag racing to frenetic scampers through freeway traffic by hurried drivers jockeying for lane position, might be viewed as preludes to aggression or akin to the stereotyped routines of intra-species animal conflict. However, excitement, acceleration, and the prescribed competition of street cultures do not equate with or automatically convert to assaultive, harm-doing behavior or the threat of such behavior. Aggressivity is not foreign to automobile driving, but predisposing conditions and precursors must be distinguished from behavior intended to cause distress, injury, or damage.

Episodic sprees of freeway shootings in the United States have received extensive media attention, thus there is some tendency to think of roadway aggression primarily in terms of that form of occurrence. However, there are a number of other aggressive behavior forms which occur on the road, and these can be seen to differ in morphological, motivational, and contextual characteristics. In addition to "freeway shootings"[3] or other projectile attacks between drivers, roadway aggression also occurs as assaults with the vehicle as a weapon, roadside confrontations outside of vehicles, sniper/robber attacks by non-drivers, drive-by shootings, and suicide/murder single car crashes. This article provides a typology of these disparate forms and maps them with regard to dimensions of their manifestations so that they may be more clearly differentiated.

Roadway aggression has indeed been a sparse topic in academic literature, yet there has been a pioneering book (Parry, 1968) and a divergence of articles and other books that form the

---

[3]*"Freeway shootings" is being used here as a generic label for the use of firearms from a moving vehicle on a highway where the target is a person in another vehicle or on the side of the road.*

research background. Lacking in these previous works, however, is an organizing conception and an adequate scope of analysis. In fact, most of the real world forms of road aggression that are delineated here have never been addressed previously. I will review the topical background and then differentiate the various contemporary manifestations and their historical precursors. It will be evident that many present day forms of road violence which have the appearance of novelty in fact have long-standing existences.

RESEARCH BACKGROUND

Early British Studies on Road Aggression

The study of aggression on the road was inaugurated commendably by Parry (1968) who conducted a survey and interview project with samples from a London borough. He was concerned with driving safety and essentially believed that accident-proneness was a function of the driver's personality. Aggression and anxiety were the personality factors that he examined for their relationship to accident liability, as well as for their distribution among his samples.[4] Parry gathered questionnaire data on 382 drivers, 55 of whom he then selected for interviewing. The interview sample consisted of subjects with extreme scores (a low group and a high group) on his aggression/anxiety index. He also conducted interviews with various professionals: eleven police officers, five driving instructors, and an unspecified number of insurance men.

---

[4]*Parry obtained three samples in Hornsey: one was produced by stopping the driver of every tenth vehicle at a chosen spot; a second came from registered voters; and a third consisted of motorists who volunteered to complete questionnaires. Very few differences were found between these samples in their questionnaire responses. The subjects were 279 males and 103 females, ranging in age from 17 to 70 years of age.*

Parry's main questionnaire consisted of 75 forced-choice items (50 aggression and 25 anxiety)[5] that were generated from motorists' responses to open-ended questions in a pilot survey (N = 50) and then pre-tested in a preliminary study with a small sample (N = 25). The questionnaire also obtained the respondents' reports of accidents and their severity. Generally, he found that aggressive sentiment was relatively prevalent among drivers, as 9% of the males and 1% of the females had been in a fight with another driver; 7% of the males and 2% of the females had deliberately driven at another vehicle in anger; and 15% of the males and 11% of the females stated that "At times, I felt that I could gladly kill another driver." Aggression scores, quite predictably, were highest for males between the ages of 17 and 35. Importantly, high aggression, with or without high levels of anxiety, was related to higher accident liability.

Approximately eleven weeks after completing the questionnaire, 55 selected motorists were interviewed by Parry, whose interview procedure (one to two and a half hours) included a sentence completion form given at the outset (e.g., "For me to be provoked when driving is...;" "If the traffic-lights change to red as I approach them, I usually...") Parry qualitatively judged that subjects responded consistently to the questionnaire and the sentence completion. In his reports of the interview, the subjects give elaborate justifications for their aggressivity. He states:

> Interview after interview with motorists brought forth expressions of justification for aggressive behavior...Not one of the people interviewed in this category (high aggression, high anxiety) admitted that he was, in any way, the guilty party. Not one admitted to having learnt a lesson as a

---

[5]*Only 45 items (30 aggression and 15 anxiety) are used by Parry as relevant for analysis. He is unclear about the status of the items and does not say how the 45 relevant ones were selected.*

consequence of which he had made a conscious effort towards becoming a better motorist. Almost all agreed that they would again do the same thing in like circumstances" (p. 34).

The relationship between aggression and accident liability that Parry found in his questionnaire and interview data was corroborated in his interviews with the professional sample. As one police inspector said, "Without any hesitation, I would say that most of the accidents I've witnessed in my capacity as a law officer were caused by young people, men, in some aggressive act or another" (p. 50-51). Parry's report of his interviews with the various professionals is abbreviated and without analytic tabulation. Nonetheless, he concluded from them as well that aggressive personalities, dangerous driving, and accident proneness were integrally related.

Parry's descriptive research made no attempt to account for causal variables and was without theoretical direction, and because it appeared outside of mainstream psychological literature, most aggression researchers missed this rich source of ideas for naturalistic studies. Similarly, another major work that escaped attention was Whitlock's (1971) monograph, which involved an archival analysis of mortality statistics from 26 countries, mapping associations between road deaths and various forms of violence. Whitlock indeed emphasized the personality of the driver as a critical factor in road accidents, thus continuing Parry's theme, although developing his own research from a much larger literature spanning driver characteristics, accident proneness, traffic safety, and aggressive behavior.

Whitlock's research was ambiguously guided by theory, but he extensively used aggression concepts (principally, psychodynamic and ethological) to account for obtained relationships between road deaths and violence indices. His hypothesis that the higher the incidence of intrasocial aggression, the higher the rates for death and injuries on the road received support across numerous correlational analyses; however, his analytical method is flawed by failure to control for co-linearity and spurious effects.[6] Whitlock argued that "road violence is one aspect of social violence" (p. 125), and he explained aggression on the road in terms of instinctive drive and territoriality.[7] Surprisingly, his elaborately developed speculation, given after presenting his findings, was not at all articulated with his elaborate introductory chapters concerning psychopathology of drivers, accident proneness, and suicidal tendencies.

The territorial defense thesis, prompted by the writings of ethologists such as Lorenz (1966) and Tinbergen (1951), need not be wedded to ideas of aggressive instinct. Aggression is obviously functional in defending territory, and the automobile is unmistakably a chunk of mobile property, often highly personalized. Marsh and Collett (1986) wrote colorfully about the car as a special territory with personal space zones, the encroachment of which provokes anger and aggression. Yet directly stimulated by

---

[6]*Whitlock used simple correlation and some multiple regression for his statistical methods. His analytical task, however, calls for times-series methodology.*

[7]*He gives an elaborate and quite eloquent rationale for the territorial defense thesis, referring to the writings of Lorenz, Andrey, Storr, Wynne-Edwards, and others in building his argument that aggressivr drives that are normally devoted to the aquisition and protection of home property are transfered to the automobile. Young men, who typically do not own houses or land, are thereby more likely to be aggressive on the road. Whitlock does acknowledge that frustration-aggresion is a viable hypothesis, although he discounts it and others in favor of the aggressive drive territoriality thesis.*

Whitlock's propositions[8], Richman (1972) conducted a participant observation and unstructured interview study of Manchester traffic wardens[9], investigating whether aggressiveness on the road was primarily a function of the driver being male, young, and of low socio-economic status (indexed by size of car). These factors were treated as operational variables for territoriality -- that is, conditions under which road aggression as territorial defense would be potentiated. His categorical data on traffic warden's views of "the errant motorist" found little support for these operational variables. However, among the problems in this study are the status of the respondents and their customary field of observation Although the hypothesis of road aggression as territorial defense can be expected to have boundaries in its range of applicability, it nonetheless merits more sophisticated testing.

---

[8]*This refers to Whitlock's thesis that the absence of real estate produces territorial aggressiveness in conjunction with the automobile, especially for young males of low socio-economic status.*

[9]*These are parking control officers, who in Manchester were a civilian force that encountered friction from both the Police Federation and civil liberties groups. They are males and females, they deal with stationary cars and cannot punish violators beyond a fixed-penalty ticket; and they provoke anger by their assigned duties. Richman's sample of 107 subjects was roughly half male and half female. The problem is that Richman's inferences concern the drivers of automobiles ("errant motorists"), whereas his data are supplied from interviewing these traffic wardens, who are not unbiased or trained observers. Marsh and Collett (1986) also convey that traffic wardens are "regular target(s) for the wrath of drivers" (p. 163) because they challenge the automobile's territory. "British traffic wardens have demanded danger money rather than weapons. At a recent conference in London, their delegation told of how they had been pelted with eggs, spat upon, and drenched with water. One warden told how a motorist had driven a car straight at him and three of his colleagues. Not content with this tactic, the driver made a u-turn and scattered them all again (Marsh & Collett, 1986, p. 164).*

Personality and Accident Liability

Vehicular homicide is the predominant form of negligent manslaughter, comprising over 90% of the cases (Newman, 1978). In a study of 119 vehicular homicides occurring in Columbus, Ohio, over a three year period, Michalowski (1975) found that a significant proportion of the offenders had a prior history of criminal aggression. His analysis was guided by Wolfgang and Ferracuti's (1967) concept of violent subcultures. While 19% of the accident victims had criminal records, 41.5% of the perpetrators had prior criminal offenses, and 36.9% had committed some crime against persons. Of the perpetrators who had criminal records, 89% had been arrested at least once for a crime of violence, and 63% had been arrested exclusively for violent crimes. Finding also that nearly all the multiple violent offenders were multiple traffic offenders, Michalowski confirmed his hypothesis that "perceptions favorable to aggressive behavior influence the way an individual drives as well as the way he behaves in face-to-face interactions" (p. 41). He therefore concluded that violence on the road is linked to violent subcultures as much as is routinely recognized violence.

The accident liability theme of the Whitlock (1971) and the Michalowski (1975) studies, whereby aggressive personality characteristics are associated with road safety risk, had in fact been pursued in earlier research in the psychiatric literature (e.g., Conger, Gaskill, Glad, Hassel, Rainey & Sawrey, 1959; Kole & Henderson, 1966; Schuman, Pelz, Ehrlich, & Selzer, 1967; Selzer, Rogers & Kern, 1968; Tillman & Hobbs, 1949). In this literature, it had been found that accident repeaters had poor control of hostile impulses and have antisocial tendencies. Non-technical works, such as Skillman (1965), often used anecdotal accounts of anger/aggressive dispositions and provocation episodes as accident risk factors. For Skillman, the experience of anger was one type of "vulnerability" for a collision.[10] Impulse expression (anger reactions) in driving situations was found by Schuman et al. (1967) to be related to accident frequency and moving violations among young male drivers, but their criterion data are confounded with number of miles driven. With some exceptions (i.e., Tillman & Hobbs, 1949), this body of psychiatrically oriented research is characterized by weak methodology and rudimentary statistical analyses. Low magnitude correlations without controlling for confounding variables are the typical findings. Consequently, one must wonder about the empirical versus the mythological basis for the linkage of aggressivity with driving safety.[11]

Among the measures encountered in this literature are projective techniques, and "aggression" was sometimes found to be unrelated to driving outcomes. For example, Panek, Wagner, Barrett & Alexander (1978) found that automobile accidents were not associated with Hand Test aggression scores, and insignificant results were also found in later analyses of moving violations for this

---

[10] *Skillman's (1965) book was published by "the Re-Appraisal Society", which is a name that cognitive mediation theorists would find appealing.*

[11] *Quite unfortunately, Whitlock (1971) misrepresents the findings of other authors in a number of places in his book. Egregios errors occur, for example, in his summarization of Conger et al. (1957) when he states that they found "that accident-repeaters showed poor control of hostility and were more overtly aggressive than the accident-free control group" (p. 34). Conger et al. (1957) found no such thing, as they had no hostility control or overt aggression measures. Whitlock (1971, p. 35) also distorts the findings of the Conger et al. (1957) study and the Selzer et al. (1968) study by referring to variables not in those studies and to findings as being significant that are not. In another instance (p.22), he refers to Tillman and Hobbes (1949) as concluding things about "latent tendencies" that they do not say. Other occurences of inaccuracies also appear in the text, which raise doubts about the vigor of Whitlock's book.*

female driver sample (Panek & Wagner, 1986). One psychoanalytic report (Hamilton, 1967) of three case histories involving rear-end collisions was based on extensive psychodynamic data, including projectives, and strongly implicated aggressive themes. Hamilton concluded that the rear-end accidents "may be regarded as an attempt to master the passive fear of anal rape by the father via identification with the aggressor in the striking of another car from behind" (p. 198). These cases were clinically evaluated as having poor internalized controls and extreme difficulties in dealing with aggressive impulses (in addition to chaotic sexual identities, castration anxiety, and latent homosexual fears). That analysis would seem to stretch the boundaries of inferential leaps. In something of the same spirit, Kole and Henderson (1966) developed a "Cartoon Reaction Scale" that discriminated (although not well) problem drivers from nonproblem drivers. The problem drivers (New Jersey point system violators) found the cartoons of driving situations less funny. Although these authors developed their scale as a projective test pertinent to aggression, they oddly never stated the expected direction of their results or provided a logic for differential reactions to the cartoons vis-a-vis aggression and driving behavior.

At the front of this literature pertaining to aggression and driving safety is the early study by Tillman and Hobbs (1949), which was admirably done and showed considerable inventiveness. They pursued the idea of "accident-proneness" that had emerged from a study of British munitions workers after World War I, studies of British bus drivers, and a study of Connecticut drivers which all found that accident liability is not distributed by chance. Tillman and Hobbs, seeking to study the personalities of London, Ontario, bus drivers with high accident records, were thwarted by labor/management problems, so they turned to taxi drivers.

However, unlike the bus companies which had extensive records tallied by the authors, taxi firms kept poor records. Nevertheless, Tillman and Hobbs resourcefully used information from insurance firms and interviews with drivers and managers (cross-checked) to isolate groups of high vs. low accident drivers. Extensive field interviews, observations of driving behavior, and information from criminal justice and social agencies found that the high accident drivers had significantly higher childhood aggression, truancy and disciplinary problems, AWOL rates in the Armed Services, family disharmony, sexual promiscuity, bootlegging on the job, and a number of other dysfunctional characteristics. Their driving habits, compared to the low accident group, were characterized by irritability, distraction, horn-honking, competitiveness, and lack of concern with the mechanical limitations of the car. Being mindful of the methodological weaknesses of their procedure, the authors then compared high accident and low accident male drivers from the general population with regard to frequencies of contacts with correctional, public health, and social service agencies. Although there are unaddressed variable contamination problems in Tillman and Hobbs' use of credit bureau difficulties, social service agency contacts, and even venereal disease records as indicators of personality predisposition for high accidents, the significant findings for Juvenile Court and Adult Court (non-traffic) offenses are corroborative of their findings for the taxi drivers.

Inspired by Tillman and Hobbs (1949) and various social deviance theorists, Macmillan (1975) pursued the hypothesis that motoring offenses and accidents are symptomatic of social maladjustment and deviance. Citing cases of dangerous driving, he argued that these are voluntary acts associated with more generalized risk-taking tendencies. The failure to adjust to society is seen to produce frustrations, and the person's maladjustment carries over to the driver role. He refers to a "temporary accident proneness" that results from emotional stress and the disorganization of skilled functioning. Macmillan's study involved a questionnaire interview with 809 drivers from Croydon, Reading, and Southhampton, which resulted from a random sampling of 1000 license holders in these three towns. The interviews were conducted by Macmillan himself and 27 part-time interviewers. In addition, the records of 12 social agencies were checked for contacts, as did Tillman & Hobbs (1949).

Part of Macmillan's questionnaire concerned driver attitudes. He performed a cluster analysis and identified a set of 15 items that represented a "competitive" approach to driving. It was primarily associated with young males (ages 16-20). Example items are: "I sometimes try to get the better of other drivers;" "It is annoying to be overtaken by an inferior car;" and "I like taking corners as fast as possible." While young male drivers had the highest cluster scores, males across all age groups who were categorized as "competitive" had significantly higher convictions for motoring offenses and higher numbers of accidents. Similarly, his cluster analysis produced a set of 24 items for an "aggressive" attitude toward driving (some overlap with "competitive" items), which also resulted in significant differences for motoring offenses and accidents among males, controlling for driver age. Examples of "aggressive" attitude items are: "It is each man for himself on a roundabout;" "One cannot avoid taking risks on the road today;" "If you are stuck in the wrong lane, you may have to cut across in front of other cars;" "I would rather accelerate than brake to get out of a difficult situation;" and "I would overtake when there are two vehicles in front with no gap in between."

Macmillan's analysis of social maladjustment produced mixed results, as he examined non-motoring convictions, contacts with social agencies, and scores on a social problems index. While there were no effects associated with accidents, there were significant associations for these measures with motoring convictions, and the effects strengthened as the number of convictions increased. Thus, social deviance was not related to accidents, but it was related to motoring offense convictions, which partially supported his social maladjustment hypothesis.

Regarding accident risk, Macmillan primarily found effects related to age and gender; neither education nor occupation were related to accidents. The overall results indicated that it is young males who are fast drivers, competitive, aggressive, and willing to take risks and that these characteristics are associated with accidents and convictions for motoring offenses. He also noted an instability of mood and a tendency to rationalize among drivers; for example, he reports the comments of one driver who said, *"What I think is not always what I do*...what I do depends on my frame of mind at the time and how 'stable' I feel" (p. 138). Like the other British authors who have produced such monographs, Macmillan's work offers a number of suggestions for road aggression research. His interview sampling approach is admirable, and although there were indeed some difficulties with interviewer quality, his questionnaire has many valuable components.

Aggressivity and Drunk Drivers

The themes of driving safety and aggressive personality tendencies certainly converge with regard to drunk drivers, whose histories have been found to be marked by antisocial behavior (McCord, 1984). Public outcry for retribution is indeed strong when drunk driving has lethal consequences for innocent victims. Many people respond to the harm-doing behavior as tantamount to a willful act. Extreme cases, such as that of the intoxicated, wrong way driver who collided head-on with a school bus in Kentucky

(May 14, 1988), killing 24 teenagers and three adults, bring immediate calls for the death penalty. In that case, the defendant was convicted of second-degree manslaughter and several other offenses and was sentenced to 16 years in prison.

While drunk driving is beyond the scope of this paper, the longitudinal study by McCord (1984) focused on the aggressive disposition theme. That study involved a sample of the 466 males from the Cambridge-Somerville Youth Project[12] who were located in 1975 in a follow-up study. Of those men, 36 had been convicted for driving while intoxicated (DWI), although family background data was available on only 18 of them. Discriminant analyses found that those convicted of DWI were more likely to have reported getting into fights and to be more likely to act rather than talk when angry. They also had been "reared in families characterized by conflict, aggression, paternal rejection and paternal alcoholism and criminality" (p. 319). Those convicted of DWI were more likely to have been convicted for serious crimes against property and crimes against persons. McCord concludes, "Their history of antisocial behavior belies a view that these men have inadvertently risked the safety of others during an unaccustomed lapse in self-control" (p. 319).

---

[12]*The Cambride-Sommerville Youth Project, well known to community psychologists, was begun in 1936 as an attempt to prevent deliquency. Seven hundred boys living in those Massachusetts areas began as participants in the original design, which included both "difficult" and "average" youngsters born between 1925 and 1932. Because of problems with staffing and travel during World War II, the program was reduced to 506 boys (252 matched pairs from 466 families, and ultimately only one boy from each family was used in the evaluation). As a primary prevention project, the intervention produced meager results. The McCord (1984) study used data from the 1975 follow-up project which located 98% of the sample and had a 75% return rate on a mailed questionnaire.*

The personality traits of drunk drivers were cluster analyzed by Donovan and Marlatt (1982) who found an aggressive subtype having a significantly higher risk of accidents. They found that some of Parry's (1968) items, along with measures of competitive speed, sensation seeking, and subscales of the Buss-Durkee hostility inventory (Buss & Durkee, 1957) identified this aggressive subtype of risk-enhancing traits.

From the standpoint of targeted aggression, stern societal reactions to drunk driving, especially when there are death victims, stand in contrast to relatively lenient reactions for *deliberate*, assaultive use of one's vehicle (see later section). This is another version of the irony in criminal justice between the intentions versus the consequences of aggressive behavior, as is the case when happenstance (e.g., how fast the paramedics arrive) determines whether the charge is murder or assault. Thus, that Kentucky drunk driver was held responsible for the carnage he produced (as indeed he should), but he did not target those school bus passengers. In contrast, drivers who go on rampages with their vehicles, targeting other drivers, cyclists, or pedestrians, receive relatively light sentences when, by the stroke of luck, they do not kill anyone.

Field Experiments

There have been a number of social psychological field experiments on roadway aggression, and these have understandably used analogue measures of the criterion variable. In nearly all of these studies, horn-honking has been the surrogate measure, prompted by the procedure of Doob and Gross (1968). One exception was the study by Hauber (1980), who used several aggressive driving indices in a pedestrian crossing situation and also followed-up with a provoking telephone call. These quasi-experimental investigations obviously are a large step removed from the harm-doing behavior that alarms communities, however, they do examine variables that plausibly influence serious aggression.

The Doob and Gross (1968) study pioneered this set of investigations, and their project itself was part of the lineage of the *Frustration and Aggression* monograph. Their study focused on the status of the frustrator as an inhibitor of horn-honking. Because high status persons have the power to exercise sanctions, fear of retaliation can be thought to generalize from other situations. They experimentally created a frustrating condition by capitalizing on a familiar traffic scenario -- i.e., a car, stopped at a traffic light, which does not move when the signal changes. Status was manipulated by using two categories of automobile for the stopped vehicle: a new luxury car (a black 1966 Chrysler Imperial) versus an older car (a rusty 1954 Ford station wagon or a grey 1961 Rambler). More honking and shorter latencies of honking occurred in the low status condition. Additionally, as can be expected, male drivers honked more quickly.

The status effect found by Doob and Gross, which also had been obtained in laboratory experiments (e.g., Hokanson & Burgess, 1962), was not replicated by Deaux (1971), although her status manipulation can be faulted for using less than optimal automobiles (an unspecified model Pontiac and a Camaro). Instead, Deaux found effects for the sex of the frustrating driver as more honking and shorter latency of honking occurred when the driver of the stopped car was a female. This was interpreted in terms of "damn female driver" stereotyping. However, neither sex of subject driver nor sex of target driver (here labeled) effects were found in the Chase and Mills (1973) replication effort. These investigators did obtain a status effect, but it was opposite to that of Doob and Gross (1968), although their "high status" car was a 1972 Mercury (model unspecified). Aside from apparent lapses in duplicating the status condition, regional variation in driver attitudes might account for the discrepant findings, since the Doob and Gross study was done in California (Palo Alto), while the other two studies were conducted in Ohio (Dayton and Toledo).

This research methodology was elaborated more fully by Turner, Layton, and Simons (1975), who proficiently incorporated the Doob and Gross procedure, the background of Parry (1968) on aggressive driving reactions, and the aggressive cues concept of Berkowitz (1962; 1973), particularly concerning the debated "weapons effect" (Berkowitz & LePage, 1967). Turner et al., who conducted their three-part study in Salt Lake City, began by administering Parry's driving survey to 93 randomly selected residents in their homes. Finding that there was a sufficient level of anger and aggressive responses in this sample, they then conducted two field experiments of considerably greater complexity than the previously reviewed studies or those which follow. Turner et al. used a pick-up truck for the stopped vehicle and added aggressive cues by means of a rifle in a gun rack and a bumper sticker that said "vengeance" (versus one that said "friend"). They also manipulated victim visibility by either opening or closing a curtain in the pick-up truck's back window. The highest rate of horn-honking (76.5%) occurred in the condition where the curtain was closed and both the rifle and the bumper sticker were present. The rifle itself and its combination with the "vengeance" bumper sticker added to the horn-honking rate compared to control conditions.

Because the rifle and the vengeance sticker were not independently manipulated (the sticker was not present without the rifle), Turner et al. followed with another study. This time those conditions were orthogonal, and the rear window was closed for all subjects in order to minimize inhibitory influences of victim visibility.[13] In addition, male drivers of older vehicles and female drivers were also used, having been excluded from the previous study because they were expected to inhibit horn-honking. Unfortunately, different (and newer) pick-up trucks were used by the confederate victims. The results of this second field experiment were that the combination of the rifle and the vengeance sticker increased horn-honking for male drivers in newer cars while it was significantly lowered for male drivers in older cars. There were no effects for females or for either the rifle or sticker alone. The vengeance sticker was viewed as heightening the aggressive meaning of the rifle, and Turner et al. explained their findings largely in terms of inhibitory processes: ". . . if male drivers of old vehicles perceived themselves to be of lower status than the confederate, they might have inhibited horn-honking as an aggressive response due to fears of retaliation from the high status driver in front of them" (p. 1106).

An attempt to replicate the Turner et al. (1975) results was made by Halderman and Jackson (1979) who found no effects for the presence of a rifle. They conducted their study in Hays, Kansas, using a pick-up truck with its driver obscured from view

---

[13]*With the curtain closed, a honk is arguably even more likely to be merely a signal given to an inattentive driver, rather than an "aggressive" behavior. However, this argument against the validity of the dependent measure does not account for the differences obtained in the experimental conditions--i.e. there is no apparent reason to believe that the presence of rifles and "vengeance: bumper stickers raise the probability of courteous signaling. Also in the Doobs and Gross (1968), Deaux (1971), and Kenrick and MacFarlane (1986) studies, significant effects were found for frequency and latency of horn honking, which argues against interpreting horn honking in the procedural context as merely a signal to the non-proceeding driver.*

by a curtain. They had no status or bumper sticker manipulations, but they added a condition in which a rifle was carried by a pedestrian.[14] However, there were no differences in horn-honking between the no rifle, rifle in gun rack, and pedestrian with rifle conditions. In fact, only 11% of the subjects honked in the 12 second interval for the green light, which is far below the rates reported by the studies discussed above. The authors interpreted the absence of effects as being due to the lessened cue value of a rifle in a rural community where guns are common.

The Doob and Gross procedure was also used in a more recent study by Kenrick and MacFarlane (1986) who utilized this methodology to investigate another phenomenon from the aggression literature -- that is, ambient temperature effects. Just as Turner et al. used this field-experimental paradigm to study Berkowitz's aggressive cues idea and the Berkowitz and LePage (1967) "weapons effect," Kenrick and MacFarlane examined ambient temperature, following the work of Baron and his colleagues (Baron, 1972; Baron & Bell, 1976; Baron & Lawton, 1972). They saw the Doob and Gross procedure as a methodology to balance the control of laboratory studies with the ecological validity of field data. In view of the problems with the Baron and Ransberger (1978) investigation of aggression and heat using archival data (as critiqued by Carlsmith and Anderson, 1979), the field experimental approach was a sensible tact.

Kenrick and MacFarlane (1986) conducted their study in Phoenix and used a 1980 Datsun 200SX with a female driver in the thwarting vehicle. There were no manipulated conditions, as they used a multiple regression design with frequency, latency, and

---

[14]*Halderman and Jackson (1979) refer to Stoltman (1978) as the originator of this procedural nuance.*

duration of honking as criterion variables regressed on temperature, humidity, and assorted subject vehicle characteristics as predictors. Ambient temperature was found to be the best predictor of a composite criterion measure, especially for those subjects having their windows open. A temperature and humidity discomfort index produced similar results. Moreover, they found the relationship between horn-honking and the environmental variables to be linear[15], and this was true across all their criterion measures. Striking effects in this regard were graphed for duration of honking across temperature ranges from 86° to 115° Fahrenheit. Because horn-honking is instrumental to escape, the linearity effect is to be expected in this procedural context.

Before discussing the criterion validity issue pertaining to horn-honking as a dependent measure of aggression, there is one additional study in this field experimental category. Hauber (1980), who conducted his study in some unspecified location in The Netherlands, used several aggressive driving indices in conjunction with an experimentally created pedestrian crossing situation. Stimulated by the work of Parry (1968), Macmillan (1975), and Whitlock (1971), among others, Hauber sought "empirical support for the supposition that there is widespread aggression in road traffic" (1980, p. 462). He selected the pedestrian crossing situation, because pedestrians have legal priority and a driver has responsibility for an accident.

---

[15]*This linearity effect for ambient temperature on aggression stands in contrast to the curvilinear effect found by Baron and his colleagues in laboratory studies, but it is consonant with other naturalistic data for the variables (Anderson and Anderson, 1984; Carlsmith and Anderson, 1979). Kenrick and MacFarlane acknowledge the instrumentality problem of horn honking in their procedure.*

At a predetermined point for an approaching car, an experimental confederate pedestrian entered the crossing. The driver's behavior was dichotomously scored (by an inconspicuous observer) as aggressive or non-aggressive, based on whether they failed to stop, gesticulated/remarked at those in the crossing, or sounded their horn. Hauber does not give the frequency distribution for these response possibilities. After recording the behavior of 966 drivers in this situation, 128 were contacted by telephone for an annoyance-type manipulation (the method for the selection of the subsample is unspecified). In this procedure, an experimenter telephoned the driver twice in succession, persistently asking for a fictitious person. In addition, these telephoned drivers were then sent a letter recruiting them for a personal interview, and amazingly 124 (97%) volunteered.

In the pedestrian crossing situation, the behavior of 25.4% of the drivers was classified as aggressive. Much of this behavior apparently was fist-shaking, invectives, and horn-blowing. However, Hauber said that occasionally the experimenters had to run for their lives." He found no significant differences for male versus female drivers, but there were effects for age (older or younger than 40) standardly found in aggression/violence studies. Younger men were of course more aggressive than older women, but younger women were more aggressive than were older men. The pedestrian's gender also produced the expected effects, as aggression occurred nearly twice as often when the pedestrian was male. Time of day also was significant, with aggression occurring more frequently in the afternoon than in the morning[16].

The second part of Hauber's study involved the telephone manipulation. He reports that those drivers who had telephones were less aggressive in the crossing than those without telephones (21.6% vs. 41.2%), which may be a function of socioeconomic status or age. Because in the Netherlands it is customary for someone answering the telephone to give their name, Hauber was able to verify driver identities indirectly. Aggression on the telephone consisted of "becoming abusive," "banging down the telephone receiver," and "strongly marked irritation" (no procedure is given for coding or reliability assessment). Of the 128 drivers contacted, 14 (10.9%) responded aggressively, and aggressive telephone responding was significantly associated with driving aggression.

In the third part of the study, these telephone-contacted drivers were contacted by letter, requesting a personal interview by the university researchers. The rationale for this interview is unspecified by Hauber (1980), but he reports that 14 persons (11.3%) behaved in an aggressive manner during the interview, although this was not associated with the two prior measures of aggression. Various items of response content related to aggression in the home and to aspects of driving behavior were found to be related to the pedestrian crossing aggression.

The Hauber study incorporated some inventive methodology, although the lack of specificity in procedural description is a considerable liability. Combined with the methodology of Doob and

---

[16]*Consistent with the effect for greater aggression in the afternoon, my own reserach on traffic congestion and stress has found the evening commute to be more aversive than the morning commute and more strongly related to negative mood at home (Novaco, Stokols, & Milanesi, 1990).*

Gross (1968) and that of Turner et al. (1975), there appear to be fruitful ideas in the literature for an experimental procedure for research on roadway aggression, although present-day regulations regarding the use of human subjects are more restrictive than when those studies were conducted. To be sure, horn-honking is easily questioned as an index of aggression, but the use of such surrogate measures and attenuated provocations in doing field experiments is necessitated by ethical considerations. One could forgo experimental manipulation of variables by studying naturally occurring behavior, but aggression on the road is not easily observed and archival data are not without validity problems.

VALIDITY ISSUES IN ROAD AGGRESSION RESEARCH

Conducting research in naturalistic settings does not guarantee external validity any more than one can assume internal validity for a measure like horn-honking. Matters of generalizability always require attention to the actors, behaviors, and settings involved, as simply going to the field is not enough (Dipboye & Flanigan, 1979). While aggressive driving may seem to be a prevalent phenomenon, violent actions are relatively low base rate events, hence naturalistic observation of the various forms of roadway aggression is generally not feasible. The Doob and Gross methodology is appealing because its procedural context models a routine thwarting that does elicit antagonistic behavior and hostility which often are preludes to physical confrontation and violence on roadways; but the criterion validity of the horn-honking measure is the salient issue.

As an index of aggression, horn-honking may be questioned on at least two counts: (1) it alternatively may be a behavior intended as a signal, without aggressive qualities (annoyance, castigation, or threat communication); and (2) even if it is performed as an antagonistic behavior, it is certainly mild, is of little consequence, and is only infrequently related to the acts of road aggression that merit community concern. Everyone knows that drivers do blow their horns in annoyance, as a response to frustrations in road travel, but the use of this measure as an experimental variable requires greater clarification.

The signalling function of horn-honking clearly weighs against its interpretation as a (mild) aggressive act, and this becomes especially ambiguous in the Kenrick and MacFarlane (1986) ambient temperature study. Turner et al. (1975) acknowledged this problem but only dealt with the criterion validity issue by pointing to variations in responding between their conditions of aggressive stimuli. They do say that "...drivers may become frustrated and angry at other drivers, and this anger or frustration can lead to various hostile reactions such as light flashing, swearing, or hand gestures. Presumably, horn-honking might also be perceived as an aggressive response by subjects, especially in the presence of aggressive stimuli" (p. 1106). Such statements, however, justify horn-honking as an *anger* measures more than as an aggression measure and raise the question of whether it is the intention of the honker or the perception of the target that is the issue. Precisely because aggression may remain under inhibitory control, even when anger is aroused to moderate or even strong levels of intensity, the horn-honking measure has transparent shortcomings as an aggression index. Since Turner et al. use inhibition concepts to explain differences in horn-honking rates among their status conditions, the anger vs. aggression distinction made here is all the more salient.

Another threat to validity is presented by cultural and regional variations in horn-honking, which have not been studied empirically but are quite easy to observe with a modicum of travel. In traffic-congested cities (e.g., New York or Rome), horn-honking is quite prevalent yet seems to reflect both the signalling and anger expression functions, rather than be a first step in an escalating aggressive sequence. The driver honks but is primarily interested in moving on, rather than remaining for a protracted confrontation with the offender. Contrastingly, in gentle surroundings (e.g., in certain California cities such as La Jolla or Carmel), horn-honking is deviant and looked at askance. Aggression and anger are very much inhibited, so the blowing of one's horn is done for signalling and rarely at that. The provocative potential of a honked horn is a function of its meaning in the collective consciousness, as well as the immediate situational context. Considering such contextual differences, it is quickly seen that there is variation in the phenomenology of both the target of the honking and the honker which merit validational assessment.

Despite the signalling function, the argument might still be made that horn-honking is oftentimes an antagonistic behavior and that it has a functional relationship to aggressive behavior--that is, it is activated by aggressive cues, its probability is increased by the arousal of anger, and it can be a prelude to more highly antagonistic behaviors in an escalating provocation sequence. As an action having a distant family relationship to aggression, horn-honking is not a behavior that draws community concern about harm-doing, except as a disturbance of the peace in residential neighborhoods or other established behavior settings where tranquility prevails. It significance, then, hinges on its empirical relationship to higher magnitude aggressive behaviors.

Some data bearing on the relationship between horn-honking and other angry or aggressive driving behaviors has been gathered in a questionnaire study that I am conducting, which is still in progress. Here, only a small portion of the data are presented to address the horn-honking validity issue. The subjects are participants in "traffic school," which is a municipal court-approved option for traffic law violators to clear their offense without a fine and without insurance company notification. In Orange County, a driver is eligible for traffic school only once in a two year period, and judges do not grant this option for serious driving offenses (such as reckless driving or multiple violations). Both traffic school administrators and Department of Motor Vehicles officials state that traffic school participants are representative of the normal driving population. While this remains to be substantiated, the background information provided by the questionnaire respondents suggests that although it is a younger population, they do not have an unusually high offense rate.

Four traffic school classes in two municipal courts were involved in the data collection (N=412). The class instructor introduced me as a university professor doing research on aggression and driving behaviors, and then a brief presentation of the research interest was given. Participation was completely voluntary and anonymous. The importance of accuracy and honest responses was emphasized, and after the completed questionnaires were collected, there was a discussion of the research topic and related topics, such as traffic congestion and stress. All indications were that the subjects enjoyed their participation, as there was considerable involvement in the subsequent discussion.

The demographic characteristics of the 412 respondents are that they have an average age of 31.7 years (27.4 yrs. median), were 55.3% male, and 48.1% single (35.4% married). The median length of driving experience was 11 years, and 70.8% drive more than 10,000 miles per year. Their traffic accident history is unremarkable, as 84.6% have had two accidents or less (zero accidents, 34.5%; one accident, 27.7%; two accidents, 22.1%). Counting the present violation, the median number of traffic tickets in the past five years is 1.3, as 65.3% had received two tickets or less and 82.1% had three tickets or less. One can infer that a primary motivation for attending traffic school is to clear the violation so that the driver's insurance company is not notified of the infraction. This is a common understanding, and it is interesting in this regard that, considering the five year median of 1.3 offenses, 79% of the respondents had one violation in the previous year.

The questionnaire inquired about numerous forms of aggressive behavior in driving, with regard to aggression both experienced as a victim and perpetrated as an actor. A full presentation of results is not attempted here, however, some descriptive data on victimization is easily presented. Of the 412 respondents, 150 (36.4%) have had an object thrown at them while driving, 56 (13.6%) have been bumped or rammed, 18 (4.4%) have been threatened with a gun while driving, 5 (1.2%) report having been shot at while driving, and 181 (43.9%) indicate that they have been chased by another driver. The respondents themselves are not without aggression histories as drivers. Forty-eight (11.7%) have thrown an object at another car, 21 (5.1%) have bumped or rammed someone, 5 (1.2%) say that they have threatened another driver with a gun, 3 (.7%) report that they have shot at someone on the road, and 128 (31.3%) have chased another driver. Other indices of aggression concerned verbal arguments and fights, for which 140 (34%) reported having been in an argument where physical violence was threatened and 32 (7.8%) indicated that they had been in a fight with another driver where physical contact was made. Although the rate of aggression is predictably higher for males, a considerable amount of aggressive behavior is reported by females.

Returning to the horn-honking issue, the participants were asked how often they honked their horns *in annoyance* at another driver. Responding to a nine-point scale with verbal anchors at each point ranging from never to daily, the median response was "3 or 4 times per year." A total of 48 respondents (11.9%) gave responses of daily, 2 or 3 times per week, or once per week. The correlation of the horn-honking measure to other items regarding aggression in driving is given in Table 1. Annoyance-motivated horn-honking has small but significant (p < .001) point-biseral correlations with ever having chased another driver and having been in a verbal argument on the road in which physical violence was threatened. It is not significantly correlated with the other more serious acts of aggression, throwing objects, bumping/ramming, threatening with a gun, shooting, and physical fighting. Horn-honking is, however, significantly correlated with other "low grade" aggressive behaviors that are apt to occur in driving (the "hostile reactions" to which Turner et al. referred). Strong relationships were found with shouting or yelling at other drivers, abruptly cutting off other drivers, flashing high beams, deliberately riding someone's bumper, and giving obscene or provocative gestures. These findings suggest that horn-honking is part of a family of annoyance-expressive behaviors whose link to serious acts of aggression is through their escalation potential.

The questionnaire data presented here to address validity issues in the use of horn-honking as a dependent measure in roadway aggression field experiments obviously must also be scrutinized on matters of validity, given the sample characteristics. However, a *Los Angeles Times* poll (Clifford, 1989) of 2,032 residents of Southern California had findings comparable to my questionnaire results on two of the three items having similarity. Their poll results indicated that 5% of drivers carry a gun in their car, while my community sample was 2.9%. Having made an obscene gesture to another driver was reported by 38% in the newspaper's poll, while I found 34.2% to report doing this "once a

Table 1
Correlations of Annoyance Motivated Horn-Honking with Other Aggressive Driving Behaviors

I. Aggressive Driving Behaviors (Ever Performed)	r	p
Thrown object at another driver	.15	
Bumped or rammed another driver	.12	
Threatened another driver with a gun	.07	
Shot at another driver	.15	
Given chase to another driver	.25	<.001
Argument on road threatening physical violence	.26	<.001
Fight on the road with physical contact	.11	
II. Aggressive Driving Behaviors (Scaled Frequency)		
Abruptly cutting off another driver	.45	<.001
Shouting or yelling at other drivers	.30	<.001
Abruptly stopping in front of another car	.15	
Deliberately riding the bumper of another car	.37	<.001
Flashing your high beams at car in front	.45	<.001
Obscene or provocative gestures	.50	<.001

Note. The correlations in section I are point-biseral coefficients, as the tabled aggressive behavior measures are dichotomous variables, while the horn-honking measure is a nine-point scale. Those in section II are Pearson coefficients. The section II variables are scaled with the same units as the horn-honking item. For this simple analysis without covariates, only the higher coefficients are noted for significance.

Aggression on Roadways

year" or less, 20.4% "hardly ever," and 43.9% "never." Twelve percent of the poll respondents reported having had a fight with another driver in the *last year*, with 1% saying the fight was physical. My findings were that 7.8% had *ever* had a physical fight with another driver and 34% had *ever* been in a verbal argument that threatened physical aggression. Differences in questionnaire wording made it difficult to directly compare results on fighting history.

A TYPOLOGY OF ROADWAY AGGRESSION

Aggressive behavior occurs in a variety of forms in the roadway context. Classification is often the first step in scientific analysis, and indeed roadway aggression can usefully be categorized morphologically and differentiated on dimensions that pertain to the dynamics of aggression and victimization. Six varieties of roadway aggression can be identified: (1) roadway shootings/throwings, (2) assault with the vehicle, (3) sniper/robber attacks, (4) drive-by shootings, (5) suicide/murder crashes, and (6) roadside confrontations. Each of these forms has contemporary manifestations, and several have had historical precursors predating the automobile.

These various forms of roadway aggression are presented as a typology in with regard to six contextual factors: (1) *target location*, whether inside or outside a motor vehicle; (2) *aggressor location*, also whether inside or outside a motor vehicle; (3) *target identity*, which may be anonymous or personal; (4) *temporal interval* between (provocation) cue and attack, either immediate or delayed; (5) *intentional quality*, whether premeditated or impulsive; and (6) *traffic relevance*, pertaining to the potential involvement of traffic circumstances (especially traffic congestion) in the aggressive episode. Since aggressive behavior in driving is sometimes attributed to traffic conditions, this factor is hence categorized as relevant or irrelevant. Each roadway aggression form will be described and then discussed in terms of these contextual factors.

The typology is concerned with acts of physical aggression, and thus excludes verbal threats and symbolic gestures. The focus on physical aggression is done for simplicity and because such behaviors generally have more serious implications. However, it is not assumed that physical aggression necessarily results in greater harm than verbal or symbolic aggression. Someone who shoots a gun at another car may only intend to frighten and thus aim above the car, whereas someone making an obscene gesture may cause a fatal collision, perhaps becoming a victim of their own anger[17]. Verbal and symbolic aggression may be involved in any of the six roadway aggression forms given in the typology which distinguishes physical morphological characteristics.

Descriptive classification rather than explanation is the objective here. These diverse forms of aggression on roadways differ considerably in their motivating and activating circumstances, yet they each occur in the roadway context which, given its centrality to everyday life, merits our attention. This classification will hopefully be useful for future studies of aggression. One step in the direction of explanation, however, is attempted by the account of disinhibitory influences given later.

---

[17] *An example of this latter possibility happened to a 62 year old man on the I-395 freeway near Washington, D.C. in 1988. Frustrated by the slow moving vehicle in front of him, he pulled alongside and made an obscene gesture; but the vehichles collided, and the gesturing driver's car jumped a median strip, hit a third car, and fatally crashed into a concrete abutment (Jenkins, 1988).*

Roadway Shootings/Throwings

Considerable publicity has been given to freeway shooting episodes, especially the one that occurred in California in the summer of 1987, which received some international as well as extensive national news coverage. As a contagion episode, the publicity hypothetically contributed to the diffusion of the shootings between mid-June and the end of August, when there were approximately 70 shootings and one serious stabbing on southern California roads reported in newspapers. Over 100 shootings were reported in newspapers throughout the state, and a cursory tabulation was made of them. The incidents were evenly distributed across days of the week, with no distinct pattern for the time of day, although most of the shootings occurred during the afternoons or in the evenings before midnight. Most of the incidents occurred on freeways, but about 25% took place on surface streets. Although males and females were victimized, the victims were males, predominantly. The assailants were all males, with female companions in a few cases. At times there were groups of three or four assailants[18]. The shots were fired from cars, trucks, and motorcycles, although pick-up trucks were involved disproportionally.

The potential public health consequences of this outbreak of violence on regional freeways led the Los Angeles County Department of Health Services to invite the Center for Disease Control to investigate the problem. Onwuachi-Saunders, Lambert, Marchbanks, O'Carroll, and Mercy (1989) reported the findings of this investigation which concerned firearm assaults on Los Angeles

---

[18]*Gang related incidents, known as "drive-by" shhotings are excluded here, as they are separately classified. They, in fact, infrequently occur on freeways, as they are closely tied to matters of territoriality.*

roadways (freeways, highways, and surface streets), excluding gang related incidents and those related to pre-existing domestic quarrels. Their analyses, however, do include brandishing incidents, which represent 54 (39%) of the 137 incidents that they tabulated. They obtained the assault data from regional law enforcement agencies for the summer 1987 episode (June 18 - August 31), comparing this period with 1985 and 1986 data, and also did a simple examination of the association of the 1987 assaults with traffic congestion.

The majority of the firearm assaults occurred on surface streets (63%), with 36% on freeways and 1% on other highways. Of the 137 incidents, seventeen resulted in injuries, two of them fatal. Although the weapon used was not always identified, it was a handgun in the majority of cases (64%), but long guns were also used (15%). From the data available on victim characteristics, the victims were mostly young adult white or Hispanic men. In 38% of the incidents, the victim reported some type of driving confrontation with the suspect (17% were unsure). Being based on victim's reports, that percentage is likely to be an underestimate. My analysis of newspaper accounts, which also rely on victim reports, found that in the majority of cases, there was some prior dispute about road space or privilege.

The analysis by Onwuachi-Saunders et al. of time trends for the June-August 1987 period compared these findings with those for 1985 and 1986, although no statistical analyses were conducted. They found that firearm assaults increased over these years (32, 91, and 137, respectively), and this was also true for the portion on freeways (4, 15, and 49, respectively). The increase occurred for both brandishings and shootings, and the increase in each category is roughly proportional. No inferential statistics were computed (three data points will not do for a time series), but the authors stray from their purely descriptive format when they try to associate the firearm assaults with traffic congestion. Unfortunately their "congestion" index (vehicle miles traveled) is seriously flawed because they do not consider roadway capacity. The spurious nature of their "positive association" with traffic congestion is reflected in their own findings that 69% of the 1987 incidents occurred during non-peak hours of travel (although what is needed here is a conditional probability).

In discussing their findings from a public health standpoint, Onwuachi-Saunders et al. suggest that given the relatively small number of injuries and deaths, the national and local concern about the roadway assaults incidents was misplaced, since over 1000 homicides and 40,000 aggravated assaults occur in Los Angeles County each year. This is indeed a telling comparison. However, they indicate that the full public health impact has not been assessed, considering that the roadway assaults could have affected drivers emotionally, although it is not clear how one would gauge such impacts. In this regard, the media play an important role in how the community is affected during the occurrence of a violence contagion episode, which will be discussed later in terms of disinhibition mechanisms.

Sequential outbreaks of roadway shootings have periodically occurred in other metropolitan areas, and aggression on highways, shootings and non-shootings, occur more frequently than is generally or officially recognized. During 1982 in Houston, when there was a large influx of newcomers and very congested freeways, there were 12 traffic-related homicides. Another dozen of such homicides happened over the next four years, and shootings were more numerous. In one newspaper account during the initial period in Houston, the chief of the major assaults division of the Houston Police Department stated that someone is beaten, stabbed, or shot on an average of 16 times per month, and he estimated that "for every one reported, 40 or 50 go unreported'" (Tempest, 1982). This police division chief also indicated that horn-honking was among the most common causes of traffic violence, which he and others viewed in terms of norm variations between newcomers (who honked) and Houstonians (who took umbrage at being honked).

In the past two years there have been other sprees of freeway shootings in St. Louis and in Detroit, which received far less notoriety than the California 1987 summer contagion. Diminished publicity of such events is indeed desirable, however, my speculation is that the reduction in news coverage was not a function of concern about social well-being but rather a matter of "news" appeal. There is considerably more of that for a "California wacko fad"[19] than for precisely the same behavior in two mid-west industrial cities.

The St. Louis episode began on October 22, 1987, with a homicide, and there were 22 confirmed shootings through December[20]. As to be expected with contagion phenomena, the shootings declined the following year, although there were seven others by June 1988. One was a homicide that involved a protracted escalation between drivers. The Detroit shootings were not as numerous, but they extended over a longer period with sporadic sprees. They began on August 17, 1987 (as the California contagion had cooled), when a man driving a pick-up truck in the left lane

---

[19] *Chicago Tribune* columinst, Mike Royko (*known for his pithy phrases*) said as much in characterizing the California 1987 summer shootings (August 4, 1987). Yet the *Chicago Tribune* gave virtually no attention to the St. Louis shootings in the months that followed.

[20] *This information was obtained from* St. Louis Post Dispatch *news archives and telephone interviews with its reporters. Similarly, the Detroit shooting information was obtained from the* Detroit Free Press *and telephone interviews with reporters.*

was shot by two young men in a Corvette, with whom he had an exchange about passing. Only one other shooting happened that fall (October 21), but then the next year a spree of three shootings and one brandishing occurred during one week in April[21] (including a woman shot in the neck), another took place in August, two happened in two days in November (one was fatal, and the second was a sniping of five cars and one driver), and then two roadway shooting homicides occurred in the following January, 1989. Thus, the wave of shootings on California freeways were not at all unique.

Nor have the incidents of roadway aggression on California freeways abated. Indeed, the number of closely patterned homicides has reduced, and their news worthiness has changed, but the rate of aggressive behavior has not diminished, according to tabulated data obtained from the California Highway Patrol (CHP)[22]. Although the individual incident data must be subjected to detailed analyses, the CHP tabulations of statewide incidents show an upward slope from January 1988, when they began to record "freeway violence" incidents, having then received funds for supplemental personnel from the California legislature. Although the majority of incidents are the brandishing of a weapon or throwing of objects, these forms of aggressive behavior are not inconsequential and the trend is upward. For example, after a rise and decline in the first half of

---

[21]*Curiously, in one <u>Detroit Free Press</u> story (April 19, 1988), a police lieutenant was quoted as saying, "...for years at this time of the year, we get groups of teens driving through the subdivisions shooting out windows of parked cars. Maybe they are getting bolder, and now they are shooting at motorists on freeways." His "rite of spring" explanation, however, falters quickly with the August, November, and January shootings.*

[22]*I thank Commander Susan Cowen-Scott for providing these data which will receive a proper detailed analysis in a subsequent paper. I also thank Officer R. Findlay for his tabulations.*

1988, the CHP tabulations indicate 114 and 98 incidents in July and August of 1988 and then show a steady rise to 250 and 325 for June and July of 1989. There are indeed regional variations, and the data require scientific scrutiny, but the point here is that this respected police agency in no way considers aggressive behavior on roadways to have been a passing fad.

In the roadway aggression typology given in Table 2, roadway shootings/throwings are arrayed with the six contextual factors. Although shootings readily receive media attention, throwings are more common and not necessarily less dangerous. In 1988, according to Associated Press reports, there was a "veggie-tossing" gang in London's East End. One man, who was hit by a turnip thrown from a car, was knocked to the ground, received a broken rib and ruptured spleen, and he died from respiratory problems. Scotland Yard did not find the incident amusing at all. To cite an Orange County, California example, on April 16, 1989, two young Vietnamese men in a sports car were trading insults with four Latinos in a station wagon, as they drove down a city street in late evening. The passenger in the sports car, who was a juvenile, threw a lead pipe at the station wagon, smashing its windshield, which caused it to collide with the sports car, which then crashed into a tow truck stopped at a traffic light. The driver of the sports car was killed.

The targets of this category of roadway aggression behaviors are typically inside a vehicle, although the London man above was a pedestrian, and there have been a number of shooting incidents in California where the victim was on the side of the roadway. Even California Highway Patrol officers have been fired upon, and in 1988 a young Garden Grove woman was fatally shot from a passing pick-up truck in an apparently random attack as she sat inside her car on the shoulder of a highway checking a map.

Table 2
Roadway Aggression Typology

	Target Location	Aggressor Location	Target Identity	Temporal Interval	Intentional Quality	Traffic Relevance
Roadway Shooting/ Throwing	inside (typically)	inside	anonymous	immediate	impulsive	yes
Assault with Vehichle	inside or outside	inside	anonymous or personal	immediate or delayed	impulsive	yes or no
"Sniper"/ Robber	inside	outside	anonymous	delayed	premeditated	yes
Drive-By Shootings	outside (typically)	inside	personal	delayed (typically)	premeditated	no
Suicide/ Murder Crashes	inside	inside	personal	delayed	premeditated	no
Roadside Confrontations	outside	outside	anonymous	immediate	impulsive	yes

The aggressor is inside (or onboard) a vehicle, and the target's identity is categorized as anonymous, because personal identity is typically not a factor in the decision to attack. The temporal interval between provocation or stimulus cue and attack is more or less immediate, and the intentional quality is impulsive rather than premeditated. Because regional conditions of traffic density can create generalized states of frustration and the base rate for aversive driving experiences can be expected to increase with traffic volume, traffic is relevant to this form of roadway aggression, although a traffic *jam* is an unlikely place for a shooting.

Assault with a Vehicle

Using the vehicle as a weapon is an unmistakable form of roadway aggression, although it has received little scholarly attention. Incidents of notoriety, however, are sure to receive press coverage. Among the most notable in the Los Angeles area occurred during the 1984 Olympics, when Daniel Lee Young went on a sidewalk rampage, killing one person and injuring 48. He was judged to be sane and was sentenced to 106 years in prison. Periodically, a truck driver will go on a rampage, as did one on California's Hollywood freeway in 1988 smashing his rig into 23 cars sequentially, which was followed several months later by a similar event in Texas. One very dramatic episode in southern California in 1988 involved a man who took a Caterpillar road grader off a construction site, and after knocking cars, trucks, and a motorcyclist off a highway, drove onto the Chino airport chased by a caravan of police cars and a police helicopter. He turned the huge machine (turbo charged) around many times and began to chase the police cars (about 10). He only smashed one airplane, but did smash into the side of a building, driving 30-50 feet into it. Over 25 bullet holes were found in the cab of the bulldozer, although he received only two thigh wounds. He said that he had had an argument with his wife that morning.

Other than Michalowski's (1975) study of vehicular homicide cases in Columbus, Ohio, discussed earlier regarding aggressive personalities, there is virtually no scientific research done on this topic, British authors have also made contributions that provide some direction in this area. Marsh and Collett (1986) give some mention to deliberate lethal driving, but this topic is specifically addressed in a criminal law review by Spencer (1985). Reviewing cases of British drivers who deliberately drove their vehicles at pedestrians and cyclists, Spencer argues that these persons who have used their vehicles as weapons receive very lenient punishment, because they are treated as motoring offenders -- they are prosecuted for manslaughter rather than murder and typically receive light sentences. However, a cursory review of United States cases heard in various State Supreme Courts and Appellate Courts[23] is at variance with Spencer's contention that those who use their vehicles as weapons do not receive punishment in proportion to the crime.

First, several U.S. courts have maintained that an automobile is a deadly weapon. In several cases, defendants have appealed their convictions of assault with a deadly weapon on the grounds that the automobile is not a "deadly weapon" *per se*. For example, in *Parrish v. the State of Texas* (November 18, 1982), the appellant's arguments were based on Texas Penal Code definitions of deadly weapons. The court found that this contention was without merit and upheld the conviction. Similar rulings occurred in *People v. Claborn*

---

[23] *John Monahan's assistance in locating these cases is gratefully acknowledged.*

(California, January 2, 1964) and in *Blalock v. the State* (Georgia, January 31, 1983), where it was held that "An automobile is not *per se* a deadly weapon, but may become one depending on the manner and means of the vehicle's use" (p. 270).

Secondly, first and second degree murder convictions are not uncommon in U.S. courts. Such judgments have been affirmed on appeal in *Jackson v. the State of Georgia* (May 16, 1957), *People of the State of Illinois v. Nathan Brown* (September 28, 1962), *State of New Mexico v. Reynaldo Montoya* (May 20, 1963), *Tom Blackwell v. the State of Alabama* (May 24, 1956), *State of North Carolina v. John C. Ferdinando* (December 4, 1979), and *Faulcon v. State of Maryland* (October, 1956). The presence of malice aforethought was judged to have been established in these cases, justifying the murder convictions instead of manslaughter. In the *Faulcon v. Maryland* case, the appellant argued both that the vehicle was not a deadly weapon *per se* and that the state penal code only stipulated manslaughter as the crime for causing death by operating a vehicle in a grossly negligent manner. The Maryland Supreme Court ruled against these claims, stating with regard to the vehicle as weapon, "Even though an automobile may not be a deadly weapon, *per se*, yet if it is used in such a wilful or calculated manner to produce death, the trial judge may well find that death was intended" (p. 260). Having found premeditation established, the court upheld the first degree murder conviction.

Three dramatic cases occurred recently in Orange County, California. On Labor Day weekend of 1988, a 37 year old woman was run down by an intoxicated 19 year old driver whom she was trying to halt, because he was driving too fast in an alley near her house. The incident, including her two young sons watching in horror, was captured on videotape by a *passenger* in the car. In May, 1989, the driver was sentenced to 10 years in prison for gross vehicular manslaughter, as the jury had rejected the second degree murder charge. Two months later, another 19 year old was convicted of first degree murder for the 1988 killing of another young man whom he had chased in his car. After knocking down the victim, who was on a motorcycle, the assailant ran over him, then made U-turns to run over him twice again. The U-turns indeed influenced the jury to convict him of murder instead of manslaughter, according to a juror's statement. The third case (February, 1990) involved a ghastly incident in which a jilted suitor parked his car across from the home of his loved one, a young woman who recently announced her engagement to another man. As she entered her car, the spurned lover accelerated at high speed, smashing her car broadside, knocking it over the curb onto a lawn. He then doused her car with charcoal lighter fluid and set it afire with her in it, killing her. Dazed and bloodied, he was caught fleeing the scene on foot.

It is apparent from these various cases of the use of a vehicle (car, truck, and bulldozer) as a deadly weapon, that roadway violence is by no means limited to shooting incidents. This subset of road aggression merits further study, especially since the law review article by Spencer (1985) concerned British cases, which had different judicial outcomes than many U.S. cases.

In the typology, assault with a vehicle is a form of roadway aggression that targets victims who are both inside and outside other vehicles, while the aggressor is obviously inside the vehicle. While target identities are often anonymous to the aggressor, especially in rampaging cases, in several of the court cases cited above, the vehicle assault was a retaliatory attack against someone in particular. This in turn bears on the temporal interval being either immediate or delayed, but even when the assault is temporally removed from the triggering circumstances, the use of the vehicle as a weapon seems to have an impulsive rather than a premeditated quality in most cases. Because various vehicle smashings occur in conjunction with traffic frustrations, the traffic context is seen as relevant, although when target identity is personalized, traffic is irrelevant.

Sniper/Robber Attacks

This form of roadway aggression refers to attacks on motorists by non-motorists. There are no studies in the literature on such behavior, yet it has a long historical tradition. During the 14th century, robbery on the king's highways was a particular cause of worry, hence the tale of Robin Hood. Bellamy (1985) in his analysis of the *Gest of Robyn Hode*, calls attention to the statute of Wincester (1285) which states the official concern with sudden attacks from the woods. Then, "in the later 1340s the king and the judges seem to have been eager to invest highway robbery with greater heinousness than it had hitherto possessed; there was even an attempt to have a particular type of that crime rated as treason. Later in the century a not uncommon afforcement of a highway robbery indictment was a statement the accused was known as a 'common ambusher of roads'" (p. 61). To be sure, most roadway aggressors of this sort, then and now, are not at all of the Robin Hood variety.

Attacks on motorists by non-motorists are common enough, ranging from juveniles throwing stones from freeway overpasses to actual rifle shooting, as occurred in the Detroit contagion discussed earlier, where one man shot at many cars, seriously injuring one driver and hitting five cars. The California Highway Patrol receives several reports every week of someone throwing something from an overpass, but injuries to motorists are rare. However, a 35 year-old man was killed on a Los Angeles freeway (February, 1990) when he was hit by a brick that crashed through his windshield.

In large urban areas, it is not uncommon for motorists who have exited from freeways to surface streets in blighted areas to be set upon by robbers and vandals. Tom Wolfe's recent book *Bonfire of the Vanities* pivots on an event of this kind. More systematically, however, there was a highway robbery contagion in south Florida in 1985 when over 100 motorists were ambushed and robbed on Interstate 95 between Ft. Lauderdale and Miami. The various attackers, who were called "smash and grab" bandits, would select cars stuck in traffic jams or vehicles deliberately disabled by debris put on the roadway. The robber would first throw a heavy object like a brick through the windshield, then rob the driver of purse, briefcase, or wallet. Heavy police patrols and some improved lighting were activated by considerable public alarm[24].

Turning to the typology's dimensions, this form of roadway aggression definitely targets drivers or passengers who are inside vehicles and is perpetrated by aggressors who are outside vehicles. The targets are anonymous, the motivating circumstances are temporally distant, hence the delayed interval categorization, and the intentional quality of the act is typically premeditated. However, some instances of throwing objects at cars and even robbery are likely to be impulsive attacks cued by immediate circumstances. Traffic conditions are categorized as relevant, since stalled, slow-moving, or diverted traffic presents opportunities for sniper/robber attacks.

---

[24]*Information on this highway robbery contagion was obtained from* Miami Herald *archives and interviews with* Ft. Lauderdale News *reporters. I Thank Kevin Davis and Renee Krause for their assistance.*

Drive-By Shootings

This is a form of roadway aggression that has resurfaced in recent years in a highly circumscribed way. In southern California, especially in East Los Angeles and more recently in the Orange County city of Santa Ana, Latino gangs perpetrate homicides from passing vehicles. The behavior is highly related to territoriality and to the subculture's norms of retribution, whereby the drive-by shooting is an act of retaliation. This has become a prototypical aggressive behavior, and during 1988 and 1989 the prevalence has escalated. During 1989, virtually every weekend there was a homicide from a drive-by shooting. Often, the victims are innocent children who are inside the house but are felled by shots aimed at someone on the sidewalk. There were 353 gang violence homicides in Los Angeles County in 1988, and the 1989 total exceeded 400.

The drive-by shooting form seems to have been initiated by New York and Chicago gangsters in the 1920s. In October of 1924, Legs Diamond was gunned down from a car that pulled alongside as he drove down Fifth Avenue. This event is described by Hammer (1975), who also gives an account of a ten-car motorcade with protruding gun barrels that blasted the Capone gang who were in a crowded restaurant in 1926, and this was a retaliation for two drive-by attacks a month earlier. Other accounts of shooting attacks from moving automobiles can be found in Nelli (1976). The famous St. Valentine's Day massacre (*New York Times*, February 15, 1929), which might be thought to be a drive-by, was actually perpetrated by gunmen on foot, although it did occur in a Chicago garage.

Although the contemporary form of drive-by shooting (which is here synonymous with a gang-related shooting from a vehicle) has become quite prevalent in southern California, there are few reports of similar routine elsewhere. It is very surprising that there are no existing studies of this phenomenon in the literature.

The great tragedy of this particular form of roadway aggression is that the victims are often not the targets. The use of semi-automatic weapons and automatic assault rifles by the aggressors has commonly resulted in the shooting of innocent victims inside residential dwellings, sometimes asleep in their beds. The "gang bangers" rack-up new victims every week and are apparently undeterred by the highly publicized tragic deaths of non-targets. A few years ago, drive-by shootings were for the most part restricted to Los Angeles areas, but the phenomenon has moved south and is now prevalent in Orange County.

Regarding the typology dimensions, the targets of drive-by shootings are typically outside of vehicles, often on sidewalks, porches, or inside houses in particular neighborhoods. Some drive-by shootings do target victims in other vehicles, however, as periodically someone is tailed and shot. The targets are typically rival gang members, although there are instances of "random" drive-bys which involve the deliberate shooting of a spontaneously chosen target. In such cases, the victim seems to be someone who was in the wrong place at the wrong time. For example, one man with no gang connections was killed in 1989 in Pacific Palisades as he just happened to be at a cul-de-sac admiring the view, when a car of gang-bangers, well outside of their territory, just happened to be driving by.

Aside from these occasional spontaneous shootings, this form of roadway aggression has a premeditated quality whereby motivating circumstances of retaliation are temporally distant from the situation of enactment. As well, a cruising carload of gang members that "spontaneously" shoots is predisposed to aggress by smoldering turf wars and by recent grievances. The need to maintain territorial control activates vigilance for provocation cues in particular stimulus categories, so their behavior has less of an impulsive quality. Traffic conditions are irrelevant to this road violence form.

Suicide/Murder Crashes

Another type of roadway aggression about which little is known concerns suicide/murder crashes. The work of Phillips (1974; 1979) on suicide and motor vehicle fatalities is the primary research in this area. In a series of studies, Phillips has found suggestive effects of published suicide stories, first with regard to increases in suicide cases and then with motor vehicle fatalities. The methodology for the aggregate mortality data on suicide and homicide used by Phillips (Bollen & Phillips, 1982; Phillips, 1983) has been criticized by Baron and Reiss (1985) to have produced artifactual results, however, the motor vehicles fatality findings appear to be more robust.

Regarding the motor vehicle research (Phillips, 1979), an exhaustive list of front page suicide stories (1966-73) was obtained from the five newspapers in California with the largest circulation, and Phillips then examined their association with subsequent motor vehicle fatalities. The analyses, which controlled for potentially confounding factors, systematically showed the effects of suggestion. Phillips found that motor vehicle fatalities increase markedly right after publicized suicides (not before); the magnitude of the increase is correlated with the degree of publicity; the increase is geographically localized in association with the published story; single-vehicle crashes are most affected; age of suicide victims and age of driver are linked; and stories about *murder and suicide* tend to be followed by multiple vehicle crashes involving *passenger* deaths. This latter discriminant association is relevant to concerns about artifactual findings. Phillips' research indicates that suggestion and modeling influences affect violent behavior on roadways, but in light of the critique of Baron and Reiss (1985), the hypothesis merits a rigorous time series investigation.

The dynamics of this form of roadway aggression are likely different from that found in the other forms, although this remains a matter for research. Those engaging in this behavior may indeed have aggressive histories, perhaps even aggressive driving histories. On the other hand, this means of suicide may simply be a matter of convenience. A seven-year-old girl in Los Angeles who miraculously survived her mother's suicide/murder crash attempt (July, 1988) reported that her young mother turned to her and said, "I'm sorry I have to do this," then drove off the road at a high rate of speed into Malibu Canyon.

Regarding the typology dimensions, suicide/murder crashes are easily categorized. The targets are inside a vehicle, as even when the suicidal driver intends to kill someone not in his own car, the other person is unlikely to be a pedestrian, since such collisions tend to have insufficient force to kill the driver. The target identity is personal, and the motivating circumstances are temporally removed from the aggressive act, which would seem to be premeditated. Traffic conditions are not relevant to the instigation, although one might suppose that suicidal crashes would not be perpetrated during peak traffic periods.

Roadside Confrontations

Traffic disputes that are extended by the participants outside the vehicle are here called "roadside confrontations." In these events, one of the disputants may have a weapon in their vehicle, which they retrieve only after the conflict escalates and they are not able to terminate the other's aversive behavior by verbal persuasion or threat. Following a dispute about road space or privilege, one driver may force another off the road or may simply be in a position to stop and thereby impede the other's movement, setting the stage for confrontation.

This type of roadway aggression may also occur in conjunction with the sprees of roadway shootings that appear as community contagions. For example, during the California 1987 summer episode, there was a stabbing in Newport Beach that left a man in critical condition after two men who were on a motor scooter began to scuffle with two men who had been in a Corvette. The following January, an irate motorist got out of his car to confront another motorist, who was a pregnant woman. He pushed her against the freeway railing, punched her, and tried to throw her over the railing but was deterred by six passing motorists who received humanitarian awards. Similarly, there were two serious injury (one fatal) roadside confrontations that were extensions of traffic disputes which occurred during the Detroit episode in late 1988 and early 1989. The man who died was pursued off the Interstate after he and his companions made obscene gestures. He died from kicks to the head and neck. In the other case, the man was forced off the road and was very badly slashed with a knife. Such events suggest that the observed increases in roadway violence during community contagions are more than mere "copy cat" behaviors, since the actions involved are not replications of random shootings on open freeways.

One striking illustration in this roadway aggression category is the case of Arthur Salomon, a Wall Street investment banker and the grandson of Percy Salomon, one of the founders of the Salomon Brothers. This prominent 52 year-old, seemingly model citizen, shot an unarmed college student on June 19, 1987 in a road dispute on the Hutchinson River Parkway (Stone, 1987). The conflict began with some friction over the right to pass on the freeway. It escalated to verbal exchanges on the side of the road and ended with the shooting of the young man by Salomon, as the victim was walking back to his car, saying that he had the license plate of Salomon's Mercedes. Mr. Salomon is reported to have been under strain at the time and was also highly involved with law enforcement hobbies. Although he was known to be stubborn, he was also well-known for his generosity, and he loved to work in his garden (Stone, 1987). Thus, here is a case of a distinguished citizen becoming ensnared in a road dispute, using a gun that he carried for protection to shoot an unarmed person who was walking away.

In the typology set forth, roadside confrontations have both the aggressor and the target outside of vehicles. The target's identity is anonymous, the temporal interval is immediate, and the intentional quality is impulsive. Traffic conditions are often relevant to the conflict, as restrictions in road space lead to disputes about right-of-way and impedance of movement.

Theoretical Perspective: Disinhibition of Aggression

Roadway aggression can usefully be understood in terms of the disinhibition of aggression concept, which can be traced to the classic *Frustration and Aggression* monograph (Dollard, Doob, Miller, Mowrer, and Sears, 1939), was used by Turner et al. (1975) to explain their horn-honking effects, and is an integral part of the social learning perspective of Bandura (1983). Since Bandura's account of acquisitional mechanisms centrally involves observational and symbolic learning, the combination of those processes with the disinhibition concept allows for the explanation of diffusion or contagion phenomena which hypothetically have occurred for roadway shootings in various communities and have been postulated by Phillips (1979) to have occurred for suicide car crashes.

Community sprees of roadway assaults appear to be a form of violence contagion, bearing similarities to urban rioting in the 60s or to airline hijackings before airport security systems were installed. Violence contagion is a rapid social transmission of aggressive behavior. The spreading of a novel behavior throughout a social system is a diffusion process that is facilitated by communication channels. The diffusion of new ideas or innovations (kindergarten, modern math, health practices, fashion, etc.) has been studied by communication theorists such as Rogers and Shoemaker (1971) who examined structural and personality factors affecting rates of adoption. Hypothetically, the California summer 1987 episode was a diffusion pattern, and a similar process occurred in the Houston and St. Louis shootings. The cluster of over 100 freeway ambushes in South Florida on Interstate 95 in 1985 when gridlocked or deliberately disabled vehicles were set upon by assaultive robbers was apparently another contagion instance.

The central concept is the disinhibition of aggression - the weakening of restraints against harm-doing. One mechanism for disinhibition is exposure to unpunished aggressive behavior by others, especially if there is some novelty involved. However, our society has many disinhibitors or releasers that override the otherwise inculculated prohibitions against aggression. Cinematic portrayals, alcohol or drug use, violence-prone subcultures, the erosion of community values, etc. can combine with the anonymity of freeways, the likelihood of escape, and carrying firearms in vehicles to lessen inhibitions. The physiological arousal induced by driving a car, per se, as well as by exposure to thwartings in transit, contributes to the override of inhibitory factors in a context that is conducive to aggressive responding. Road violence is a product of weakened social controls and personal controls, which can act in concert with arousal-inducing environmental circumstances, such as traffic congestion, work pressures, or family strain.

The spread of violence as a contagious phenomenon was discussed by LeBon (1895/1960) in his classic work on group behavior. He saw human groups as being in a state of expectant attention, susceptible to suggestion, and as thinking in terms of images, which can evoke destructive impulses. A crowd is influenced by example, and imitation was viewed by LeBon as a natural tendency. For him, contagion was a fundamental and powerful process by which ideas, sentiments, and emotions spread. However, he gave no account of contagion mechanisms, except to allude to microbial analogy and refer to imitation. Behavioral contagion as a group phenomenon was later examined by Redl and his associates (Polansky, Lippitt, & Redl, 1949) as behavior change occurring in social interaction that is linked with impulse expression. In historical writings on emotion, the idea of contagion can be found in Hutcheson's (1742) treatise on "passions."

The contagion concept has been utilized in analyses of increases of criminal violence (Berkowitz & Macaulay, 1971), urban rioting (Mazur, 1972; Midlarsky, 1978), and aircraft hijacking (Bandura, 1983; Holden, 1986). The basic concept in these analyses is the social diffusion of violence. Bandura, following his research on observational learning of aggressive behavior (Bandura, 1973), later approached the contagion effect in terms of symbolic modeling whereby new behavior is spread by a salient example. Observational learning is also the basis for how Berkowitz and Macaulay (1971) account for the sharp increases in violent crime following the Kennedy assassination in 1963, the Speck murder of 8 nurses in Chicago in 1966, and the Whitman shooting of 45 persons from the University of Texas tower in 1966. Various occurrences of copycat violence, or what the French sociologist, Tarde, in 1890 called "suggesto-imitative assaults," have often been reported following major crimes and movie theater showings of violent films.

Midlarsky's (1978) mathematical analysis of the contagion of urban disorders also conceives of the spread as an observational learning process.

It is not enough to understand contagion in terms of modeling influences. Wheeler (1966) argued that contagion was a social influence process mediated by restraint reduction. He asserted that contagion would not occur unless restraints were reduced - i.e., the lessening of fear, guilt, and regret for engaging in the behavior. Conditions of deindividuation or the feeling of anonymity were also thought by Wheeler to reduce restraints.

Disinhibition of Aggression During Driving: Multiple Influence Channels

As suggested above, roadway violence has many determinants and a roadway violence contagion is a community phenomenon of social transmission and escalation of an aggressive behavior prototype. The diffusion of the "innovation" can be understood in terms of communication processes, norms, and other social system variables as have been delineated by Rogers and Shoemaker (1971) regarding the adoption of other innovative practices. The focus here, though, is not on the social transmission but on the psychological processes entailed in particular aggressive behaviors, with disinhibition as a central concept. Modeling influences through mass communication channels is one disinhibiting influence that affects imitation or adoption of a prototype behavior. However, the modeling effects hypothetically act in conjunction with other converging facilitators, such as the physiological arousal associated with driving, the anonymity of freeways, escape potential, cinematic scripts that have pre-programmed the mind, alcohol or drug abuse, the occurrence of thwartings by "inconsiderate" drivers that "justify" aggression, and the carrying of firearms, which under conditions of arousal and anger can activate aggressive counter-responding. Such factors act as releasers that override the otherwise inculculated prohibitions about aggressive behavior.

Given that aggressive behavior is restrained by social norms and by legal penalties in the general case, and that this is quite specifically so in driving situations, the delineation of disinhibiting influences is a plausible approach to understanding various forms of aggression on roadways. The following categorization of multiple influence channels is a step in this direction.

Physiological Arousal

The activation of physiological arousal systems increases the probability of impulsive behavior by over-riding restraints and heightens the probability of aggression by constituting a precondition for anger. Although anger is neither necessary nor sufficient for aggression, the role of anger as an activator of aggression has been unmistakably demonstrated in experimental laboratory research, and it is quite clearly a core ingredient of both individual and collective violence (Novaco, 1986). Physiological arousal is a defining property of anger; and as the theory and research of Zillmann (1971; 1983) has shown, arousal which has not been induced by anger provocation can add to that which has been provoked by annoying or irritating circumstances, thereby increasing the probability of aggression. Zillmann has called this process "excitation transfer." Thus, the transfer of excitation or arousal from non-provocation sources enhances or intensifies the experience of anger and the occurrence of aggression in some immediate situation where the person's emotional experience and behavior are guided by environmental stimuli linked with antagonism. Konecni

(1975) has shown that cognitive "labeling" or arousal as anger is central to the enhanced aggression effect[25].

Driving an automobile involves many conditions of arousal activation. Merely driving a car is arousing. Passing, braking, turning, attending to other cars, unexpected occurrences, etc. are even more potent activators of arousal. Extensive research on human factors in automobile driving has demonstrated this quite clearly (cf. Stokols & Novaco, 1981). The research that Stokols and I have conducted with regard to chronic exposure to traffic congestion has found highly significant increases in baseline blood pressure, lowering of frustration tolerance, increases in negative mood, and aggressive driving habits to be associated with traffic exposure in long distance commuting. Moreover, we have found highly significant stress effects for travel impedance on both a physical or objective dimension and a perceived or subjective dimension. This is described further in the next section.

The Transportation Context of Driving

Very little is known about the prevalence of hostile reactions while driving. Turner et al. (1975) found that 23% of the men and 18% of the women stated that they are easily provoked when driving. Actually chasing an annoying driver was reported by 12% of the men and 4% of the women. A higher prevalence for chasing was found by Marsh (1986), who reported that a study in Scotland found that 25% of drivers in the 17 to 35 age group admitted

---

[25]*Koneci (1975) found that arousal-inducing physical stimulation (averse auditory tones) heighten aggression when conjoined with psychosocial aversiveness. Conditions of insult provided a "cognitive label" for the combined arousal state (aversive tones and aversive interpersonal interaction), resulting in greater retaliatory aggression than for insult alone or for auditory aversiveness alone (very loud and complex tones).*

chasing drivers who had offended them. This is very comparable to the results of my own surveys which for university students found 29.6% reported having chased someone (for males, the rate was 42.9%) and for community drivers, 31.3% had chased someone. From several studies, then, a significant number of drivers report strong negative feelings regarding road situations, and such anger or irritation may lead to actual physical aggression.

Traffic congestion has become a conspicuous and bothersome feature of the urban landscape. As an inevitable constraint on mobility in metropolitan areas, traffic congestion is now a major concern of communities throughout the United States and abroad, although congestion as a hindrance to mobility is not unique to automobile travel, having also occurred with horse-drawn vehicles in ancient Rome and in many 19th century European and American cities (Smerk, 1974). Our research on traffic congestion as a stressor that impacts well-being (Novaco, Stokols, Campbell, & Stokols, 1979; Novaco, Stokols, & Milanesi, 1990; Stokols, Novaco, Stokols, & Campbell, 1978; Stokols & Novaco, 1981) has examined transportation experience in the interactive context of personality, residential, and employment variables in addition to travel conditions.

Traffic congestion is viewed as a stressor in terms of the concept of *impedance,* a behavioral constraint on movement and goal attainment. We have operationalized impedance as a physical or objective dimension in terms of the distance and time parameters of commuting and with regard to exposure to road interchanges as nodes of congestion. We also have examined impedance as a perceptual or subjective dimension in terms of perceived aspects of travel constraints. Both the physical and the perceived dimensions of impedance have been found to impair personal well being, job satisfaction, and quality of home life, and we have developed an ecological model for understanding these effects (Novaco et al, 1990). Our research has shown that the transportation environment is reciprocally linked with characteristics of home and work environments, as well as with personality factors. We have also found that seemingly "low stress" personalities can be strongly affected by high impedance commuting.

Among our research procedures with Irvine industrial area commuters was a questionnaire measure of impatient/antagonistic driving habits. This involved 16 forced-choice items concerning behavioral tendencies in traffic situations (e.g., responses to a yellow light at an intersection, someone cutting in front, someone following too closely, having to yield the right-of-way, someone not moving when a stop light changes, and so on). A summary index of impatient/antagonistic responses to these sampled situations was significantly correlated with a number of stress and anger measures obtained from a variety of methodologies (physiological, performance, and self-report) and at several different points in time. In addition to being significantly associated with diastolic blood pressure, anger, impatience, low frustration tolerance, negative mood on arrival home, and alcohol consumption, the driving habits index was also positively correlated with level of education ($r = .23$, $p < .03$) and socio-economic status ($r = .31$, $p < .004$). Consequently, one should not think of antagonistic driving as a working class, aggressive subculture phenomenon. Moreover, our findings on the driving habits variable reflect environmental influences, because persons who were otherwise *not* time-urgent, impatient, or hostile[26] had high impatient/antagonistic driving habits scores when they were also high impedance commuters.

The traffic context can shape driving dispositions over the long-term, thereby making aggressive responding more prepotent. Elevations of arousal, negative mood, and impatience work against restraints on aggression, which are further weakened by the anonymity of roadways and the escape potential provided by the automobile. Characteristics of anonymity indeed mark the experiences of urban dwellers (Milgram, 1970), and it has been theorized by Zimbardo (1969) that conditions of anonymity (along with group presence and altered responsibility) can produce a state of deindividuation that raises the probability of impulsive, irrational behavior. Although some laboratory aggression experiments simulating deindividuation conditions have had mixed results (Diener, 1976; Diener, Dineen, Endresen, Beaman, & Fraser, 1975), it seems more than plausible that a driver's lack of social connectedness to targets of aggression, relative concealment of identity, and the ability to escape by speeding away and exiting all lessen the restraining influences of social norms, social controls, and personal controls.

Cognitive Scripts of Aggression

Roadway assaults are in part a product of personal experience and exposure factors that script the individual towards aggression and lower restraints against harm-doing. Elements of the social fabric that have led to a desensitization towards violence and

---

[26]*The **personality** factor was coronary-proneness Type A/Type B variable, as measured by the Jenkins Activity Survey (cf. Stokols et al., 1978). Type As scored significantly higher than Type Bs on the driving habits index in our low and medium impedance conditions, but the reverse was true for high impedance subjects.*

the presence of violence-prone subcultures add to the facilitation equations. Drive-by shootings, for example, are a routine behavior for Southern California gangs. The regular occurrence of such incidents may further establish freeway shootings in the repertoire of other drivers, or the gang behavior itself might be transposed to freeways and to other targets. The mock war games being conducted in wilderness areas with thousands of sport combat participants (many of whom are white-collar professionals) shooting paint balls at one another certainly does not diminish the concern about disinhibition and the recurrence potential of roadway shooting contagions.

In situations where there are salient cues for aggressive behavior, cognitive scripts of aggression embedded in the experience of the individual can potentiate an aggressive behavior chain. The psychological idea of a script pertains to how social information is cognitively represented and organized (Abelson, 1976; Bower, Black, & Turner, 1979; Higgins, Herman, & Zanna, 1981) and has alternatively been called a "social episode" by Forgas (1979; 1986), referring to cognitive representations of stereotypical interaction sequences. Forgas (1986) has begun to study implicit representations of aggression situations for understanding everyday reactions. The script idea, however, was implied in Toch's (1969) analysis of violent men, for example, when he wrote that violence was habit forming, viewed violent incidents as composed of stages, and asserted that offenders saw themselves as participants in violent games. "Most importantly, they start seeing elements of past violent encounters as they approach fresh situations and begin to respond routinely" (p.186). An elaborate model of cognitive scripts for aggression has also bee developed by Huesmann (1988).

The concept of an aggressive script then is that of a mental programming of antagonistic behavior in a particular context whereby situational cues activate various subroutines for an actor's responses. Automobile driving is indeed impregnated with cues linked to aggressive scripts. In addition to the themes of automobile symbolization, traffic context, anger provocation, and personal histories of aggression previously discussed, there have been countless media portrayals of aggression in driving scenarios-- for example, the prototypic chase scenes of *Bullitt* and *The French Connection*.

Exposure to scripts which suggest or even legitimize violence have reduced inhibitions as well as programmed the mind with mental images. The modeling effects of media portrayals of violence surely are not irrelevant. I am not saying that someone tails and blasts at other motorists simply or mostly because of watching too many movies with hyped-up chase scenes or avenging angel storylines. Of course, it's more complicated, and to be sure it involves the breakdown of community values and the relative improbability of punishment for violent behavior. Yet we might understand the road assaults as an antisocial dramaturgy played out with tragic consequences. Combined with other disinhibitory influences, cognitive scripts for antagonistic behavior may be particularly potent in driving situations, making aggression difficult to deter (cf. Huesmann, 1988 regarding retrieval processes).

Criminologists have argued that criminal sanctions are too distant and too improbable to deter offenders and that "punishment" has the least effect on those we want to punish most. With regard to the roadway assaults, the force of their argument depends on who is doing the shooting. If the freeway shooter is someone who is otherwise violent and law-breaking, it cannot be expected that he will be much deterred by new laws or even broadcasts of increased police presence[27]. However, if the prospective shooter is someone who is otherwise law-abiding and has a gun in the car for protection or someone not ordinarily violent but is considering "having some fun," then legislative and law enforcement responses may have a sobering influence. People do not rationally calculate the probability of getting caught or suffering the consequences (an argument used by deterrence opponents against harsher penalties), and a media report of one arrest may deter those whose inhibitions can be activated when there are no tangible rewards to over-ride them. Legislative responses reported in the media may be a visible way to operationalize community concern and disapproval of the deviants' behavior, thereby affirming community norms and leading to internalized personal control. Some freeway shooters described their actions as only intended to scare the victims--as if the bullets would never hit anyone. Perhaps this is a fiction used to exonerate themselves, but it may be that they did not comprehend that real people were involved who would be harmed. Destructive impulses must be kept in check by convergent inhibitory forces.

On the other hand, expressions of community concern, publicized arrests, and judicial penalties have had little, if any, deterrence effect on drive-by shootings southern California. The "accidental" killing of young children by stray bullets that penetrate the walls of their homes and the deaths of numerous innocent bystanders evidently have not induced sentiments that can compete with violence subculture norms. Even condolence-givers leaving the home of a recently slain person's family were themselves fired-upon and critically wounded. The development and maintenance of these

---

[27]*Despite the augmented police patrols, less than 10 arrests were made in more than 100 shootings, which translates to better than a 9 in 10 chance of escaping.*

subcultural norms beckons for study, particularly in view of the contemporary ethnic specificity of this aggressive behavior script -- i.e., this is primarily a Latino gang phenomenon. There are many Asian gangs in the region, but they do not do drive-by shootings. And although there are periodic instances of drive-bys done by Caucasians or Blacks, this form of road aggression is today a Latino gang trademark.

Contagion Mechanisms

The diffusion or contagion effects of mass media communication were discussed earlier. Calls for media downplay of violent incidents are commonly heard, and this seems relevant to slowing the social transmission; yet the media have a responsibility to report the news. However, there has been curious variation in the length and positioning of road shooting stories. During the California contagion, stories of freeway shootings gradually moved off the front page, partly by editorial judgment and partly displaced by other news. To illustrate, on August 26, two months after the shootings began, an arrest of an injury shooting suspect and the death of a victim of another shooting received two small paragraphs of coverage in the *Los Angeles Times* on an interior page. In contrast, a shattered window incident early in the episode received a full story on a regional front page.

Some acts of road violence may be attempted for publicity, but very few have this calculating quality, being instead of an "impulsive" nature. The stimulational and suggestive influence of the media seems unmistakable, as does the commercial value of sensational stories. However, the effect of media reportage on roadway aggression remains to be demonstrated. One experimental study (Greenberg & Wotring, 1974) of exposure to television violence on driving behavior found no effects, although both the violence exposure and the driving elements were simulations performed with driver education students. In contrast, a naturalistic but correlational study by Smith (1969) found that aberrant drivers tended to watch violent television programs. Although there is obviously a dearth in research on viewers' roadway behavior, a different tact could be taken by focusing instead on media personnel behavior and decision-making.

One way to investigate the hypothesized role of the news media in the social transmission of roadway aggression during a contagion episode would be to study the behavior and decisions of those who construct news stories. In addition to an exacting analysis of all regional newspaper stories and videotapes of television news broadcasts, interviews might be conducted with each of the reporters of road aggression incidents, as well as with editorial decision-makers (e.g., assistant city editor, city editor, news editor, and managing editor). Such interviews could examine how the news item comes to their attention, what makes it "news," how they pursue the story, what factors determine the aspects of the story that are reported, and how it is reported. Their views on the role of media reporting as a mechanism of contagion could be examined directly in terms of policy decisions.

SUMMARY

Aggressive behavior has had a recurrent association with automobile driving reflected in our symbolization of cars and trucks, as well as being rooted in psychosocial experiences on congested roadways. Dramatic occurrences of violence such as freeway shooting episodes have been thought to be idiosyncratic events but instead need to be understood in their historical and phenomenological context. Freeway shootings are only one type of aggression occurring on roadways and are in no way unique to any regional area.

A typology of six types of roadway aggression was presented, mapping the range of contemporary forms of this behavior with regard to various characteristics of targets, perpetrators, and context. Most of these roadway aggression forms have received sparse academic attention, despite having high social and scientific relevance. A theoretical perspective on the determinants of roadway aggression was also offered.

The concept of disinhibition was central to this analysis of roadway aggression. The disinhibition of aggression was seen to result from multiple influence channels associated with physiological arousal, traffic context, aggressive scripts, and contagion mechanisms linked with the mass media. Modeling and suggestion are thought to have an important role during the diffusion of an aggressive behavior prototype.

Findings from previous research and from an ongoing survey project on road aggression indicate that antagonistic behavior in driving is relatively prevalent and that provocative and self-endangering actions are perpetrated by both male and female drivers. While it would be an exaggeration to say that antagonism and aggression are a routine part of automobile driving, the findings of the preliminary surveys indicate that such behavior is not uncommon. The topic of aggression on roadways merits continued study independent of shooting contagions. In addition to field experiments and archival data studies, it is suggested that news reporting behavior and decision-making be examined.

REFERENCES

Abelson, R. P. (1976). Script processing in attitude formation and decision making. In J. Carroll & J. Payne (Eds.) *Cognitive and Social Behavior*. Hillsdale, NJ: Laurence Erlbaum Associates.

Anderson, C. A., & Anderson, D. C. (1984). Ambient temperature and violent crime: tests of the linear and curvilinear hypotheses. *Journal of Personality and Social Psychology, 46*, 91-97.

Bandura, A. (1973). *Aggression: A Social Learning Analysis*. Englewood Cliffs, NJ: Prentice Hall.

Bandura, A. (1983). Psychological mechanisms of aggression. In R. G. Green & E. I. Donnerstein (Eds.) *Aggression: Theoretical and Empirical Reviews, Volume 1*. New York: Academic Press.

Baron, R. A. (1972). Aggression as a function of ambient temperature and prior anger arousal. *Journal of Personality and Social Psychology, 21*, 183-189.

Baron, R. A. (1976). The reduction of human aggression: A field study of the influence of incompatible reactions. *Journal of Applied Social Psychology, 6*, 260-274.

Baron, R. A. and Bell, P. A. (1976). Aggression and heat: The influence of ambient temperature, negative affect, and a cooling drink on physical aggression. *Journal of Personality and Social Psychology, 33*, 245-255.

Baron, R. A. and Lawton, S. F. (1972). Environmental influences on aggression: The facilitation of modeling effects by high ambient temperatures. *Psychonomic Science, 26*, 80-83.

Baron, R. A. and Ransberger, V. M. (1978). Ambient temperature and the occurrence of collective violence: The "long hot summer" revisited. *Journal of Personality and Social Psychology, 36,* 351-360.

Berkowitz, L. (1962). *Aggression: A Social Psychological Analysis.* New York: McGraw-Hill.

Berkowitz, L. (1973). Words and symbols as stimuli to aggressive responses. In J. F. Knutson (Ed.) *Control of Aggression: Implications from Basic Research.* Chicago: Aldine.

Berkowitz, L. and LePage, A. (1967). Weapons as aggression-eliciting stimuli. *Journal of Personality and Social Psychology, 7,* 202-207.

Berkowitz, L. and Macaulay, J. (1971). The contagion of criminal violence. *Sociometry, 34,* 238-260.

Bower, G. H., Black, J. B., and Turner, T. J. (1979). Scripts for memory in text. *Cognitive Psychology, 11,* 177-220.

Buss, A. H. and Durkee, A. (1957). An inventory for assessing different kinds of hostility. *Journal of Consulting Psychology, 21,* 343-349.

Carlsmith, J. M., & Anderson, C. A. (1979). Ambient temperature and the occurrence of collective violence: A new analysis. *Journal of Personality and Social Psychology, 37,* 337-344.

Chase, L. J. and Mills, N H. (1973). Status of frustration as a facilitator of aggression: A brief note. *Journal of Psychology, 84,* 225-226.

Clifford, F. (1989). Traffic or no, we love our autos. *Los Angeles Times,* October 4, 1-3.

Conger, J. J., Gaskill, H. S., Glad, D. D., Hassel, L., Rainey, R. V., and Sawrey, W. L. (1959). Psychological and psychophysiological factors in motor vehicle accidents. *Journal of the American Medical Association, 169,* 1581-1587.

Deaux, K. K. (1971). Honking at the intersection: A replication and extension. *Journal of Social Psychology, 84,* 159-160.

Diener, E. (1976). Effects of prior destructive behavior, anonymity, and group presence on deindividuation and aggression. *Journal of Personality and Social Psychology, 33,* 497-507.

Diener, E., Dineen, J., Endresen, K., Beaman, A., and Fraser, S. (1975). Effects of altered responsibility, cognitive set, and modeling on physical aggression and deindividuation. *Journal of Personality and Social Psychology, 31,* 328-337.

Dipboye, R. L. and Flanigan, M.F. (1981). Research settings in industrial and organizational psychology: Are findings in the field more generalizable than in the laboratory. *American Psychologist, 34,* 141-150.

Dollard, J., Doob, L., Miller, N., Mowrer, O., and Sears, R. (1939). *Frustration and Aggression.* New Haven: Yale University Press.

Donovan, D. M. and Marlatt, G. A. (1982). Personality subtypes among driving-while- intoxicated offenders: Relationship to drinking behavior and driving risk. *Journal of Consulting and Clinical Psychology, 50,* 241-249.

Doob, A. and Gross, A E. (1968). Status of frustrator as an inhibitor of horn-honking responses. *Journal of Social Psychology, 76,* 213-218.

Forgas, J. P. (1979). Multidimensional scaling: A discovery method in social psychology. In G. P. Ginsburg (Ed.) *Emerging Strategies in Social Psychology.* London: Academic Press.

Forgas, J. P. (1986). Cognitive representations of aggression. In A. Campbell & J. Gibbs (Eds.) *Violent Transactions: The Limits of Personality.* Oxford: Basil Blackwell Ltd.

Greenberg, B. S. and Wotring, C. E. (1974). Television violence and its potential for aggressive driving behavior. *Journal of Broadcasting, 18,* 473-480.

Halderman, B. L. and Jackson, T. T. (1979). Naturalistic study of aggression: Aggressive stimuli and horn-honking: A replication. *Psychological Reports, 45,* 880-882.

Hamilton, J. W. (1967). The rear-end collision. *Journal of the Hillside Hospital, 16,* 187-204.

Hammer, R. (1975). *Gangland U.S.A.* Chicago: Playboy Press.

Hauber, A. R. (1980). The social psychology of driving behaviour and the traffic environment: Research on aggressive behaviour in traffic. *International Review of Applied Psychology, 29,* 461-474.

Higgins, E. T., Herman, C. P., and Zanna, M. P. (1981). *Social Cognition: The Ontario Symposium, Volume I.* Hillsdale, NJ: Laurence Erlbaum Associates.

Holden, R. T. (1986). The contagiousness of aircraft hijacking. *American Journal of Sociology, 91,* 874-904.

Huesmann, R. (1988). An information processing model for the development of aggression. *Aggressive Behavior, 14,* 13-24.

Hutcheson, F. (1942). An essay on The nature and conduct of the passions and affections. Gainesville, Florida: *Scholars' Facsimiles and Reprints,* 1962.

Jenkins, K. (1988). Fatal Va. crash follows obscene gesture. *Washington Post*, December 7, D3.

Kenrick, D. T. and MacFariane, S. W. (1986). Ambient temperature and horn- honking: A field study of the heat/aggression relationship. *Environment and Behavior, 18,* 179-191.

Kole, T. and Henderson, H. L. (1966). Cartoon reaction scale with special reference to driving behavior. *Journal of Applied Psychology, 50,* 311-316.

Konecni, V. J. (1975). The mediation of aggressive behavior: Arousal level versus anger and cognitive labeling. *Journal of Personality and Social Psychology, 32,* 706-712.

LeBon, G. (1895/1960). *The Crowd.* New York: Viking Press.

Macmillan, J. (1975). *Deviant Drivers.* Westmead, U.K.: Saxon House, D. C. Heath Ltd.

Marsh, P. and Collett, P. (1986). *Driving Passion.* London: Jonathan Cape.

Mazur, A. (1972). The causes of black riots. *American Sociological Review, 37,* 490-493.

McCord, J. (1984). Drunken drivers in longitudinal perspective. *Journal of Studies on Alcohol, 45,* 316-320.

Michalowski, R. J. (1975). Violence in the road: The crime of vehicular homicide. *Journal of Research in Crime and Delinquency, 12,* 30-43.

Midlarsky, M. I. (1978). Analyzing diffusion and contagion effects: The urban disorders of the 1960's. *American Political Science Review, 72,* 996-1008.

Milgram, S. (1970). The experience of living in cities. *Science, 167,* 1461-1468.

Nelli, H. S. (1976). *The Business of Crime.* Chicago: University of Chicago Press.

Novaco, R. W. (1986). Anger as a clinical and social problem. In R. Blanchard & C. Blanchard (Eds.) *Advances in the Study of Aggression, Volume II.* New York: Academic Press.

Novaco, R. W. (1989). *Automobile Driving and Aggressive Behavior: Effects of Multiple Disinhibitory Influences.* Paper presented at UCLA Symposium, "The car and the city," April 9-10, 1988.

Novaco, R. W., Stokols, D., Campbell, J., and Stokols, J. (1979). Transportation, stress, and community psychology. *American Journal of Community Psychology, 7,* 361-380.

Novaco, R. W., Stokols, D. S., and Milanesi, L. (1990). Objective and subjective dimensions of travel impedance as determinants of commuting stress. *American Journal of Community Psychology, 18, 231-257.*

Onwuachi-Saunders, E. C., Lambert, D. A., Marchbanks, P. A., O'Carroll, P. W., & Mercy, J. A. (1989). Firearm-related assaults on Los Angeles roadways. *Journal of the American Medical Association, 262,* 2262-2264.

Panek, P. E. and Wagner, E. E. (1986). Hand Test personality variables related to automotive moving violations in female drivers. *Journal of Personality Assessment, 50,* 208-211.

Panek, P. E., Wagner, E. E., Barrett, G. V., and Alexander, R. A. (1978). Selected Hand Test personality variables related to accidents in female drivers. *Journal of Personality Assessment, 42,* 355-357.

Parry. M. (1968). *Aggression on the Road.* London: Tavistock.

Phillips, D. P. (1974). The influence of suggestion on suicide: Substantive and theoretical implications of the Werther Effect. *American Sociological Review, 39,* 340-354.

Polansky, N., Lippitt, R., and Redl, F. (1950). An investigation of behavioral contagion in groups. *Human Relations, 3,* 319-348.

Redl, F. (1949). The phenomenon of contagion and "shock effect" in group therapy. In K. R. Eissler (Ed.) *Searchlights on Delinquency.* New York: International Universities Press.

Richman, J. (1972). The motor car and the territorial aggression thesis: Some aspects of the sociology of the street. *Sociological Review, 20,* 5-25.

Rimm, D. C., deGroot, J. C., Boord, P., Heiman, J., & Dillow, P. V. (1971). Systematic desensitization of an anger response. *Behavior Research and Theory, 9,* 273-280.

Rogers, E. M. and Shoemaker, F. F. (1971). *Communication of Innovations.* New York: The Free Press.

Schuman, S. H., Pelz, D. C., Ehrlich, N. J. and Selzer, M. L. (1967). Young male drivers: Impulse expression, accidents, and violations. *Journal of the American Medical Association, 200,* 1026-1030.

Selzer, M. L., Payne, C. E., & Westervelt, F. H. (1967). Automobile accidents as an expression of psychopathology in an alcoholic population. *Quarterly Journal of Studies on Alcohol, 28,* 505-516.

Selzer, M. L., Rogers, J. E., and Kern, S. (1968). Fatal accidents: The role of psychopathy, social stress, and acute disturbance. *American Journal of Psychiatry, 124,* 1028-1036.

Skillman, T. S. (1965). *Road Safety.* London: Reappraisal Society.

Smerk, G. M. (1974). *Urban Mass Transportation: A dozen Years of Federal Policy.* Bloomington: Indiana University Press.

Smith, J. R. (1969). Television violence and driving behavior. *Educational Broadcasting Review, 3,* 23-28.

Spencer, J. R. (1985). Motor vehicles as weapons of offence. *Criminal Law Review*, January, 29-41.

Stokols, D. and Novaco, R. W. (1981). Transportation and wellbeing: An ecological perspective. In I. Altman, J. Wohlwill, & P. Everett (Eds.) *Human Behavior and Environment: Advances in Theory and Research, Volume 5*. New York: Plenum Press.

Stoltman, J. J. (1978). *Naturalistic Studies of Aggressive Behavior: A Modified and Partial Replication*. Paper presented at the meeting of the Southwest Psychological Association, New Orleans, April, 1978.

Stone, M. (1987). Incident at Exit 20. *New York*, October, 5, 50-56.

Tempest, R. (1982). Houston traffic: Wild West lives on freeways. *Los Angeles Times*, December 25, Part I, p. 10.

Tillman, W. A. and Hobbes, G. E. (1949). The accident prone automobile driver. *American Journal of Psychiatry, 106,* 321-331.

Tinbergen, N. (1951). *The Study of Instinct*. London: Oxford University Press.

Toch, H. (1969). *Violent Men*. Chicago: Aldine Publishing Company.

Turner, C. W., Layton, J. F., & Simons, L. S. (1975). Naturalistic studies of aggressive behavior: Aggressive stimuli, victim visibility, and horn-honking. *Journal of Personality and Social Psychology, 31,* 1098-1107.

Wheeler, L. (1966). Toward a theory of behavioral contagion. *Psychological Review, 73,* 179-192.

Whitlock, F. A. (1971). *Death on the Road: A Study in Social Violence*. London: Tavistock.

Wolfgang, M. E. and Ferracuti, F. (1967). *The Subculture of Violence: Towards an Integrated Theory of Criminology.* London: Tavistock.

Zimbardo, P. (1969). The human choice: Individuation, reason and order versus deindividuation, impulse, and chaos. In W. J. Arnold & D. Levine (Eds.) *Nebraska Symposium on Motivation, Volume 17.* Lincoln: University of Nebraska Press.

8

Violence Toward Clinicians
Burr Eichelman

There is a dark side to the treatment of the mentally ill. Not only does this "side" require the training in aggression management for therapists and aides, it also carries with it real risks to therapists for their own safety, and their assumption of the role of victim coincident with that of caregiver. Acknowledgement of the reality of assaults upon mental health professionals has been relatively sparse and only recently has there been consciousness-raising in this area, as illustrated by the book edited by Lion and Reid, *Assaults within Psychiatric Facilities* (1983), and the recently formed American Psychiatric Association task force on clinician safety.

One explanation for this silence may be related to the protectivenes of mental health workers who wish to "play down" the violence of psychiatric patients due to the troublesome old stereotype of the "raving maniac" and the stigmatization of the mentally ill as a class. A second explanation, however, could be that mental health workers refuse to acknowledge the potential dangerousness of their vocation and utilize a basic psychological defense of denial. Case review of clinician fatalities lends some credibility to this latter hypothesis. Review of the working conditions where clinician assault occurs also suggests that they may not have the direct control over their environment needed to successfully cope with the reality of assault by altering dangerous architecture or increasing staff to patient ratios. These same clinicians will acknowledge that stressed or threatened individuals who cannot find concrete coping strategies to reduce the risk of harm will be more likely to utilize basic psychological defense mechanisms like denial.

One could even argue that psychiataric diagnostic nosology abets this clinical denial. DSM IIIR (1987) has multiple ways to diagnose disorders of affect associated with depressed mood and suicidal behavior. There are organic depressions (293.83), major depression (296), dysthymic disorder (300.40), depressive disorder NOS (311), and adjustment disorder with depressed mood (309). In contrat, DSM IIIR diagnoses for which aggressive behavior is a major component are limited, given the spectrum of violence which the clinician sees: organic personality disorder (310.10), intermittent explosive disorder (312.94), antisocial personality disorder (301.7), the conduct disorders (312), and adjustment disorder with disturbance of conduct (309.30). Problem behaviors such as spouse abuse and child abuse for which treatment is sought either through court order or voluntary initiative do not even qualify for a diagnosis. They are, rather, given a "V code" listing.

Depressed schizophrenics can receive a dual diagnosis for their schizophrenia (e.g. chronic undifferentiated schizophrenia) and for their depression (e.g. depressive disorder NOS). Angry, aggressive schizophrenics cannot be codified, diagnostically, any differently than nonviolent schizophrenics. Is this denial of patient violence even built into our diagnostic nosology?

THE REALITY OF PSYCHIATRIC PATIENT VIOLENCE IN THE U.S

Psychiatric patients in the United States exhibit a substantial amount of violent behavior. Violent behavior is a significant behavior appearing prior to psychiatric hospitalization. Binder and McNeil (1986) observed that 15% of patients admitted to a university hospital psychiatric service had been violent within two weeks prior to admission. In this study, as well as Tardiff's (1984), more than 50% of these assaults were directed against family members - another target of assault for psychiatric patients.

Once hospitalized, violent behavior continues to occur. In a study of U.S. hospitals, Reid and Kang (1986) compared the frequency of assaults, calculated as assaults/bed/year, which ranged from 1.2 for private hospitals to 6.9 for high security hospitals. State hospitals registered 3.3 assaults per bed per year. This figure is roughly consistent with other reports in the literature e.g. Camarillo State Hospital at 3.4 assaults/bed/year (Liberman, Marshall and Burke, 1981). It is also consistent with current data generated at Dorothea Dix Hospital, a North Carolina state facility, that averages 3 assaults/day/670 beds or 1.6 assaults/bed/year (Eichelman, 1988).

These numbers as they are summed throughout a hospital system become immense. The New York hospital system reported 12,000 assaults annually (New York State Senate Select Committee on Mental and Physical Handicaps, 1975-1976). The Veterans Administration reported 12,000 assaults during a five year period (Lion & Reid, 1983). Both of these figures may represent substantial underreporting. Lion et al.. (1981), from a study of a Maryland state hospital, suggest that underreporting may exist by a factor of five, potentially quintupling the figures cited above.

Not only are psychiatric hospitals or general hospitals the sites for patient assault. Substantial assaultive behavior occurs within mental retardation centers. Hill et al. (1985) report that 30% of institutionalized retardation patients in their survey exhibited assaultive behavior. Comparable figures exist for nursing homes. Rovner et al.. (1986) note that 26% of nursing home patients surveyed display assaultive behavior and 24-34% manifested loud, disruptive, or threatening behavior.

THE CLINICIAN-VICTIM

While not all patient violence in a hospital or clinic setting is directed agaist therapists and aides, a substantial amount is. Nevertheless, studies obtaining incidence rates of assault for mental health professionals are few. Madden et al.. (1976) surveyed psychiatrists with appointments at the University of Maryland. From a 100% response rate of 115 psychiatrists they observed that 48 (42%) had been assaulted at some time in their career. The attacks came primarily from patients in treatment. In a Canadian survey, Tardiff and Maurice (1977) surveyed 210 Vancouver psychiatrists. One hundred responses (a 48% response rate) indicated that 40% of the psychiarists had sustained one or more attacks thus far in their careers. In a broader survey, Whitman et al. (1976) surveyed 184 mental health workers - psychiatrists, psychologists and social workers in the Cincinnati, Ohio, area. They requested information concerning threats and assaults during a one year period. The response rate for this questionnaire was 55%. Of 6,720 patients, the respondents felt that 1.9% (126) posed a physical threat to the therapist and 42 (0.63%) actually assaulted the therapist. Thirty-four per cent of the psychiarists, 20% of the social workers and 7% of the psychologists were assaulted during the one year period. Fifteen per cent of the psychiatrists and five per cent of the social workers had been assaulted more than once. Bernstein (1981) surveyed psychotherapists in the San Diego area. This study surveyed 988 clinicians. There was a response rate of 46%. Fourteen per cent of the respondents reported having been assaulted at least once. The extrapolated incidence of assault for psychiatrists from this study was 42%. On the East coast, Hatti et al. (1982) surveyed psychiatrists in the greater Philadelphia area. Six hundred fifty psychiatrists were polled, with a response rate of 60%. Twenty per cent of the respondents reported having been assaulted.

Trainees may be particuarly vulnerable to assault. In a study of psychiatric residents at Los Angeles County Hospital, Ruben et al. (1980) found that 15 of 31 residents (48%) had already been assaulted during their residency. Moreover, two had been hit twice and two had been hit three times. Similarly disturbing data was reported by Fink (1989) in a survey of Pennsylvania psychiatry residents. In this study of 333 residents with a response rate of 47%, 41% of the residents reported assaults and eight percent of the residents sustained five or more assaults.

Statistically, most assaults to clinicians are minor (Haller and Deluty, 1988. Reid and Kang (1986) questioned 470 psychiatrists, 150 psychologists and 350 family practice physicians regarding "serious" attacks. Serious attacks were defined as an attack resulting in one or more days lost from work. One third of the psychiatrists and family practioners responded as did two-thirds of the psychologists. Three percent of psychiatrists and family practitioners reported having been seriously attacked. One percent of the psychologists reported being attacked.

Major injuries as well as death can be the sequellae. Lanza (1985) reported a survey of Veterans Administration nursing staff. Ninety-one assaults upon sixty-seven staff were noted. The "attack distribution" was significantly skewed. Fifty-eight percent of the attacked nurses had been attacked from one to three times. Thirteen percent had been attacked four to six times. Three percent had been attacked seven to ten times. Four percent reported being attacked by patients more than ten times! Forty of the staff were interviewed. Significant serious injuries were reported. In addition, nursing staff appeared to carry psychological sequellae of a post-traumatic nature for periods of time far longer than their absence from work.

Within an American forensic facility, Carmel and Hunter (1989) examined serious patient assaults for all inpatient staff, including psychiatric technicians. Serious attacks were defined by injury leading to time off, loss of consciouness, subsequent restriction of work or motion, termination or transfer from a position, or receipt of medical treatment beyond first aid. Of the sample of nursing staff (RNs, supervisors, and psych techs) six percent reported patient attacks directed personally towards them. Ten percent reported injuries which occurred while controlling patient violence. In this survey, "professionals" (psychiatrists, psychologists, social workers, and rehabilitation therapists) reported no serious attacks which were personally directed, but two percent of staff reported injury while controlling patient violence.

There is no formal registry of clinicians who are killed or seriously injured by patients. Clinicians in the United States who study violence often are contacted about such deaths. Occasionally individual cases are reported in the literature (Annis and Baker, 1986) or in professional newspapers (APA News). Often public review of a clinicians's death can be impeded by wrongful death suits against the institution which then is advised by legal counsel to make no pubic comment on the clinician homicide (Eichelman, unpublished observation).

Is there a profile for the clinician victim? At this time there has been no study describing the behavior or psychological profile of mental health personnel who frequently are the victims of assault. Since there appears from at least three studies (Rubin, et al., 1980; Fink, 1989; Haller and Deluty, 1988) to be strong data suggesting that some staff are attacked more frequently than others, this should be an encouraged "risk management" exercise. Some clinicians believe they could have anticipated the attack (Madden et al.. 1976) and describe clinical errors such as acting provocatively, making unfavorable interpretations, or setting too many or too few limits. They also believe that they were overly insistent that certain clinical material be examined. They noted that at times transference and counter-transference issues were not adequately addressed.

From an interpersonal perspective, Rubin et al.'s study (1980) asked the residents about their behavior outside of the hospital. Those residents who said they would physically resist a threat (as opposed to fleeing) were essentially those who had been assaulted (83%) in the clinical setting versus those who would flee (38% assaulted).

Inexperience of the therapist and placement of inexperienced therapists into high-risk areas, more than anything else, appear to be the reasons for much clinician assault. This seemed true in Madden's et al. study (1976) where most of the reported assaults occurred in the early period of psychiatric training at a time when such psychiatrists were more likely to be in contact with violent patients (Tardiff, 1974). At this time, therapist gender does not appear to be a significant variable. However, a report by Levy and Hartocollis (1976) where male aides were removed from wards and staffing was totally female led to a substantial reduction in patient assaults.

COPING STRATEGIES TO REDUCE VIOLENCE TOWARD CLINICIANS

Many different approaches have been instituted by clinicians in the attempt to cope with violence directed towards them. These include attempts to characterize the "typical" violent patient, attempts to delineate the time and location of most inpatient violence, and attempts through case review to analyze ways in which violent episodes could have been prevented. Training programs in violence intervention have been developed and implemented. Technical and architectural changes have been proposed. Lastly, legal assistance has been attempted to prosecute certain mentally ill assaulters.

If clinicians could delineate one diagnostic group as responsible for most assaults, this might afford some possibility of special learning and intervention with such a patient group. Studies that have focused on diagnostic category have been inconsistent. Kermani's review (1981) suggested that psychotic or depressed patients were most at risk as assaultive, and suggested the patients at greatest risk to be young schizophrenic males with paranoid ideation. Shader et al.'s (1977) review of 79 violent patients at a teaching hospital showed a preponderance of schizophrenics (57%) with an overrepresentation of schizo- affective patients. Nevertheless 43% were not schizophrenic. Tardiff (1983) listed patients with many diagnoses (e.g., nonparanoid schizophrenia, organic brain syndromes, other psychoses, and mental retardation) in his survey of assaults in a chart review of over 5000 patients. Interestingly, over 20% of the assaultive patients in this study had seizures. Adler, Kreeger, and Ziegler suggested that manic patients, regressed schizophrenic patients and adolescents were the most likely groups to be assaultive. Diagnostic category does not seem to be of great assistance in predicting assault upon clinicians.

Depp (1983) attempted to examine, within a hospital setting, the time and situation for the greatest number of assaults. He found for his hospital a high incidence of assault beteen 6:00 and 8:00 a.m. when patients were getting breakfast and in close proximity to one another. He also noted that 10 of 60 assaults occurred during staff limit-setting, specifically with the denial of privileges. Conn and Lion (1983) noted that approximately one third of the assaults occurred during seclusion procedures, 20% were associated with a verbal argument, 16% were associated with a denial of privileges. They felt that 20% were "unpredictable".

Among outpatients, Hatti et al. (1982) reported that 24% of the assaults were related to a conflict in the therapy, 22% related to paranoid ideation of the patient, 10% related to problems in the transference, 11% occurred under the influence of drugs, and in 40% the precipitant could not be delineated. In Dubin et al.'s (1988) survey of outpatient assaults (91 seriously assaulted respondents from a solicitation of 3800 psychiatrists), forty percent of the assaulting patients were schizophrenic and ten percent manic. Thirty-five percent carried a personality disorder diagnosis. It is noteworthy that 36% of the assaulting patients had been in therapy for more than a year. Ten percent of the assaults were committed by patients who had never been in treatment with the victimized psychiatrist.

Thus, strategies to predict the perpetrator of violence toward clinicians by diagnosis have been generally unsuccesful. Also unsuccessful has been the attempt to profile a specific high risk time or occurrence when such violence will occur. Such violence can occur under many circumstances.

As noted in the papers cited above, clinician assault can occur on inpatient units, in outpatient clinics, in the emergency room, or at the clinicians's home office. In Hatti et al.'s (1982) survey, guns and knives were weapons of outpatient assault while fists, furniture, or ashtrays were the weapon of inpatient assault.

A predictor (and coping strategy) which may work in the emergency room uses the patient's prior behavior. Thus, patients with a previous assault are considered high risk patients. This strategy can be linked to either manual or computerized "flagging" of a patients's medical record to put the clinical staff on alert. Such a mechanism has been decribed by Sparr et al. (1989) as used in the Portland, Oregon Veteran's Administration hospital. Using such a method, emergency room assaults decreased to 25% of baseline following implementation.

Staff training should have a significant impact in reducing assaults upon clinicians. However, data demonstrating the efficacy of training is sparse. In a comparative study there was a ten-fold difference in the assault rate on the untrained compared to the trained inpatient staff (Infantino & Musingo, 1985). A similar reduction in assault rate was observed in a mental health center following formal staff training (Gertz, 1980).

There are many adequate training sources already in the literature. These materials discuss verbal strategies to reduce anger and establish rapport (Tardiff, 1989), as well as indications and methods of physical restraint (Tardiff, 1984). Many hospitals have developed their own training programs for verbal and physical interventions with potentially violent patients. Commercial "travelling road shows" are also available for training of staff. Unfortunately, many clinical training programs do not appear to utilize such training programs. In Fink's survey of Pennsylvania psychiatry residents, the mean time spent in training the management of the violent patient was three hours (Fink, 1989).

It would appear that such training is useful to provide technical expertise. In Dubin et al.'s survey (1988) the investigators divided psychiatrists' responses into positive, talking strategies, neutral strategies (e.g., fleeing) or a verbal or physically aggressive response. While no psychiatrists were injured using positive, talking strategies, one third of those using an aggressive reponse were injured.

It is also important to deal with the issue of clinician denial. Cornfield and Fielding (1980) noted that clinician apathy and emotional detachment as well as narcissistic self-absorption contributed to assaults upon clinicians. They also noted elements of displaced affect and mutual criticism in trainees. They proposed staff sensitivity sessions, educational programs, "community" discussion and senior staff consultation in the handling of dangerous patients.

Clinician denial can be illustrated by the following case report (Annis and Baker, 1986) and by findings in the survey of Dubin et al. (1988). In the case report a psychiatrist was alone in his office. A patient came to his receptionist in the adjacent room. The patient carried a shotgun. He told the receptionist that he wanted to see the psychiatrist. The receptionist over the intercom advised the psychiatrist that "Mr. Doe" was in the waiting area, that he was angry, and that he was carrying a shotgun. The psychiatrist came out of his office to greet Mr. Doe. He attempted to persuade Mr. Doe to hand over the gun and was immediately shot and killed by his patient.

While retrospective analysis is always easier and safer than prediction, it is apparent that the psychiatrist did not need to leave his office. He had many alternatives to obtain help without making himself available as the primary target. One must speculate that 1) he did not believe he would (could?) be shot and killed by the patient; and 2) believed that he was so skillful that even if the patient intended to kill him, he could talk the patient down. Elements of denial and grandiosity certainly seem possible.

Even after a violent episode, clinicians appear to exercise significant denial. In the survey by Dubin et al. (1988), in 42% of cases where the psychiatrist experienced personal injury, the psychiatrist continued to treat the patient! More astoundingly, 21% never subsequently discussed the episode with the patient and 39% reported making no changes in the treatment plan for the patient, the setting for the therapy, or in the safety precautions taken.

A final case example (Eichelman, unpublished observation) may serve to illustrate, again, the sense of denial ("not to me", "not here") and "supertherapist" stance which can be endangering to life. A second year female resident (who, during her first year had received the "outstanding first year award" in her class) was treating a young male schizophrenic. She and her classmates had been concerned about the violent patient at the adjacent VA hospital and resident concern had been instrumental in that hospital's placement of behavioral emergency buzzers and the development of a behavioral emergency "Code Orange". Such concerns had not been expressed for the university hospital clinic and no comparable safety alerts were in place. The young male schizophrenic had become noncompliant with medication and was no longer taking antipsychotic medication. He had also become noncompliant with his visits and had not been seen regularly or frequently. Nevertheless, he had written to the resident and provided pictures which (in retrospect) appeared violent in nature. The resident had not obtained an existing past history of the violent behavior of this patient while he resided in California, and she had not required him to become compliant with medication in order to be seen.

One morning he appeared at 7:30 a.m. at the outpatient clinic and found the resident there. He requested an "emergency" appointment. This early in the morning the clinic was only sparsely staffed. The resident apparently made no brief assessment of the patient, but took him to her office at the end of a long unattended corridor. Though not observed, apparently the patient suddenly drew a .22 caliber handgun and shot the resident in the heart, then turned the gun on himself. Both were killed.

Review of this case (again with the advantage of hindsight) suggested that the resident could have taken a more complete violence history from the patient, and should have persisted in obtaining medical records from his past therapists. The resident could have rated this patient a "new" patient (since he had been noncompliant with medication and therapy) and seen him in the emergency room, where greater security and staff support could have been available. Lastly, the institution could have had an emergency alarm system which might have signalled help sufficiently soon as to interrupt the violence. This, again, appears to be a "not me, not here" scenario.

ADMINISTRATIVE INTERVENTIONS TO REDUCE VIOLENCE TOWARD CLINICIANS

In addition to the encouragement of training for staff in the techniques of verbal and physical intervention, mental health administrations and hospital administrations can also assist staff with additional "coping" strategies. Such strategies include architectural changes in the emergency room and in hospital ward design. These include the installation of surveillance equipment and alarm systems. They include the implementation of employee assistance programs for assaulted staff. Finally, administrations can support their staff in pressing criminal and civil action against assaultive patients.

Architecturally, emergency room space for psychiatric patients should be somewhat removed from the mainstream of the

ER, but not at the end of the longest corridor (where such space is often allocated since these patients are "so disruptive"). The room should be violence-proofed with the removal of hard or sharp objects which could be used a weapons. An intensive care room with lots of glass, needles and scalpels is not an appropriate interview room. Safety can be enhanced by having the room visible to staff outside. Half windows can afford the privacy of conversation, but allow other ER staff to monitor threatening behavior. The installation of an intercom system which can be turned on for monitoring should the clinician feel it necessary is also a support. Finally, there should be an alarm system operated through the telephone or an alarm button which can institute a centralized behavioral emergency alert, bringing help to the area initiating the signal.

Outpatient rooms should also be violence-proofed. Those therapists who see a significant number of violent patients should seriously consider designing their offices with two doors. They can develop a communication system with their receptionist so that the receptionist can unobtrusively signal to the therapist a threatening demeanor of a registering patient, or so that the receptionist can unobtrusively request of the therapist assistance with a threatening patient.

Inpatient units should be designed with maximum visibility and no blind corners. In older or poorly designed wards, surveillance equipment such a convex mirrors or TV monitors can be installed to reduce the risk of surprise encounters with patients.

Staffing ratios with high staff to patient numbers allow staff to respond early to behaviorally escalating patients. Sparsely staffed units where nursing staff must be concerned with the ward routine only (feeding, mediating, and assisting with personal hygiene) have little time to observe the subtle signs of behavioral escalation until they become irreversible and spill over into assault.

A final administrative issue which is becoming more prominent is the pressing of charges against violent inpatients for whom staff feel there is some degree of behavioral control and recognition of responsibility. Phelan et al. (1985) suggest that pressing charges may have a therapeutic effect on the patient, with a subsequent deterrence from assault, and may also provide some appropriate response on the part of the victimized staff, who cannot respond violently in kind to the patient. In general, most states with a NGRI (Not Guilty by Reason of Insanity) defense still allow for many mentally ill patients to be held legally responsible if they were *able to understand the wrongfulness of their behavior and are deemed able to conform their behavior to the standards of the law.* However, in certain jurisdictions, such legal action has been met with resistance on the part of the courts. In two Carolina cases the judge commented during the trials that "If you were a soldier and sent to Vietnam, you expected to be shot at. If you went to a bar you expected to meet up with drunks. And, if you worked at (the state psychiatric hospital) you should expect to be assaulted." Such judicial denial or excusing of criminal behavior is demoralizing for psychiatric caregivers. It raises a threatening specter for hospital administrators that staff will take the law into their own hands and either retaliate directly with undue violence or more subtly with the sabotaging of treatment plans or over-medication. Clearly, education of the judiciary must occur.

FUTURE CONCERNS

There appear to be several issues which bode poorly for a future reduction in violence toward clinicians in this country. General resources for health care are being capped. Significant health care dollars are being required to deal with AIDS and the drug epidemics. This poses the likelihood that mental health funding will not increase on a per capita basis, and will not keep pace with inflation. These factors, coupled with the drive to deinstituionalize patients, could lead to a relative decrease in mental health resources for the community. This in turn, could lead to further depleting of staff/patient ratios in inpatient settings and to understaffed emergency rooms servicing mental health patients.

Coupled to limited mental health resources for the impoverished mentally ill is the question of whether a non-violent mentally ill patient can receive voluntary inpatient treatment. State hospitals filled to capacity and understaffed are reluctant to admit voluntary patients who are not a danger to themselves or others. They are referred to the community mental health center, perhaps to a long waiting list. Clinicians should examine whether the "triage" system actually fosters violent behavior that may serve as the "ticket for admission", or for the prolongation of hospitalization.

Increased substance abuse including alcohol, cocaine, narcotics and phencyclidine all pose the risk of greater violence associated with drug intoxication or withdrawal. Overcrowding in the criminal justice system may force the premature release of mentally ill patients, and put legally responsible violent patients back into the mental health system. Such crowding may also impede the legal action taken by clinicians against assaultive patients. Overburdened District Attorneys and judges with overbooked dockets may have little patience for such cases.

Finally, the high technical cost of a health care system that provides trauma helicopters, NMRs, and SPECT, for example, may reduce the funding that can be made available for mundane or boring items like safer interview rooms and "trivial" warning systems for behavioral emergencies.

The future suggests that violence toward clinicians will remain a significant part of American health care for years to come. Clinician safety will continue to rest predominantly in the hands of the clinician directly. Training and constant vigilance regarding this reality remain the most reliable and successful strategies.

REFERENCES

Adler, W. N., Kreeger, C. and Ziegler, P. *Patient Violence in a Private Psychiatric Hospital.* Unpublished observation. (pp. 81- 89).

Annis, L. V. and Baker C. A. (1986). A psychiatrist murder in a mental hospital. *Hospital and Community Psychiatry, 37,* 505-506.

American Psychiatric Association: *Diagnostic and Statistical Manual of Mental Disorder, Third Edition, Revised.* Washington, D.C., American Psychiatric Association, 1987.

APA News 17 (2) pp. 1 and 10. January 15, 1982.

Bernstein, J. A. (1981). Survey of threats and assaults directed toward psychotherapists. *American Journal of Psychotherapy, 35,* 542-549.

Binder, R. and McNeil, D. (1986). Victims and families of violent psychiatric patients. *Bulletin of the American Academy of Psychiatry and the Law, 14,* 131-139.

Carmel, H. and Hunter, H. (1989). Staff inquiries from inpatient violence. *Hospital and Community Psychiatry, 40,* 41-46.

Conn, L. M. and Lion, J. R. *Assaults in a University Hospital.* Unpublished observation, pp 61-69.

Cornfield, R. B. and Fielding, S. D. (1980). Impact of the threatening patient on ward communications. *American Journal of Psychiatry, 137,* 616-619.

Depp, F. C. *Assaults in a Public Mental Hospital.* Unpublished observation, pp. 21-45.

Drummond, D. J., Sparr, L. F., and Gordon, G. H. (1989). Hospital violence reduction among high risk patients. *Journal of the American Medical Association. 261,* 2531-2534.

Dubin, W. R., Wilson, S. J. and Mercer, C. (1988). Assault against psychiatrists in outpatient settings. *Journal of Clinical Psychiatry, 49,* 338-345.

Eichelman, B. Unpublished observation.

Eichelman, B. Paper presented to the North Carolina Mental Health Study Commission, 1988.

Fink, P. Paper presented at the meeting of the American Psychiatric Association, San Francisco, May, 1989.

Gertz, B. (1980). Training for prevention of assaultive behavior in a psychiatric setting. *Hospital and Community Psychiatry, 31,* 628-630.

Haller, R. M. and Deluty, R H. (1988). Assaults on staff by psychiatric inpatients: A critical review. *British Journal of Psychiatry, 152,* 174- 179.

Hatti, S., Dubin, W. R. and Weiss, K. J. (1982). A study of circumstances surrounding patient assaults on psychiatrists. *Hospital and Community Psychiatry, 33,* 660-661.

Hill, B. K., Balow, E. A, Bruninks, R. H. (1985). A national study of prescribed drugs in institutions and community residential facilities for mentally retarded people. *Psychopharmacology Bulletin, 21,* 279-284.

Infantino, J. A. and Musingo, S. (1985). Assaults and injuries among staff with and without training in aggression control techniques. *Hospital and Community Psychiatry, 36,* 1312-1314.

Kermani, E. J. (1981). Violent psychiatric patients: A study. *Journal of Psychotherapy, 35*, 215-225.

Lanza, M. (1985). Nurses react to assault. *Journal of Psychosocial Nursing, 23*, 6-11.

Levy, P, Hartocollis, P. (1976). Nursing aides and patient violence. *American Journal of Psychiatry, 133*, 429-431.

Liberman, R. P., Marshall, B. D., Burke, K. L. (1981). Drug and environmental interventions for aggressive psychiatric patient. In R. B. Stuart (Ed.) *Violent Behavior: Social Learning Approaches to Prediction, Management and Treatment*, (p. 229). New York: Bruner/Mazel, Inc.

Lion, J. R. and Reid, W. H. (Eds.) (1983). *Assaults Within Psychiatric Facilities*. New York: Grune and Stratton.

Lion, J. R. and Reid, W. (1983). *Preface in Assaults Within Psychiatric Facilities* ed. by J. R. Lion and W. Reid. (p. 1X) New York: Grune and Stratton.

Lion, J. R., Snyder, W., Merill, G. (1981). Underreporting of assaults on staff in a state hospital. *Hospital and Community Psychiatry, 33*, 497-498.

Madden, D. J., Lion, J. R. and Penna M.W. (1976). Assaults on psychiatrists by patients. *American Journal of Psychiatry, 133*, 422-425.

Miller, R D. and Maier, G. J. (1987). Factors affecting the decision to prosecute mental patients for criminal behavior. *Hospital and Community Psychiatry, 38*, 50-55.

New York State Senate Select Committee on Mental and Physical Handicap. Senator James H. Donovan, Chairman (1975-1976). Violence revisited...a report on traditional indifference in state mental institutions towards assaultive activity.

Phelan, L. A., Mills, M. J. and Ryan, J. A. (1985). Prosecuting psychiatric patients for assaults. *Hospital and Community Psychiatry, 36,* 581-582.

Reid, W. H. and Kang, J. S. (1986). Serious assaults by outpatient or former patients. *American Journal of Psychotherapy, 40,* 594-600.

Reid, W. H. *Assaults in Hospitals.* Portion of a CME course "The Management of the violent patient, given at the American Psychiatric Association Meeting.

Rovner, B. W., Kafonek, S., Filipp, L., Lucas, M. J., Foltein, M. F. (1986). Prevalence of mental illness in a community nursing home. *American Journal of Psychiatry, 143,* 1446-1449.

Rubin, I., Wolkon, G., and Yamamoto, J. (1980). Physical attacks on psychiatric residents by patients. *Journal of Nervous and Mental Disease, 168,* 243-245.

Shader, R. I., Jackson, A. H., Harmatz, J. and Appelbaum, P S. (1977). Patterns of violent behavior among schizophrenic inpatients. *Diseases of the Nervous System, 38,* 13-16.

Tardiff, K. (1989). *Assessment and Management of Violent Patients.* Washington, D.C., American Psychiatric Press.

Tardiff, K. (Ed.). (1984). *The Psychiatric Uses of Seclusion and Restraint.* Washington, DC: American Psychiatric Press.

Tardiff, K. (1984). Characteristics of assaultive patients in private hospitals. *American Journal of Psychiatry, 141,* 1232-1235.

Tardiff, K. (1983). A survey of assault by chronic patients in a state hospital system. In *Assaults within Psychiatric Facilities,* Ed. by J. R. Lion and W. H. Reid, (pp. 3-19), New York: Grune and Stratton.

Tardiff, K. and Maurice, W. L. (1977). The care of violent patients by psychiatrists: A tale of two cities. *Canadian Psychiatric Association Journal, 22,* 83-86.

Tardiff, K. (1974). A survey of psychiatrists in Boston and their work with violent patients. *American Journal of Psychiatry, 131*, 1008-1011.

Whitman, R. M., Arms, B. B. and Dent, O. B. (1976). Assault on therapist. *American Journal of Psychiatry, 133*, 426-431.

9

Gay-Bashing: Violence and Aggression Against Gay Men and Lesbians
Peter M. Nardi and Ralph Bolton[1]

INTRODUCTION

Violence, threats of physical harm, verbal abuse, and other types of aggression directed against individuals because of their sexual orientation or perceived sexual orientation, often referred to collectively as "fag-bashing" or "gay-bashing," are commonplace in contemporary American society. From locker room to board room, from the pulpit to the courts, and from newspaper opinion columns to late-night comedy shows on television, the vilification of gays and lesbians is popular sport. In a recent public service announcement, comedian Bob Hope stated that he had become aware of the seriousness of the problem of attacks on gays and lesbians, which he deplored-after many years of engaging in bigoted humor

---

[1]*The authors wish to thank Gail Orozco and Lynn L. Thomas for their assistance in preparing the manuscript and Kevin Berrill of the NGLTF for providing materials on anti-gay violence and aggression. Seniority of authorship of this article was determined by the flip of a coin.*

that was derogatory toward gays. His public service announcement was arranged as a form of penance. The fact is that each year tens of thousands of gay men and lesbians become the victims of aggression and discrimination because of their sexual orientation, while millions of others live with the fear and knowledge that they, too, are at risk of being the targets of hate crimes and of discriminatory actions such as the loss of a job, of housing, and of child custody rights, without legal recourse in many jurisdictions. Indeed, as a report prepared for the U.S. Department of Justice noted, members of the gay minority in this country are more likely than are members of ethnic and religious minorities to be attacked because of their minority status (Finn and McNeil, 1987).

Although the focus of this report is on individual gay-bashing, this social phenomenon cannot be understood fully until it is placed in the context of institutionalized gay-bashing which will also be discussed in this chapter and in which even the behavioral sciences themselves have participated, overtly through theorizing that contributes to the stigmatization of homosexuality (deviance theories, for example, and the medicalization of homosexuality) and covertly by failing to acknowledge and examine the problem of anti-gay violence. The theoretical literature produced by specialists on violence and aggression is replete with discussions of the related issues of anti-semitism and racism, but with almost no attention paid to gay-bashing (cf. Weiner, Zahn, and Sagi, 1990). What little work has been done on anti-gay violence and homophobia has generally been reported in nonmainstream journals (e.g., the Journal of Homosexuality). Thus, the pervasive homophobic milieu of the society at large and of the academic community itself has resulted in both the neglect and the ghettoization of this important problem.

It needs to be underscored at the outset that aggression and violence against gays and lesbians take many forms from the obvious, such as physical attacks, insults, and vicious jokes, to the subtle but equally pernicious, such as the refusal to recognize the existence and legitimacy of the gay community and gay culture, the re-writing of verse by famous poets to obscure references to same-sex love, and the genocidal failure by the American government to fund AIDS prevention efforts at an adequate level.

Debates within scholarly circles over the causes of variations in sexual orientation continue to rage, with essentialists and social constructionists battling each other in a replay of the nature-versus-nurture controversy that has afflicted the social sciences in many domains of scientific inquiry (Weinrich, 1987; Greenberg, 1989). However, certain important facts, supported by cross-cultural and cross-historical research by anthropologists and social historians, seem to be beyond reasonable dispute.

The first of these facts is that erotic attraction and sexual behavior between individuals of the same genetic sex are present in most societies in which sexuality has been studied carefully, and, indeed, it is quite possible that homoeroticism is a cultural universal, present to one degree or another in all societies at all times (Blumenfeld and Raymond, 1988; Ford and Beach, 1951; Herdt, 1987a; Whitam, 1987). The second fact is that how societies construe homoeroticism varies greatly; in particular, the roles in which homosexual practices are embedded and the practices themselves differ from culture to culture. In some societies in New Guinea and Africa homosexual behavior is not only expected during at least a portion of the life cycle of males, it may be required in ritual contexts of all males (Herdt, 1984, 1987b), whereas in others the commitment to and involvement in homosexual behavior is seen as a significant, permanent characteristic of a minority of individuals for whom sexual orientation becomes one component of the personal identity, as is the case in Northern European and white American cultures. In still other societies, only some individuals who participate in homosexual activity are thereby defined as "homosexual", such definition depending on the role the individual plays in homosexual encounters (Carrier, 1980, 1989). A third compelling fact is that sexual orientation is not a matter of choice for most individuals; instead, it is a given in the same way that skin color and handedness are, though, like the latter, its expression can be facilitated or suppressed.

The fourth fact is that the level of acceptability or unacceptability of homosexual behavior varies tremendously from culture to culture (Carrier, 1980; Crapo, n.d.; Werner, 1979) and even over time within the same culture (Boswell, 1980). If one examines this phenomenon at the level of present-day nation states, one can see the sharp contrasts that exist. At one extreme on the acceptability dimension are the Scandinavian countries, especially Norway and Denmark. In the former, not only are gays and lesbians guaranteed the same legal rights as other citizens, but in addition Norwegian laws protect them against homophobic attacks (Pedersen, 1985). It is illegal to incite animosity or violence against the gay community, and the law has been used to prosecute a radio evangelist for making anti-gay remarks over the public airwaves. Denmark in 1989 became the first country to permit legal marriages between individuals of the same sex.

At the other end of the scale one finds countries such as Iran and Saudi Arabia where homosexual acts are punishable by death (Gmunder and Stamford, 1988; IGA, 1985). However, the most extreme official persecution of gays in the present century took place in Nazi Germany where thousands of gays, forced to wear a pink triangle, shared the fate of Jews, gypsies, and others who were considered in the Third Reich to be expendable (Heger, 1980; Plant 1986; Rector, 1981). The gay liberation movement, which had been strong in post-WWI Germany was destroyed, along with the leading pro-gay institution of the time, the Institute of Sexual Science in Berlin, founded by Magnus Hirschfeld. In addition to being largely ignored by subsequent scholarly research on Nazi genocide, gays who survived concentration camps, in contrast to other survivors of the Holocaust, were never given reparations; they remained the forgotten victims.

Historically, the fate of homosexuals has run parallel to that of Jews in European societies, their oppression waxing and waning in tandem. Both groups served as scapegoats during various periods. Following a period of toleration in the Middle Ages, toward the middle of the twelfth century hostility toward gays increased, and they were subject to the death penalty (Boswell, 1980).

ANTI-GAY VIOLENCE AND AGGRESSION IN CONTEMPORARY AMERICA

By contrast with the virulence of anti-gay attacks in the past and in a few cultures today, the present situation for gays and lesbians in the West may seem benign. But the appearances are somewhat deceptive. Laws on the books in some states continue to make felons of those engaging in homosexual acts, and the penalties for consenting homosexual behavior can be as severe as 20 years in prison, although these laws are rarely enforced. They function more as mechanisms of psychological aggression and intimidation. However, violence, threats of physical aggression and verbal abuse are significant risks in the lives of many gays and lesbians.

These dangers are often present even within the families of origin of gays and lesbians. Frequently, gay youths are rejected and abused by parents, siblings and other kin because of their homosexuality. Thus, where other minority youth generally do not face problems with racism and religious intolerance within their own families, for gays and lesbians often abuse begins at home. Many such youths even fear disclosing who they are to parents because of the possibility of rejection. In many cases, aggression against gay youths takes the form of expulsion from the childhood home and a severance of ties and financial support by unsympathetic parents. These young men and women then end up, in many cases, on the streets where they are targets for further violence.

EXAMPLES OF GAY-BASHING

Many cases of gay-bashing that occur today are reminiscent of the worst incidents of racial violence and harassment that were common before the successes of the civil rights movement. A few examples will suffice to illustrate what is often involved in gay-bashing.

Case 1. In 1986, a gay man living in Sacramento walked to the corner store one evening. Two men walking in the opposite direction passed him, and as they did so, he heard one of them mutter, "Too many faggots moving into the neighborhood". He continued on his way, ignoring the comment, until he heard footsteps behind him. As he turned around to look, he was struck on the shoulder by one of the men and thrown to the ground where he was kicked repeatedly in the face. His attackers retreated shouting, "queer, queer, queer." When he got up, he discovered that he was bleeding and had been stabbed. He managed to crawl to his apartment complex before losing onsciousness. He was found by a neighbor who called for medical assistance. His stab wound was

1/16th of an inch from a carotid artery, but he survived. His assailants were never identified.

Case 2. On May 13, 1988 two lesbians were hiking along the Appalachian trail in Pennsylvania when they were shot by an assailant who had been stalking them for a day. The women had camped in a secluded area when the man, hiding in the woods about 80 feet away, opened fire on them. One of the women died at the campsite of back and head wounds; the other walked four miles with wounds in the head, face, upper arm, and neck before she got help. The attorney for the murderer claimed that the women had provoked the attack by performing sexual acts in front of the man. They had made love by the campfire unaware that they were being watched.

Case 3. A fraternity at the University of Vermont used a stamp that read "Drink Beer, Kill Queers" on the hands of students attending a fraternity party, and the same slogan was painted on a fraternity bus during a spring trip to Florida. Sanctions were applied to the fraternity by the university (probation, community service, and attendance at seminars on discrimination). (Reported in *The Advocate, Issue #100,* June 7, 1988, p. 34).

Case 4. Following a series of three gay-bashings in Laguna Beach, California, in August 1988, several shots from a high-powered rifle were fired into an area in which several gay businesses and a gay bar are located. No one was injured and the attackers were not caught (Reported by the *Los Angeles Times*, August 14, 1988).

Case 5. A heterosexual male tourist in San Francisco in July, 1987 was stabbed in the face and abdomen. He died two hours later. His attackers had shouted "faggot" and "fruit" at him during the assault, mistakenly identifying him as gay. The police determined that he had done nothing to provoke the attack: He was, in their words, "at the wrong place at the wrong time" (NGLTF, 1988).

Case 6. At Columbia University, in October 1988, a football coach filed an official complaint against a male cafeteria worker whom he saw kissing another male friend goodbye. The employee was verbally harassed by members of the football team during "Training Table." Anonymous complaints were also filed by team members, stating, "Get homo's [sic] out of the kitchen, you are encouraging AIDS die [sic]!" and "Get rid of the fags who serve during Training Table." The attacked employee is heterosexual (NGLTF, 1989).

These and many similar incidents, ranging from homicide to verbal insults, represent a category of violence called "hate crimes" which are generating increasing attention and concern among citizens and law enforcement officials. In a report submitted to the U.S. Department of Justice (Finn and McNeil, 1987: p.1), these incidents have been described as widespread and increasing:

> Bias crimes, or hate violence, are words or actions designed to intimidate an individual because of his or her race, religion, national origin, or sexual preference. Bias crimes range from threatening phone calls to murder. These types of offenses are far more serious than comparable crimes that do not involve prejudice because they are intended to intimidate an entire group. The fear they generate can therefore victimize a whole class of people.

The report concluded that homosexuals were "probably the most frequent victims" of hate violence and bias crimes (Finn and McNeil, 1987: p. 2). Yet, many statutes and policies continue to exclude sexual orientation as a category or motivating factor in bias crime reporting. The reasons for this and the organized responses to it are discussed below.

DEFINITIONS

Gay-bashing involves acts of aggression committed against people because of their actual or perceived sexual orientation. Such acts are in many respects similar to hostile behavior displayed toward members of ethnic, racial, and religious minorities. Beginning in the late 1970s and early 1980s, a new category of crime was developed, primarily in response to increasing reports of violence committed against racial minorities. This development emphasized the importance of focussing attention on the victims of crimes rather than studying only the characteristics of those committing them. Various terms, including hate violence, bias crime, civil rights violations, human relations incidents, bias-related violence, and several other combinations of these words, have been used to index criminal episodes that fit into this new category.

While a standard definition of this new category does not exist, most definitions of bias crime incorporate several criteria for recognizing a crime as a bias crime. These include the presence of verbal abuse or physical actions, threatened, attempted or carried out, directed against individuals or group, or an attack on their property, motivated, all or in part, by the actual or perceived ethnicity, race, national origin, religion, sex, age, disability, or sexual orientation of the target, with such acts intended to intimidate not just individuals per se, but the entire group to which the victim is thought to belong. While these elements appear in almost all definitions of bias crimes, controversy typically focuses on which categories should be included. The inclusion of both race and religion is almost universal; some definitions include age, sex, and disability; but only a few have included sexual orientation.

The New York State Governor's Task Force on Bias-Related Violence (1988: p. 2) adopted the following definition:

An act of bias-related violence is an act or a

threatened or attempted act of intimidation, harassment or physical force directed against any person, or group, or their property or advocate, motivated either in whole or in part by hostility to their real or perceived race, ethnic background, national origin, religious belief, sex, age, disability, or sexual orientation, with the intention of deterring the free exercise or enjoyment of any rights or privileges secured by the Constitution or the laws of the United States or the State of New York whether or not performed under color of law.

The Los Angeles County Commission on Human Relations (1989: p. 5), in its report, Hate Crime in Los Angeles County in 1988, defined hate crimes as "acts directed at an individual, institution, or business expressly because of race, ethnicity, religion, or sexual orientation." The report specifies a number of guidelines to be used in determining if a crime is a hate crime. To be designated as such, the crime "must involve a specific target;" "bigotry must be the central motive for the attack;" if graffiti is involved the "graffiti must be racial, ethnic, religious, or homophobic in nature;" and, for assaults in which no other motive is present, the assault must be initiated with epithets. Vandalism to organizations as well as threatening phone calls are considered hate crimes, also, when racial, ethnic, religious, or homophobic language is employed as part of the act.

The California Racial, Ethnic, and Religious Crimes Project, according to a report prepared by Abt Associates for the U.S. Department of Justice (Finn and McNeil, 1987: p. 18), defines bias crime as "any act to cause physical injury, emotional suffering, or property damage, which appears to be motivated, all or in part, by race, ethnicity, religion, or sexual orientation." The International Association of Chiefs of Police uses a definition developed by the National Organization of Black Law Enforcement Executives, which focuses on racial and religious incidents: "an act or a threatened or attempted act by any person or group of persons against the person or property of another individual or group which may in any way constitute an expression of racial or religious hostility" (as quoted in Finn and McNeil, 1987: p. 18). This definition, as well as the ones in statutes in Maryland and Pennsylvania, does not include sexual orientation as a motivating factor.

The use of different definitions of bias crime leads to a number of problems, of course. For example, comparing data from different locales is made difficult, and even comparing data for a given locale over time is problematic when changes are made in the criteria for inclusion or exclusion of an event in the records intended to monitor bias-related aggression and violence. Increases or decreases in incidence, under such circumstances may be real or they may be artifacts of changes in data-collection procedures. Work in this area is hampered by divergent definitions and agreement is needed on an "accurate and workable definition of bias crime" (Finn and McNeil, 1987: p. 18). Whether or not to include sexual orientation in the definition continues to be a highly debated issue.

Another important step in arriving at a working definition is to state what is not included as hate violence or bias crime. The Los Angeles County Commission on Human Relations (1989) excludes actions, such as graffiti on freeway overpasses and public phone booths, that are not directed at a specific target; interracial crimes not motivated by race, ethnicity, religion, or sexual orientation; intragroup acts; name calling not accompanied by assault; and rallies and leafletting by hate crime groups.

TYPES AND INCIDENCE OF BIAS CRIMES

During the 1985 hearings on Intro 2, the New York City Council bill to prohibit discrimination in housing, employment, and public acommodations on grounds of sexual orientation, one of the arguments used by the bill's opponents was that data did not exist to prove the need for the bill, i.e., that there was not sufficient evidence available to show that discrimination against gays and lesbians occurs. The same could have been said about anti-gay violence and aggression until very recently---a lack of data. Fortunately, some local governments and gay organizations have begun to remedy this situation by collecting systematic information on this problem. The results of these studies are discussed in this section. Although better data from more localities are definitely needed the pattern that emerges from existing studies indicates the magnitude of the problem of anti-gay violence and aggression.

According to the Los Angeles County Commission on Human Rights (1989, 1990a, 1990b) hate crime in Los Angeles County escalated between 1980 and 1982, levelled off until 1985, increased again in 1986, and then reached record levels between 1987 and 1989. In 1989, there were 167 reported race- based incidents, 125 religion-based incidents, and 86 bias-crime incidents related to sexual orientation. The victims of the racial incidents were as follows: Blacks, 57.5%, Latinos, 13.2%, Asians, 11.3%, Armenians, 6.0%, Arabs, 4.2%, others, 7.8%. Jews were the targets of 88.0% of the incidents based on religious intolerance; Catholics were the victims in 5.6% of the bias crimes based on religious preference.

The bias incidents most frequently cited in the racial and religious categories involved graffiti and hate literature, 32.3% (race) and 56.0% (religion) respectively. (See Table 1). Assaults and attempted assaults were uncommon as bias crimes based on religion,

TABLE 1

Hate Crime Incidents Reported in Los Angeles County, 1989

Racial (n=167)
Graffiti/hate literature:	32.3%
Assault/attempted assault:	31.8%
Property vandalism:	13.2%
Criminal threats:	11.3%
Vandalism plus graffiti:	7.2%
Other:	4.2%

Religious (n=125)
Graffiti/hate literature:	56.0%
Criminal threats:	15.2%
Assault/attempted assault:	8.8%
Property vandalism:	7.2%
Vandalism plus graffiti:	5.6%
Arson:	3.2%
Other:	4.0%

Sexual Orientation (n=86)
Assault/attempted assault:	62.8%
Graffiti/hate literature:	30.2%
Property vandalism:	2.3%
Criminal threats:	3.5%
Arson:	1.2%

only 8.8%. They were more frequent in the racial category, 31.8%. The pattern is different for crimes related to sexual orientation. Almost two-thirds of the bias crimes related to sexual orientation involved an assault or an attempted assault, whereas graffiti and hate literature accounted for less than one-third of the reported incidents (Los Angeles County Commission on Human Rights, 1990a).

In general, shouted epithets and verbal abuse are the single most commonly reported type of incident for all of the categories (race, religion, sexual orientation), but these incidents are typically not recorded in the statistics of bias crimes. What is clear from the comparative data is that violent forms of bias crime are more likely to be committed against gay men than against individuals because of race or religion. (In 1989, 93.0% of the victims of the sexual orientation incidents were gay men, and only 7% of the victims were lesbians). As the Los Angeles County report (1989: p. 14) noted: "The term [gay bashing] is disturbingly accurate, as the great majority of these incidents involved assaults."

In general, bias crime reporting and investigating began by focusing on violence directed at Blacks and Jews. Most of these incidents were committed by individuals and small groups rather than by organized hate groups, such as the Ku Klux Klan and white supremacist groups. The overwhelming majority of those arrested for these crimes are white males between the ages of 16 and 25. In New York City, 70% of arrests for bias crimes between 1980 and 1987 involved persons under 20 years of age (Finn and McNeil, 1987).

While most hate crime is committed by people who do not know their victims, in many cases of anti-gay violence the victim knows the assailant. A 1984 survey conducted by NGLTF (reported in NGLTF, 1989), found that 34% of gay men and lesbians had been verbally harassed by relatives and 7% had been physically assaulted by family members because of their sexual orientation.

Physical and sexual abuses committed in prisons against people because of their race, ethnicity, religion, or sexual orientation are poorly documented (Governor's Task Force, 1988). While there is considerable violence along racial lines, much of that may be related to the disproportionate number of incarcerated minority individuals, rather than to overt racial prejudice (Governor's Task Force, 1988). But violence in such settings appears to be especially problematic and severe for gay prisoners. NGLTF (1989: p. 22) reports that "There are few settings where anti-gay violence is more trivialized than in prisons and jails, and none where it is more inescapable." Wooden and Parker (1982) document some of the types of sexual exploitation that routinely occur in prisons, especially against gay men.

As data collection efforts improve, reports of hate violence and bias crimes against Hispanics, Southeast Asians, and homosexuals have increased. Racial incidents are more likely to be underreported than religious ones, due to the lack of familiarity with the laws by immigrants and non-English speakers. Sexual orientation cases are also underreported due to the victims' fears of disclosure and to police difficulties in identifying gay men and lesbians.

Although few organizations have kept detailed records on incidents related to gay men and lesbians, the National Gay and Lesbian Task Force (NGLTF) has been documenting such cases since 1982 and has issued reports annually since 1985. The latest is entitled Anti-Gay Violence, Victimization and Defamation in 1988. According to NGLTF figures (1989), which in 1988 came from 120 organizations in 38 states and the District of Columbia, 7,248 incidents were reported, a 3% increase over 1987, due primarily to an increase in the number of organizations reporting, especially campus groups and gay churches. The pattern of incidents has remained relatively constant over the past several years. As Table 2 shows, the most common type of incident involves verbal harrassment or threats of violence, followed by physical assaults.

TABLE 2
Anti-Gay Incidents Reported to NGLTF

	1988 (n=7248)	1987 (n=7008)	1986 (n=4946)
Verbal harassment/ threats of violence	77%	78%	70%
Physical assault	12%	12%	15%
Vandalism	6%	5%	4%
Police abuse (physical/ verbal)	3%	3%	8%
Homicides	1%	1%	2%
Other	1%	2%	1%

NGLTF (1989: p. 8) notes that these statistics sharply underestimate the actual extent of anti-gay harassment and violence that occurred in the United States in 1988. Anti-gay episodes in the vast majority of U.S. towns and cities, and in 12 states...were not reported to NGLTF in 1988." Furthermore, the majority of the 120 reporting organizations had not systematically collected statistics on anti-gay incidents. In addition, these figures exclude suicides due to anti-gay oppression, reports of discrimination in employment, membership in the armed forces, child custody decisions, housing, and so forth, and cases of harassment and violence that did not appear to be motivated by anti-gay prejudice. In short, as one group indicated to NGLTF (1989: p. 8), these figures "don't even scratch the surface of the problem."

Other studies of anti-gay hate crimes corroborate these findings and conclusions. In a survey released by NGLTF in 1984 more than 90% of 2074 people (654 lesbians and 1420 gay men) in Atlanta, Boston, Dallas, Denver, Los Angeles, Seattle, and St. Louis reported having experienced some type of harassment, threat, or assault; more than 30% said they had been threatened with violence; almost 25% of the men and 10% of the women had been physically assaulted; approximately 33% were verbally abused and 7% were physically abused by relatives; and 20% of the women and almost 50% of the men reported they had been threatened, attacked, or harassed in junior or senior high school because they were perceived to be gay or lesbian.

NGLTF (1989) reviewed several other unpublished studies of anti-gay violence conducted in Philadelphia, Washington, DC, and Baltimore in 1988. These studies found that between 9% and 18% of those surveyed had experienced one or more physical assaults because of their sexual orientation. Since several of these studies are based on samples of gay people over time, rather than tabulations of reported bias crime incidents, some trend comparisons can be made. Herek (1989: p. 950) concluded that these studies "support the hypothesis that victimization is increasing."

Furthermore, NGLTF (1989: p. 12) reports that the Philadelphia study compared Pennsylvania rates with criminal victimization rates in a Bureau of Justice statistical study and concluded:

> When annual rates of criminal violence in the Pennsylvania study are compared with Department of Justice estimates of the number of adult Americans who experienced criminal violence in

1986, gay men in Pennsylvania (excluding Philadelphia) were victimized 9 times more often, and Pennsylvania lesbians (excluding Philadelphia) were victimized 7 times more often, than the average rate for the U.S. adult population (i.e., those who live in rural, suburban or urban settings). Gay men and lesbians in Philadelphia only were victimized 10 times and 7 times more, respectively, than the average rates for men and women living in U.S. major cities.

Since the Pennsylvania data are primarily from respondents who are white and above average in affluence and education and since the risk of victimization is greater among minorities and low income people, these figures are undoubtedly underestimates of the amounts of anti-gay violence and harassment experienced by the gay and lesbian community as a whole.

Another survey of anti-gay violence (Comstock, 1989) confirms many of the figures presented above. In that study, questionnaires were distributed to 700 people in gay meeting places and through ads in gay publications, with a 42% response rate (usable questionnaires from 166 gay men and 125 lesbians). The sample was 77% white, 11% Black, and 8% Hispanic; 39% of the respondents were between 21 and 30 years of age, 39% between 31 and 40, and 17% over 40. Comstock (1989) found that the types of victimization included a) being chased or followed (32%); b) objects thrown at them (21%); c) punched/kicked/hit/beaten (18%); d) vandalism/arson (16%), robbed (12%); e) raped (8%); f) assaulted with weapon (7%); and g) spit at (7%). While the order was similar for whites and people of color, people of color were more likely than whites to have been chased/followed (43% vs. 29%) or have objects thrown at them (31% vs. 18%).

In the Comstock study, differences by gender were statistically significant: men were more likely than women, a) to have been chased/followed (36% vs. 28%); b) to have objects thrown at them (27% vs. 14%); c) to have been punched, kicked, hit or beaten (24% vs. 10%); d) to have been robbed (19% vs. 2%); e) to have been raped (10% vs. 5%); and f) to have been assaulted with a weapon (11% vs. 2%).

Overall, 59% of the respondents reported being victimized in public gay areas (such as gay bars or gay neighborhoods), 31% in public nongay areas (such as on public transportation or in nongay neighborhoods), 26% in home settings (parents' or relatives' homes, their own homes), and 25% in schools (high school and college). Men were more likely than women to report victimization in gay public areas (66% vs. 45%), while women were more likely than men to report attacks in public non-gay areas (42% vs. 26%) and in home settings (30% vs. 24%).

While these figures may reflect some increased tendency on the part of individuals who have been victimized in anti-gay attacks to complete a questionnaire on the subject, these numbers are probably closer indicators of the true rate of anti-gay victimization than are those obtained from police records and from the recording of incidents by various agencies. Evidence for this is the finding from Comstock's questionnaire that 73% of the respondents never reported the incident to the police. Most of those not reporting the crime said that they perceived or experienced the police to be anti-gay (67%). And 40% of those not reporting attacks to police said that they feared disclosure of sexual orientation. Of those who did report the incident to the police (and, again, only 27% chose to do so), 51% found the police to be courteous, 67% reported the police to be indifferent, 23% said the police were hostile, and 5% said they were abusive (these were not mutually exclusive items).

Herek (1989), too, noted that several surveys of gay-bashing victims discovered that only between 10 and 23% of the victims reported the incident to the police or other agencies. Berrill (1986: p. 6) concludes that victims of anti-gay violence are less likely than others to report to the police: "Current research indicates that at least three quarters of anti-gay violence victims fail to notify police, while half (52%) of the victims of violent crimes fail to do so." Anderson (1982) describes the results of a 1979 study in Minneapolis in which two-thirds of the lesbians and gay men who were victims of assault took no action in reporting the incident and only 9.3% reported it to the police.

Research by Comstock (1989), NGLTF (1989), and several other unpublished studies (as quoted in NGLTF, 1989), all point in similar directions. It is, of course, impossible to get accurate data on crime; all data must depend on what is reported. It is even more difficult to obtain accurate data on gay-related crimes when the fear of reporting such crime may be greater. Furthermore, it is impossible to generate a random sample survey of gay people. Consequently, all findings must be based on those responding to surveys, who are usually middle-class, white, educated, urban, and open about their sexual orientation. Similarly, figures based on data gathered from organizations reporting to a central clearinghouse are limited to the number of organizations that choose to record the hate crimes reported to them and then, in turn, choose to report those data to the central agency (in this case, NGLTF).

In short, the numbers presented above should be viewed as relative indicators of what bias crimes are being committed, how frequently, and against whom, rather than as absolute levels. Clearly, though, there is a significant problem of violent crimes being perpetrated against gay men and lesbians because of their sexual orientation. How this problem is being handled by the criminal justice system, the media, and other organizations is the focus of the discussion that follows.

THE CRIMINAL JUSTICE SYSTEM AND GAY BASHING

From law enforcement practices to the role of the prosecutor's office to the attitudes of the judge to law makers in state and national government, dealing with bias crimes is generally hampered by prejudice, misinformation, and few guidelines. Of all the groups affected by bias crimes, gay men and lesbians appear to be most vulnerable and ill-treated by the various components of the criminal justice system, largely because of the familiar process known as "blaming the victim."

Police

Many professionals in the law enforcement field do not view bias crimes as a serious problem (Finn and McNeil, 1987). In New York State, the response to bias crime "is uneven and inadequate. Few of the 600 police agencies have any awareness of or focused response to bias crimes" (Governor's Task Force, 1988: p. 105). The New York State report continues: "Despite the widespread inability for police agency officials to specify the incidence of bias crime, evidence suggests that it is widespread in the state" (Governor's Task Force, 1988: p. 106).

While some of the perception that bias crime is not a significant problem is due to the fact that many groups fear reporting incidents, ignoring bias crime is also related to the fact that some law enforcement personnel do not take it seriously. Since much hate crime is committed by teenage boys and young adults, it is often considered just an adolescent "prank" or something done by a basically "good kid" (Finn and McNeil, 1987; Governor's Task Force, 1988). Confusion over the definition and identification of hate crimes is also part of the problem. In addition, some police departments are reluctant to develop a whole new category of crime which will require more paperwork and necessitate the allocation of time and funds to handle, in most instances diverting them from other projects (see Finn and McNeil, 1987).

The New York State Governor's Task Force (1988: p. 134) reported that "Allegations of bias-related violence by police officers were among the most disturbing to come before the Task Force. Many of those incidents marked by the tragedy of death involve law enforcement officers." Public testimony to the Task Force described improper police use of force against Blacks, Hispanics, Asians, and gays and lesbians. In this connection it is worth reiterating that Comstock's (1989) study, cited above, found that the most common reason given by respondents for not reporting incidents of gay-bashing to police was a perceived or experienced anti-gay attitude by police. Fear of police abuse was also claimed by 14% of the respondents. Police harassment and abuse accounted for 205 incidents (almost 3%) of the total number of cases reported to NGLTF (1989) for 1988, including such cases as the verbal abuse and clubbing of patrons by police in a Pittsburgh gay bar, police name-calling and striking a suspect perceived to be gay, and security guards yelling "faggot" and "queer" at protestors in a Massachusetts state senate gallery demonstration.

Prosecutors

Intimidation by some police forces is only the beginning of the problems in the criminal justice system. Prosecutors are also likely to ignore bias crimes or not to see them as a major problem: there is "a low level of awareness of bias crime in many DAs' offices" (Governor's Task Force, 1988: p. 147). Prosecutors who do comprehend the seriousness of such crimes may find their efforts hampered for various reasons. The police, for example, may not gather all the necessary evidence or they may fail to bring cases to be prosecuted; sometimes victims may want to drop the case in order to avoid the risk of public exposure with a trial; plea-bargaining may diminish the civil rights charges in some cases; and smaller cities and towns, especially those without a bias-crime focus in the police force, may not have sufficient resources to allow them to respond to hate crimes (Finn and McNeil, 1987).

Judiciary

But even if the police and the district attorney's office are successful in bringing a case to court on a bias-crime charge, problems in the judiciary often change the focus. A typical reaction is to acquit the defendant or to hand down a lenient sentence on the basis of the so-called "homosexual panic" or "gay advance" defense. In these cases, self-defense or temporary insanity is claimed as a result of an actual or perceived sexual advance by the victim (Finn and McNeil, 1987). A widely-reported example of this phenomenon was the December 1988 sentence hearing of a man convicted of murdering two gay men in Dallas. The defendant was sentenced to 30 years in prison rather than a life sentence as sought by the prosecution. According to an Associated Press report (Los Angeles Times, 1988), State District Judge Jack Hampton said: "These two guys that got killed wouldn't have been killed if they hadn't been cruising the streets picking up teenage boys." Hampton claimed that the homosexuality of the murder victims entered into his decision to give the killer a lighter sentence. He said he would have given a harsher sentence if the victims had been "a couple of housewives out shopping, not hurting anybody." The Texas Commission on Judicial Conduct is investigating this case.

In another incident in Broward County, Florida,

Circuit Judge Daniel Futch jokingly asked the prosecutor when the anti-gay nature of a beating death outside a Fort Lauderdale gay nightclub was brought up, "That's a crime now, to beat up a homosexual?" (as reported in NGLTF, 1989: p. 25). In this and many similar cases, the "homosexual panic" defense is used as a way of shifting responsibility to the victim and away from the defendant. The assumption is "that gay people are sexually aggressive and predatory, and [this] has been used most successfully when the victims are dead and therefore unable to answer the defendant's allegations" (NGLTF, 1989: p. 25). Although NGLTF reports that this type of defense has failed to exonerate defendants in most cases, the fact that it is used speaks to the problems anti- gay violence victims must confront and the prejudices some judges and prosecutors bring to their cases.

The case of the assassination of San Francisco Supervisor Harvey Milk and of Mayor George Moscone in 1978 by Dan White, is perhaps the most famous example of light sentences given to violent offenders when their victims are gay or lesbian. Although this case is better known for its so-called "Twinkie defense", rather than for the use of a "homosexual panic" tactic, the outcome, which was a miscarriage of justice, was generally perceived to be heavily influenced by the fact that one of the victims was a gay man (Shilts, 1982).

These examples could be multiplied manyfold to illustrate the point that the judicial system has a tendency to treat the perpetrators of anti-gay violence with leniency, which serves to reinforce homophobic ideas that gay-bashing is not a serious crime.

Legislation

Appropriate legislation could help to deter anti-gay violence. However, the same kinds of prejudices and assumptions that influence police, prosecutors, and judges also are found among legislators, many of whom maintain that existing laws already apply and that newer, more specific ones therefore do not need to be enacted. Some object to the special protection nature of bias crime laws, while others are concerned about First Amendment issues related to criminalizing verbal harassment (Finn and McNeil, 1987).

The central issues that need to be addressed by legislators include raising the charges from misdemeanors to felonies; increasing the penalties for convictions; using civil rights injunctions more frequently; mandating bias crime education, especially targeted to minorities; requiring the collection of bias-crime data; and the most controversial, adding "sexual orientation" as a category in the list of groups included in bias crime bills (see Finn and McNeil, 1987; Governor's Task Force, 1988). The Governor's Task Force (1988: p. 218) reported that:

> no single statute in New York State addresses acts of violence which are motivated in whole or in part by prejudice against the victim's race, religion, creed, color, age, disability, national origin, sex or sexual orientation. A number of existing statutes do offer some relief, but only to victims of some types of bias-related violence. Of particular note is omission of anti-gay/lesbian violence from the protection now provided by the existing statutes.

New York is not alone in this regard. Depending on the state, legislation aimed at bias crimes varies in what is covered, which groups are included, and what kinds of penalties are imposed. Property damage statutes (especially aimed at religious buildings and cemeteries) are in effect in 21 states; some states have raised the penalties for assault to a felony if the assault is due to bias

(Minnesota, California, and Wisconsin have such laws); some states have statutes forbidding interfering with someone's civil rights; and a few states require police departments to collect bias-crime data at the local and state level (Connecticut and Minnesota have such laws). But as of late 1989, only California and the city of Seattle prohibit acts motivated by the sexual orientation of the victim. Leaders of the Republican Party in the New York State Senate--despite the recommendation from the Governor's Task Force, passage by the State Assembly, and support from Governor Cuomo--blocked the passage of a bias-crime bill which contained "sexual orientation" as a category.

According to NGLTF (1989), Michigan's state senate removed a sexual orientation provision from a hate crimes bill although it had been included in the House version of the bill. At the city level, Oklahoma City included sexual orientation as a minority group protected from harassment in its bill; Columbus, Ohio, despite the Mayor's request to drop gays from its bill, voted to increase penalties for bias crimes including those based on sexual orientation; and San Francisco, San Diego County, and Montgomery County, Maryland have required data collection on bias crimes including those committed against gays and lesbians.

At the federal level, the Hate Crime Statistics Act (HR. 3193; S. 702) which would require the collection of statistics at the federal level on crimes based on race, religion, ethnicity, and "homosexuality or heterosexuality," passed the House of Representatives by a large margin (383- 29) in May 1988, but was blocked in the Senate by Jesse Helms, despite passing unanimously in the Senate Judiciary Committee. The bill, re-introduced in February 1989, passed in the House in June 1989 (386-47) and in February 1990 in the Senate (92-4). At this writing, it is on President Bush's desk awaiting his signature (he backed the bill).

Sexual orientation has also been included in a model hate-crime statute developed by the national Anti-Defamation League of B'nai B'rith. This model proposes enhanced criminal penalties for bias-motivated crimes, a civil cause of action for victims, and mandatory data collection by law enforcement agencies (NGLTF, 1989).

The inclusion of "sexual orientation" as a category in bias crime bills has led to the rejection of proposed statutes in many locales. The Governor's Task Force (1988: p. 219) recognized the greater likelihood of a bias crime act being passed if lesbians and gay men are excluded, but strongly states:

> the Task Force believes that excluding anti-gay/lesbian violence victims from the protection of the Act would be wrong. To do so would give the false impression that such conduct is either condoned by the state or that such acts of bias-related violence do not exist. Neither of these notions is correct.

The New York state bill was defeated because of the sexual orientation provision.

THE CAUSES OF ANTI-GAY AGGRESSION

The deficiencies in the criminal justice system outlined above clearly serve as contributory factors in gay-bashing. If anti-gay crimes tend not to be reported, if the offenders tend not to be apprehended, if legislators have not provided the legal tools for penalizing offenders, and if the sentences meted out to those successfully prosecuted for such offenses tend to be light, then the possibility for deterring individuals who might commit bias crimes is small. But the other causes of anti-gay aggression are complex and legion. Some of the factors responsible for attacks on gays and lesbians are unique to this category of victims, but others are identical to the factors generally implicated in violence and aggression targeted to minorities in general. Most of the theories used to explain racism and religious intolerance can be applied to understanding gay-bashing, but a comprehensive theory of anti-gay aggression must include variables that are specific to this category of victim.

The sociopolitical climate of the 1980's in the United States certainly contributed to the increasing severity of the problem of hate crime in general. The Anti-Defamation League of B'nai B'rith has documented a five-year high in anti-semitic incidents in 1988, an increase of 19% in vandalism and 41% in harassment over the preceding year (as reported in NGLTF, 1989). Other organizations (such as the Center for Democratic Renewal, the National Institute Against Prejudice and Violence, and the Southern Poverty Law Center) which monitor racial and religious bias also have reported increases, leading NGLTF (1989: p. 30) to conclude that "growing reports of hate violence suggest that the pluralistic fabric of our society may be unravelling, a trend that should alarm all those concerned about human and civil rights."

SOCIAL AND CULTURAL CAUSES

Finn and McNeil (1987: p.1), in their report for the Department of Justice, suggested that, while some increases in bias-crime statistics are related to more accurate reporting and clearer definitions, the widespread problem is due to "increased economic competition from minorities, visibility of gay men, ethnic neighborhood transition, and a perceived decrease in government efforts to prevent discrimination in education, housing, and employment." The rhetoric of white supremacist groups and the failure of local and national leaders to condemn these groups more strongly also contribute to the increase in bias-motivated incidents.

Los Angeles County's Commission on Human Rights (1989) suggested that the causes of increases in hate crimes include rapid ethnic demographic change, ongoing intergroup tension, international events, and entrenched bigotry in some segments of the population, and the New York State Governor's Task Force (1988) concluded that broad social forces, such as the failure of schools to educate about diversity and anti-bias, the failure of the media to provide accurate portrayals of ethnic and racial groups, and the perpetuation of segregated housing which denies minorities equal access to housing, are responsible for the increase in bias crimes. Many of these factors are relevant to the situation of gay men and lesbians as well as that of other minorities.

Although there have been increases in the 1980's in hate crimes generally, within American society over the past 30 years the acceptability of overt racism and anti-semitism has declined. A similar magnitude of decline in negative attitudes towards gays and lesbians and in values related to homosexuality is difficult to document. For many of the religious denominations in this country, for example, homosexuality remains a sin. While a few Protestant denominations have been moving toward full equality and acceptance for gays and lesbians, the Catholic Church's anti-homosexual stance has become vocally more strident in recent years, with Vatican spokesmen and some leading figures in American Catholicism, such as New York's John Cardinal O'Connor, actively expressing their opposition to the gay subculture.

During the two decades since the Stonewall Rebellion in 1969, the gay rights movement has pushed for equal rights for gays and lesbians. As a result, gays and lesbians have become more visible to the general public, augmenting considerably the awareness of homosexuality as a significant phenomenon in American society that resulted from the research by Kinsey and his associates which demonstrated that homosexual behavior was much more widespread than had been thought previously. The struggle for gay rights brought with it an increase in anti-gay rhetoric on the part of both religious and political leaders, and this rhetoric, too, must be seen as a major contributor to gay-bashing, fueling overt hostility and violence against the gay minority. While various denominations in the past justified discrimination against and hostility toward members of racial and religious outgroups, such as Blacks and Jews, citing biblical scriptures to justify bigotry, few do so today. Opposition to homosexuality, however, continues to be based in religious beliefs. Therefore, some of the same groups that in the past supported civil rights for ethnic groups are strongly opposed to equal rights and protections for gays and lesbians.

Highly visible attacks on gays are made with regularity by influential politicians and political commentators. These attacks by Senators and Congressmen such as Jesse Helms and William Dannemeyer and by political commentators such as Patrick Buchanan continue a long tradition in which gays and lesbians have served as scapegoats and targets of opportunity. An alleged association between homosexuals and communists was stressed during the McCarthy era when gay-bashing in Congress was especially serious, with careers and lives ruined by the attacks during that witchhunt aimed at ridding American society of undesirables and unpopular beliefs. The second-class status of gays and lesbians persists today inasmuch as laws which prevent them from exercising the same rights as other citizens are still on the books and are often enforced. Discrimination continues with respect to membership in the armed forces, security clearances, immigration and naturalization, child custody and visitation rights, adoption and foster care, housing and public accommodations, marriage, and inheritance (Stoddard et al., 1983). While the civil rights protections of other minorities may have eroded to some degree during the 1980's, the gay minority has still to attain many of the rights and protections guaranteed to members of ethnic and religious minorities.

In one sense, the gay minority's victimization rises and falls along with the victimization of other minorities in response to the increase or decrease in the factors that have an impact on attacks on outgroups generally. However, it is also likely that as other minorities are perceived as less legitimate targets of attack (condemned by opinion molders in the society), gays and lesbians will become more and more the victims of hate crimes. Indeed, with the current changes in Eastern Europe and the Soviet Union and the resultant decline in anti-communism, it is also quite conceivable that intolerance will focus attention more strongly on gays and lesbians.

STEREOTYPING AND THE ROLE OF THE MEDIA

Stereotypes of gay men, and perhaps to a lesser extent of lesbians, play a key role in the etiology of gay-bashing, just as stereotypes of other minority groups are implicated in bias crimes committed against their members. Furthermore, the perpetuation of these stereotypes in the media as well as the media's handling of gay-bashing merit examination as indirect causes of bias crimes. Newspapers, television, and other public forms of communication can provide useful information about bias incidents, yet they can also create images about the groups involved that provoke new incidents.

The Governor's Task Force (1988) studied 10 daily newspapers throughout New York State and concluded that the media was not performing a positive function with respect to bias violence. More specifically, the report found that newspaper coverage emphasizes physical violence out of proportion to actual rates; that bias incidents are portrayed as isolated from normal, everyday life; and that violence against some groups is systematically underreported, "particularly true of attacks on gays and on Asians and other ethnic groups with a high proportion of recent immigrants....No reports of anti-gay violence were found in the sample of newspapers in this study even though gays and lesbians may be the most victimized group in the nation" (Governor's Task Force, 1988: p. 228).

The Task Force saw this in part as a reflection of the underreporting of gay violence to police by the victims and the dependency of media on police reports for information. Also, The Governor's Task Force (1988: p. 229) concluded,

> The failure of the media to report about anti-gay and anti-lesbian violence on a regular basis may also reflect the continuing reluctance of the media to acknowledge that anti-gay actions are as serious as actions motivated by hatred of a person's race, religion, or ethnicity.
> In this respect the media are reflecting what is often considered to be the prevalent social attitudes toward lesbian and gay men. The existence of the gay community was frequently ignored by the media prior to the onset of the AIDS crisis; only in the last few years have the media begun to acknowledge that a significant minority of Americans face unique concerns related to their sexual orientation. The violence resulting from hostile attitudes toward lesbians and gay men has still failed to attract media interest.

Further findings about media coverage by the Governor's Task Force (1988: p. 232) include the dependence on official sources for perspectives and viewpoints on the incident; attempts to delegitimate the victims by questioning the honesty of the victim's version and focusing on motives and character; and frequent attempts to deny the bias motivations in the incident by framing it in terms of youhtful perpetrators "protecting their turf" or the protection of property.

There has also been an increase in radio and television talk shows which perpetuate "false and sometimes vicious myths that reasonable and sensitive listeners take to be anti-Jewish, anti-Black, anti-gay, and anti other groups" (Governor's Task Force, 1988: p. 235). Coupled with low minority representative among media employees and the almost exclusive use of whites in advertisements, the media rarely portray minorities in everyday life situations, thereby enhancing the out-of-context aspects of bias crimes when they are reported. Defamatory remarks by public figures in the media against lesbians and gay men are not included in the bias incident statistics. Yet, many of these statements can be viewed as the source of subsequent assaults (NGLTF, 1989). They are included here as a means of illustrating the context in which gay-bashing incidents occur and to show how they may be related to the violence which occurs soon after they are aired.

The NGLTF report quotes an article in the Boston Gay Community News about Philadelphia city councilmember Francis Rafferty's statement opposing Gay Pride Month by declaring that gays have nothing to be proud about because they are spreading AIDS. Soon after that, "a Philadelphia gay activist was beaten by two men who began their attack by claiming that 'We're for Rafferty and we're for the majority'" (NGLTF, 1989: p. 28).

The case of Andy Rooney is instructive. Rooney, a CBS commentator, made anti-gay remarks in his syndicated columns and also on a television special in December 1989. Subsequently, he was reported to have made racist remarks as well, which he denied. He was suspended from his job for three months by CBS. Newspaper reports seemed to suggest that the suspension came not because of his admitted inflammatory anti-gay remarks but because of his alleged racist comments. In any case, his early reinstatement following a public outcry in his favor sent a message that both homophobic and racist attacks are acceptable.

Other media incidents reported to NGLTF ranged from a comedy album by Sam Kinison that blames AIDS on gay men having intercourse with monkeys; a song, "Homesick Heroes," on an album by country and western singer Charlie Daniels which encourages punching out "sissy" gays and sending them back "where women are women and men are men;" a radio disc jockey in Connecticut who stated that "fags" should be castrated to prevent AIDS from spreading, followed soon by a gay man with AIDS being chased by teenagers screaming that he didn't deserve to live since the deejay said "queers" spread AIDS; a Miami radio station advertising a nightclub offering special activities including "beating up queers;" and an HBO television comedy special which had comedian Damon Wayans talking about gay-bashing as he "wobbled feyly across the stage while rolling his eyes and swishing his wrists" (NGLTF, 1989: p. 29). Although such incidents are not included when defining or recording bias crime incidents, the media are being monitored for anti-gay remarks and stereotyping by various chapters of the Gay and Lesbian Alliance Against Defamation and protests against such incidents are being lodged with media representatives and program sponsors, since their impact on gay-bashing is far from negligible.

Aspects of the widespread stereotype of gay men in American culture may also contribute to gay-bashing. These include the perception of gay men as feminine and weak, as men who engage in unmanly occupations such as hairdressing, interior decorating and the arts, which are of lesser value to society than stereotypical, straight male occupations. The general tendency of the media is to focus on those segments of the gay community that conform to this pattern. There is very little effort made to portray gays who do not conform to the swishy stereotype. If gay men are portrayed as feminine and weak, it is natural for gay-bashers to perceive them as easy targets and a safe outlet for thrill-seeking.

In addition to seeing gays and lesbians as cost-free targets, there is a widespread perception that homosexuality is illegal, and therefore, attacks on gays and lesbians can be justified as attacks on criminals. While homosexual behavior is a felony in some states, this perception persists even in states where homosexuality has been decriminalized for almost two decades. A common misunderstanding of the Bowers v. Hardwick sodomy case decided by the Supreme Court in 1986 is that the ruling handed down outlawed homosexuality, whereas it simply made it permissible for states to have laws of that type. While that case did not make homosexuality illegal, the fact that it did uphold the rights of states to outlaw homosexual behavior can be interpreted as institutional gay-bashing by giving permission to withhold equal rights, even the right of the gay minority to exist. It is noteworthy that reports of gay-bashings increased significantly in many locales after news of that decision appeared in the media.

Other dimensions of the gay stereotype are also worth mentioning. Gay men are often viewed as hypersexual, their lives being defined by their sexuality. They are seen as highly promiscuous, an image that was exacerbated by AIDS reporting which stressed the number of partners some gay men have.
They are seen as incapable of maintaining relationships, and their intimate life is interpreted as involving lots of sex but no love. The image often portrayed is one of well-to-do, self-indulgent hedonists without the responsibilities of mature heterosexual men. Moreover, the belief that gay men recruit new members by seducing young

boys is widespread. And long after the psychological professions removed homosexuality from the list of mental illnesses, the stereotype of gays and lesbians as mentally disturbed or sick individuals persists. Some elements of this stereotype, gays share with other minorities, e.g., hypersexuality and unstable relationships with Blacks, wealth with Jews (see Adam, 1978).

While some media producers have made some efforts to portray gays and lesbians in a more positive light (PBS, in particular, in some cities), the efforts are insufficient to eliminate erroneous elements in the popular gay stereotype and to counter the anti-gay material broadcast on radio and television.

Explanations for anti-gay sentiments and gay-bashing need to take into account the negative stereotypes, which are perpetuated by the media, as does the work by Harry (1982: p. 546) who discusses the concept of "derivative deviance" which he defines as "that subset of all victimizations which is perpetrated upon other presumed deviants who, because of their deviant status, are presumed unable to avail themselves of civil protection." He distinguishes two kinds: cultural derivative deviance and opportunistic derivative deviance. The former occurs when the victim is unknown to the assailant who relies on stereotypes of appearance and place. This kind of victimization results in assaults and robberies, what Harry (1982) calls "fag-bashing." The latter type occurs when a pre-existing relationship is present and the victim has trustingly shared his or her stigmatized status with the perpetrator. This kind typically leads to incidents of extortion or blackmail.

Harry's (1982) data support the idea that "fag-bashing" is more likely to occur in gay-defined areas and when the person conforms more to cultural stereotypes (39% of the self-defined effeminate men were assaulted versus 22% of the masculine and

17% of the very masculine self-defined men). Similarly for cases of blackmail: the more effeminate and those not attached to a reference group of other gays were more likely successfully extorted. Thus, Harry (1982: p. 560) concludes that "those who most conform to stereotypes of deviants appear to bear the brunt of derivative victimization, both cultural and opportunistic."

Although Harry found that marginal gays were more likely to be blackmailed, he was unable to show a significant relationship between those gays unattached to a large gay network and increased assaults, thus contradicting the findings of Miller and Humphreys (1980: p. 177) whose data suggested that homosexual marginals, i.e., those who operate "on the periphery of gay institutions and social networks," are more likely to be victims of violent crimes. Rather, attachment to a visible gay community and participation in activities in gay areas make gay men and lesbians more vulnerable to identification and possible victimization.

Given that most anti-gay incidents are committed by young males, Herek (1984) believes that the pressure among peers to accept masculine gender role traits and to solidify group membership by affirming masculinity through violence should be considered as a possible explanation in our culture. More and more, "sexual orientation is becoming the component defining masculinity" (Franklin, 1988: p. 163). As this happens, heterosexuality becomes increasingly relevant as the core idea of masculinity; the pressure to deemphasize homosexuality and intimacy between men increases; and the devaluing of feminine behaviors in men continues. In such a cultural climate, young males are more likely to target openly gay men, males perceived to be more feminine in appearance and behavior, and anyone else perceived to be non-conforming to gender roles.

Thus, from a sociological perspective, crimes committed against lesbians and gay men are related to cultural stereotyping, opportunities to identify people as stigmatized by seeing them participate in gay contexts, and other social definitions of what constitutes appropriate gender behavior as perceived especially by young males.

ANTI-GAY ATTITUDES AND HOMOPHOBIA

The negative stereotype of gays discussed above tends to be accompanied by anti-gay attitudes on the part of a significant proportion of the American population, and in more extreme cases by homophobia, a concept used to designate irrational fear of and hostility toward homosexuals. Evidence of the magnitude of homophobic attitudes in this society is provided by many studies. Results from a few of these studies can be described here. Inasmuch as young males tend to be the chief perpetrators of anti-gay violence, an understanding of homophobia in that segment of the population is essential. A survey of the attitudes of 2823 junior and senior high school students in 20 school districts in New York State, conducted by the Governor's Task Force (1988) provided data on anti-gay hostility. The report (1988: p. 97) concluded that:

> One of the most alarming findings in the youth survey is the openness with which the respondents expressed their aversion and hostility toward gays and lesbians....the students were quite emphatic about their dislike for these groups and frequently made violent, threatening statements. Gays and lesbians, it seems, are perceived as legitimate targets which can be openly attacked.

One of the findings from this survey clearly showed gender differences in attitudes toward gays. While 74% of the boys agreed that it would be "bad" or "very bad" to have gays move into the neighborhood, 48% of the girls checked those attitudes. Overall, between 69% and 91% of the students rejected the idea of having gays as neighbors. Only 12% believed it would be "very good" or "good" to have a gay person move into their neighborhood. For purposes of comparison, 50% to 60% said it would be "very good" or "good" to have neighbors of ethnic and racial minorities (Blacks, Hispanics, Asians, Jews). When comments were made on the questionnaires by the students, most were positive about interracial and intercultural interactions. However, when the comments were about gay people, they "were often openly vicious. Emphasis was frequently added to the negative responses and a number of students threatened violence against gays" (Governor's Task Force, 1988: p. 84).

Data from 64 higher education campuses in New York State show similar results. In a survey of official representatives of four-year colleges and universities, 20% perceived that gay and lesbian students were rejected by fellow students, 37% felt that they were avoided by others, and 23% believed they were ignored by other students. In other words, 80% reported that they perceived gay and lesbian students as being rejected, avoided, or ignored; the next closest group was Black students perceived to be avoided or ignored by 55% of the administrators. As the Governor's Task Force (1988: p. 55) stated: "No other group is defined as rejected in institutional authorities' perceptions. This refusal to accept gay and lesbian students leads all too frequently to active rejection....active rejection of other groups is not normative on campus."

In addition, 35% of these 64 administrators, report that anti-gay and lesbian incidents have occurred on their campuses, 60% believe there is anti-gay sentiment, and 32% say they have policies against gay bias. The Governor's Task Force (1988: p. 56) concludes:

> The pattern seems clear. Many campuses in New York experience anti-gay/lesbian incidents and even more have anti-gay/lesbian feelings. In the face of this, most have no organizational support and few have experimented with promising policies to alleviate this problem.

From a psychological viewpoint, the concept of homophobia is given much prominence as a driving force in the development of negative and violent behavior toward homosexuals. Homophobia has generally been perceived as a unidimensional trait of personality, often unrelated to the social context in which prejudicial attitudes (including racism and sexism) develop and are maintained.

In another study (D'Augelli, 1989), this one of students at a major university who had applied for the position of resident assistant, all of the subjects indicated that they had heard disparaging remarks made about gays and lesbians, 83% of them indicated that they heard such remarks often, and indeed, most of the subjects admitted that they themselves had made such remarks. Furthermore, the subjects all agreed that harassment of gays and lesbians was likely on their campus, with 52% believing that harassment, threats of violence, or physical attack are "very likely."

Herek (1984) provided a list of factors that correlate with the holding of negative attitudes toward lesbians and gay men; according to his review of the literature, those with more negative attitudes, 1) have had less personal contact with gays and lesbians, 2) have themselves not engaged in homosexual behavior and to identify themselves as gay or lesbian, 3) tend to perceive that their peers hold anti-gay attitudes, 4) tend to live in areas of North America where negative attitudes towards gays have been found to be more prevalent, 5) tend to be older and low in educational level, 6) tend to more religious, to be more frequent churchgoers, and to believe in more conservative religious ideology, 7) tend to hold traditional sex-role attitudes, 8) tend to be more negative about sexuality generally and to express more guilt about sexuality, and 9) tend to score high on authoritarianism and related personality measures.

In Herek's (1984) view, attitudes serve as strategies for meeting a variety of psychological needs in different social contexts. Homophobic attitudes, in particular, can serve various functions for different people. Herek (1984) sees three major needs being met by three types of attitudes: those which categorize reality based on past interactions (experiential), those which are used to cope with conflicts and anxieties by projecting them onto others (defensive), and those used to express abstract ideological concepts which are closely linked to notions of self (symbolic). These explain the variation in findings from studies about attitudes toward homosexuals.

The persistence of anti-gay attitudes and their effects on aggression have been supported in other research. Using male college students, San Miguel and Millham (1976) studied the interactive effects of attitudes, type of contact, perceived similarity, and sexual orientation on aggressive behavior and attitudes. Despite a limited sample and an absence of measures on actual violence, they found that there was significantly more aggression expressed toward homosexuals than heterosexuals. In addition, they (1976: p. 26) concluded that "homosexuals who are perceived by a heterosexual as personally similar to himself are likely to experience heightened rather than diminished aggressiveness from that person." In addition, aggression was not attenuated among heterosexuals who held prior negative attitudes towards homosexuals even after experiencing a positive cooperative interaction. In short, homosexuals "are subject to higher levels of aggression than are their normative counterparts" (San Miguel and Millham, 1976: p. 26).

Clearly the question of how attitudes toward homosexuality and gays and lesbians are formed and maintained is an important one in understanding anti-gay violence, especially from a psychological perspective. Since many people hold favorable attitudes toward gays and lesbians, even in a social and cultural context less supportive of homosexuals, personality traits and attitude formation become salient variables in explaining bias crimes.

AIDS AND GAY BASHING

The AIDS epidemic added to the problems confronting the gay community in the 1980's. On top of having to cope with a rising death toll and to make critical changes in patterns of behavior related to HIV transmission, gay men (and lesbians as well) became concerned about the possibility of a backlash and heightened homophobia and anti-gay violence. Originally labelled GRID (Gay-Related Immune Deficiency), AIDS became associated with homosexuality in the U.S. because the first cases were recognized in gay men living in major urban areas, notably in cities with large gay populations (New York, San Francisco, and Los Angeles). The high case fatality rate, ignorance about the etiology and the means of transmission of the disease, failure by the Reagan administration to deal with the epidemic, and sensationalist reporting by the press (when they were not ignoring the epidemic entirely), all helped to generate hysteria, a secondary epidemic sometimes referred to as "AFRAIDS". Political and religious opponents of the gay community were quick to use AIDS as a weapon, blaming AIDS on the sinfulness of gays and citing AIDS as justification for continued oppression of the gay minority (see Lang, 1989). To what extent, then, does AIDS serve as a cause of gay-bashing?

NGLTF (1989) reports that 17% of all incidents in their files were classified by local groups as "AIDS-related." Typically this designation refers to incidents involving verbal references to AIDS by assailants or actions directed against persons with AIDS because of their condition. While this percentage has been fairly consistent over the years (15% in 1987; 14% in 1986), it is probably underestimated since many organizations do not question victims about whether AIDS was a factor in the incident, many victims do not include AIDS as a variable when reporting, and many times it goes unspoken yet may be an underlying motivating factor.

However, AIDS is probably less a direct cause of the aggression than an excuse to allow the assailant to justify committing the hate act. Data from studies completed before AIDS became an issue provide evidence that anti-gay violence (in particular, physical assaults) existed as a serious problem even before the AIDS era. This is not to say that verbal harassment and property vandalism have remained steady, however. Again, problems in wording, categories used, and sampling prevent definitive conclusions from being made about rate changes over the years. In their 1969 survey (pre-gay liberation) of San Francisco Bay Area homosexuals, Bell and Weinberg (1978) found that 38% of the gay white men, 21% of the gay Black men, 2% of the white lesbians, and 5% of the Black Lesbians reported they had been robbed or assaulted one or more times because of their homosexuality. They also report that 35% of 458 Chicago gay white men in a 1967 pilot study said that they had been assaulted or robbed because of their homosexuality.

Anderson (1982) reports the results of a study conducted in Minneapolis of 289 gay men and lesbians in 1979. About 23% said they had experienced physical assault and almost 6% stated they were raped because of their sexual orientation. In a 1978 study of 1600 gay men (91% white) in Chicago, Harry (1982) found that 27% of those living in a gay neighborhood and 20% of those living in non-gay areas reported that they had been assaulted because of their homosexuality. These pre-AIDS figures, while difficult to compare exactly with the current figures because of the use of different categories of incidents, are not significantly different from the data reported by NGLTF, by Comstock (1989), and in the summary of unpublished studies analyzed by Herek (1989).

Thus, AIDS may not be a direct cause of violence. However, the AIDS epidemic has certainly made the gay community more visible, and this enhanced visibility could heighten the likelihood of gays and lesbians increasingly becoming targets of bias aggression. A reasonable though untested hypothesis can be advanced to account for the increases in anti-gay aggression of recent years, to wit, that the behaviors are justified by the attackers in terms of AIDS but they are produced by changes taking place in the total configuration of potential minority group targets seen as appropriate by intolerant individuals and by the greater visibility and accessibility of gays and lesbians due to the public attention they attract in their efforts to combat AIDS. As Herek (1989: p. 951) says,

> Much of the variance in AIDS-related bigotry
> is explained by antigay attitudes, which presumably
> predate the epidemic. Thus, AIDS may be
> less a cause of antigay sentiment than a focal
> event that crystallizes heterosexuals'
> preexisting hostility toward gay people.

While AIDS may have contributed in the early years of the epidemic to increased hostility toward gays, it is important to point out that the opposite reaction has also occurred. As NEWSWEEK (March 12, 1990, p.21) reported recently, "the devastation AIDS has created has led to greater sympathy in the straight world, and gays' responsible handling of the crisis has led to new respect for the community." Ironically, then, on balance in the long run, AIDS may contribute to a reduction in the incidence of gay-bashing.

RECOMMENDATIONS AND PROPOSALS

In order to reduce anti-gay violence, attention must be paid to a complex set of issues related to hate crime. The first task is to gain acceptance by a variety of constituents for the development of strong bias-crime laws and policies. Second, where not already included, sexual orientation needs to be added as a category of bias crime. Third, comprehensive efforts must be made to reduce homophobia and negative attitudes towards homosexuality. Fourth, educational efforts must be intensified to improve the public's understanding of AIDS. And fifth, the needs of the victims of bias crimes should be addressed through the provisioning of appropriate services, and the treatment of victims by law enforcement agencies and mental health care facilities should be improved.

Legislation

At the top of the list of recommendations is the enactment of the federal Hate Crime Statistics Act which would require the collection of statistics on hate crimes at the national level. States and local communities must also be required to criminalize bias-motivated crimes and upgrade charges from the category of misdemeanor to that of felony. Mandatory data collection at the local and state level is also necessary to insure that hate violence receives the attention it merits. Sexual orientation, of course, must be included as a category in these laws. The enactment of a national law prohibiting discrimination on the basis of sexual orientation in housing, employment, public accommodations, and other aspects of life, and the repeal of sodomy laws in those states where they still exist would further serve to ameliorate the problem of anti-gay aggression.

Victim Services

The New York State Governor's Task Force (1983: p. 3) discusses the "rediscovery" of the victim and points to the need for policy makers and practitioners "to constantly improve their awareness of victims' needs and [to] pioneer innovative assistance programs." The report further states that some victims' experiences, such as those of the victims of bias-related violence, are so traumatic that special help should be given.

In a survey conducted by the Governor's Task Force (1988) in New York State, 46% of the district attorneys perceived that the essential services were available and were being delivered to the victims of hate crimes, and 81% agreed that bias-crime victims need special services. Additionally, the Task Force found that stereotypical handling of bias-crime victims existed, that few victim programs actually included any special effort to assist bias-crime victims, and that these individuals, rather than their assailants, were often blamed for the criminal event.

Anderson (1982) delineated some of the unique problems experienced by victims of assaults, especially sexual assaults against gay men, noting that the stages an assault victim goes through parallel those of female rape victims: the set-up (power ploys), the attack, and the aftermath (shock, denial, shame, guilt, self-blame, embarrassment, fear, suspicion, depression, low self-esteem). The content and intensity of such attacks may vary depending on whether the victim is a woman, a gay male, or a straight male perceived to be gay, but in general, victims of hate crime, and in particular of physical and sexual assaults, must deal with the larger issues of sexual identity and gender in ways that the victims of non-bias-related assaults do not. The special problems raised by gender and sexual orientation must be taken into consideration when exploring ways to create appropriate services for the victims of bias-related violence.

Education and Prevention

The primary goal, of course, is to prevent bias crimes rather than to deal with them after they have been committed, and crucial to the achievement of this objective is education on this issue for all segments of society, but most notably for those most closely linked to the problem, and that includes junior high and high school students, college students, police, prosecutors, judges, legislators, mental health personnel, and media professionals. The focus of such educational efforts needs to be on prejudice and the questions of racism, sexism, anti-Semitism, religious intolerance, and homophobia. The enactment and enforcement of effective bias-crime legislation nationwide is likely to depend on massive educational campaigns on these core topics.

Education should also include ways to identify bias crimes, training law enforcement personnel in sensitive methods of interviewing victims, the development of strategies to encourage individuals to report incidents with confidentiality, getting prosecutors and judges away from a "blame-the-victim" mentality, informing people of the seriousness of prejudice-motivated incidents, and aiding law enforcement agencies in working with community-based organizations representing various ethnic, racial, religious, and gay constituencies. Finally, prevention programs, training programs, effectively enacted legislation, and good data collection all require funding and a commitment from the government to support them. Nothing short of this will bring about any change in the widespread and continuing problem of bias-related violence.

Perhaps the most succinct way to end this chapter is to quote from the conclusion of a recent NGLTF (1989: p. 34) report:

> In assessing the impact of anti-gay violence, statistics alone fail to adequately do the job. Statistics do not measure the anguish, suffering, and rage experienced not only by the survivors but by the larger lesbian and gay community. As with other crimes motivated by prejudice, anti-gay attacks are acts of terrorism aimed at discouraging lesbians and gay men from exercising their rights to freedom of speech, association and assembly. On a more basic level, anti-gay violence seeks to deny to lesbians and gay men the essential right to live and love as they choose....The slowness of government on every level to acknowledge and combat anti-gay violence parallels its willful failure to deal with AIDS in the early stages of that epidemic. Some leaders in government, law enforcement, civil rights and religion have begun to address this issue. Their efforts, however, are frequently met by fierce--and often successful--opposition on the part of those who seek to exclude gay men and lesbians from protection in laws and programs aimed at combatting hate violence. The denial of such protections to gay people is a legal and moral disgrace that must be challenged by all people of conscience.

REFERENCES

Adam, B. (1978). *The Survival of Domination.* New York: Elsevier.

Anderson, C. (1982). Males as sexual assault victims: Multiple levels of trauma. *Journal of Homosexuality, 7:2/3*, 145-162.

Bell, A., & Weinberg, M. (1978). *Homosexualities: A Study of Diversity Among Men and Women.* New York: Simon and Schuster.

Berrill, K. (1986). Anti-Gay Violence: *Causes, Consequences, Responses.* Washington, DC: National Gay & Lesbian Task Force.

Blumenfeld, W. J., & Raymond, D. (1988). *Looking at Gay and Lesbian Life.* Boston: Beacon Press.

Boswell, J. (1980). *Christianity, Social Tolerance, and Homosexuality: Gay People in Western Europe from the Beginning of the Christian Era to the Fourteenth Century.* Chicago: The University of Chicago Press.

Carrier, J. M. (1980). Homosexual behavior in cross-cultural perspective. *In Homosexual Behavior: A Modern Reappraisal.* (Ed. by J. Marmor). Pp. 100-22. New York: Basic Books.

Carrier, J. M. (1989). Sexual behavior and spread of AIDS in Mexico. *In The AIDS Pandemic: A Global Emergency.* (Ed. by R. Bolton). Pp. 37-50. New York: Gordon and Breach.

Comstock, G. D. (1989). Victims of anti-gay/lesbian violence. *Journal of Interpersonal Violence, 4:1,* 101-106.

Crapo, R. H. (n.d.). *Factors in the cross-cultural patterning of homosexuality: A reappraisal of the literature.* Unpublished manuscript.

Davis, D. L. & Whitten, R.G. (1987). The cross-cultural study of human sexuality. *Annual Reviews in Anthropology, 16,* 69-98.

D'Augelli, A. R. (1989). Homophobia in a university community: Views of prospective resident assistants. *Journal of College Student Development, 30,* 546-552.

Finn, P., & McNeil, T. (1987). *The Response of the Criminal Justice System to Bias Crime: An Exploratory Review*. Submitted to U.S. Department of Justice. Cambridge, MA: Abt Associates.

Ford, C. S. & Beach, F. A. (1951). *Patterns of Sexual Behavior*. New York: Harper & Row, Publishers.

Franklin, C. W. (1988). *Men and Society*. Chicago: Nelson-Hall.

Gmunder, B. & Stamford, J. D. (1988). *Spartacus Guide for Gay Men. 17th Edition*. Berlin: Bruno Gmunder Verlag.

Governor's Task Force on Bias-Related Violence. (1988). *Final Report*. Albany, NY.

Greenberg, D. (1989). *The Construction of Homosexuality*. Chicago: University of Chicago Press.

Harry, J. (1982). Derivative deviance: The cases of extortion, fag-bashing, and shakedown of gay men. *Criminology, 19:4*, 546-564.

Heger, H. (1980). *The Men with the Pink Triangle*. Boston: Alyson Publications, Inc.

Herdt, G. H., Ed. (1984). *Ritualized Homosexuality in Melanesia*. Berkeley: University of California Press.

Herdt, G. H. (1987a). *Homosexuality. Encyclopedia of Religion, Vol. 3*. New York: Macmillan.

Herdt, G. H. (1987b). *The Sambia: Ritual and Gender in New Guinea*. New York: Holt, Rinehart, & Winston.

Herek, G. (1984). Beyond "homophobia": A social psychological perspective on attitudes toward lesbians and gay men. *Journal of Homosexuality, 10:1/2*, 1-21.

Herek, G. (1989). Hate crimes against lesbians and gay men. *American Psychologist, 44:6*, 948-955.

IGA, International Association of Lesbians/Gay Women and Gay Men. (1985). *IGA Pink Book 1985: A Global View of Lesbian and Gay Oppression and Liberation.* Amsterdam: COC-magazine.

Lang, N. G. (1989). AIDS, gays and the ballot box: The politics of disease in Houston, Texas. In: *The AIDS Pandemic: A Global Emergency.* (Ed. by R. Bolton). Pp. 111-117. New York: Gordon and Breach.

Los Angeles County Commission on Human Relations. (1989). *Hate Crime in Los Angeles County 1988.* Los Angeles, CA.

Los Angeles County Commission on Human Relations. (1990a). *Hate Crime in Los Angeles County 1989.* Los Angeles, Ca.

Los Angeles County Commission on Human Relations. (1990b). *Hate Crime in the 1980's: A Decade of Bigotry.* Los Angeles, Ca.

Los Angeles Times. (1988). *Dallas gay leader angry at Judge over his remarks on murder case.* December 17.

Miller, B., & Humphreys, L. (1980). Life-styles and violence: Homosexual victims of assault and murder. *Qualitative Sociology, 3:3,* 169-185.

National Gay & Lesbian Task Force (NGLTF). (1987). *Anti-Gay Violence, Victimization and Defamation in 1986.* Washington, DC: NGLTF.

National Gay & Lesbian Task Force (NGLTF). (1988). *Anti-Gay Violence, Victimization and Defamation in 1987.* Washington, DC: NGLTF.

National Gay & Lesbian Task Force (NGLTF). (1989). *Anti-Gay Violence, Victimization and Defamation in 1988.* Washington, DC: NGLTF.

Pedersen, L. (1985). The anti-discrimination law: the experience so far. *In The IGA Pink Book 1985.* (Ed. by IGA). Pp. 117-19. Amsterdam: COC-magazine.

Plant, R. (1986). The Pink Triangle: *The Nazi War Against Homosexuals*. New York: Henry Holt and Company.

Rector, F. (1981). *The Nazi Extermination of Homosexuals*. New York: Stein and Day.

Renzetti, C. (1988). Violence in lesbian relationships: A preliminary analysis of causal factors. *Journal of Interpersonal Violence, 3:4*, 381-399.

San Miguel, C., & Millham, J. (1976). The role of cognitive and situational variables in aggression toward homosexuals. *Journal of Homosexuality, 2:1*, 11-27.

Shilts, R. (1982). *The Mayor of Castro Street*. New York: St. Martin's Press.

Stoddard, T.B., Boggan, E.C., Haft, M.C., Lister, C., & Rupp, J.P. (1983). *The Rights of Gay People: An American Civil Liberties Union Handbook. Revised edition*. Toronto: Bantam Books.

Weiner, N.A., Zahn, M.A., & Sagi, R. J., (Eds.) (1990). *Violence: Patterns, Causes, Public Policy*. San Diego: Harcourt Brace Jovanovich, Publishers.

Weinrich, J. D. (1987). *Sexual Landscapes*. New York: Charles Scribner's Sons.

Werner, D. (1979). A cross-cultural perspective on theory and research on male homosexuality. *Journal of Homosexuality, 4:4*, 345-362.

Whitam, F. L. (1987). A cross-cultural perspective on homosexuality, transvestism and trans-sexualism. *In Variant Sexuality: Research and Theory*. (Ed. by G.D. Wilson). Pp. 176-201. London: Groom Helm.

Wooden, W., & Parker, J. (1982). *Men Behind Bars: Sexual Exploitation in Prison*. New York: Plenum Press.

10

Aggression by Women: Mores, Myths, & Methods
Luci Paul and MaryAnn Baenninger

Females are traditionally considered to be the less aggressive sex (Maccoby & Jacklin, 1974). Most investigators have adopted this tradition to such an extent that reports of violent crime by females have been relegated to footnote status or to short "asides" in discussions of the more prevalent male aggression (Campbell, 1982; Rosenblatt & Greenland, 1974). Information about the victims or objects of female crime or aggression has been similarly scarce.

A further consequence of the anomalous way that female violence has been perceived is that historically it has taken on a sensational flavor (Macaulay, 1985; Rosenblatt & Greenland, 1974), or has been viewed as supernatural, as evidenced by the social construction of witches (Karlsen, 1987). This sensationalism has continued in the media in the twentieth century, and has been reflected in the public's avid interest in recent reports, nonfiction "novels", and made-for-television movies, about violent females and mothers who kill their children. It is safe to say that "Bonnie and Clyde" had more mystique than if they had been Joe and Clyde, and Jean Harris got more attention in the press for killing the "Scarsdale diet doctor" than the male doctor would have gotten if he had killed her.

Also related to the low probability of female violence is the idea that the actions of a woman committing violent or aggressive acts are seen as more aberrant, and therefore more heinous than similar actions by a male. Women who murder, for instance, are thought to be different in motivation and psychological profile and to employ different weapons than men (Sparrow, 1950).

Recently there has been evidence to suggest that the relative probability of male versus female violent crimes has been shifting, however slowly. McClintock reported in 1963 that only 5.4% of violent crimes were committed by females, contrasting with Rosenblatt & Greenland's (1974) report of 14% in 1969. In addition, the rate of violent crimes committed by women is on the increase, in contrast to a decreasing rate of violent crime committed by men (Rosenblatt & Greenland, 1974). The most likely explanation for this turn of events is change in social norms and early experience and upbringing that permit women to be more equal to men in all respects. While becoming "equal" in the number of violent crimes is a regrettable form of equality, it nevertheless parallels evidence that social and cognitive characteristics of women and men are converging (e.g., Baenninger & Newcombe, 1989; Hilton, 1985). These changes no longer permit researchers to downplay the importance or relevance of aggressive and violent acts committed by females.

Of course aggressive actions are not restricted to the category of violent crime. Researchers, often developmentalists, have examined sex differences in less dramatic forms of aggressive behavior, such as children's fighting and aggressive interactions, and have concluded almost unanimously that boys are more aggressive than girls (see Maccoby & Jacklin, 1974; Hyde, 1984;1986, for comprehensive reviews). An examination of the *Child Development Abstracts* for the years since 1986 indicates researchers' acceptance of this idea. The majority of studies listed under the category of "aggression" include only males or almost all males as subjects. Thus, the a priori assumption that females are not aggressive occurs even in the developmental literature, an indication of the belief that either females are biologically nonaggressive, or that the social mores governing gender differences in aggression begin very early. While that may be so, gender differences decrease in later years (Hyde, 1984).Because researchers rarely include female subjects, there has been little cause to discuss the targets of females' aggression.

More recent reviews of literature concerning aggression by adults (Eagly & Steffen, 1986; Frodi, Macaulay, & Thome, 1977) seemingly contribute additional evidence to the general consensus that males engage in significantly more aggressive behaviors than females in experimental situations designed to provoke aggression. Nevertheless, many females are quite capable of aggressive behavior in the laboratory (see Eagly & Steffen, 1986), on city streets and in social situations (Campbell, 1982) and some commit violent crimes (Rosenblatt & Greenland, 1974). It is time to realize that "who aggresses more?", is no longer an appropriate question. Believing that males aggress more than females promotes an implicit ignorance and lack of interest about the situations in which females do aggress, the characteristics of their aggressive behavior, and the profiles of those who are their victims. This ignorance is perpetuated by myths, by the failure to examine social mores that dictate the modes of aggressive expression, and the use of scientific methodology that does not tap a full range of aggressive behavior. This chapter is organized around two basic goals. First, it offers some reasons for prior inadequacies in the study of female aggression, and makes some suggestions for future research directed at correcting these inadequacies. Second, it describes a single program of research on interfemale competition and aggression that is an example of the "new direction" in the study of human female aggression.

MORES, MYTHS, AND METHODS

Mores

Within the confines of the experimental situation, few researchers have considered the relevance of social norms in regulating sex differences in aggression (Macaulay, 1985). The influence of the social environment on aggressive behavior can be seen as either accounting for the existence of aggressive behavior (as in learning theories of aggression), or as modifying the expression of aggression (in biological theories of aggression). In either case, the social milieu greatly influences the appearance of aggression either in ecologically natural situations or in the laboratory. The structural or social approach, for instance, views aggression largely as role behavior regulated by social norms (Eagly & Steffen, 1986).

Females' social role, or gender role, stresses the importance of caring and empathetic qualities that may not be compatible with aggression (Eagly & Steffen, 1986). This incompatibility logically dictates that aggression and empathy will not occur simultaneously. Unfortunately, experimental paradigms directed at studying aggression have not also been directed at limiting empathic responses. The most commonly used measure of aggression, willingness to deliver shocks via the "aggression machine" (Buss, 1961), directly pits empathy against aggression. If women are less willing than men to deliver shocks in these situations, it may be because the social role of women is in part defined by empathy.

In contrast, most people expect men to behave more aggressively than women (Cicone & Ruble, 1978). That is, people believe that males' social role is in part defined by aggressiveness. Males' social role is also defined by "chivalry." Thus, if experimental paradigms were to force men to choose between showing aggressive behavior and chivalrous behavior, we might well see a reduction in males' aggressive responses (Eagly & Crowley, 1986). If males were to respond with chivalry, rather than aggression when this hypothetical paradigm was used, it is doubtful that researchers would conclude that males are unaggressive. Ironically, experiments which have placed empathy for the victim in direct contest with the subject's willingness to shock a victim (as it would in almost every case), have left us with a body of literature that attests to the unaggressiveness of females. Suppose a female subject was told her "victim" was a child abuser or a wife beater. In a case such as this, where levels of empathy would be likely to be low, one would expect higher levels of aggressive responses, even from females.

Other social roles involving the target of aggression are gender-related. For instance, women report more guilt and anxiety about behaving aggressively (Frodi et al., 1977). This is a force which may exert inhibitory control over the expression of aggression, and predicts that women may choose forms of aggression that ameliorate potential guilt, but does not define women as unaggressive. A way of ameliorating guilt, for instance, would be to turn an aggressive act into a defensive act, such as sabotaging a coworker's image as a way of saving one's own job, or acting against a third party to retain one's relationship with a mate or spouse (see below). A second, extreme way of absolving onself from guilt is to turn an aggressive act into an empathic one, as in the case of two women who killed their own children for reasons such as protecting them from lives of poverty and the need to become prostitutes (Rosenblatt & Greenland, 1974). Aggression by women sometimes comes to the surface in socially acceptable or anonymous situations. A very popular 1987 film, "Fatal Attraction", concerned a triangular relationship in which the wronged wife killed the "other woman". American theaters resounded with cries of "Kill the bitch!", and "Shoot her" as the wife pointed a gun at her competitor, and both male and female theatergoers applauded when the desired act was done (Baenninger & Baenninger, 1988). Can one doubt the suppressed aggressiveness in this population of theatergoers?

In addition to experiencing more guilt, at least for exhibiting overt aggression, women are more likely to expect recrimination or retaliation for their aggressive actions than are men (Eagly & Steffen, 1986). Given this expectation, one might predict that women would be less likely to aggress when the target is more powerful (as is the case when the target is a male), or when the target has the potential for retaliation. Evidence for the effect of the fear or expectation is that men are aggressed upon more than women in the laboratory, but not in the field (Eagly & Steffen, 1986). In the laboratory, unlike field situations, the aggressor is often unknown or unavailable to the "victim", thus reducing the aggressor's fear of retaliation. In the real world, women's violent crimes are almost always committed against the less powerful--their children, younger siblings, or elderly parents-- freeing the female aggressor from harmful retaliation (Rosenblatt & Greenland, 1974).

Finally, in naturalistic situations, females report their unwillingness to fight or show aggressive responses when there is an audience (Campbell, 1982). This is in contrast to males for whom audiences appear to be reinforcing. Women, then, may feel inclined to behave aggressively, but suppress this urge when others besides the victim are present.

Thus, the social influences that impinge on a potential aggressor, including gender-related mores and feelings regarding the target, are worthy of examination. However, classic interpretations of aggressive behavior have set the stage for examining "sex" as an explanatory variable, resulting in the notion that females are unaggressive. This is to say that sex has been seen as the *cause* of one's aggression or the lack of it. Social influences then are often examined only in terms of their accounting for individual differences in aggressive behavior in men. Another way of saying this is that if women are believed to be nonaggressive by nature, there is little reason to examine the variables that affect the expression of aggression in women.

Myths

"Myth" is defined by *Webster's New Riverside University Dictionary* as "a real or fictional story that appeals to the consciousness of a people by embodying its cultural ideals or by giving expression to deep, commonly felt emotions." The emphasis here is placed on myths about female aggression that may be true or false; the most profound one is that females are not aggressive.

Social mores as discussed above, combined with methods not suitable for controlling the effects of those mores, have played a part in the perpetuation of several myths about the circumstances under which females will and will not aggress. One of the purposes of this chapter is to stress the point that researchers should take advantage of social myths involving female aggression in planning their research strategies. These myths should become the basis for hypotheses about the nature of females' aggression, and most lend themselves to empirical consideration. Some of these myths are discussed below. (See also Macaulay, 1985, for an excellent and systematic treatment of these issues.)

The most pervasive myth is that women are not aggressive. This is an hypothesis that lends itself to empirical investigation, but perhaps with more creative or less constrictive paradigms than have been used in the past. Researchers might ask themselves what the value is in perpetuating this myth. Perhaps perpetuating this myth, consciously or unconsciously, is of particular value to men. Clearly in any relationship or social group, the person seeking or already holding power benefits from the nonaggressiveness of others. Since women in most cases do not benefit from their own nonaggressiveness, it seems likely that men might. If women's aggression is suppressed by this or other myths women are less likely to contest men's desires or actions. Such a pervasive myth as this acts to influence social norms that may regulate women's (and men's) behavior and may also impact directly in the experimental situation. This can take the form of an a priori assumption that women are not aggressive, or by a more subtle lack of attention to social constraints that may be operating in the experimental situation, or a failure to include a variety of dependent measures of aggression.

Another myth is that women's aggression is not open and direct, but rather is sneaky, underhanded and derisive. Such tactics include verbal assaults (Feshbach, 1970), secretive sabotage in the workplace or in social situations (see below), or competitive responses, such as accentuating their own feminine characteristics in an attempt to "steal" a man (Horner, 1972; Joseph, 1985) This myth also appears to be supported in our own research, as we will discuss. However, regardless of its validity, traditional paradigms have not been directed at examining this myth, except in the case of sex differences in verbal aggression which favor females (Frieze, Parsons, Johnson, Ruble, & Zellman, 1978; Tavris & Offir, 1977). Nevertheless, contrary findings, showing no sex differences, or more verbal (and physical) aggression by males are not rare (McCabe & Liscomb, 1988; Parke & Slaby, 1983; Williams, 1977).

A third myth takes the position that females are aggressive, but only when defending their offspring (e.g., Moyer, 1974; see also below). Such "maternal aggression" is seen as biologically-based, and intimately tied to a woman's identity as a woman (Macaulay, 1985). Interestingly, this myth fits women's social role as well, but quite possibly because it does not disrupt the potential benefits to men of the first myth discussed here, that females are not aggressive. Maternal aggression is the one form of aggression that is indeed beneficial to males-- it is clearly of reproductive advantage to have a mate who will protect one's offspring.

All of the myths described above, as well as several others, have an impact, along with social mores, on the methods of studying aggression chosen by researchers. The following section addresses the issue of how these myths often impede that research, but also how these myths, if carefully considered and operationally defined, can serve as excellent heuristic devices for generating hypotheses about women's aggression.

Methods

The earlier sections on "mores" and "myths" have addressed theoretical concerns about the nature of womens' aggression. This section is devoted to empirical concerns, some of which follow directly from the earlier discussion of myths and mores.

Many researchers have operationally defined aggression as the willingness to inflict noxious stimuli upon another (e.g. Buss, 1961). These stimuli are most often physical, frequently in the form of "shocks". Understandably, one reason to use these methods is that they allow for facility of measurement and recording, but they are not ecologically valid (see Baenninger, in the final chapter of this volume, for a discussion of the *lack* of actual physical aggression in western societies). But, this definition has been qualified by the notion that noxious stimuli delivered in the context of a social role are not necessarily aggressive. This is to say that one's social role may define the aggressiveness of an act. Conversely, if an individual's social role is incompatible with the expression of aggressive responses *in a specific behavioral setting*, as women's social roles often are, aggressive responses will not be emitted. This means only that the individual may not respond aggressively in that specific experimental context, not that the individual is unaggressive, or incapable of aggressive acts given the appropriate social context.

The above formulation is evidence that the influence of social norms has not been ignored in classical considerations of the situational determinants of aggression. However, the viewing of the subject's sex as a "normative consideration", i.e. as an addition or precursor to contextual constraints, is problematic. Such constraints include the "lawful status of the act,... the degree of personal responsibility,...[and] the degree of emotional disturbance" (Feshbach, 1971). It is argued here that social or contextual constraints similar to these govern women's behavior such that they inhibit the expression of aggression, particulary in laboratory settings. It is exactly when social role expectations are salient that sex differences in aggression in the laboratory are accentuated (Eisenberg & Lennon, 1983). When one treats sex as a separate "normative constraint", as most researchers have done, it becomes an explanation for why aggression does not occur in a specific subject population, in this case women, and allows researchers to ignore situational constraints that happen to be gender-related. Such situational constraints are often experimental versions of gender-related social norms. Upon examination, these situational constraints may in fact be better predictors of aggressive behavior than a subject's sex alone.

The first of several needed methodological changes in the study of womens' aggression is to expand the range of operational definitions of aggression. For example, situations might be devised in which subjects have the opportunity to inflict emotional, rather than physical, harm. Reports of emotional (angry) or cognitive (blaming) components of aggressive responding could serve as dependent variables. Acts which cause harm by limiting another's reproductive potential could be included. Examples are actions that make it more difficult for another to secure a mate or acts which decrease another's fertility.

Another alternative would be to examine the influence of the victim on the subject's willingness to inflict harm, physical or otherwise. This could be accomplished by varying the victim's characteristics, or the victim's supposed infraction.

A third, less conventional, way of decreasing methodological constraints on the study of aggression is to use nonexperimental forms of investigation whenever possible. While a bit of rigor is lost, much can be gained in the way of ecological or contextual validity (Eagly & Steffen, 1986; Macaulay, 1985). For instance, self-report data on subjects' actions in potentially aggressive situations are particulary helpful. Not only do these data provide evidence of aggressive expression in naturalistic situations, but they also have heuristic value for future experimentally constrained investigations. We have found subjects' self-reports, as well as their reports of how males and females are expected to behave in potentially aggressive situations, to be extremely enlightening. Some of this research is discussed later in successive parts of this chapter.

Often the problems with methodology are problems of assumptions. These assumptions include the impression that cultural mores surrounding aggression are the same for both sexes, and the a priori idea that specific myths about women's aggression are either true or not true.

AGONISTIC BEHAVIOR IN FEMALES: AN EVOLUTIONARY PERSPECTIVE

An evolutionary perspective is helpful in specifying the situations likely to evoke agonistic behavior in women and the targets of such behavior. Presumably, a woman's biological fitness is increased by choosing a male with signs of "good genes" and by choosing one who can provide resources and protection to her and to her offspring (e.g., Alcock, 1989; Daly and Wilson, 1983; Hrdy, 1981). Since males differ in these characteristics it is reasonable to assume that females will compete for males with desirable characteristics. The competitive strategies should involve techniques both to attract a male and to reduce or eliminate competition from other females.

Once a male is acquired, a threat to the relationship from another female poses a severe threat to the fitness of the original female. She stands to lose the male's "good genes" and she stands to lose, in part or entirely, the resources and protection she has assumed the male will provide. Short of a threat to her offspring, there is no situation which poses more of a threat to a woman's fitness. Consequently, we would expect from women considerable aggressive behavior supported by appropriate emotion when an established relationship is threatened by a female rival. Finally, since a woman's fitness depends on the survival and reproductive success of her children, women should show considerable competitive and aggressive behavior that has as its focus the woman's children. More particularly, such behaviors should be evoked when the life of a woman's child is endangered or when the success of a child is endangered through competition with other children.

We have begun a systematic program of research to investigate women's agonistic behavior in these situations which threaten a woman's fitness. Initially, we conducted a large number of interviews with women, young and old, married and unmarried, with and without children, in an attempt to provide a preliminary description of targets and tactics of competitive and aggressive behavior. In some instances men, too, were interviewed. These preliminary findings are discussed below.

MATE-FOCUSED AGONISTIC BEHAVIOR
Competition in Acquiring a Mate

If some men, as mates, increase a woman's fitness more than others, some behaviors in women should increase the probability of acquiring a high quality mate. Logically, such behaviors could involve either enhancing one's own attractiveness through appearance or behavior or reducing the competitive position of others. In the former there is no focus on a particular competitor whereas in the latter case a particular competitor may or may not be involved.

1. **Enhancing personal physical attractiveness.** The competitive nature of enhancing physical attractiveness in women is obvious. As males try to excel at those activities (athletic, financial, intellectual) that mark them as desirable, so women engage in beauty contests, formal and informal. Women regularly assess their own appearance in relation to that of other women, friends aid in enhancing appearance and reassure each other about appearance, and it is as common to compliment women on their appearance as it is to compliment men on athletic skill. The advantage to enhancing appearance has been well documented. Men state a

preference for physically attractive women (e.g., Coombs and Kenkel, 1966) and physically attractive women have an advantage in selection of marital partners (e.g., Udry, 1978).

Morris (1967) popularized the idea that women make themselves more attractive by exaggerating the physical signals of femaleness such as large breasts, small waist, large hips, red lips, etc. While there is evidence to support the idea (e.g., Low, 1979; McKeachie, 1952) the matter is considerably more complex. For example, even casual observers can see that not all women take steps to enhance their physical attractiveness. "Plain Janes" are as obvious as "Betty Beauties".

Our interviews of young, unmarried men and women suggest that "Plain Jane" is a tactic which some women use to attract a mate. Men are very much concerned with a wife's fidelity (e.g., Alcock, 1989; Daly and Wilson, 1983). Women who do not use appearance-enhancers may be signalling their lack of interest in generally attracting men. In other words, they may be signalling their quality as a faithful mate. To signal faithfulness may be of special interest to those men who are less able to ensure the faithfulness of an attractive mate, less attractive males of low status. The interviews also suggested that less attractive young men were more likely to value "natural good looks" and to urge their girlfriends to cut down on the use of make-up, sexy clothing, and even under-arm deodorant. Thus, these inquiries suggest that there are several ways to compete for males' attention. The most salient method of accentuating one's feminine characteristics may not always be the best strategy. It is interesting to note that men rating slides find a woman less attractive as a potential marital partner if she is wearing tight, revealing clothing but only if that clothing is low-status clothing (Hill, Nocks, and Gardner, 1987). This is quite possibly because tight clothing, combined with low status, may be an indication of potential infidelity. Smart women, having an understanding of this, will seek to attract a man while at the same time attesting to their potential fidelity.

2. Attracting behaviors. Flirting behavior has been studied by several investigators (e.g., Eibl-Eibesfeldt, 1971; Givens, 1978). These are nonverbal displays which elicit the approach of a male and/or serve to maintain his attention and presence. A recent study (Moore, 1985) indicates that these are effective attractants. Women who used these displays more often in "mate relevant" contexts were more often approached by a man. Our interviews indicate that some women are conscious of these displays and report using them deliberately whereas others seem to be much less aware of using them. It would be interesting to know whether awareness and deliberateness of usage are correlated with the number of male approaches.

Some of our respondents also reported deliberately using what might be called "fixing" behaviors, behaviors such as staring deeply into a man's eyes, appearing excited by the man's conversation, and frequently leaning towards him as if he were a magnet. These behaviors, women said, were to indicate to the man that the woman is "fixed" to the man through fascination. As used deliberately, however, women said that such adulation serves to fix the man to the woman. Furthermore, "fixing" behaviors were used especially when the woman desired a long-term or permanent relationship with the man. Again, it would be interesting to know whether deliberate use of such behavior provides a competitive advantage to the woman. Both of these attracting behaviors could be methodically observed, an example of how what we already know about social behavior can operate as a heuristic for future research.

3. Reducing competition. Women and girls are prone to use "indirect" aggression rather than the "direct" physical assaults associated with male aggression (e.g., Lagerspetz, 1988). Such indirect aggression may be directed at particular rivals. To illustrate, one young woman toured singles bars and other "mate-relevant" sites with a friend. She confessed that she often complimented her "friend" on her appearance when it was less than optimal. Yellow clothing made her friend's complexion look dull and washed-out, yet our informant regularly told her what a good color yellow was for her. The informant stated that she was enhancing her own prospects of attracting the more attractive males.

Sometimes women target any other women, as if they were attempting to reduce the population of rivals. An example is an informant who worked at a fast-food establishment. She and her coworkers always urged desserts on the young female customers. Why? "To make them fat and unattractive." Even if they weren't acquainted? "Sure. We didn't want anyone more attractive than us."

Indirect aggression for the purpose of eliminating the competition is an area that deserves systematic investigation. Research should focus not only on description of techniques but also on assessment of the effectiveness of such techniques. Is the propensity for indirect aggression directed at potential and actual rivals correlated with the characteristics of mates finally procured? The question is whether such behavior is best characterized as advantageous or spiteful.

Indirect aggression may lead to direct aggression. A study of 16-year-old-schoolgirls illustrates the point (Campbell, 1982). The most frequent cause of physical fighting was a verbal assault on a girl's reputation such as an insult to sexual reputation or remarks impugning the girl's personal character (intelligence, courage, etc.). Because it is a leading cause of physical attack, indirect aggression probably is advantageous in eliminating competition. Otherwise, countering it should not be so prominent a response.

Guarding the Mate

Considerable attention has been paid to mate-guarding by males and very little attention to mate-guarding tactics used by females. Mate-guarding by women is demanded by an evolutionary view. If a "good" mate is scarce and difficult to acquire and if competitors for a woman's mate exist, then the evolution of guarding behavior should have occurred.

Flinn (1988) reported the absence of mate-guarding by women in a Caribbean village as assessed by overt agonistic interactions. However, measures of indirect aggression might reveal its presence, especially because Flinn reported that men did not approve of overt competition. Women we interviewed were familiar with mate-guarding and described several tactics:

1. Blocking access to the mate. Some examples are: ensuring that one's husband does not spend a long time in conversation with another woman at a party, and never inviting single women to social gatherings.

2. Checking up on the whereabouts of one's mate.

3. Threatening the mate with the consequences of unfaithfulness. Commonly, women threaten to leave the man.

4. Making it psychologically/emotionally costly for the man to show any interest in another woman. Women may flirt with another man, cry, withhold sex, etc.

5. Women threaten potential rivals. For example, a study of institutionalized adolescents noted that the girls ranking high in dominance, whose boyfriends were always themselves high in dominance, warned all newcomers away from the boyfriends with threats of bodily harm (Deutsch, Esser, and Sossin, 1978). Some of our informants reported similar acts.

Sexual Jealousy

The threat to an established relationship by a rival defines the stimulus for sexual jealousy. For a woman, the threat is severe. If the man deserts to her rival she loses the "good genes" of the man. The threat of such a loss is not trivial because older and previously married women haven't the range of choice than young, unmarried women do. Even if he does not desert her, he may divert substantial amounts of resources and protection to her rival or her rival's children. We can expect natural selection to have provided women with appropriate emotions (anger and fear of loss should be the principle ones) to guide behavioral strategies to diminish the threat.

Men, too, experience sexual jealousy. However, the threat to fitness posed by a male rival is quite different from the threat posed to a female by her rival. The threat to a man's fitness is that he will invest in offspring which are not his, that he will provide resources and protection to the children of another man, thus wasting his parental investment. The threat, then, rests not only in the rival but also in the man's mate.

Accordingly, sociobiologists such as John Alcock (1984, 1989) and Daly and Wilson (1983, 1988) have suggested a sex difference in both the amount and the content of sexual jealousy. Primarily based on the argument that maternity is certain, paternity uncertain, a man's fear of cuckoldry is said to lead to a higher level of sexual jealousy on the part of males. In support, they point to higher rates of spousal homicide by husbands, the tendency of men to be profoundly disturbed by the rape of their wives, the sexual double standard about adultery which is a cross-cultural universal, and laws which make adultery a defense for wife-murder. Such data attest to the strength of male jealousy. They do not necessarily reflect less jealousy on the part of women. As we argue below, sex differences in aggression may reflect the suppression of women's aggressive tendencies, a suppression which is accomplished with tools such as the sexual double standard and legal codes favoring male interests.

With respect to a difference in content of jealousy, Daly and Wilson cite one study of fantasies about hypothetical situations which supports the idea that for men, jealousy should be focused on the act which produces a threat of loss; for women, jealousy should be focused on the threatened loss, not on the act that produces the threat. We cannot agree with this reasoning.

In fact, the matter of sexual jealousy is more complicated. Our research points to two major factors, neglected in previous discussions, which are critical to the targets and content of aggression motivated by sexual jealousy. First, the content of sexual jealousy, including the targets of aggressive actions, ought to depend on the stage of relationship, courtship vs. commitment. Second, men take steps to prevent aggressive action on the part of their sexually-betrayed female partners.

During courtship, infidelity on the part of one's partner signals the likelihood of subsequent infidelity and consequent loss as described above. Thus, during courtship, infidelity should be a cue for terminating the relationship and continuing the search for a "good" partner. The logic applies to both sexes. During courtship the anger of both men and women should be directed more at the offending partner than at the rival and terminating the relationship should be likely. At a cognitive level, to support termination of the relationship, we would expect the offended individuals to "blame" their partners more than their rivals. Neither men nor women should be particularly sad or distressed at the loss of an unfaithful partner at this stage of the mating game (although distress might depend on resources expended). Rather, the offended parties, regardless of sex, might be expected to take the attitude of "Better now than later."

Following a commitment such as marriage, however, the situation is different for male and female. For a man, the threat of loss (inappropriate paternal investment) derives from the wife who may bear another man's child. Therefore, the husband's anger should be directed at his wife at least as much, if not more, than at his rival. But for the woman whose husband is unfaithful, the threat of loss (husband's "good genes", his resources) derives from the rival who may acquire the husband or part of his resources. The threat to the wife's fitness can only be removed by overcoming the competition. There are two general ways for her to achieve that goal. She may get rid of her rival or she may tighten the bond that ties her husband to her. Therefore, a wife's anger should be directed primarily at her rival. Cognitively, she should blame the rival rather than her husband for the infidelity, allowing her to take aggressive action against the rival and to take steps to strengthen her husband's tie to her. Anger toward the mate would not be beneficial, because it could result in loss of the mate. Only in special circumstances might anger directed at her mate be a beneficial strategy. For example, her anger might deter him from continued or future infidelities. Or, if there were other partners available, her anger might motivate a search for a "better" man and termination of the current marriage. Furthermore, unlike the courting woman, the married woman might well be obsessed with loss of the relationship, loss of resources, and the fate of her children.

The second factor which our research suggests determines the response to infidelity concerns the interests of the unfaithful mate. The latter are served if no aggressive action, against either the rival or offending mate, is taken by the betrayed mate.

Aggressive action could harm the offending mate or the rival and aggressive action could deter either the offending mate or the rival from continuing the relationship. Think of a wife becoming angry at sexual betrayal. She may berate her husband and make him suffer emotionally in order to prevent future betrayal. If she is successful he loses future reproductive opportunities. Worse (from his point of view), she may leave him. If so, he would lose any reproductive effort he had put into courting her and supporting her. Should her anger and aggressive action be focused on her rival, her husband stands to lose the reproductive effort he put into her rival.

How can an unfaithful spouse minimize retaliatory action by the offended spouse? Preventive action could be taken at an individual level by, e.g., hiding the adulterous liaison or threatening the offended spouse with physical aggression. There are possibilities at a societal level as well. Cultural practices, belief systems, and legal codes are powerful tools serving individual fitness (Alexander, 1987, Daly and Wilson, 1988, Lumsden and Wilson, 1981). But whose interest would these tools serve, the adulterous spouses or the betrayed spouses, women's interests or men's interests? In cases of conflict of interest, the same set of beliefs and "morality" cannot serve the interests of both parties to the conflict. In general, cultural practices and beliefs should serve the interests of those with the greater power. The powerful can dictate self-serving beliefs and practices, regardless of the interests of the less powerful. Manipulation and exploitation, deception and hypocrisy are, in the words of E. O. Wilson (1975), "very human devices for conducting the complex daily business of social life." Thus, accepted cultural practice may sometimes reflect nothing more than exploitation, belief nothing more than deception. In our culture, and many others, males hold more power than females. Therefore, we would expect "morality" regarding adultery to serve male interests, in effect, a sexual double standard, and we would expect beliefs to discourage aggressive action on the part of women. If women are told, and believe, that they are passive, not prone to violence, that anger and fighting are not appropriate for women, then women will be less likely to take aggressive action against their spouses or their rivals. If women are told, and believe, that male sexual betrayal is to be expected or even condoned, women will be less likely to take any action. If such beliefs are supported by a legal system which, for example, makes it easy for a man to divorce an adulterous wife but not vice versa and which permits male violence in retaliation for adultery, but does not permit retaliatory female violence, then women should be even less inclined to take aggressive action for lack of legal support for the action. Such belief systems with their support in the legal system are common (Alexander,1987; Daly and Wilson, 1988).

If beliefs and legal codes operate as proposed, women's sexual jealousy, expressed by word or action, would be suppressed. Measures of sexual jealousy would often show more jealousy on the part of men, even if, other things being equal, there were no sex difference in sexual jealousy. How can we decide whether a sex difference in expressed sexual jealousy represents a genuine sex difference or a gender difference due to suppression of female sexual jealousy? There are several possibilities which would suggest the latter. In some situations the belief system or the legal system may be loosened due to large changes in the social structure of a society, allowing women to express their sexual jealousy in ways otherwise rarely encountered. In other situations a woman's fitness may depend so heavily on, e.g., elimination of a rival, that she would act against the traditional belief system. Or, discrepancies may arise between the sexes in their judgments or perceptions about sexual jealousy in a way that suggests the belief system is biased toward male interests.

The few relevant studies of sexual jealousy support our view that the content of sexual jealousy in women depends on the stage of the relationship and on the conditions of society which make it more or less costly for women to express their sexual jealousy. First, there is evidence that, during courting, men and women are equally jealous and that their partners are the targets of their anger as much or more than are their rivals. In contrast, women in long-term committed relationships direct their anger principally at their rivals.

In a study by Paul, Foss, Fiorito, and Baenninger (in preparation) college students answered questions about two situations involving sexual transgressions, when a partner flirts with another and when a partner cheats. The latter was defined as deceit about serious matters such as having sexual intercourse with someone else or going out a number of times with another. We used two questionnaires to provide three independent assessments of the amount and content of sexual jealousy and one assessment of attitudes about sexual jealousy. One questionnaire asked people to make judgments about what they thought was appropriate, reasonable, or right when a partner flirted or cheated and also to indicate what they thought was generally true of others when their partners flirted or cheated. Each of the sexes made these judgments about their own sex and the opposite sex. Other students were asked to respond to similar questions, but they were asked to report on their own feelings and actions if they had had flirting or cheating partners. If they hadn't had experience with a flirting or cheating partner, they were asked to answer the questions according to what they thought they would do if they discovered their partner flirting or cheating. A number of questions about the content of jealous reactions were asked. The discussion here will be limited to answers related to aggression: feelings of anger, cognitions of blame, and aggressive thoughts or actions.

The results supported our view of the similarity of the sexes' jealous reactions during courting. No matter how measured (people's perceptions of others' reactions, what was reported by those with betraying partners, and what the inexperienced expected to happen), there were no (with one minor exception) gender differences in the amount of anger and blame directed at partner or rival. Apparently, both young women and men became quite angry, even at the minor transgression of flirting (all mean anger scores were above 4 on a 7-point-Likert scale) and they were somewhat angrier with their partners than with their rivals. Blame was placed heavily on the partner and, as we expected, breaking up the relationship was likely. About one- quarter of those women and men who had the experience broke up over flirting and more than half broke up over cheating.

Other research indicates that in a long-term relationship like marriage, in contrast with men, women focus their anger and aggression on their rivals rather than on their betraying spouses. Baenninger and Baenninger (1988) reported that women's attitudes were more negative about a woman's rival than about a betraying husband. Women and men were asked questions about their reactions to the protagonists in the film, "Fatal Attraction," which provoked unusually intense and vocal emotional reactions in audiences. Many more women reported disliking the "other woman" compared to those who said they disliked the straying husband. Furthermore, while women were able to identify with the wife (finally, a murderess--of her rival), and some could identify with the husband, not a single woman was able to identify with the wife's rival. It is interesting to note that the story line of "Fatal Attraction" is in line with our hypothesis that older, married women usually try to get rid of their rival and remain with their husband.

A study by Schuster (1983) documented in real life the violence of betrayed women against their rivals. Schuster surveyed cases of physical aggression by Zambian women induced by sexual jealousy. The attacks involved slapping, kicking, and biting - deep biting in which pieces of ear or lip were bitten off. Weapons used included knives, axes, broken bottles, and boiling water. Chili pepper was sometimes rubbed into the victim's wounds. Female-female aggression is a fact of modern Zambian society, Schuster claimed, and these physical battles were most often initiated by a wife against a rival for her husband's attention and resources. She comments that the rival, if known, was attacked physically and, if unknown, the rival was attacked through magic or the use of drugs which are thought to induce illness or sterility or other harm. In these instances the husband was not a target of aggression. The reason appears clear. Women in Zambia are economically dependent on males. For the poor, the husband's income is a matter of survival; for those women and their children above this poverty (survival) line the male income determines social class and life style. In such circumstances, it is crucial for the woman with a rival to get rid of that rival and maintain her relationship with her husband. The cases documented by Schuster are remarkable for the extreme violence employed by women. They are not unique (see Hupka, 1981). Such data do not fit well with the older myths of woman's pacific nature nor do they fit well with more modern views of woman as less aggressive than man. These data do fit our view that women's aggressiveness is suppressed in many cultures by beliefs and legal codes favoring male interests, and that women will be aggressive, and even violently so, when their fitness is critically dependent on aggression.

In support of this hypothesis are some data that contrast with Schuster's. Flinn (1988) observed all individuals in a small (pop.=342) Caribbean village. He reported that, in contrast to males, females courting the same male did not have higher rates of agonistic interaction with each other than they had with other females who were not rivals to them. The discrepancy is probably related to male control of female behavior. Flinn suggests that there is competition between women for the same man. But, he notes, men in the village "express a dislike of overt female competition, and this probably affects female behavior." Fights and quarrels embarrass the man and may lower his chances of maintaining polygynous relationships. In other words, a jealous female's actions against her rival(s) are probably effective in putting off the rival, thereby lowering male fitness. It is not surprising, then, that males counter the woman's action against her rivals. Since males typically control much of the economic resources available to women, males are able, individually and collectively, to suppress women's agonistic behavior.

However, when diversion of resources to a rival represents a strong threat to the woman's fitness, as in the Zambian case, there may be greater benefit to action than to passive acceptance of male wishes. Flinn notes that the village women are more likely to have antagonistic interactions with their mates when he diverts resources to another woman rather than when there is only sexual activity with another. While these data seem to support Daly and Wilson's (1983, 1988) thesis that the jealous male focuses on the sexual act while the jealous female focuses on loss of attention and resources, they are open to interpretation. It may be that the jealous woman is angry about the sexual betrayal, that she would like to make her mate suffer for his betrayal and get rid of her rival, but that the proscriptions on her aggressive behavior are obeyed until there is clear threat to her fitness.

Finally, we have evidence that attitudes about what reactions are appropriate when a partner is unfaithful follow lines of self interest. In the work described above by Paul, Foss, Fiorito, and Baenninger, young women and men judged the amount of anger and blame appropriate to partner and rival when a woman or a man discovers a flirting or cheating partner. Each sex thought that more anger, toward partner and rival, was appropriate to own sex than to opposite sex. Self interest also characterized judgments of blame. That is, women thought less blame should be placed on a female partner who transgressed than should be placed on a transgressing male partner. Men thought the opposite. These data certainly support the idea that "morality" is a matter of self-interest (e.g., Wilson, 1978; Alexander, 1987). It is a small step to propose that, when self-interest of subgroups conflict, the "morality" of the society will suit the interests of the subgroup holding more power. If so, the views of males should prevail; that a large amount of anger is not appropriate to a woman betrayed by her man and that she is not justified in placing considerable blame on her man or her rival. Data from the Paul et al. study supported this view. Women who had had experience with transgressing partners reported being angrier at their rivals than either the amount of anger other women thought appropriate or than the amount of anger nonexperienced women expected to feel. In other words, the societal standard for aggression governed women's expectations but not their experience. Interestingly, the opposite was true for men. The nonexperienced men thought they would be angrier at their rivals than the experienced men reported being. Nevertheless, there were no significant gender differences in the number of experienced individuals who took steps to hurt their rivals, either physically or emotionally. If the myths and mores call for a lack of physical violence on the part of women, one might expect women to turn to indirect aggression. Women tended, more often than men, to think about and imagine hurting their partners emotionally. More women than men said they took steps to do so, but the difference was not significant. However, significantly more women than men flirted with someone else as a way of getting even with their partner. One may view such actions as indirect aggression.

As a whole, these studies suggest two major conclusions. First, women's aggression in response to sexual jealousy may, under many circumstances, be suppressed or indirect in conformity with prevailing myths and mores. Ultimately, however, women will act in self-interest. They will break up with unfaithful partners before commitment limits their choice and they will act against rivals when the rival poses a clear threat to a long-term relationship.

Child-Focused Agonistic Behavior

Human females make enormous parental investment in their offspring. This occurs over many years of childhood and, consequently, the reproductive ceiling of women is low under the best of circumstances (Trivers, 1972, Daly and Wilson, 1983). It may not be feasible to rear successfully more than one or two children, as appears to be the case in our society. At least among our women students the preference is for that number because, they say, it is too costly to have more children. With fitness dependent on so few offspring, it would be surprising if women did not show considerable competitive and aggressive behavior to ensure the survival and social and economic success of their children (Hrdy, 1981).

In our interviews, we asked mothers, and some fathers, to relate their feelings, thoughts, and actions in reply to three questions. How do you and other parents behave if your child is competing with another child? Do you compete with other mothers in ways that put your child in a better position? If your child's life was ever endangered, what did you do? Women are quite aware of their child-focused competitive behavior and the strategies they use to further their child's success. Below is a very preliminary classification of situations and behavioral strategies used.

I. Child-child competition. In numberless situations a woman's child is in direct competition with another child or children. Some examples are two children fighting over a desirable toy, competition for a place on the sports team or a part in the school play, and academic competiton. Three major strategies to further offspring success have emerged.

1. Removal of the opponent. These responses are overtly aggressive (even if only in fantasy) and appear designed to remove the offspring's competitor. "I might bad-mouth the other child," said one woman about her child's competition for a particular place on a sports team. "I fantasized that the other child got very sick and so she was out of the running," said another woman.

2. Self-sacrifice. All women interviewed agreed that they are willing to make considerable sacrifices in money, time and energy in order to ensure that their child succeed. The family's finances are funneled into the child's "needs" (e.g., the latest styles in footgear and t-shirts) and women join the P.T.A., sew costumes for the school play, and drive their children to innumerable lessons and activities. There is an element of female-female competition in the self-sacrifice. Women are aware that other women are so engaged and indicate that so, too, must they be, because the others are doing so.

3. Political maneuvering. Persuasion, exchange of favors, hints of unpleasant consequences, etc. are all much a part of child-focused competition. "I'd tell other parents why my child was best for the part and then get them to speak to the teacher." "I told the coach I'd do whatever I could to help." "I let her know that I'd make trouble if my child didn't get it."

II. Direct inter-female competition. Mothers have said that they compete directly with other mothers, for example, in trying to give the best birthday party for their child, by allowing their child to do things another child is not permitted, giving presents to other children, being the best-liked mother, etc.

III. The endangered child. Almost all parents have gone through a time when their child was severely ill and many have children who were accidentally injured. Often, when immediate, decisive action was required to rescue their child, women reported a state of consciousness similar to the "peak performance" (Browne and Mahoney, 1984) state described by athletes. For example, one woman's child fell out of a window onto a sloping roof and another woman saw her child's hand stuck to a red-hot barbecue grill. In such instances women reported instantaneous assessment of the situation and rapid, appropriate action. Details were blurred except for their child upon whom they were totally focused. In one case, the child appeared perceptually larger than normal. Usually, the woman had a sense of time slowing down. If immediate action was not demanded, women said that they rationally and logically assessed the situation to determine what action to take to aid their child. Once they decided on a course of action, they pursued it in determined fashion. In all of these crises women told us that all other concerns were put on hold, that they were certain in their determination to pursue a course of action, and that in no other situation had they felt so energized, fearless, tireless, and determined to overcome all obstacles. Several targets of aggression can be involved:

a) **Individuals who can help the child.** Such people become targets of, first, assertive action and then, if necessary, aggressive action to ensure their aid to the child. One woman became extremely assertive when her daughter was suddenly rushed to hospital with an illness. She wouldn't wait in the waiting room, badgered doctors and other hospital personnel for information, refused to leave her daughter's room at night, and doggedly checked on all details for the duration of her daughter's stay. This was quite unlike her usual compliant behavior with physicians, as she remarked while shaking her head in emphasis.

b) **The bearer of bad tidings.** The individual who brings the bad news about the child may suffer physical or verbal aggression. For example, one woman reported that it was all she could do to withhold a physical attack on the woman who brought her the news that her daughter had been in an automobile accident.

c) **Those responsible for endangering the child.** One woman developed the belief that her common-law husband was going to steal their new-born child. She tried to prevent him entering her hospital room and began to growl if he came near the infant. The growls, she said, were loud, from deep in the throat, and they made her husband nervous enough to stay away. (After a few weeks her fear disappeared and so did her growling. Eight years later, the three live happily together.) Another woman shook with emotion, eleven years after the incident, as she related what happened in a custody battle. Her husband "stole" their son and refused to tell her where the child was. Reasoning that the child was probably with her mother-in-law, the mother confronted her mother-in-law who denied knowing the child's whereabouts. However, her son, who was in an upstairs bedroom, heard his mother at the door and called to her. Her mother-in-law tried to prevent her going to him. "Get out of the way or I'll kill you," was the mother's response. Her mother-in-law backed off, knowing that she meant it.

While such cases attest to women's aggressive potential in support of their children, the potential may not always be realized. We cannot be sure, but we suspect that men attempt to suppress women's aggression even in cases of endangered children. Two women told us that their husbands tried to stop them from badgering physicians about their hospitalized children. In one case, the woman said that she never forgave her husband, for if she hadn't badgered, another specialist would not have been consulted, an operation would not have been performed, and her son would have died. Additionally, some men we have interviewed said that they were the ones who responded to the crisis while their wives "fell apart." Their wives don't agree. Could these men be acting to strengthen the belief system of unassertive, ineffective, hysterical women? Certainly, we have yet to interview a woman who has fit that stereotype when her fitness was at stake.

SUMMARY AND CONCLUSIONS

This chapter is directed at providing an overview of some of the factors that are responsible for, and impact on, the perpetuation of the belief that women are not aggressive creatures. These include social mores, myths, possibly true or false, about the existence or nature of women's aggression, and stilted methodological constraints which have made it almost impossible to discover women's aggression when it may exist. We have also provided a large amount of evidence, most empirical (although not all is "experimental"), and some anecdotal, about the circumstances under which women do aggress, or express an intense desire to aggress. The heuristics that aided in generating our hypotheses in some cases grew out of the very myths that may have perpetuated the idea that females are not aggressive.

Social mores serve to define the situations under which women will be aggressive. The idea of past researchers that "sex is a normative constraint" in predicting aggressive behaviors, has resulted in lack of attention to the variables which may predict aggression **within** populations of women. It is our belief that researchers need to step beyond this normative constraint in planning research strategies. Foci in future research could include the role of empathy in constraining aggressive responses, the potential threat that the victim poses to the aggressor in later interactions, and the role of an audience in promoting or inhibiting aggressive responses.

Myths have greatly influenced and constrained the expression of aggression by women. The biggest myth, which is likely to be in service of mens' traditionally dominant role, is that women are not aggressive. This serves to protect men's power in society by making women feel guilty and unfeminine for ever aggressing. Research findings that perpetuate this myth merely strengthen it and increase its value to men. Another important myth is that women are only aggressive when they are considering their children's protection or best interests. This myth is interesting in that it is also in the service of men, because it ensures the fitness of their offspring without necessitating that they provide the protection. In addition, this myth is interesting because it is partly true-- women are aggressive in defense of their offspring, and partly false-- this is not the only form that women's aggression takes.

The methodological problems with much of the study of women's aggression to this date stem from the social and mythological constraints discussed above. It has been suggested here that researchers take several new directions in the study of aggressive behavior in women. First, they should broaden the range of operational definitions of aggression, understanding that it can take more forms than previously thought. Second, as discussed above, researchers should systematically vary some of the social constraints that may influence the expression of aggression. Finally, more ecologically valid methods of research should be used, especially while trying to discover variables that could later be studied systematically. It is the latter approach that we have taken in the research described in this chapter. We have used self-report and interviews of both women and men to examine a variety of circumstances in which women might be aggressive, as well as subjects' understanding of when aggression is appropriate, and for whom, and against whom it is appropriate.

Specifically, we have examined the aggressive responses produced by women when their relationships are threatened by rivals and when their children are endangered. These finding are enlightening and not always in line with expectations.

Women actively compete in acquiring mates. They not only compete against specific rivals, but also against the entire population of "other women." Their strategies often include enhancing their own physical attractiveness in a kind of offensive, rather than defensive, form of aggression. Paradoxically, one approach to this strategy is to adopt a "plain Jane" look to convince males that they will be a faithful partner. Women also use "fixing" behaviors and "flirting" behaviors to acquire and keep men. Perhaps the most aggressive form of competition for mates is aimed at reducing the competition, often in underhanded ways, like recommending clothing and makeup that reduces the attractiveness of a rival, or hoping that other women will do things like eat too much and become unattractive. A final competitive strategy involves guarding the mate in order to shield him from opportunities for interaction with other women.

Another area to which we have devoted considerable investigation is the area of sexual jealousy. In our formulation, contrary to Daly and Wilson's, sexual jealousy is directed against the mate, by both men and women during courtship, but directed against the rival after marriage or commitment. The reason for this is that before commitment, the needs of both men and women could best be served by getting rid of the errant mate, before a commitment is made. In contrast, after marriage or commitment, especially if children are involved, it is imperative for the wronged spouse to get rid of the rival, rather than the errant spouse, in order to protect any prior or future reproductive investment. Our evidence comes from interviews, questionnaires describing hypothetical situations, as well as a "projective" test that used a popular film as the focus of subjects' feelings toward their partner, (or any errant partner), and the rival.

Finally, we have presented a preliminary classification of how women might aggress or work in service of protecting their children. These include involvement in child-to-child competition, removal of opponents from the child's social world, self-sacrificing behaviors directed toward the child, political maneuvering to enhance a child's position, and direct competition with other mothers. In addition, we present several ways in which a mother may aggress against various targets if her child is actually physically or emotionally endangered. Any one or all of these classification, gathered from our interviews could serve as heuristics for future reseach.

The present chapter, we hope, represents a new tradition in examining sex differences in aggression (see Macaulay, 1985). By this we mean a move away from traditionally confined methods, an attention to the social mores that impact on women's (and men's) aggression, and an evaluation and closer examination of the myths surrounding it.

REFERENCES

Alcock, J. (1984). *Animal Behavior: An Evolutionary Approach* (3rd ed.). Sunderland, MA.: Sinauer Associates.

Alcock, J. (1989). *Animal Behavior: An Evolutionary Approach* (4th ed.). Sunderland, MA.: Sinauer Associates.

Baenninger, M. & Baenninger, R. (1988). *Interfemale aggression: A consequence of the male shortage?* Presented at the European Meetings of the International Society for Research on Aggression, Swansea, Wales.

Baenninger, M. & Newcombe (1989). The role of experience in spatial test performance. *Sex Roles, 20,* 327-344.

Browne, M. A. & Mahoney, M. J. (1984). Sport psychology. In M. R. Rosenzweig & L. W. Porter (Eds.), *Annual Review of Psychology,* vol. 35 (pp. 605-626). Palo Alto: Annual Reviews.

Buss, A. H. (1961). *The Psychology of Aggression.* New York: Wiley.

Campbell, A. (1982). Female aggression. In P. Marsh & A. Campbell (Eds.), *Aggression and Violence* (pp. 137- 150). New York: St. Martin's Press.

Cicone, M. V. & Ruble, D. N. (1978). Beliefs about males, *Journal of Social Issues, 34,* 5-16.

Coombs, R. H. & Kenkel, W. F. (1966). Sex differences in dating aspirations and satisfaction with computer selected partners. *Journal of Marriage and the Family, 28,* 62-66.

Daly, M. & Wilson, M. (1983). *Sex, Evolution and Behavior* (2nd ed). Boston, MA: Willard Grant.

Daly, M. & Wilson, M. (1988). *Homicide.* New York: Aldine de Gruyter.

Deutsch, R. D., Esser, A. H., & Sossin, M. (1978). Dominance, aggression, and the functional use of space in institutionalized female adolescents. *Aggressive Behavior, 4,* 313-330.

Eagly, A. H. & Crowley, M. (1986). Gender and helping behavior: A meta-analytic review of the social psychological literature. *Psychological Bulletin, 100,* 283-308.

Eagly, A. H. & Steffen, V. J. (1986). Gender and aggressive behavior: A meta-analytic review of the social psychological literature. *Psychological Bulletin, 100,* 309-330.

Eibl-Eibesfeldt, I. (1971). *Love and Hate.* New York: Holt, Rinehart and Winston.

Eisenberg, N. & Lennon, R. (1983). Sex differences in empathy and related capacities. *Psychological Bulletin, 94,* 100-131.

Feshbach, S. (1971). Dynamics of morality of violence and aggression: Some psychological considerations. *American Psychologist, 26,* 281-291.

Flinn, M. V. (1988). Mate guarding in a Caribbean village. *Ethology and Sociobiology, 9,* 1-28.

Frieze, I. H., Parsons, J. E., Johnson, R. B., Ruble, D. N., & Zellman, G. L. (1978). *Women and Sex Roles: A Social Psychological Perspective.* New York: Norton.

Frodi, A., Macaulay, J., & Thome, P. R., (1977). Are women always less aggressive than men? A review of the experimental literature. *Psychological Bulletin, 84,* 643-660.

Givens, D. (1978). The nonverbal basis of attraction: Flirtation, courtship, and seduction. *Psychiatry, 41,* 346-359.

Hill, E. M., Nocks, E. S. & Gardner, L. (1987). Physical attractiveness: Manipulation by physique and status displays. *Ethology and Sociobiology, 8,* 143-154.

Hilton, T. L. (1985). National changes in spatial-visual ability from 1960-1980. *Research report: Educational Testing Services,* Princeton, New Jersey.

Horner, M. S. (1972). Toward an understanding of achievement-related conflicts in women. *Journal of Social Issues, 28,* 157-176.

Hrdy, S. B. (1981). *The Woman that Never Evolved.* Cambridge, MA.: Harvard University Press.

Hupka, R.B. (1981) Cultural determinants of jealousy. *Alternative Lifestyles, 4,* 310-356.

Hyde, J. S. (1984). How large are gender differences in aggression? A developmental meta-analysis. *Developmental Psychology, 20,* 722-736.

Hyde, J. S. (1986). Gender differences in aggression. In J. S. Hyde & M. Linn (Eds.), *The Psychology of Gender: Advances Through Meta-Analysis* (pp. 51-66). Baltimore: Johns Hopkins University Press.

Joseph, R. (1985). Competition between women. *Psychology: A Quarterly Journal of Human Behavior, 22,* 1-12.

Karlsen, C. F. (1987). *The Devil in the Shape of a Woman:* Witchcraft in Colonial England. New York: Norton.

Lagerspetz, K. M., Bjorkqvist, K., & Peltonen, T. (1988). Is indirect aggression typical of females?: Gender differences in aggressiveness in 11-year-old to 12-year-old children. *Aggressive Behavior 14,* 403-414.

Low, B. S. (1979). Sexual selection and human ornamentation. In N. A. Chagnon, W. Irons (Eds.). *Evolutionary Biology and Human Social Behavior.* North Scituate, MA.: Duxbury.

Lumsden, C. & Wilson, E. O. (1981). *Genes, Mind, and Culture.* Cambridge, MA.: Harvard University Press.

Macaulay, J. (1985). Adding gender to aggression research: Incremental or revolutionary change? In V. E. O'Leary, R. K. Unger, & B. S. Wallston, (Eds.). *Women, Gender, and Social Psychology* (pp. 191-224). Hillsdale, N.J.: Erlbaum.

Maccoby, E. E. & Jacklin, C. N. (1974). *The Psychology of Sex Differences.* Stanford, CA.: Stanford University Press.

McCabe, A. & Liscomb, T. J. (1988). Sex differences in children's verbal aggression. *Merrill-Palmer Quarterly, 34,* 389-401.

McClintock, F. H. (1963). *Crimes of Violence*. London: Macmillan.

McKeachie, W. (1952). Lipstick as a determiner of first impressions of personality: An experiment for the general psychology course. *Journal of Social Psychology, 36*, 241-244.

Moore, M. M. (1985). Nonverbal courtship patterns in women: Context and consequences. *Ethology and Sociobiology, 6*, 237-248.

Morris, D. (1967). *The Naked Ape: A Zoologist's Study of the Human Animal*. New York: McGraw-Hill.

Moyer, K. E. (1974). Sex differences in aggression. In R. C. Freedman, R. M Richart, R. L. Vanderwiele, & L. O. Stern (Eds.), *Sex Differences in Behavior*. New York: Wiley.

Parke, R. D. & Slaby, R. G. (1983). The development of aggression. In E. M. Hetherington (Ed.), *Handbook of Child Psychology: Volume IV, Socialization, Personality and Social Development*, Fourth Edition (pp. 547-641). New York: Wiley.

Paul, L., Foss, M., Fiorito, J. & Baenninger, M. (in preparation). *Sexual jealousy in young women and men: Attitudes, perceptions, and actions.*

Rosenblatt, E. & Greenland, C. (1974). Female crimes of violence. *Canadian Journal of Criminology, 16*, 173-180.

Schuster, I. (1983). Women's aggression: An African case study. *Aggressive Behavior, 9*, 319-332.

Sparrow, G. (1950). *Women Who Murder*. London: Baker.

Tavris, C. & Offir, C. (1977). *The Longest War: Sex Differences in Perspective*. New York: Harcourt Brace Jovanovich.

Trivers, R. L. (1972). Parental investment and sexual selection. In B. Campbell (Ed.), *Sexual Selection and the Descent of Man 1871- 1971*. Chicago: Aldine.

Udry, J. R. (1978). The importance of being beautiful: A reexamination and racial comparison. *American Journal of Sociology, 83,* 154-160.

Williams, J. H. (1977). *Psychology of Women: Behavior in a Biosocial Context*. New York: Norton.

Wilson, E. O. (1975). *Sociobiology: The New Synthesis*. Cambridge MA: Harvard University Press.

Wilson, E. O. (1978). *On Human Nature*. Cambridge MA: Harvard University Press.

11

Violence, Aggression, and Targets: An Overview
Ronald Baenninger

At a meeting of the International Society for Research on Aggression several years ago a group of us were talking informally about our own personal aggressive interactions. We had not lived sheltered lives, and several of us had done field work in dangerous places. All of us had been robbed at least once, but most of us (all males) could not recall any serious incidents as adults in which we were either the target of violence, or the aggressor. Three men still recalled fistfights as children on the school playground. While aggression researchers may be atypical, my long observation suggests to me that we are rather like most other people except for our preoccupation with the topic of aggression. Our lack of direct, personal experience with violence and aggression as adults may have been rather typical (at least for white male professionals).

Stephen Jay Gould (1988) recently suggested that human aggressive interactions are statistically rare events, not nearly as common as kind and cooperative acts. Certainly every reader of newspapers, or every viewer of the TV news, is aware of violent acts committed on a daily basis, but despite the muggings, bar fights, spouse and child abuse, the assaults, rapes, etc., that are described daily by the media, Gould asserted that we are normally a relatively peaceable (and even amicable) species. We may have confounded the dramatic nature of interpersonal violence with its frequency.

Bender (1969), an eminent psychiatrist who specialized in treating disturbed children for many years, concluded that "destructiveness and hostile aggression in a child is a symptom complex caused by developmental pathology which disorganizes the normal constructive patterned drives...". Bender posited 1) an inherent drive for normality determined by goal-directed biological maturation, 2) an inborn capacity to relate and identify with other humans so that experiences of love, social relations, communication and language are possible, and 3) an inborn capacity for fantasy, symbol formation and projection. She suggested that a constellation of several factors is required to produce violent, potentially dangerous individuals. These factors include "endogenous pathology", unfavorable social environment, an irritating victim or target, a lethal agent, and a lack of protection. Bender (1969) found "no place" for the psychoanalytic concepts of universal inborn aggressive or death instincts or death wishes. While such assertions (like the psychoanalytic concepts they criticize) are not supported by formal scientific data, they are the result of long experience with a large sample of children who were sufficiently disturbed to receive psychiatric attention. Surely they merit our attention.

Even on a group, regional, or national level significant physical aggression is rare. Certainly there are violent strikes, disputes between rival groups over economic matters, and wars in which religious, tribal, or nationalistic differences result in acts of violence and aggression. But such events are rare enough to be newsworthy. Consider the number of adults in a major American city, and multiply that by the number of interpersonal interactions each of them has each day. The result is an enormous number of interactions; even if many of those interactions are characterized as hostile or angry only a small subset of them involve physical aggression or violence. Is it any wonder that even aggression researchers find it difficult to recall the times when they have resorted to physical aggression? We may be assertive, but that is not the same thing at all.

The concept of personality rests on the fact that people are remarkably consistent in their behavior. Those who show little physical aggression remain generally peaceable even when provoked. In modern, stable societies such people are in the vast majority - employed, middle class, with a home address where they live their lives in mundane pursuits with a circle of friends and a minimum of drama.

Those who do engage in violent behavior are also consistent, whether the reasons for doing so are inherited, due to a difficult life history, or due to frustrating circumstances of unemployment, poverty, homelessness, or the lack of a restraining social network. Such people may be in the minority, but constitute the majority of those who act aggressively in ways that the rest of us hear about.

Those who are consistently violent and physically aggressive are perceived by the rest of us as unusual. Aggression researchers have undertaken the task of trying to understand the causal factors behind the actions of these problem people, and perhaps ultimately to restore them to the consistent peaceableness of the rest of us. Thus, we have focussed on this minority, and this focus may have distorted our vision.

ANIMAL AGGRESSION

Another source of our preoccupation with a statistically rare kind of behavior may be our reliance on data from animals. Individual members of many animal species must engage in some overt, physically violent competition, predation, or parasitic behavior just in order to survive as an individual, and contribute genetically to offspring. While symbiotic behavior and even friendship certainly exist in other species, especially among primates (Smuts, 1987), Tennyson's "Nature, red in tooth and claw" is widely believed to describe species other than ourselves. The fact is that very few animal behaviorists have studied peaceful attachments or the analogues of friendship among members of other species.

Most books on aggression and violence in humans at least note the superficial similarities between human and animal aggression, and describe animal "models". Particularly in our attempts to understand the physiology and neuroscience of aggressive behavior in humans these models have had a powerful influence on our thinking. Some, like Konrad Lorenz, Desmond Morris, and Robert Ardrey have emphasized possible functional similarities, and have mistaken metaphorical analogies and convergences for legitimately homologous similarities. But there are also many differences in the form and content of human and animal aggression - the weapons, the stimuli, the outcomes, and what they fight about - and these have sometimes been ignored. In many other species the males are considerably larger and more aggressive than the females and the general perception exists that males are endowed by their evolution and testosterone levels with a violent nature. Dramatic examples of sexual and behavioral dimorphism in species like Northern elephant seals (LeBoeuf, 1971) contribute to the belief that males fight overtly, while females are simply attractive, receptive, and nurturant. One of the earliest empirical studies to question the universality of this view was Ewer's extensive field study of *Rattus rattus* (the black, or "plague" rat) in African villages (1971). She found that free-living female roof rats accounted for most of the aggressive interactions. According to Woolpy's studies of wolves (1968) the aggressive, intrasexual competition among females is a primary determinant of female mating success in this carnivore. DeWaal's studies (1982) of non-human primates in semi-natural environments certainly found aggression and violence among females. The view that females are normally peaceful, while males do all the violent fighting, has nevertheless taken on the character of a myth. In Chapter 9, Paul and M. Baenninger point out that such a myth may be self-serving for males, and is an inaccurate portrayal of human females.

THE ROLE OF SOCIAL, ECONOMIC, AND POLITICAL RULES

It is also worth remembering that the resources animals fight over - e.g. food, shelter, dominance status, mate competition - are normally allocated by economic, political and social arrangements among humans. The rules, laws, police, militia, and even the armies of civilized nations have evolved to minimize overt aggression and physical violence between people competing for the resources that they require. Even such a simple device as a traffic light is responsible for reducing massive struggles for access among motorists at intersections. Like traffic lights, these systems sometimes break down, especially at the international level, but they normally work surprisingly well in preventing violence.

Through the acquisition and expenditure of money much of the human competition for resources is eliminated, or changed into a less physical competition for an abstract resource, a secondary reinforcement. While some use force or violence to acquire money, thereby risking prison sentences, the majority of people are willing to provide their labor, goods or services in exchange for money in conventional ways according to economic rules, although cheating and guile certainly occur. This is not possible for species that lack our ability to develop abstract rules and concepts. Especially at times when a resource is scarce animals must compete directly for it with conspecifics, or with members of other species. A gull which finds an edible item on the beach must almost invariably contend with other gulls bent on taking it for themselves; in a monetary system the price of a rare item rises until only those few with lots of money can afford to have it, thus averting physical aggression.

Even in non-monetary situations we humans have developed social rules of decorum that inhibit violence. Competition at a cocktail party for the last caviar canape does not normally resemble the screaming attacks of gulls attempting to grab a clam from a conspecific. It is a violation of the social rules to resort to physical violence, or even shoving, in such situations. The host or hostess can gain preclude violent competition and gain status by providing enough caviar for everyone, which may be a reason for having the cocktail party in the first place.

As much as we may decry political bickering the deals, discussions, trading of favors, and the Byzantine intrigue of political activity all have the virtue of avoiding physical violence. Most of us would prefer that people, groups, or nations whose interests are opposed should be talking rather than fighting. The military historian von Clausewitz (1780-1831) described war as a continuation of state policy (or politics) by other means; our species is fortunate (and perhaps different from most others) in that we have a political alternative to violence or warfare. Conciliation and peace-making may occur in nonhuman primates as well (DeWaal,

1989), although their abstract communication abilities are not as highly developed as ours.

HOSTILITY AND ANGER

Thus, economic, social, and political conventions have developed partly to reduce overt aggression in our species. In the absence of violence and aggression there may still be human emotions such as hostility and anger. These emotions may lead to overtly aggressive actions, but they do not necessarily do so in properly socialized adults. Clearly, among children this is not yet true. In Chapter 2, Olweus describes the extent of one kind of childhood aggression in Scandinavia, and the way in which a rational campaign of education may decrease it. While Norway and Sweden are relatively homogeneous societies, not notable for adult violence, the reductions in bullying brought about by nationwide awareness of the problem are impressive. Such results are a testimonial to the extent to which inevitable childhood anger and hostility may be brought under control, so that they no longer lead to aggressive persecution of victims.

Aggressive acts by psychiatric patients toward clinicians are examined by Eichelman in Chapter 7. This topic has rarely been described in the general literature, for a variety of reasons addressed by Eichelman. We do not know, for example, whether such attacks on clinicians occur with a frequency higher than the frequency of interpersonal attacks in the general population. Aggressive psychiatric patients are poorly socialized and unable to deal with their angry, hostile feelings in non-aggressive ways. Obviously, not all psychiatric patients suffer from similar maladies and some may be less-than-normally likely to use overt aggression as a way of coping with their feelings. Eichelman reports that young paranoid males may be a particularly risky population for clinicians to deal with because of their pervasive anger and hostility.

INSTITUTIONS THAT CONDONE AGGRESSION

One unfortunate consequence of having peace-keeping organizations, designated by a society to minimize overt aggression by its citizens, is that these organizations may resort to violent means. Brutality toward individuals and certain minorities by police, the judicial system, and the army do occur. The victims of such institutional, organizational aggression may have some redress if they have political power in the larger society. Peace-keeping organizations may also aggress passively against certain individuals or groups. As Bolton and Nardi discuss in Chapter 8, certain minorities may be at risk because the larger society is intolerant of them; as a result, these minorities are helpless against attacks unless they defend themselves. Violence and aggression toward sexual minorities appears particularly likely to be condoned by the majority; as Bolton and Nardi point out, violence toward homosexuals is frequently treated as less serious by the police, and is prosecuted less vigorously by the judicial system.

When violence and aggression toward particular targets is condoned or even encouraged by a society there is a risk to the very foundations of the larger society. Normally nonviolent minority groups that are consistent targets of active or passive aggression, whether they are defined ethnically, culturally, economically, by their religious beliefs, sexual preference, or by some other criterion, are eventually going to either leave the larger society, change it by political means, or retaliate with violence of their own.

Hyman, in Chapter 4, discusses the brutality toward school children that occurs in institutions that are not normally devoted to peace-keeping. School systems, with their teachers and administrators, have an educational function. But education of children may be difficult in chaotic situations; a certain amount of peace-keeping and policing may be necessary in order that teachers and students can engage in the educational enterprise. Victims of the kind of bullying described by Olweus find learning difficult when they live in constant fear of the their peers. Corporal violence by educators toward students is not condoned in most American schools, but Hyman points out quite dramatically that it does occur. Interestingly, the ages of children attacked by bullies and by teachers are similar; in both cases the frequency of attacks increases to a peak early in childhood and then declines. This may suggest that both bullies and teachers attack relatively helpless targets, whose retaliation would be neither serious nor painful. This is an issue to which we will return.

When institutions condone, or even encourage, aggressive acts the responsibility for protection is given back to individuals and the social contract is broken. Schools that permit or encourage violent acts toward young students by teachers, administrators, or older student bullies are undercutting faith in the ability of societal institutions to defend the victims. In addition, such schools are presenting a violent, aggressive model of society, a model for students in how to deal with conflict. The same is true for other societal institutions as well; they have a responsibility to model as well as protect. Police attacks on individuals or groups call into question that institution's ability to protect people even-handedly from the attacks of other individuals or groups.

One may ask why a society or its institutions might condone violence and aggression against individual or group targets. One answer may be that it lacks the power to stop individuals from their attacks. There are not enough police officers to prevent attacks by each and every aggressively hostile citizen. But why are such attacks infrequently prosecuted? It is possible that the hydraulic model of aggressive motivation is widely accepted. This pernicious model, as discussed by Lorenz (1966) and Storr (1968), suggests that motivation to aggress against something or someone is a form of life energy that wells up in individuals. Acceptance of this model implies that attacks in circumscribed situations, or on certain targets, will ultimately benefit the majority by providing outlets for the aggressive motivation, drives, or instincts of those who must express them. Lorenz (1966) maintained that this was a major function of sports, a view that those who have studied violence in sports do not share (e.g. Russell in Chapter 5).

As Bolton and Nardi point out in their chapter, restoring the faith of homosexuals in the willingness of the legal system to protect their rights is an important matter. Without such faith by members of a persecuted minority, they are tempted to undertake their own defense against attacks condoned by the sexual majority. When a church or religious institution condones violence toward a rival religious organization, or a religious minority, there is a similar modeling effect. After centuries of persecution as a minority it was inevitable that a Jewish Defense League should eventually appear to defend Jews against the attacks of majority religions or political groups. Many Jews simply lost faith in the willingness of non-Jews to protect their rights, based primarily on the treatment of Jews in Nazi Germany, and the JDL was the predictable result.

Human violence and aggression toward members of other animal species is a special case, with a unique solution. Animals themselves do not band together as a persecuted minority in their own defense; instead, people who empathize with their plight have organized on the animals' behalf, motivated by their own anthropomorphic sentiments. The humane movement would surely not have occurred without the perception of its members that domestic animals were suffering and persecuted. As I documented in Chapter 1, societies for the prevention of cruelty to animals were contemporaneous with the anti-slavery movement in Great Britain and the United States, and preceded societies for the protection of another helpless minority - human children. As the chapters by Knutson, Schwartz & Zaidi(Chapter 3), by Hyman Chapter 4), and by Olweus (Chapter 2) make clear, children are still subject to violence by parents and relatives, by the schools, and by older children. But there are now societal institutions for child protection, and they no longer suffer the virtual enslavement that occurred during the Industrial Revolution and its aftermath. If we humans are unique in having devised the concept of slavery (Barnett, 1988) we are also unique in experiencing the moral revulsion that led to its eventual abolition in most of the industrialized world. It is also true, of course, that machines for manufacturing and agriculture led to a decline in the need for the labor of human slaves, children, and animals. Aggression and violence toward them declined as a result.

RETALIATION BY TARGETS OF AGGRESSION AND VIOLENCE

While slaves frequently fought back and revolted against their captors and masters, children and animals that were taken advantage of did not. This may have been due to their inability to organize, or to their perception that they were helpless against the majority in the societies that condoned their persecution. The targets of aggression discussed in most of the contributed chapters of this book share this inability to retaliate. It is an important issue.

There are laboratory analogs to some of these matters, where animals are the experimental subjects. In my own early research on aggression in animals I was interested in the effects of punishment on aggressive behavior. Normally, punishment has a suppressing effect on the behavior that is punished (Solomon, 1964), but painful stimulation is one of the principal stimuli for aggression (Hutchinson, 1972). The prediction that punishment of aggressive acts with aversive, painful stimuli might actually increase it was borne out in a number of experiments (Baenninger & Grossman, 1969; Ulrich and Azrin, 1962). The target of an aggressive attack can punish the attack by retaliating aggressively, a situation that may increase the aggressiveness of the original aggressor (Baenninger, 1974).

If the target of an aggressive attack can retaliate by a counterattack on the aggressor this constitutes an experimentally uncontrolled source of punishment for the aggressor, as well as an instigating stimulus for further aggression. When a mouse-killing rat attacks his victim there is little that the mouse can do to retaliate; thus, the experimenter can exert nearly complete control over the consequences for the rat of attacking the mouse. Painful electric shock consequent on a rat's attempts to kill mice suppressed his attacks for long periods of time, although this effect was rarely permanent (Baenninger, 1970). Arousing stimuli, even painful ones, reinstated the attacks on mice by killers who had suppressed their attacks (Baenninger & Ulm, 1969). When punishment for attacking mice was discontinued most killer rats eventually begin to kill again. In the absence of any consequences for their attacks mouse-killing rats would continue until they appeared exhausted, killing every mouse presented to them. I eventually came to believe, incidentally, that the benefits of this research program no longer outweighed the suffering and death of so many mice.

Children, domestic animals, and the victims of bullies have little or no ability to inflict punishment on those who behave cruelly toward them. An external agent must be prepared to do so, or internal inhibition of attacking must develop. For example, in a predominantly heterosexual society that condones violence toward homosexual men and women, such behavior will occur unless people find it morally reprehensible. As Russell points out in Chapter 5, athletes are frequent targets of hostility and even violence by fans; while athletes can (and do) retaliate against attacks by other athletes on the playing field, it is difficult or impossible for them to retaliate against the fans who fill the stadium.

Weapons give aggressors the ability to aggress safely, and without punishment against targets who lack weapons. Objects that are hurled, or bombs that are dropped, as well as arrows, bullets, and cannon shells all permit an aggressor to remain at a distance from a victim. The ability to make and use weapons is one of major differences between the aggression of humans and animals. Teeth and claws are the only weapons of most mammals (Matthews, 1964), and even non-human primates that allegedly wield weapons remain in potential contact with their targets. Our uniquely human ability to deliver injurious stimuli while some distance away means that human aggressors need not risk injury themselves, unless their opponents are similarly armed. They may also be spared direct sensory evidence of their attacks in the form of hearing the screams, or seeing gory injuries and the mutilation of their victims. While aggressors may experience these things in imagination, that is not certain, and punishment in the form of remorse or guilt do not necessarily occur. I suspect that most sane humans find direct evidence of their own violence to be aversive, although that is an empirical question (for which little evidence exists one way or the other). But it is certainly true that distance weapons endow aggressors with greater power and effectiveness in damaging their targets, without danger of retaliation.

In Chapter 6, Novaco examines the use of vehicles as instruments of aggression. From the classification that he has worked out it is clear that automobiles and trucks may serve as powerful destructive weapons, or as a mobile refuge from attempts by victims to retaliate. Roadway aggression could provide a useful paradigm for studying the importance of retaliation in the inhibition of aggression. Would people in traffic jams behave as aggressively as people on the open highway? An aggressive act, such as intentionally ramming another car, shooting, or even verbal abuse exposes the aggressors to retaliation by their targets if they are all together in a stationary traffic tie-up. For most people outside the clinical professions the idea of a relatively helpless patient, whether institutionalized or not, attacking an authority figure such as a psychotherapist is likely to be unexpected because the roles of attacker and helpless victim are somehow reversed. Staff abuse of helpless patients is a concern of institutions for children, the aged, or the mentally ill. But bringing an aggressive psychiatric patient to trial is unlikely, and there may be minimal consequences for the patient who attacks a clinician. As Eichelman points out, the psychotherapist or clinician may be the helpless party in such situations.

SUMMARY AND CONCLUSIONS

This overview of the diverse chapters in this book began with the assertion that the daily lives of most people contain few overtly aggressive interactions. Despite the preoccupation of aggression researchers, and the attention to violence that is evident in the media, personal experiences of behaving aggressively are infrequent for most people. If that is true, we must ask the counter-intuitive question: Why is there not more individual violence and aggression? What do ordinary adults do with feelings of anger and hostility that are aroused by the stress and frustration of daily life?

Humans, as distinct from most other species, normally use economic, social, or political means for settling disputes, instead of overt aggression. Economic weapons, social rules and conventions, and political dialogue serve as substitutes for naked violence. Psychologically, successful socialization enables most developing adults to cope with their feelings of anger and hostility without resorting to actions more serious than threat displays, occasional temper tantrums, or displacement of aggression (more accurately called "re-directed aggression" by earlier ethologists).

In this chapter two additional, related answers have been proposed to the question of why aggression is not more prevalent in our species. First, it appears that aggressive attacks toward certain targets may be implicitly condoned, in the sense that legal consequences for the attacker are haphazard, unpredictable, and frequently absent entirely. As the chapters on "gay-bashing", aggression on the highway, violence toward clinicians, violence toward athletes, and bullying of school children make clear there is a degree of societal or institutional acceptance of such acts in some Western societies. People can get away with attacking such targets.

Second, even when legal consequences for aggressive attacks are lacking certain targets may be unable or unwilling to retaliate personally when they are attacked. Cruelty toward animals and abuse of children by families or educators are not universally perceived as crimes, although enactment and enforcement of prohibitions for such aggressive acts have increased during the last century. While cruelty to animals or children, especially attractive ones, may evoke public censure there is rarely any vigorous prosecution by legal agents. And since intentional retaliation by animals or children themselves is usually an impossible fantasy there is little but internal inhibition to prevent attacks on them.

The targets of violence and aggression described in this book all share the characteristic that they are either helpless and unable to retaliate, or that attacks on them do not reliably produce serious consequences for the perpetrator of the attacks. Those who do attack such targets presumably lack the internal inhibitions on violence that successful socialization engenders. Or they may believe that there will be no legal or personal repercussions or punishment for their attacks.

If those with the power and motivation to attack are held in check by external or internalized inhibitory mechanisms, what about their potential targets? Why do the targets of violence and aggression discussed in this book - the victims of bullies, abused children, gay people, clinicians, athletes, or abused wives - so rarely attack their persecutors? Do they lack feelings of hostility and anger, or are they morally superior? Although such retaliation does occur it is remarkably rare. Clearly, such attacks are inhibited by the fear of repercussions by those who are powerful, organized and aggressively uninhibited. Thus, the infrequent attacks by helpless targets of aggression and violence emphasizes the importance of aversive consequences in controlling aggression.

There is thus a strong cognitive component that emerges in this discussion of human aggression. The implication is that potential aggressors assess the consequences of their attacks. If retaliation by a target is unlikely, or if such attacks are societally condoned, then the likelihood of violence and aggression toward that target is increased. Those who study aggression cannot ignore this rational, cognitive analysis and concentrate solely on emotional aspects of human aggression. The targets tell us a great deal about aggression.

REFERENCES

Ardrey, R. (1967). *The Territorial Imperative*. London: Collins.

Baenninger, R. (1970).. Suppression of interspecies aggression in the rat by several aversive training procedures. *Journal of Comparative and Physiological Psychology, 70,* 382-388

Baenninger, R. (1974). Some consequences of aggressive behavior: a selective review of the literature on other animals. *Aggressive Behavior, 1,* 17-37.

Baenninger, R. and Grossman, J.C. (1969). Some effects of punishment on pain-elicited aggression. *Journal of Experimental Analysis of Behavior, 12,* 1017-1022.

Baenninger, R. and Ulm, R. (1969). Overcoming the effects of prior punishment on interspecies aggression. *Journal of Comparative and Physiological Psychology, 69,* 628-635.

Barnett, S.A. (1988). *Biology and Freedom*. Cambridge: Cambridge University Press.

Bender, L. (1969). Hostile aggression in children. In Garattini, S. and Sigg, E.B. (Eds.). *Aggressive Behavior*. Amsterdam: Excerpta Medica.

DeWaal, F. (1982). *Chimpanzee Politics*. New York: Harper & Row.

DeWaal, F. (1989). *Peacemaking Among Primates*. Cambridge, MA: Harvard University Press.

Ewer, R.E. (1971). The biology and behaviour of a free- living population of black rats (Rattus rattus). *Animal Behaviour Monographs, 4,* 127-174.

Gould, S.J. (1988). Ten thousand acts of kindness. *Natural History, (Dec.).,* 12-17.

Hutchinson, R.R. (1972). The environmental causes of aggression. In J.K. Cole & D.D. Jensen (Eds.) *Nebraska Symposium on Motivation*. Lincoln: University of Nebraska Press.

Le Boeuf, B. (1971). The aggression of the breeding bulls. *Natural History, 80,* 83-91.

Lorenz, K. (1966). *On Aggression*. London: Methuen.

Matthews, L.H. (1964). Overt fighting in mammals. In Carthy, J.D. & Ebling, F.J. (Eds). *The Natural History of Aggression*. London: Academic Press.

Smuts, B. (1987). What are friends for? *Natural History, (Feb.),* 36-44.

Solomon, R.L. (1964). Punishment. *American Psychologist, 19,* 239-253.

Storr, A. (1968). *Human Aggression*. New York: Atheneum.

Ulrich, R.E. and Azrin, N.H. (1962). Reflexive fighting in response to aversive stimulation. *Journal of Experimental Analysis of Behavior, 5,* 511-520.

Woolpy, J.H. (1968). The social organization of wolves. *Natural History, (May),* 46-55.

Author Index

Abelson, R.P., 312, 318
Achenbach, T.M., 125, 141
Adam, B., 384, 396
Adam, H., 112, 152
Adler, W.N., 334, 343
Agathonos, H., 112, 152
Ageton, S.S., 83, 100
Ainsworth, M.D.S., 114, 141
Alberts, J.R., 109, 141
Alcock, J., 412, 414, 418, 436
Alderfer, C.P., 222, 247
Alexander, R.A., 262, 323
Altemeier, W.A., 116, 155
Alves, W.M., 215, 247
Ammerman, R.T., 107, 120, 121, 141, 142
Andereck, N.D., 110, 150
Anderson, C., 268, 392, 394, 396
Anderson, C.A., 272, 318, 319
Anderson, D.C., 318
Anderson, E.A., 129, 144
Anderson, R.D., 226, 250
Annis, L.V., 232, 337, 343
Appelbaum, P.S., 346
Ardrey, R., 446, 459
Arkowitz, H., 129, 155
Arms, B.B., 347
Ascione, F., 23, 37
Authier, K.J., 120, 148
Azar, S.T., 106, 118, 142, 153
Azrin, N.H., 454, 460

Back, G., 219, 221, 247
Baenninger, M., 401, 402, 406, 423, 424, 427, 436, 440, 447
Baenninger, R., 1, 2, 3, 5, 7, 17, 26, 27, 32, 37, 406, 409, 424, 436, 443, 454, 459
Baker, C.A., 332, 337, 343
Balow, E.A., 344

Bandura, A., 128, 142, 167, 168, 196, 242, 247, 303, 305, 318
Barahal, R.H., 118, 142
Barden, R.C., 117, 142
Barkley, R.A., 122, 145
Barloy, J.J., 20, 37
Barnes, J., 238, 247
Barnett, D., 114, 144
Barnett, S.A., 453, 459
Baron, R.A., 109, 142, 237, 247, 272, 300, 301, 318, 319
Barrett, G.V., 262, 323
Barth, J.T., 215, 247
Bathurst, J.E., 23, 38
Baumrind, D., 95, 100
Beach, F.A., 21, 38, 251, 398
Beaman, A., 311, 320
Beck, F.W., 120, 145
Bell, A., 391, 396
Bell, R.C., 109, 142
Belsky, J., 105, 142
Bender, L., 444, 459
Benton, A.L., 215, 247
Benton, D., 2, 3
Berger, A.M., 104, 134, 137, 142, 143
Berkowitz, L., 109, 143, 237, 247, 270, 272, 305, 319
Berline, S., 120, 149
Berlyne, D.E., 228, 247
Bernard, J., 229, 248
Bernstein, J.A., 331, 343
Berrill, K., 368, 397
Berts, M., 57, 64, 100
Bettelheim, B., 18, 38
Binder, R., 329, 343
Bjorkqvist, K., 57, 64, 100, 439
Black, J.B., 312, 319
Black, H., 194, 197
Blackman, N., 25, 40
Blehar, M.C., 114, 141
Boggan, E.C., 400
Bolton, F.G., 117, 143

Author Index

Boord, P., 324
Borden, R.J., 240, 248
Boriskin, J.A., 108, 120, 123, 148
Boswell, J., 352, 353 397
Bower, G.H., 312, 319
Brain, P.F., 2, 3
Braucht, G.N., 107, 143
Braudel, F., 11, 38
Braunwald, K., 114, 144
Breitenbucher, M., 114, 146
Brock, T.C., 124, 143
Brookhouser, P.E., 120, 122, 143, 148
Brossard, S.D., 105, 143
Brown, M., 223, 252
Brown, M.M., 130, 146
Browne, M.A., 430, 436
Bruninks, R.H., 344
Brunnquell, D., 106, 113, 146
Bryant, B.K., 22, 38
Burgess, R., 128, 143
Burgess, R.L., 129, 144
Burgess, R.S., 127, 129, 144
Burke, K.L., 329, 345
Buss, A.H., 109, 144, 268, 319, 404, 409, 436

Camblin, L.D. Jr., 120, 144
Cameron, J., 231, 249
Campbell, A., 401, 397, 406, 416, 436
Campbell, D.T., 100
Campbell, E.A., 216, 248
Campbell, J., 7, 38, 309, 321, 323
Campbell, J.R., 10, 38
Campbell, S.B., 122, 144
Caras, R.W., 5, 38
Carlsmith, J.M., 272, 319
Carlson, V., 114, 115, 144
Carmel, H., 332, 343
Carr, W.G., 7, 38
Carrier, J.M., 352, 397
Cassisi, J.E., 107, 141
Casson, I.R., 216, 248
Ceresnie, S., 117, 156
Chase, L.J., 269, 319
Chisholm, L.D.J., 215, 251
Cicchetti, D., 104, 114, 118, 139 144, 150
Cicone, M.J., 404, 436
Clark, J., 159, 175, 181, 182,183, 190, 191, 193, 198, 202
Climent, C.E., 25, 38
Cohn, A.H., 108, 145
Cohn, E.S., 239, 249
Coie, J.D., 130, 145
Coleman, J.S., 229, 248

Collett, P., 259, 293, 322
Collins, G.S., 231, 249
Collmer, C.W., 104, 152
Comstock, G.D., 366-368, 370, 392, 397
Conger, J.J., 261, 320
Conger, R., 129, 144
Conger, R.D., 127, 129, 144
Conn, L.M., 335 343
Connell, D.B., 115, 152
Cook, T.D., 100
Coombes, P., 124, 145
Coombes, R.H., 414, 437
Coon, K.B., 120, 145
Coon, R.C., 120, 145
Copitch, P., 132, 156
Cornfield, R.B., 337, 343
Crapo, R.H., 352, 397
Crawford, J.S., 215, 251
Crockenberg, S., 118, 145
Crowley, M., 405, 437
Cummings, M., 115, 145
Cunningham, C.E., 122, 145
Curtis, B., 244, 248

Daly, M., 110, 157, 412, 414, 418, 419, 421, 422, 426, 428, 435, 437
D'Augelli, A.R., 388, 397
Daniel, J.H., 118, 145
Dart, R.A., 5, 38
Davis, D.L., 397
Davis, R.W., 239, 249
Deaux, K.K., 269, 320
Deci, E.L., 222, 248
deGroot, J.C., 324
Deluty, R.H., 331, 333, 344
Dent, O.B., 347
Depp, F.C., 335, 344
Deutsch, R.D., 417, 437
DeWaal, F., 447, 448, 459
Diamond, L.J., 119, 150
Dickens, C., 16, 38
DiDomenico, A., 216, 220
Diener, E., 311, 320
Dietrich, K.N., 117, 156
Dillow, P.V., 324
Dineen, E., 311, 320
Dion, K.K., 116, 145
Dipboye, R.L., 276, 320
Dishion, T., 70, 101
Dodge, K.A., 130, 146
Dollard, J., 303, 320
Donovan, D.M., 266, 320
Donovan, W.L., 148
Doob, L., 268, 269, 272, 275, 276, 303, 320

Doran, L., 125, 153
Dotemoto, S., 122, 156
Doueck, H.J., 119, 146
Downey, G., 107, 146
Droegemueller, W., 103, 150
Drummond, D.J., 344
Dubin, W.R., 335-338, 344
Dumas, J.E., 129, 146
Duner, A., 70, 101
Durkee, 268, 319
Dutile, F.N., 25, 38

Eagly, A.H., 397-406, 411, 437
Earp, J.A., 118, 146
Edelbrock, C.S., 125, 141
Edwards, D., 25, 44
Egeland, B., 104, 106, 111,
    113-115, 144, 146, 147
Ehrlich, N.J., 261, 324
Eibl-Eibesfeldt, I., 415, 437
Eichelman, B., 327, 329, 332,
    338, 344
Einbender, A.J., 108, 148
Eisenberg, N., 22, 39, 410,
    437
Ekblad, S., 59, 100
Ekman, K., 64, 100
Elliot, D.S., 83, 100
Elmer, E., 106, 107, 124, 147, 149
El-Sheikh, M., 115, 147
Emery, G.N., 42
Endresen, J., 83, 102
Endresen, K., 311, 320
Erdlen, R., 181, 198
Eron, L., 168, 199
Ervin, F.R., 25, 38
Esser, A.H., 417, 437
Evans, J., 231, 249
Evans, M.P., 21, 39
Everett, A., 223, 248
Ewer, R.E., 447, 459

Faranoff, A., 112, 147
Farber, E.A., 106, 107, 111, 147
Farley, A., 171, 200
Fasteau, M.F., 203, 248
Feiring, C., 115, 151
Felthous, A.R., 24-26, 30, 31, 39,
    40
Ferracuti, F., 226, 261
Fesbach, S., 414, 410, 437
Fielding, S.D., 337, 343
File, S.E., 109, 147
Filipp, L., 346
Finn, P., 350, 356, 358, 359, 362,
    369-371, 373, 376, 398

Fink, P., 331, 333, 336, 344
Fiorito, J., 423, 427, 440
Fisher, J., 9, 39
Flanigan, M.F., 376, 320
Flinn, M.V., 417, 426, 437
Foltein, M.F., 346
Fontana, V.J., 109, 123, 147
Ford, C.S., 351, 398
Ford, M.E., 117, 142
Forgas, J.P., 312, 321
Foss, M., 423, 428, 440
Foster, J.B., 216, 248
Foust, C.H., 25, 38
Fox, L., 118, 147
Frame, C.L., 130, 146
Franklin, C.W., 385, 398
Fraser, S., 311, 320
Friedman, S., 120, 152
Friedrich, W.N., 108, 120, 123,
    148
Frieze, I.H., 408, 438
Frodi, A., 112-114, 148
Frodi, A.M., 402, 405, 438
Furstenberg, F.F. Jr., 148

Gaines, R., 113, 148
Gaines, R.W., 107, 108, 149, 155
Galef, B.G., 109, 141
Garbarino, J., 120, 148
Gardner, L., 414, 438
Garrick, J.G., 231, 249
Gaskill, H.S., 261, 320
Geen, R.G., 238, 249
Gelles, R., 168, 185, 200, 207
George, C., 127, 129, 148
Gerak, J., 185, 199
Gertz, B., 336, 344
Gibson, I., 163, 164, 199
Gil, D., 168, 200
Gil, E., 120, 149
Gillespie, D., 120, 149
Givens, D., 415, 438
Glad, D.D., 261, 320
Gmunder, B., 352, 398
Goetsch, V.L., 115, 147
Goldberg, S., 112, 113, 149
Goldstein, J.H., 239, 249
Gould, S.J., 443, 444, 459
Grandin, T., 28-30, 39
Green, A.H., 107, 108, 113, 124,
    148, 149, 155
Greenaway, K.D., 119
Greenberg, B.S., 315, 321
Greenberg, D., 351, 398
Greenland, C., 401-403, 405, 406,
    440
Greer, D., 239, 249

Gregg, G.S., 107, 124, 147, 149
Griffin, D.R., 17, 39
Gross, A.E., 268-270, 272, 276, 320
Grossman, J.C., 454, 459
Guttmann, A., 218, 249

Haddox, V.G., 25, 43
Haft, M.C., 396
Haller, R.M., 331, 333, 344
Halperin, S.M., 124, 149
Hamilton, J.W., 263, 321
Hammer, R., 298, 321
Hampton, R.L., 111, 118, 145
Harbaugh, R.E., 215, 249
Hardman, J.M., 216, 250
Harmatz, J., 346
Harry, J., 384, 385, 392, 398
Hassel, L., 261, 320
Hastings, D.E., 231
Hatti, S., 331, 335, 344
Hauber, A.R., 268, 273-275, 321
Heger, H., 353, 398
Heinemann, P.P., 45, 47, 100
Heinman, J., 324
Hekimian, E., 118, 142
Helfer, R.E., 104, 150
Hellman, D.S., 25, 40
Henderson, H.L., 261, 263, 322
Henker, B., 122, 156
Hentoff, N., 167, 201
Herdt, G.H., 351, 398
Herek, G., 365, 368, 385, 388, 389, 392, 398
Herman, C.P., 312, 321
Herrenkohl, E.C., 105, 107, 112, 113, 117, 123, 124, 129, 149
Herrenkohl, R.C., 105, 107, 112, 113, 117, 123, 124, 128, 149
Herson, M., 142
Herzog, H.A., 28, 40
Higgins, E.T., 312, 321
Hill, B.K., 330, 344
Hill, E.M., 414, 438
Hilton, T.L., 402, 438
Hindelang, M.J., 83, 100
Hirschi, T., 83, 100
Hobbs, G.E., 261-265, 325
Hoffman, M.L., 22, 40
Hoffman-Plotkin, D., 125, 149
Holden, C., 7, 40
Holden, R.T., 305, 321
Horner, M.S., 408, 438
Hrdy, S.B., 412, 428, 438

Humphreys, L., 385, 399
Hunter, H., 332, 343
Hupka, R.B., 425, 438
Huston, A., 167, 195
Hutchinson, R.R., 454, 460
Hyams, E., 7, 40
Hyde, J.S., 59, 100, 402, 403, 438
Hyg, M.S., 25, 38
Hyman, I.A., 159, 160, 162, 164, 166, 167, 170, 172, 173, 181, 183, 185, 192, 198, 200-203
Hynan, M.T., 109, 149

Infantino, J.A., 336, 344
Ishisaka, A.H., 119, 146

Jacklin, C.N., 59, 101, 401, 402, 439
Jackson, A.H., 346
Jacobsen, R.S., 129, 150
Jacobsen, N.S., 129, 150
Jamieson, K.J., 107, 143
Jane, J.A., 215, 247
Jason, J., 110, 150
Jaudes, P.K., 119, 150
Jenkins, T.N., 15, 43
Jensen, A.G., 115, 142
Jerome, J.K., 224, 231, 249
Johnson, B., 122, 129, 150
Johnson, R.B., 408, 438
Joseph, R., 408, 439

Kafonek, S., 346
Kane, S., 117, 143
Kang, J.S., 329, 331, 346
Kaplan, S., 125, 155
Karlsen, C.F., 401, 439
Kaste, M., 401, 439
Katevuo, K., 216, 249
Kaufman, J., 118, 150
Kazdin, A.E., 132, 150
Kellert, S.R., 24-27, 30, 31, 39, 40
Kempe, C.H., 103, 104, 150
Kenkel, W.F., 424, 447
Kennell, J., 120, 154
Kenrick, D.T., 272, 277, 322
Kermani, E.J., 334, 345
Kern, S., 261, 324
Kerns, M., 239, 249
Kim, D., 219, 221, 247
Kinard, E.M., 118, 150
King, E., 57, 64, 100
Klaus, M., 112, 147

Author Index   465

Klausner, S.Z., 222, 227, 228, 248, 249
Klein, M., 112, 150
Klerman, L.V., 118, 150
Kohlberg, L., 106, 150
Kohn, A., 168, 202
Kole, T., 261, 263, 322
Konecni, V.J., 307, 322
Kourany, R.F.C., 124, 152
Knutson, J.F., 103, 104, 106, 108, 109, 115, 122, 133, 143, 157, 170, 209
Kramer, J., 122, 157
Kraus, J.F., 216, 250
Kreeger, C., 334, 343
Krieger, R., 125, 155
Kupersmidt, J.B., 130, 145
Kusel, S.J., 83, 102
Kuurne, T., 216, 249

LaCrosse, J., 106, 151
Lagerspetz, K.M., 64, 100, 416, 439
Laird, D.A., 239, 250
Lally, D., 173, 192, 202
Lamb, M.E., 109, 113, 114, 148, 151
Lambert, D.A., 285, 323
Lampert, P.W., 216, 250
Lang, N.G., 391, 399
Laner, R.H., 117, 143
Langdon, J., 11, 41
Langlois, A., 118, 147
Lansbury, C., 14, 41
Lanza, M., 331, 345
Larrance, D.T., 118, 132, 151
Lasley, J.F., 10, 38
Lauderdale, M., 111, 156
Layton, J.F., 271, 325
Leavitt, L.A., 113, 148
LeBoeuf, B., 446, 451
LeBon, G., 305, 322
Lefkowitz, M., 168, 200
Leiguarda, R., 216, 248
Lennon, R., 410, 437
Lennox, N., 168, 169, 203
Lester, D., 21, 41
Leventhal, J.M., 113, 151
Levinson, B.M., 7, 22, 41
Levy, P., 342, 345
Lewis, G., 223, 226, 250
Lewis, J.M., 232, 250
Lewis, M., 115, 151
Liberman, R.P., 329, 345
Liberman-Lascoe, R., 183, 198
Lillie, H.R., 16, 41

Lion, J.R., 327, 329, 335, 343, 345, 346
Lippitt, R., 305, 324
Liscomb, T.J., 409, 439
Lister, C., 400
Loeber, R., 70, 101, 128, 154
Long, S.H., 118, 147
Lonsdale, S., 7, 41
Lorber, R., 128, 125, 154
Lorenz, K., 1, 3, 7, 41, 446, 452, 460
Low, B.S., 414, 439
Loya, F., 107, 143
Lubetsky, M.J., 121, 142
Lucas, M.J., 346
Lumsden, C., 421, 439
Lynch, M.A., 108, 116, 117, 151
Lyons-Ruth, K., 115, 152

Macaulay, J., 305, 319, 401, 396, 404, 401, 409, 411, 435, 438, 439
Macciocchi, S.N., 215, 247
Maccoby, E.E., 59, 101, 401, 402, 439
MacFarlane, S.W., 272, 277, 322
Macmillan, J., 264-266, 273, 322
MacNeil, M.L., 221, 251
Madden, D.J., 230, 233, 345
Magnusson, D., 70, 101
Mahoney, M.J., 430, 436
Maier, G.J., 345
Main, M., 127, 129, 148
Manger, T., 77, 101
Manning, J., 166, 203
Marchbanks, P.A., 287, 323
Margolin, G., 131, 156
Marlatt, G.A., 268, 320
Marsh, P., 259, 293, 308, 322
Marshall, B.D., 329, 345
Marshall, L.F., 217, 250
Martin, H.P., 112, 118, 124, 142, 152
Matthews, L.H., 455, 460
Maurer, A., 188, 194, 203, 204
Maurice, W.L., 330, 346
Mazur, A., 305, 322
McCabe, A., 409, 439
McClaskey, C.L., 130, 146
McClelland, D.C., 222, 250
McClintock, F.H., 402, 440
McCord, J., 266, 267, 322
McCrea, R., 14, 15, 41
McGee, S., 28, 40
McGonigle, J.J., 121, 142
McKeachie, W., 414, 440
McNeil, D., 329, 343

Author Index

McNeil, T., 350, 356, 358, 359, 362, 369-371, 373, 376, 398
Meadow, K., 117, 155
Mehm, J.B., 121, 133, 157
Mehm, J.G., 135, 142, 148, 157,
Mercer, C., 344
Mercy, J.A., 285, 323
Merill, G., 345
Meurala, H., 216, 249
Michalowski, R.J., 261, 293
Midgley, M., 47
Milanesi, L., 309, 323
Milgram, S., 244, 250, 311, 322
Miller, B., 385, 399
Miller, N., 303, 320
Miller, R.D., 345
Millham, J., 289, 390, 400
Mills, M.J., 346
Mills, N.H., 269, 319
Mishkin, A., 170, 195, 203
Montague, A., 22, 41
Moore, M.M., 415, 440
Morris, D., 414, 440
Morse, C., 120, 152
Morse, H.A., 122, 130, 150
Mosher, D.L., 222, 231, 226, 250
Mosk, M.D., 125, 126, 157
Mowrer, O., 303, 320
Moyer, K.E., 1, 2, 3, 32, 42, 409, 440
Muckerman, H., 16, 42
Mulhern, R.K. Jr., 133, 139, 153
Musingo, S., 336, 344
Mussen, P., 28, 45

Nacik, E.M., 185, 200
Nakau, S., 112, 152
Neff, C., 113, 148
Nelli, H.S., 298, 322
Nelson, B.J., 103, 152
Nelson, W.E., 215, 247
Newberger, E.H., 111, 120, 145, 149
Newcombe, N., 402, 436
Newman, J.B., 130, 146
Nitecki, D.V., 26, 42
Nitecki, M.H., 26, 42
Nosanchuk, T.A., 321, 251
Nourjah, P., 216, 250
Novaco, R.W., 253, 307-310, 323, 325
Niven, C.D., 11, 14, 17, 42

O'Carroll, P.W., 285, 323
O'Connor, S., 125, 155

Offir, C., 408, 441
Olweus, D., 45-47, 48, 53, 57, 59, 64, 67-69, 71-74, 76, 77, 82, 83, 85, 93-95, 100-101
Onwuachi-Saunders, E.C., 285-287, 323
Ortega y Gasset, J., 27, 42
Ory, M.G., 118, 146

Pallack, M.S., 124, 143
Panek, P.E., 262, 263, 323
Parke, R.D., 104, 152, 409, 440
Parker, J., 363, 400
Parker, S.M., 231, 249
Parry, M., 255-258, 268, 270, 273, 323
Parsons, J.E., 408, 438
Pashby, R.C., 215, 251
Pashby, T.J., 215, 251
Passman, R.H., 133, 139, 153
Patterson, G.R., 72, 94, 102, 109, 128, 131, 138, 140, 153, 154
Paul, L., 401, 423, 427, 440, 447
Payne, C.E., 318
Pedersen, L., 352, 399
Pelcovitz, D., 125, 155
Pelton, L.H., 111, 112, 153
Peltonen, T., 439
Pelz, D.C., 261, 324
Penna, M.W., 345
Perkins, K.A., 135, 143
Perri, M.G., 106, 154
Perry, D.G., 82, 102
Perry, L.C., 82, 102
Perry, M., 125, 153
Pettit, G.S., 130, 145
Peters, D.P., 245, 251
Phelan, L.A., 341, 346
Phillips, D.P., 300, 303, 323
Pikas, A., 57, 102
Plant, R., 353, 400
Pless, I.B., 116, 153
Plomin, R., 115, 153
Plotkin, R., 118, 156
Plotkin, R.C., 106, 154
Pokalo, M., 165, 204
Polansky, N., 305, 324
Pollack, C.G., 108, 156
Pope, J.H., 109, 157
Power, E., 113, 158

Radbill, S., 164, 205
Radke-Yarrow, M., 22, 42
Rainey, R.V., 261, 320

Raundalen, M., 57, 102
Raundalen, T.S., 57, 102
Raymond, D., 351, 397
Rector, F., 353, 400
Redl, F., 305, 324
Reid, J.B., 128, 129, 131, 138, 153, 154
Reid, W.H., 327, 323, 331, 345, 346
Reidy, T.J., 126, 154
Repucci, N.D., 124, 154
Requa, R.K., 231, 249
Rheingold, H.L., 42
Richman, J., 260, 324
Ricks, D., 107, 151
Rimel, R.M., 215, 247
Rimm, D.C., 324
Ritvo, H., 14, 42
Roberts, J., 117, 152
Robins, L.N., 118, 130, 154
Robinson, D.R., 118, 142
Rogers, E.M., 304, 306, 324
Rogers, J.E., 261, 324
Rogers-Salyer, M., 117, 142
Rohrbeck, C.A., 125, 154
Roland, E., 57, 68, 76, 95, 102
Rose, T., 172, 205
Rosenberg, D., 114, 146
Rosenberg, M.S., 124, 154
Rosenblatt, E., 401-403, 405, 406, 440
Rosenthal, J.A., 110, 155
Rovner, B.W., 330, 346
Roy, S.P., 216, 251
Rubin, I., 333, 346
Ruble, D.N., 404, 409, 436
Ruff, R.M., 217, 250
Rupp, J.P., 400
Ruspoli, M., 5, 42
Russell, C.S., 117, 151
Russell, G.W., 211, 219, 239, 240, 242, 245, 248, 251
Rutter, M., 65, 102
Ryan, J.A., 346
Ryan, R.M., 222, 248
Ryan, T.V., 215, 247

Sahler, O., 120, 152
Sagi, R.J., 350, 400
Sainio, K., 216, 250
Salyer, K.E., 117, 142
Salzinger, S., 125, 126, 127, 155
Samit, C., 125, 155
Sandford, D.A., 109, 155
Sandgrund, A., 107, 113, 119, 148, 155
Sandgrund, D., 108, 147

San Miguel, C., 389, 390, 400
Sarnoff, C.A., 231, 252
Saunders, R.L., 216, 249
Sawrey, W.L., 261, 320
Schellenbach, C.J., 129, 144
Schinder, F., 129, 155
Schlesinger, H., 113, 155
Schuman, S.H., 261, 262, 324
Schuster, I., 425, 426, 440
Seaberg, J., 120, 149
Sears, R., 303, 320
Selzer, M.L., 261, 324
Shader, R.I., 334, 346
Sham, R., 216, 248
Shepard, P., 19, 42
Sherrod, K.B., 116, 155
Sherry, D., 113, 148
Shilts, R., 372, 400
Shoemaker, F.F., 304, 306, 324
Silva, J.M., 238, 252
Silver, H.K., 103, 150
Silverman, F.N., 103, 150
Simons, L.S., 270, 325
Sinclair, U, 28, 40
Sirkin, M., 222, 225, 226, 250
Skillman, T.S., 261, 324
Skinner, B.F., 170, 192, 206
Slaby, R.G., 408, 440
Smerk, G.M., 309, 324
Smith, R.E., 244, 248
Smith, M.D., 218, 240, 252
Smith, S.M., 112, 155
Smoll, F.L., 244, 248
Smuts, B., 446, 460
Snyder, W., 345
Sofer, B., 169, 207
Solomon, G., 119, 155
Solomon, R.L., 453, 460
Sossin, M., 417, 437
Sparrow, G., 402, 440
Spearly, J.L., 111, 156
Spencer, J.R., 293, 295, 325
Stahl, J., 115, 152
Stamford, J.P., 352, 398
Starr, R.H., 117, 130, 156
Stathacopoulou, N., 112, 152
Stattin, H., 70, 101
Steele, B.F., 103, 108, 150, 156
Steffen, V.J., 397, 404, 406, 411, 437
Steinmetz, S., 168, 207
Stern, L., 112, 150
Stoddard, T.B., 378, 400
Stokols, D.S., 308, 309, 323, 325
Stokols, J., 309, 323
Stoltman, J.J., 325
Storr, A., 452, 460
Stouthamer-Loeber, M., 72, 102

Straker, G., 129, 150
Straus, M.A., 112, 156
Strauss, M., 168, 200
Stulginskas, J., 116, 153

Taplin, P.S., 128, 129, 154
Taraldson, B., 104, 144
Tardiff, K., 329, 330, 333, 334, 336, 346, 347
Tarlau, M., 216, 248
Tavris, C., 408, 441
Taylor, S.P., 240, 246
Thirer, J., 229, 252
Thome, P.R., 397, 438
Thorndike, E.L., 19, 42
Tilley, P.J.B., 216, 248
Tillman, W.A., 261-265, 325
Tinbergen, N., 259, 325
Toch, H., 312, 325
Tomkins, S.S., 226, 250
Toth, S.L., 104, 144
Trivers, R.L., 428, 441
Trulson, M.E., 221, 252
Turnbull, D., 223, 252
Turner, C.W., 270-272, 276, 277, 281, 303, 308, 325
Turner, T.J., 312, 319
Tustin, R.D., 109, 155
Twentyman, C.T., 106, 118, 125, 130, 142, 149, 151, 154, 156

Udry, J. R., 414, 441
Ulm, R., 454, 459
Ulrich, R.E., 454, 460

Van Hasselt, V.B., 107, 120, 121, 141, 142
Van Houten, R., 192, 209
Vasta, R., 132, 156
Vaughn, B., 113, 147
Vietze, P.M., 116, 155
Vilkki, J., 216, 249

Waddle, H., 43
Wagner, E.E., 262, 263, 323
Wagner, W.G., 105, 143
Wahler, R.G., 129, 146
Walder, L., 166, 200
Walker, E., 107, 146
Wall, S., 114, 141
Warden, C.J., 15, 43
Warner, L.H., 15, 43
Waterman, J., 118, 142

Waters, E., 114, 141
Wax, D.E., 25, 43
Weghorst, S.J., 110, 157
Weinberg, M., 391, 396
Weiner, N.A., 350, 400
Weinrich, J.D., 351, 400
Weis, J.G., 83, 100
Weiss, K.J., 344
Wells, E., 125, 153
Werner, D., 352, 400
Westervelt, F.H., 324
Westervelt, M.O., 46
Weston, J.T., 119, 156
Whalen, C.K., 122, 156
Wheeler, L., 306, 325
Whitam, F.L., 351, 400
Whitlock, F.A., 258-261, 272, 325
Whitman, R.M., 330, 347
Whitmore, E., 122, 157
Whittaker, J.K., 123, 157
Whitten, R.G., 397
Wiehe, E., 165, 209
Wille, D., 113, 148
Williams, J.H., 408, 441
Wilson, E.O., 421, 427, 439, 441
Wilson, M., 412, 414, 418, 419, 421, 422, 426, 428, 435, 437
Wilson, M.I., 110, 111, 157
Wilson, S.J., 344
Winthrop, J., 21, 43
Wise, J., 162, 164, 167, 170, 192, 200-203
Wolfe, D.A., 125, 157
Wolfgang, M.E., 261, 326
Wolkon, G., 346
Wooden, W., 363, 400
Woolpy, J.H., 447, 460
Wotring, C.E., 315, 321
Wright, S.D., 229, 252

Yamamoto, J., 346
Yasser, R.L., 238, 243, 245, 252
Young, L., 130, 157

Zahn, M.A., 350, 400
Zaidi, L.Y., 103, 121, 134-137, 157, 168, 209
Zanna, M.P., 312, 321
Zellman, G.L., 408, 438
Ziegler, P., 334, 343
Zillman, D., 2, 3, 32, 43
Zimbardo, P., 311, 326
Zoll, D., 115, 152
Zuravin, S.J., 117, 118, 157
Zweier, D., 117, 156

Subject Index

Abuse (see child abuse)
  -family members, 354, 365
  -prisons, 363
  -spouse, 328
  -substance, 342
Accident liability, 256-258, 261-266
  -age, 266
  -gender, 266
Achenbach Child Behavior Checklist, 125
Adjustment disorder, 328
Adolescents, 72, 83
Adult-child interactions, 95
Adultery, 418, 421, 422
Aggression (see punishment, roadway aggression, violence)
  -abused children, 129
  -animals, 446
  -anti-gay, causes of, 375-379
  -children, 45-102, 402, 429, 443, 444, 449-451, 457
  -context, 410
  -direct, 415
  -evolutionary perspective, 412, 413
  -females, 401-441
  -gender differences, 403, 424, 427
  -indirect, 415-417, 428
  -instinctual, 159
  -institutionalized, 159-209
  -interspecies, 7, 27
  -management, 327
  -operational definition, 411, 434
  -psychiatric patients, 327, 329-330, 341, 449
  -situational constraints, 410
  -social roles, 404, 405, 409, 410
  -sports, 211-251
    -frequency, 218
    -location, 230-235
    -sources, 235-245
  -toward homosexuals, 349-400, 450
Aggressive personality pattern, 70-72, 95
Agonistic behavior, 412-432
AIDS, 351, 356, 380-383, 390-393, 396
Alarm systems, 345, 340
Alcohol abuse (Alcoholism), 71, 168,
Alzheimers disease, 217
America
  -colonial, 162, 166, 167
American Psychiatric Association Task Force on Clinician Safety, 327
American Society for the Prevention of Cruelty to Animals, 14
Analog parenting tasks, 133, 134, 137, 137
Anglo-Saxon tradition, 162, 163
Animals
  -cognitive processes, 19
  -domestic, 11, 12, 32
  -humane treatment of, 8-15, 23, 28, 29
  -hunting, 12, 27, 28, 3042
  -mistreatment of, 9, 36
  -models in science and medicine, 7
  -pets, 6, 18, 23, 24, 30,
  -possession of intelligence, 19
  -possession of moral sense, 20, 21
  -possession of soul, 19, 20
  -protection of, 12-15

Subject Index

-symbols in art and religion, 7
-trapping of, 12, 27
-wild, 6, 12, 27
46
Annals of Philadelphia and Pennsylvania, 166
Anthropomorphism, 8, 18, 19, 38
Anti Defamation League, 375, 376
Anti-gay attitudes, 386-390
Anti-social behavior, 70, 75, 83, 84, 93
Antisocial personality disorder, 328
Anxiety, 69, 70, 74, 405
Anxious personality pattern, 69
Aristotle, 11, 21
Arousal jag, 228
Arson, 361, 366
Assault
  -on clinicians, 327-336, 339, 341, 342
  -on educators by students, 162
  -on homosexuals, 355, 358-368, 373, 381, 384, 385, 391, 392, 394, 397
  -on students by educators, 194
  -underreporting, 329
Assessing Environments III, 134, 135
Attachment
  -mother-child, 113-117, 119
    -disruption, 114, 117, 119
  -to animals, 64
Attacks
  -on athletes, 235-244
    -frequency, 237-244
    -intensity, 235-244
    -source, 235-244
    -type, 237-244
Attention deficit hyperactivity disorder, 121, 122
Attitude, 49, 65, 68, 69, 71, 74, 75, 82, 93
Attracting behavior, 415
Attractiveness, 413, 414, 434
Attrition, 81
Automobile, 253-255, 259, 262, 269, 282, 293, 294, 298, 308, 309, 311, 313, 316, 317
  -deadly weapon, 293, 294
  -territory, 259

Balzac, 12
Baptists, 165
Beatings, 162, 167
Bed-wetting, 29
Behavioral dimorphism, 446
Behaviorism, 170
Bias crimes, 356-370, 373-377, 379, 381, 382, 393, 397
Bible belt, 166
Bigotry, 358, 377, 378, 392
Biting, 425
Blackmail, 384, 385
Black's Law Dictionary, 194
Blaming the victim, 369
Bowers v. Hardwick, 383
Boys Town National Research Hospital, 121
Bruises, 160, 175, 183, 191
Buddhism, 8
Bull-baiting, 11, 13
Bully, 45-102
  -aggressive personality pattern, 70-72, 95
    -development of 71-72
  -alcohol abuse, 70
  -boys, 46 50, 54, 58, 59, 67-72, 78, 85
  -characteristics of, 46, 66 67, 69, 77, 97
  -child-rearing methods, 46, 67, 72, 73
  -class size, 64 65
  -competition hypothesis, 67
  -criminality, 70, 71
  -direct, 48, 58, 59, 62, 81, 92
  -dirty gestures, 48
  -disciplinary problems, 84
  -empathy (lack of), 70
  -failure/frustration hypothesis, 67
  -family problems, 73
  -followers, 70
  -frequency, 50, 51, 53 57, 61, 65, 77, 97
  -girls, 50, 54, 58, 59, 79, 85
  -henchmen, 70
  -impulsivity, 70
  -indirect, 48, 58, 59, 62, 82, 92
  -intervention, 46, 75-98
    -components, 75-77
    -goals, 75, 76
    -inventory, 76, 83, 84
    -key principles, 94-95

Subject Index 471

-sub-goals, 97, 98
-mobbing (mobbning), 45, 47
-negative actions, 47, 48
-open attacks, 48, 58, 62, 82
-oppression, 75
-passive, 70
-perpetrators, 58, 59
-physical contact, 48
-punishment, 72, 98
-school size, 64, 65
-self-reports, 46, 82, 83, 93
-social contagion, 73
-targets, 58, 67, 74
-Total Scale of Antisocial Behavior (TSAS), 84
Burnout (teacher), 159
Butler, Samuel, 163

California Racial, Ethnic and Religious Crimes Project, 358
Canadian Opthalmology Society, 215
Cartoon Reaction Scale, 263
Catholic theology, 164, 165
Center for Abused Handicapped Children, 121
Center for Democratic Renewal, 376
Child abuse, 103-157, 160, 162, 194, 328
-attention deficit hyperactivity disorder, 121, 122
-attractiveness, 117
-childhood illness, 116
-handicapping conditions, 119-123
-parental characteristics, 104
-premature infants, 112-114
-risk factors, 103, 105-109, 112, 113, 116, 123-131
-scapegoat hypothesis, 123
-teacher ratings, 126, 127
-transgenerational hypothesis, 133, 134
-unplanned pregnancies, 117
-victim characteristics, 105-116, 118, 126, 130, 131, 134, 137, 141
Child
-black, 172

-development, 163, 170
-hispanic, 172, 175
-rearing practices, 46, 67, 72, 73, 163, 166
-vulnerability hypothesis, 115
-white, 171, 172
Childhood conditions, 73
Chivalry, 405
Christian
-schools, 164
-theology, 164
Civil rights violations, 357
Class meetings, 98
Class size, 64, 65
Closed institutions, 160
Communist societies, 163
Competition, 404, 412-417, 428-430, 434, 435
-acquiring mate, 413-417, 434
-child-focused, 428-430, 435
-inter-female, 430
Competetive responses, 408
Correctional institutions, 160
Counselor, 171
Counter-transference, 333
Court conviction, 72
Criminality, 70, 72
Criminal justice system
-gay bashing, 369-375
Cruelty
-to animals, 5-43

Death, 180
Death penalty
-homosexuals, 353
Deindividuation, 306, 311
Dementia pugilistica, 216
Demon theory of deviance, 164
Denial
-clinicians, 327, 328, 337, 338, 341
Depressive disorder NOS, 328
Derivative deviance, 384, 385
-cultural, 384, 385
-opportunistic, 384, 385
Descartes, 11, 18
Deviant behavior, 164
Devil, 164, 165
Dickens, Charles, 159, 162
Direct bullying, 48, 58, 59, 62, 81, 92
Dirty gestures, 48
Discipline, 159-162, 169, 171, 172, 175, 178, 185,

Subject Index

172, 175, 178, 185, 188, 192, 193, 195
Disinhibition of aggression, 287, 303-307, 312, 317
Discriminatory actions, 350
Divorce, 73
Dosage-response relationships, 94
Drugs, 335
Drunk drivers, 266-268
DSM IIIR, 328
Dysthymic disorder, 328

Education, 366, 373, 376, 387, 389, 393, 397, 396
Education level, 170
Educator, 160, 161, 172-174, 176, 178, 180, 182, 184-187, 192-194, 196
Eighth Amendment, 193
Empathy, 70, 404, 405
Endogenous pathology, 444
Evangelical, 164, 165
Excitation transfer, 307
Exclusion, 48, 58, 62, 82

Faadelte schools, 63
Fag bashing, 349, 384
Fair Labor Standards Act, 15
Family
 -childhood conditions, 73
 -child-rearing practices, 46, 66, 72, 74
 -conditions, 66
 -divorce, 73
 -freedom, 72
 -love, 72, 73
 -overprotective mother, 69
 -parents, 45, 49, 60, 62, 63, 69, 72-74, 76, 77, 95, 97, 98
 -primary caretaker, 71, 95
 -problems, 73
 -siblings, 69, 71
Fatalities
 -clinicians, 327
 -from corporal punishment, 180
Fire-setting, 29
First Amendment, 373
Fixing behaviors, 415, 434
Flirting, 415, 423, 424, 427- 434
Flogging, 61, 166, 167
Followers, 70
Fourteenth Amendment, 193, 194

Fraud, 84
Friend, 68
Friendship, 98
Frustration-aggression perpective, 237
Fundamentalist theology, 164, 165

Gangs, 286, 290, 298, 299, 312, 321
 -drive-by shootings, 298, 299, 312
Gallup poll, 160, 164
Gay bashing, 349-400
 -individual, 350, 356-358
 -institutional, 350, 358, 382
Gay liberation movement, 353
Gay youths, 354
Graffitti, 358-362
Guilt, 405, 406, 433

Hand Test, 262
Harassment, 47, 48, 69, 74
Harris poll, 160
Hate crimes, 350, 356, 358-362, 365, 368-371, 374, 376, 377, 379, 393-397
Hate literature, 360-362
Hebrews, 164
Henchmen, 70
Highway robbery (see roadway aggression)
Hobbes, Thomas, 253
Holocaust, 353
Homicide, 261, 287-289, 293, 298, 300, 332
 -clinicians, 332
 -homosexuals, 356, 364
 -vehicular, 261, 287, 293
Homoeroticism, 351
Homophobia, 386-390
Homosexual behavior, 351-353, 378, 383, 388
Homosexual panic, 371, 372
Hormonal assays, 46
Horn-honking (see roadway aggression)
Hospitalization
 -from corporal punishment, 175
Hudibras, 163
Humane movement, 8-15
Human relations incidents, 357
Human rights committee, 195
Humiliation, 76, 167

Hunting
   -dominionistic, 27, 28
   -naturalistic, 27
   -utilitarian, 27
Hypermasculinity, 223, 226
Hypersexuality, 384

Impulsivity, 70
Inclusive fitness, 35
Indirect bullying, 48, 58, 59, 82, 92
Infidelity, 415, 419, 420
Infractions
   -nonviolent, 183
   -violent, 183, 190
Ingraham v Wright, 194
Injuries
   -from corporal punishment, 175-178
   -requiring medical attention, 179, 183
   -to athletes, 213-218, 231, 234, 237, 246
Insecurity, 69, 70, 74
Institute of Sexual Science, 353
Intermittent explosive disorder, 328
International Association of Chiefs of Police, 358
International Society for Research on Aggression, 443
Interpersonal relationships, 73
Interspecies interaction, 5, 7
Intervention
   -effects, 80
   -groups, 81, 93
   -program, 75-98
Isolation, 48, 58, 62, 82, 168

Jainism, 8
Jewish Defense League, 452
Jews, 165
Judeo-Christian religions, 9
Junior high school, 49, 50, 54, 57-62, 64, 74, 78, 171, 187

Kicking, 425
Killing
   -ritualistic, 9, 30
Ku Klux Klan, 362

Leather strap, 173
Legal sanctions, 159

Legislation, 371-375
Locke, John, 10
Los Angeles County Commission on Human Relations, 358-360, 362, 377
Love, 72, 73
Literalism, 165
Luce Press Clipping Service, 174
Luther, Martin, 164
Lutherans, 165

Machismo, 34, 223, 226
Macho personality, 222-226
   -components, 225, 226
Major depressions, 328
Mann, Horace, 167
Marriage, 420, 424, 435
Master, 53, 60, 162, 166
Mate guarding, 417
Materialist, 16
McNaughton Rule, 20
Mensur, 223-225
Mental health facilities, 180
Mental health professionals, 327, 330
Mental retardation, 165, 180, 334
Methodists, 165
Ministry of Education, 46
Minorities, 172, 350, 357, 366, 373, 376, 377, 379, 381, 384, 387
Mistress, 53, 60
Mobbing (see bully)
Mobbning (see bully)
Modeling theory, 161, 165, 167-170, 172, 191, 196
Monitoring student activities, 94
Morality, 421, 427
Mores, 397, 403-407
Mother, 171
Motivation, 402
Murder
   -by females, 402, 424

Myth
   -of female aggression 401, 403, 407-409, 412, 425, 432, 433, 436

National Center for the Study of Corporal Punishment and Alternatives in Schools (NCSCPAS), 182
National Child Labor Commission, 14

Subject Index

Force (NGLTF), 363
National Institute Against Predjudice and Violence, 376
National Organization of Black Law Enforcement Executives, 358
Natural selection, 418
Nazi Germany, 353, 452
Negative actions, 47, 48
New York Society for the Prevention of Cruelty to Children, 14
New York State Governor's Task Force on Bias-Related Crimes, 357
New York State Senate Select Committee on Mental and Physical Handicaps, 329
Nonparanoid schizophrenia, 334

Ocker, 223
Office of civil rights, 184
Old Testament, 163, 166
Open attacks, 48, 58, 62, 82
Open institutions, 161
Oppression, 75
Organic brain syndromes, 334
Organic depressions, 328
Organic personality disorder, 328
Original sin, 164
Outside observers, 53
Overprotectiveness, 69

Paddle, 162, 173, 174, 191
Paddling (see punishment)
Pain, 159-162, 175, 176, 192
Paranoid ideation, 334, 335
Parental stress, 168
Parents, 45, 49, 50, 60, 62, 69, 71, 73, 74, 76, 77, 95, 97, 98
Parkinson's disease, 217
Parliament, 162
Passive aggression, 450
Passive bully, 70
Passive victim, 69
Paternal investment, 420
Pathology
  -of teachers, 196
Peace keeping organizations, 450, 451
Peer ratings, 46, 57, 82, 83
Peers, 46, 47, 49, 68, 69, 71
Personality attributes, 66
Perpetrators, 58, 59
Personality, 256, 258, 261-266, 309, 310
  -accident liability, 256, 258, 261-266
Pestalozzi, 167
Pets, 6, 18, 23, 24, 30
Physical contact, 48
Plaintiff, 193, 195
Police, 355, 358, 363, 364, 367-374, 380, 397
Positive reinforcement, 192
Possession (by evil spirit), 164
Pre-adolescents, 83
Predation, 6, 7, 13, 31, 37, 42
Prejudice, 356, 363, 365, 369, 372, 373, 376, 397
Presbyterians, 165
Primary caretaker, 71, 95
Primary school, 54, 57, 62-64
Principal, 171, 175, 181, 190, 193
Project Tiger, 6
Projective techniques, 46, 70
Property damage, 358, 373
Protection
  -of another, 162, 180, 195
  -of oneself, 162
  -of property, 162
Protestant belief, 164, 165
Proverbs
  -(13:24), 163
  -(22:15), 163
  -(23:13-14), 163
Psychiatric illness, 73
Psychological aggression, 353
Punishment
  -beatings, 162, 167
  -bullying, 72, 98
  -corporal, 159-209
    -death from, 180
    -injuries from, 175-178
  -discipline, 159-162, 169, 171, 173, 175, 178, 185, 188, 192, 193, 195
  -drills, 179, 180
  -flogging, 162, 166, 167
  -humiliation, 167
  -isolation, 168
  -paddling, 168, 169, 172, 174, 176, 177, 180, 181, 184, 188, 189, 193
  -slap, 168
  -spank, 159, 168-170, 176-178, 180
  -whipping post, 166
Race, 172
Rape, 366, 367, 392, 394
Rattan, 173, 174

Rattan, 173, 174
Recess, 58, 62, 65, 66, 74, 82, 84, 93, 97
Religious ideology, 159, 167, 163-167
Retaliation, 451, 453-456
Road deaths, 258, 287, 294, 299, 300, 314, 315
Roadway aggression
- aggressive cues, 270, 272, 278
- assault with vehichle, 283, 392-296
- cognitive scripts, 311-315
- contagion, 315-316
- contextual factors
  - aggressor location, 283
  - intentional quality, 283-303
  - target identity, 283-303
  - target location, 283-303
  - temporal interval, 283-303
  - traffic relevance, 283-303
- drive-by shootings, 297, 300, 312, 314, 315
- environmental variables, 273
- gender, 266, 274
- highway robbery, 296, 297
- horn-honking, 268, 271-273, 275-278, 281, 282, 288, 303
- instinctive drive, 259
- multiple disinhibitory influences, 254
- roadside confrontations, 255, 283, 285-292
- roadway shootings/ throwings, 283, 285-292
- sniper/robber attacks, 283, 296-297
- suicide/murder single car crashes, 283, 300-301
- territorial defense, 259, 260
- traffic congestion, 279, 283, 286, 287, 304, 308, 309
Rousseau, 167
Royal Society for the Prevention of Cruelty to Animals, 135

Sadism, 162
Salt, Henry, 164
Satan, 164
Schizophrenia, 328, 334, 335, 338
School
- board, 162, 193-195

- bully/victim problems, 45-102
- class meeting, 98
- class size, 64, 65
- district, 162, 195, 196
- English, 162
- faadelte (one room), 63
- intervention program, 75-98
- junior high, 49, 50, 54, 57-61, 64, 74, 78, 171, 187
- master, 53, 60, 162, 166
- mistress, 53, 60
- nursery, 167
- personnel, 74, 76, 95
- primary, 54, 57, 69-64
- public, 159, 161
- recess, 58, 62, 66, 74, 83, 84, 93, 97
- size, 64, 65
- social hour, 98
- teacher
  - density, 65-74
  - monitoring student activities, 94
  - nominations, 46, 57
  - supervision, 65, 66, 97
Schopenhauer, 123
Separation
- mother-infant, 113
Sexual jealousy, 418-428, 435
Siblings, 69, 71
Sinclair, Upton, 28, 40
Skinner, B.F., 170
Slap, 168, 425
Slaughterhouse, 16, 28-30
Social contagion, 74
Social episode, 312
Social isolation, 48, 58, 62, 82
Social norms, 402, 404, 408, 410
Societies
- agricultural, 12
- communist, 163
- post-industrial, 23
- rural, 12
- socialist, 163
Sociobiological theory, 35, 36
Socio-economic status, 171
Southern Poverty Law Center, 376
Spank, 159, 168-170, 176-178, 180
Special education, 180, 181
Sports (see aggression)
- combatant, 214, 216, 218, 219
- contact, 215, 223, 230, 237

Staffing ratios, 340
Statistical Abstracts of the United States, 184
Stereotyping
 -of homosexuals, 379-385
Stonewall Rebellion, 377
Stress seeking, 222, 227-229, 246
Student, 161, 162, 166, 169, 171, 175, 176, 178, 180, 182-192
 -age, 182, 185-189
 -sex, 184, 185, 189, 190
Substance abuse, 342
Suggesto-imitative assaults, 305
Suicide, 46, 74, 364
Supervision, 65, 66, 73, 97
Supreme Court, 167, 194
Surveillance, 94
Surveillance equipment, 339, 340

Teacher
 -assaults on, 162
 -burnout, 159
 -use of corporal punishment, 159-209
Teaching methods, 163
Teasing, 68
Temperament, 72, 170
 -of bullies, 72
 -of victims, 72
Theft, 84
Therapy
 -for pets, 22
Time out, 162
Tolerance, 71
Total Scale of Antisocial Behavior (TSAS), 84
Transference, 333, 335
Transmigration, 8
Truancy, 93
Twinkie defense, 372

Vandalism, 84, 358, 361, 364, 366, 376, 391
Verbal abuse, 349, 353, 357, 362, 370
Verbal assault, 408, 416
Victim
 -anxious personality pattern, 69
 -attitude of, 68, 74, 93
 -behavior of, 68, 74
 -boys, 46, 50, 54
 -class size, 64, 65
 -clinician, 327, 330-333, 335, 341
 -external characteristics, 66, 67
 -frequency, 50, 51, 53, 57, 61, 65, 77, 97
 -friendships, 98
 -girls, 50, 54
 -insecurity, 69, 70, 74
 -passive, 69
 -provocative, 68
 -satisfaction with school, 84, 94
 -school size, 64, 65
 -self-report, 46, 82, 83, 93
 -suicide, 46, 74
Violence (see also aggression)
 -adolescents, 334
 -anti-gay, 349-400
 -clinicians, 327, 347
 -copy-cat, 305
 -family members, 329
 -in sports, 211-252
 -institutionalized, 159, 209
 -mental retardation, 165, 180, 334
 -mental retardation centers, 330
 -mentally ill, 327, 334, 341, 342
 -nursing homes, 330
 -outpatients, 335, 336
 -psychiatric hospitals, 329, 330, 341
 -psychiatric patients, 327, 329, 330, 341
 -sanctioned, 158
 -social diffusion, 305
 -toward homosexuals, 349-400
 -toward other species, 5-43
Violent crimes
 -females, 401-403, 406

Weapon, 402, 425, 446, 455-457
Western culture, 158, 163
Whipping post, 166
White supremacist groups, 362, 376